Word
Wealth

By **WARD S. MILLER**

HOLT, RINEHART AND WINSTON, INC., NEW YORK

WARD S. MILLER was formerly teacher of English and adviser of publications, John Marshall High School, Rochester, New York. He is now Associate Professor of English, University of Redlands, Redlands, California.

Illustrated by Johannes Troyer.

64P2

Copyright © 1958, by Holt, Rinehart and Winston, Inc.

Library of Congress Catalog Card Number: 58-5541

15734—0418

Printed in the United States of America

TO THE Teacher

WHEN the first edition of WORD WEALTH appeared almost twenty years ago, it was to some degree a pioneering venture. Grammar, punctuation, spelling, letters, newswriting, and even etiquette had been taught systematically for generations, but not the vocabulary of English. Increasing literacy and less emphasis on the study of Latin had made vocabulary building more and more important. Meanwhile, the high correlation between vocabulary and scholastic ability was recognized, and carefully controlled experiments had shown the far-reaching benefits of vocabulary training. The need for an effective method of teaching vocabulary was widely felt.

In response to this need, WORD WEALTH was brought forth, with a three-year plan for the study of a scientifically selected list of 750 base words, together with a tested and efficient method of presenting them. Ample exercise materials were provided. The book won great popularity because it was simple, practical, informal, interesting, and adapted to individual differences among students.

The present revision retains the best features of the earlier editions and incorporates more than a dozen improvements and new features, most of which were suggested by users of previous editions.

1. The list of base words has been carefully revised to make it more effective. Many words which readily exemplify common roots and prefixes have been absorbed into the new Jackpot Units, which are devoted to the study of these important word-building forms.

2. Each of the variant forms of a base word is "flagged" according to its part of speech. The red symbols (• - ■ ▶) placed before sentences illustrating variants indicate what form to

iii

look for but do not interrupt the sentences with irrelevant tags. The symbols are explained in detail on page 9.

3. The pronunciation, following the Merriam-Webster system, accompanies each base word. Where several pronunciations are possible, the one listed first in the dictionary is given here.

4. The definitions have been extensively recast to make them more precise and less abstract or pedantic, and the illustrative sentences are more specific and more varied.

5. More synonyms and antonyms are included, together with expanded practice material.

6. The material on roots and prefixes, formerly in the Appendix, has been reorganized and expanded into two groups of Jackpot Units, which appear at the end of Parts I and II. The forms are given in their most common English spelling. When two or more forms with similar meaning and a common derivation appear on the same line, they are grouped together; thus, *-solve-*, *-solu-*. When forms with similar meaning but different derivations appear on the same line, they are separated by spaced periods; thus, *uni- . . . mono-*.

7. A section on suffixes, with practice material, may be found in Appendix I.

8. Objective exercises of the types most widely used in standardized vocabulary tests are provided. These include synonym matching exercises in Part I, antonym exercises in Part II, and analogy exercises in Part III.

9. The teaser-pretests have been carefully constructed to challenge the student. If these exercises are not used as pretests, they may be used as extra practice sets or as final tests.

10. For greater ease and speed in scoring, the final tests now require recall of a base word rather than a definition. Thus, spelling is tested as well as recognition of meaning.

11. Each division test is subdivided in order to offer review tests at intervals of three or four units.

12. The units have been reorganized to provide for individual differences among students. The third practice sets and most of the teaser-pretests are intended primarily for better-than-average students. Average and slow learners may not have time to go beyond the first two practice sets. Mastering the base words will probably be sufficient for many students, but superior students may be

expected to master, in addition, the variants, synonyms and antonyms, and other supplementary material.

THE BASE WORDS AND THEIR COVERAGE

The base words, many of them taken from literature books usually read in high school English classes, have been carefully restricted to what may be called the "twilight zone" of general vocabulary. This consists mainly of words which appear in the middle range of frequency according to *The Teacher's Word Book of 30,000 Words* compiled by Edward L. Thorndike and Irving Lorge. These are the words which a high school graduate needs to understand—if not to use—in college, in business, in industry, or in other kinds of employment, as well as in the mass media and in personal communication.

In addition to the base words, typical variant forms have been included, making a total of more than 2,000 "teachworthy" words. These, plus several hundred synonyms and antonyms which are presented with the base words and fully 1,000 words unlocked by the roots and prefixes in the Jackpot Units, bring the total number of words included to approximately 4,000.

The base words are arranged to some degree in terms of frequency, difficulty, and other factors. Fortunately, the relation between frequency and difficulty tends toward concomitance.

HOW TO USE *WORD WEALTH*

The amount of class time spent in studying WORD WEALTH will undoubtedly depend on the ability and needs of the class. One or two units a month is a standard rate of progress throughout the three-year period for which this book is designed. Of course, WORD WEALTH may be used more intensively or for review purposes by superior students, but growth in vocabulary and word experience is ordinarily a gradual process, best integrated with reading and other class work.

A unit may be covered in two weeks at the rate of perhaps fifteen minutes a day, or it may be studied intensively in two or three class periods, depending on student ability and other factors.

The following suggestions for covering a unit may prove helpful to teachers using this book for the first time:

1. Use the division test as a pretest to find out, for example, whether Part I is too easy for a superior ninth grade or about right for an average tenth grade.

2. When an appropriate Part has been selected, give the teaser-pretest of Unit 1 to motivate the class and discover what percentage of the words in this unit the students already "know," at least partially. Many teachers, however, omit the pretest or use it as a final test or as an additional practice set.

3. Study the word list. Many teachers like to present, or have a student present, four or five words of a unit each day, with the pronunciations, definitions, examples, and perhaps synonyms and antonyms. The words are written on the board. The class may then collect examples from newspapers and magazines for the entire group of words, or each student may be assigned one of the words and asked to collect examples or think up uses.

4. Following the word study, do the practice sets, preferably one a day.

5. As a last check on the students' mastery of the unit, give the final test, the pretest, or one of the practice sets.

6. Give the division test when all the units in one Part have been completed. Or give a section of the division test when the units covered by it have been completed. The division tests are mostly, but not wholly, devoted to the base words.

Among other suggestions for using WORD WEALTH which many teachers have found helpful are the following:

1. It is advisable to give a standardized vocabulary test at the beginning of the year and again at the end, graphing the results against the norms for the grade and comparing them with the scores of another class not studying vocabulary systematically.[1]

2. Though students tend to consider vocabulary building more practical and, therefore, more valuable than grammar work, punctuation, and even letter writing, it is a good idea to dramatize

---

[1]Inglis Forms X, Y, and Z are excellent for slow or average students, but Forms A, B, and C are better for superior students in the junior and senior year.

their progress by having them make graphs of their scores on pre-tests and compare these with the scores they make on final tests.

3. Experience has shown that students will learn more if they score their own or each other's papers. Keys are provided in the Appendix for most short-answer and multiple-choice tests. Other practice sets can be scored readily from the word lists.

4. Encourage individual students to work on their own. Some will enjoy making notebooks or scrapbooks and devising additional exercises, games, and puzzles for supplementary use. It may be wise to divide the class into groups according to scores in order to devote more time to the group needing the most help.

5. Help students to remember that *a definition is rarely the exact equivalent of a word.* Quite a few satisfactory definitions are usually possible—even, occasionally, contradictory ones. Encourage the use of the dictionary for supplementary information.

6. Traditional methods of teaching vocabulary may be used in conjunction with this book. Students may look up and report on words found in school reading but not included in WORD WEALTH. Committees, selected in rotation, may look up and present words found in other sources. Finding words to fit a need or fill gaps in writing is good experience and exercises may be devised for such study. One of the best consists of passages from unfamiliar poems with a word or two omitted from each. Students pick a word for each blank and compare it with the one which belongs there.

The WORD WEALTH method of teaching vocabulary attempts to fulfill six requirements:

1. To enlist the interest of the student in his own progress—and dramatize that progress

2. To be practical, varied, and easy to use

3. To adapt itself readily to individual differences

4. To be objective and self-educative

5. To encourage the use of the dictionary

6. To foster creativity in the use of words

The new features which have been added in this edition will, it is hoped, further enhance the utility and popularity which the book has achieved.

W. S. M.

Redlands, California

ACKNOWLEDGMENTS

If this book should last a hundred years, it will not outlive its indebtedness to an outstanding teacher and department head who first interested the author in vocabulary building, early in his teaching career. Her name was Elizabeth LeMay Wright. Nor will the book outlive its indebtedness to James M. Spinning, formerly superintendent of schools in Rochester, New York.

The book also owes much to those teachers who, in the middle 1930's, made up the English Department of Rochester's John Marshall High School and to the hundreds of students who participated, willy-nilly but often enthusiastically, in the experiments from which the first edition of WORD WEALTH evolved. Thus the book belongs and will always belong to this school, where the author taught and learned for eleven years.

The present WORD WEALTH owes many of its new features to the detailed suggestions and criticisms of a number of people, but especially to the help of five distinguished teachers in various parts of the country. They are Kenneth L. Meinke, Director of Secondary Instruction, Hartford Board of Education, Hartford, Connecticut; Francis Reardon, Head of the English Department, Lowell High School, Lowell, Massachusetts; Miss Ruth M. Wheeler, teacher of English at Beverly Hills High School, Beverly Hills, California; Miss Dorothy M. Sullivan, teacher of English at Oceanside Senior High School, Oceanside, New York; and Miss Tannette Jaloff, teacher of English at Sir Francis Drake High School, San Anselmo, California. Appreciation is due to Mrs. Carl Gustafsson and Mrs. Richard D. Jack, who put the manuscript in final form. The author's wife, Phyllis Trayhern Miller, also helped immeasurably in preparing the book.

The decorations done by Mr. Johannes Troyer have as their theme various aspects of the development of writing and printing.

TABLE OF Contents

ADVENTURES WITH Words

Mᴏʀᴇ than three thousand years ago, a legendary Greek hero named Odysseus made a long voyage on the Mediterranean Sea. The trip was not for pleasure. Odysseus had fought in the ten-year war between the Greeks and the Trojans. With the fall of Troy, the long war finally ended, and Odysseus was free to return home to his wife and son in the Greek town of Ithaca.

According to Homer, the voyage took ten years. Odysseus lost his way, made mistakes, and had to sail where the winds took him. The enchantress Circe, who kept him on her island for a year, magically changed his men into pigs; the Lotus-Eaters almost destroyed his desire to go home; a one-eyed giant imprisoned him on the island of the Cyclops. Once, he was detained seven years by the sea-nymph, Calypso.

A modern Odysseus can travel half-way round the world in ten *days*—not ten *years*. No longer are men separated from one another, either by distances or lack of communication.

The Importance of Words. How did this earth we live on grow so small? The answer is a familiar one: this miracle was accomplished by science. Improvements in transportation and communication have brought far-away places near. The three billion or more inhabitants of the earth—more than at any previous time in history—have become as closely associated as neighbors.

Yet science could never have developed as it has if there had not been a *means of communication:* a way for men both to express their ideas and to record them for others to use. Without

1

language, scientific instruments and scientific methods would still be very rudimentary and limited in their usefulness.

Words play an equally important role in human relations. Through words, we come to understand people and discover the best way of living peacefully and productively with them. With the advent of radio, television, and high-powered advertising, words have become increasingly important as tools for shaping our moral, social, intellectual, and economic life. Words are the means to nearly all we are or hope to be on this planet.

Words: Their Nature and Development. What is the nature and origin of the words in our language? How did they get their meanings? Why and how do these meanings change?

Words themselves give a clue to the history of language. The word *brother* is a good example. It has changed its form, although not its meaning, from one language to another many times in three or four thousand years. Here are some examples:

(India) Sanskrit: *bharata*   Greek: *phrater*   Latin: *frater*

German: *Bruder*   Italian: *fratello*   French: *frère*

To a linguist (a specialist who studies language scientifically), these forms are more alike than they appear. The similarities among them tell a great deal about the development of these languages. The differences can be explained by regular and almost universal laws of language change.

When a group of languages have certain similarities in pronunciation, vocabulary, and grammar, such languages are usually related. Most of the languages spoken in Europe, America, and Western Asia belong to the Indo-European family. All are descended from an ancient language known as Primitive Indo-European. Not a single sentence of this early language has survived. However, linguists have been able to reconstruct it from a comparative study of the languages descended from it.

Experts do not agree on just where the first speakers of Primitive Indo-European lived, although a study of plant and animal names, as well as words for climatic and geographical features, seems to indicate that it was in the southern part of what is now the Ukraine. In any case, at some remote time in the past, various tribes speaking this language began to migrate from their original homeland. As each tribe lost contact with the others, it gradually drifted into its own ways of speaking the common language. Changes in pronunciation developed. New words were created by each tribe as it needed them. Familiar words took on new and different meanings. The result was that through the centuries thousands of little differences accumulated until, eventually, the dialects of Primitive Indo-European became separate and distinct languages. Members of these different tribes could no longer communicate in the original common language.

Some of these tribes settled in the forests of Germany and Scandinavia and spoke a branch of Indo-European which we now call Primitive Germanic. As groups of people broke away and lost close contact with one another, they developed their own languages, from which modern German, Dutch, English, and the Scandinavian languages are descended.

During the fifth and sixth centuries, two of these wandering tribes—the Angles and the Saxons—began to invade and conquer England. The Celtic peoples who inhabited the island were defeated and forced to withdraw to the mountains of Wales, Ireland, and Scotland. Since they had little influence thereafter, only a few Celtic words, most of them place-names, came into the English language. Although a number of tribes from the continent came to settle in England, the Angles and Saxons were the most important. The English language you speak today developed from Anglo-Saxon or Old English, which was a combination of the dialects of these two tribes.

Beginning in the eighth century, Viking raiders from Scandinavia attacked the coast of England. Later, these pirates became settlers and intermarried with the Anglo-Saxons. As a result, many Scandinavian forms and words came into English at this time, including such important words as the pronouns *they, them, their,* and the plural *are.*

A few hundred years later, in 1066, an army of Norman-French adventurers crossed the channel from France, hoping to capture the English throne for their leader, William, Duke of Normandy. The English army, which had just met and repelled an invasion of Danes in the north, hurried to meet the Normans. How the British were defeated at the Battle of Hastings is a familiar story. The victorious Normans then assumed control of the country, and French became the official language of England. Scott's novel *Ivanhoe* gives a vivid, if not always entirely accurate, picture of the period after the Norman conquest.

Gradually, as the Normans and English intermarried and learned each other's language, and as political conditions altered, English began to assert itself once more as the major language of the country—though with some changes. Thousands of French words had been added to the English vocabulary, as well as some French suffixes. Later, during the Middle Ages, many Latin words were also added, partly through French and partly as a result of the importance given to Latin in universities and churches.

In each succeeding century, the English language continued to grow. Education, the arts, travel, exploration, religion, and science—all have contributed new words. In addition, English has been enriched by a steadily growing number of foreign words. Modern English is probably one of the richest languages in the world, allowing for the expression of fine shades of meaning. The United States has done its part in developing the vocabulary of the English language and in extending its influence. American wealth, political power, and scientific achievement have helped make it one of the most widely-used languages in the world.

In spite of the very close ties which exist between the United States and Great Britain, the American language differs, in minor ways, in pronunciation, grammar, and vocabulary. Differences in vocabulary are the most obvious. For example, in England you would hear a truck referred to as a lorry, an elevator as a lift, and the local hardware store as the ironmonger's. These differences can usually be explained in one of two ways: old words either acquired new meanings or new words came into the language in one country but not in the other.

Enter Semantics. As long as a language is alive, it is in a continual state of change, both in form and in meaning. However, changes in pronunciation, spelling, and grammar come about more slowly than changes in word meanings. There are many examples of meaning change. The Anglo-Saxons applied the word *deer* to any animal. The word *starve,* which first meant "die from any cause," has now come to mean "die or perish from hunger." The word *board* has acquired a number of quite different meanings in addition to its original meaning of "plank." Here are just a few examples: board of directors, room and board, boarding school.

The study of word meanings and how they change is a part of the science called semantics. Although, at first, semantics emphasized only the study of meaning changes, it now deals with communication, the nature of words, and the "meaning of meaning." Suppose you made the statement that *girls are selfish.* If a semanticist heard you, he would point out that you were using words very carelessly. Actually, some girls are selfish and some are not. Also, what is selfishness? Where does selfishness end and thrift begin? How can you prove that someone is or is not selfish? To some degree, or in some sense of the word, isn't everyone selfish? The semanticist is aware of both the power and the limitations of words, and of the danger of using them loosely. A study of semantics can help us understand language better and use it more intelligently.

Space does not permit a full discussion of this interesting science, but the important facts about the nature of words and the insights of semantics may be summarized in a few simple principles:

1. A word is not an object or a thing. It is a sound, or group of sounds, which has become associated with an object, a situation, or an idea. This object, situation, or idea may be represented in a hundred different languages by a hundred different words, all of them subject to change. Many people become attached to words as such, or to one special pattern of words. It is important to remember that words are not unchanging, eternal objects.

2. A word usually has varied shades of meaning and is hard to define exactly. Even a simple word like *chair* may refer to any one of a number of different types and styles. If *chair* is hard to define, what about *courage?* Does *courage* mean "absence of fear" or "the will power to disregard fear"? Does it mean the same thing to a soldier on the battlefield that it does to a scientist in a laboratory? A precise definition is not easy to formulate.

3. Words belong to families and have ancestors. Many

words display some of the traits of their families and ancestors, but many of them have changed almost completely.

4. Words have connotations as well as denotations. The denotation of a word is its meaning or meanings. The connotation is what the word suggests in addition to its simple meaning: the associations which the word has acquired. For example, the denotation of the word *lake* is simply "an inland body of standing water," yet for most people, the word connotes more than that. It brings to mind memories of summer holidays, fishing trips, and so on. It suggests relaxation, natural beauty, vacation fun.

5. Words need to be used with great care, especially when they stand for abstract qualities or represent valuative judgments. When you say, "Polly gave a dollar to the Red Cross," you are making a clear statement of fact, easily verifiable. But when you say, "Polly is generous," you are going beyond fact and making a sweeping statement of opinion. Wherever possible, it is better to state facts and let people draw their own conclusions.

6. Words are alive. Try to think of them not only in terms of what they now mean but also in terms of what they are coming to mean. English is not a dead language like Latin, in which every word is, so to speak, fossilized and will continue to have the same meaning as long as the language is taught. English is alive; it is constantly growing and changing. The various definitions given in this book are a starting point only. You cannot take too great liberties with these meanings or you will fail to communicate what you have to say. However, it is your privilege to use old words in new ways if you do so intelligently and creatively.

Why a Vocabulary Builder? Since words play such an important role in the cultural, economic, and political life of the world today, it is increasingly important for you to devote time and study to their meaning and use. Already you know thousands of words, but there are thousands more you need to know.

In all your school subjects, you are constantly meeting new words. They appear on every page of the daily paper. Television and radio programs bombard the air with them. Conversations are full of them. New words confront you in factories and offices, as well as at home. Doctors diagnose your ills and prescribe cures in words you may never have heard before but which they don't bother to explain.

Words are important in business, too. Because a prospective employee's score on a vocabulary test is such a reliable clue to his abilities, many large concerns now require job-applicants to take such a test. A workman need not have a mastery of many words in order to operate a machine, but studies have shown that the workman who advances to become a foreman usually has a better vocabulary.

A scientific investigator once said:

> An extensive knowledge of the exact meanings of English words accompanies outstanding success in this country more often than any other single characteristic which the Human Engineering Laboratory has been able to isolate and measure.[1]

Words are also important in obtaining a college education. A vocabulary test is a regular part of most college entrance examinations and placement tests. Your grade on this test many determine whether you are accepted by a college and, if accepted, whether you are enrolled in the regular freshman course or in a remedial English course without credit. Previous editions of WORD WEALTH have already helped thousands of other students. This new edition, with practice material especially designed to prepare you for the College Board Examinations, should prove even more helpful.

How the Words in This Book Were Selected. You may wonder whether, in a single vocabulary book, you will find most, or a large number, of the words you need to know. On what basis were the words chosen?

In the past, a number of careful studies were made to determine which words in the English language were used most frequently in writing and speaking. From one of these studies, a list of 30,000 words was prepared.[2] Roughly one third to one half of these words

---

[1] O'Connor, Johnson, Director of the Human Engineering Laboratory, Stevens Institute of Technology, Hoboken, New Jersey.

[2] Edward L. Thorndike and Irving Lorge, *The Teacher's Word Book of 30,000 Words.*

would hardly merit special study. They are known to nearly everyone and used constantly in everyday life. The remaining ten
thousand words would fall into two groups: (1) those used too
rarely to justify inclusion in a highschool text, and (2) those which
need and deserve special study. It is from the last group—about
five thousand in number—that the words for this book were drawn.
Three criteria were used in making the final selection:

1. *Words that belong to the general vocabulary of people
who carry on the affairs of the English-speaking world.* These
words appear frequently in books and magazines, are heard on
radio and television programs, and are used in daily conversation. They have been important for hundreds of years, and will
probably continue to be important. Not included were words which
have a short life-expectancy—*quisling* and *snafu,* for example, which
were invented during World War II but are already half-forgotten.
The words in this book are of more lasting importance.

2. *Words that are applicable to a variety of situations.* Such
words have a wide, rather than a limited, usefulness and are, therefore, a speaker's or writer's stock in trade. Not included are those
words which belong to the special, technical vocabulary of a
science, sport, or hobby.

3. *Words that are important in literature.* Many of these
words were taken directly from novels and literature texts used in
school. However, only those were included which are also important in everyday life.

How the Words are Presented. The greater your mastery of words and their meaning, the more likely you are to achieve
exactness in thinking, accuracy in speaking and writing, and an
intelligent grasp of what you read. This book is organized in such
a way that word study is natural, easy, and efficient. The study lists
present nearly seven hundred *base words,* each with a standard pronunciation, a simple definition, and one or more illustrative sentences.

Many base words have *variant forms.* Where these are
important, they are presented in illustrative sentences. Each variant
form is marked with a special symbol to indicate its part of speech.

1. The verb is one of the most important forms in English. It changes to indicate person, number, and tense; for example, *go, goes, going, went,* and *gone.* Each illustrative sentence containing a **verb** form as a variant is marked with a bullet, thus: ●

2. The noun is more stable, changing in form only to indicate possession or plural. Many nouns are formed by the addition of a noun suffix to words already functioning as other parts of speech; for example, *abandon, abandonment.* Each illustrative sentence containing a **noun** as a variant is marked with a square, thus: ■

3. The adjective always accompanies another word, usually a noun. Each illustrative sentence containing an **adjective** as a variant is marked with a wedge, thus: ▶

4. The adverb also accompanies another word, phrase, or clause. Most English adverbs are formed by adding the suffix *-ly* to adjectives or participles; for example, *quick, quickly.* Each illustrative sentence containing an **adverb** as a variant is marked with a bar, thus: ▬

Many words are related in meaning. Consider *gay, happy,* and *glad,* for example. These words are alike in meaning and are called **synonyms.** Other words, such as *rude* and *courteous,* have opposite meanings and are called **antonyms.** *Sane* and *insane, regular* and *irregular* are also antonyms, developed from a base word by the addition of a negative prefix. Since each word in the language has its own shade of meaning, a mastery of both synonyms and antonyms allows the speaker or writer to express his ideas and feelings accurately and precisely.

Many words have an interesting ancestry. Frequently, an understanding of the origin of a word gives you a clue to its meaning and to the meaning of other words derived from the same parent word. For example, words like *sediment, sedentary,* and *insidious* are easier to understand and remember when you know that all three come from the Latin verb *sedere,* meaning "sit."

Roots and prefixes provide a key for unlocking thousands of words. Most of the units in this book are alike in that they contain twenty-five base words. However, at the end of Parts I and II, there are special JACKPOT UNITS which, as the name implies, "pay off" very well. Each one offers twenty-five roots and prefixes—some two hundred in all—which are the building blocks from which a large number of words are made, especially scientific and technical terms. Scientists frequently create new words from existing roots and prefixes, always in new combinations. The following are only a few of the new words created by adding the root *photo-* to other words already in use: *photochemistry, photogenic, photosensitive, photosynthesis.* To this root you might add other roots, such as *tele-* and *micro-*, to make words like *telephotography* and *microphotography.* You might also use the root *photo-* to create the name for a new machine in which light operates a feeder for chickens. You might call such a device a *photofeeder.* If the word became common, dictionaries would soon include it.

WORD WEALTH *is not a dictionary or a substitute for one.* Only a limited number of important words are included for special study, and the definitions are shorter and less detailed. The purpose of this book is to stimulate your interest in words, make you acquainted with words you need to know, and help you use your dictionary more intelligently.

A dictionary is a directory, a Who's Who among words. The men who compile a dictionary do not invent words; they simply record the words which are in use and the way they are used. No student would ever need to learn all the words in the dictionary. The number of words in a typical school dictionary may run from 50,000 to 100,000 base words, with perhaps another 50,000 variant forms. A dictionary is a reference book, not a text book.

The WORD WEALTH method helps you to learn words, not by rote but by seeing them in context and working with them in a number of different ways. Remember, this book is not intended to put you into a linguistic strait jacket. Its purpose is to teach you to use words with freedom, yet with precision. It must help you understand, think, and write *creatively* or it will have failed.

May your adventure be a pleasant one! You have a whole worldful of accumulated knowledge to cover, but you can do it in far less time than it took Odysseus to go from Troy to Ithaca.

PART **I**

ROAD SIGNS

When you see one of these symbols in front of an illustrative sentence, watch for the part of speech it denotes:

● a **verb** form of the base word

‒ an **adverb** form of the base word

■ a **noun** form of the base word

▶ an **adjective** form of the base word

For Pronouncing Key, see page 406.

UNIT DESIGNS FOR PART I

1. Alpha and Omega
2. Device of Karolus Magnus (Charlemagne)
3. The word *IRISH* in Irish letters
4. Initial, English, about 1400
5. Stone Age symbol of the sun
6. Scroll and reed pen with ink pots
7. Water-mark, 15th century
8. Monk writing
9. The Roman alphabet
10. The classical abridged form of *AND*
11. The basic forms of square, circle, and triangle
    for the Roman alphabet
12. Roman numerals

ALPHA

OMEGA

UNIT ONE

Which of the words at the right offers the best answer to each question?

1. Which word reveals a secret?

2. Which word begs?

3. Which word changes something so it is suitable?

4. Which word states or declares something?

5. Which word makes less of something?

6. Which one by its action brings more?

7. Which word compels somebody?

8. Which word postpones action?

9. Which word appoints?

10. Which word warns or advises?

11. Which one does away with something?

abolish
acquire
adapt
admonish
curtail
divulge
designate
implore
coerce
affirm
demolish
defer
elude

• Word List—VERBS

1. ABOLISH (ȧ·bŏl'ĭsh) . . . . do away with

Lincoln tried to abolish slavery without a war.

■ Is the abolition of poverty possible?

2. ACQUIRE (ȧ·kwīr') . . . . get, procure, obtain

How did you acquire so many new stamps?

■ Schools exist for the acquisition of knowledge and skills.

► An acquisitive person has a knack for acquiring property.

3. ADAPT (ȧ·dăpt') . . . . make suitable (by changing)

The two boys adapted the old car so they could sleep in it
when they went on fishing trips.

► Belonging to a large family made her adaptable (able to
adjust herself to circumstances).

■ Is adaptability always a virtue?

Cf. adjust, conform, accommodate, harmonize

4. ADMONISH (ăd·mŏn'ĭsh) . . . . . . warn, reprove; advise

Mr. Mason considered it his duty to admonish his children
about the habits they were forming.

■ The Book of Proverbs contains many admonitions.

► The highway department posted admonitory signs where
the road was under construction.

5. AFFIRM (ȧ·fûrm') . . . . declare, assert

I affirm my allegiance to the Constitution of the United
States.

■ The affirmation must be in writing.

► The affirmative team argues the "yes side" of a debate.

Opposite: ***deny***
Cf. allege, avouch, warrant, asseverate

6. **COERCE** (kô·ûrs') . . . . compel

"Please do not coerce me into going," Tony begged.
■ If you want to train a puppy, use praise, not coercion.
► Coercive treatment may break the puppy's spirit.

7. **CURTAIL** (kûr·tāl') . . . . cut down, reduce

The city must curtail its spending because the tax rate is too high now.
■ Curtailment is always difficult.

Opposites: *lengthen, amplify, expand*
Cf. shorten, abridge, abbreviate

8. **DEFER** (dē·fûr') . . . . delay, postpone

Do not defer your visits to a dentist.
■ Deferment may prove costly.

Defer may also mean "yield" or "show respect to": A boy defers to his father's wishes.

9. **DEMOLISH** (dē·mŏl'ĭsh) . . . . . break to pieces, destroy

He tried to demolish the old car with a sledge hammer.
■ The demolition (tearing down) of the theater took a week.

10. **DESIGNATE** (dĕz'ĭg·nāt) . . . . name; point out

The President will designate someone to represent us.
■ Designation of an heir is part of making a will.

Cf. specify

11. **DIVULGE** (dĭ·vŭlj') . . . . disclose, reveal

Tom would not divulge the secret hiding place.
■ The penalty for divulgence was expulsion from the club.

12. **IMPLORE** (ĭm·plōr') . . . . beg, entreat

"I implore you to save my life," she cried.

Synonyms: *beseech, entreat, importune, solicit*
Other *Plore* Words: To **deplore** a situation is to express regret about it or lament it.
To **explore** is to seek or search out something unfamiliar.

▪ Word List— NOUNS

1. AMBUSH (ăm'boͦosh) . . . . . . a lying in wait; a hiding
place for an attack

Not one man survived the enemy ambush in the woods.
● The caravan was ambushed and robbed near Bagdad.

2. CONTOUR (kŏn'toͦor) . . . . outline, profile

He scanned the jagged contour of the High Sierras.
▶ A contour map shows different levels of elevation.

3. GUILE (gīl) . . . . deceit, trickery

The man's shifty eyes gave a hint of his guile.
▶ The guileless look on Junior's face was quite misleading.

The word *guileless* often means "innocent-appearing." Junior was
probably not innocent at all.

4. HAZARD (hăz'ērd) . . . . risk; danger

No traveler is safe from the hazards of the highway.
▶ Climbing Mt. Everest is a hazardous adventure.
● The coach would not hazard an opinion on the game.

5. INTERIM (ĭn'tēr·ĭm) . . . . intervening time

In the interim between attacks, we ate our rations hastily.

Interlude has a similar meaning. (See dictionary.)

6. JARGON (jär'gŏn) . . . confusing lingo; technical words used
by a special trade or group

The jargon of baseball is hard for mothers to understand.
The agreement was full of legal jargon.

The word **cant** is applied to insincere speech or stock phrases.
Argot is slang, especially that used by criminals in the underworld.
The **vernacular** is the common language that people use every day.

7. **LABYRINTH** (lăb′ĭ·rĭnth) . . . . . maze; intricate situation

The Pentagon is a labyrinth of passages.
► Visitors often get lost in its labyrinthine corridors.

Query: Why do we speak of threading a labyrinth? Look up Theseus.

8. **MEDLEY** (mĕd′lĭ) . . . . mixture; jumble

A medley of strange noises came from the barn.
The band played a medley of military songs.

In music, the word *medley* refers to a composition made up of passages from several different compositions.

9. **RAPTURE** (răp′tŭr) . . . . ecstasy, keen delight

A splendid sunset fills one's soul with rapture.
► A good baseball game has many rapturous moments.

Transport carries one outside himself with joy.

10. **REMNANT** (rĕm′nănt) . . . . . remainder; scrap or trace

Hash often contains the remnants of a roast.
Hardly a remnant of the old man's skill was left.

11. **ROBOT** (rō′bŏt) . . . . . mechanical "man," automaton

An electronic calculating machine is one kind of robot.
► A robot pilot in a plane is an automatic mechanism that keeps the plane on its course.

The word *robot*, from the Czech *robotnik*, comes from the play, *Rossum's Universal Robots* by Karel Čapek. The play tells of the invention of robots, mechanical creatures designed to perform manual labor.

12. **VERGE** (vûrj) . . . . edge, border

Lost in a forest, the boys were on the verge of despair.
● Driving a friend's car without permission verges on theft.

13. **ZEPHYR** (zĕf′ẽr) . . . . gentle breeze

Zephyrs come in summer, blizzards in winter.

The word originally referred only to the West Wind.

FIRST PRACTICE SET

Copy the *italicized* words. Beside each, write an appropriate definition.

1. The firm *acquired* two more coal mines and did not have to *curtail* production.
2. I *implore* you not to *defer* payment of the bill any longer.
3. The coach will *adapt* his strategy to the players he has, without trying to *coerce* anyone.
4. Only a *remnant* of our striking force survived the *ambush.*
5. Each *hazard* brought him to the *verge* of destruction.
6. A *robot* is incapable of *rapture.*
7. The foreman *designated* an old white house as the one to *demolish,* but he would not *divulge* the owner's name.
8. Criminals use their own *jargon* to conceal their *guile.*
9. *Admonish* him not to enter the Devil's *labyrinth.*
10. The President *affirmed* his desire to *abolish* the department.

SECOND PRACTICE SET

Which base word in the unit best replaces each *italicized* word or group of words? Watch for tenses and plurals.

1. The article was full of *confusing lingo* about *doing away with* the sales tax.
2. After you *procure* the necessary information for your term paper, the material must be *made suitable* to your needs.
3. The *lying in wait* made it necessary to *reduce* his plans for attacking.
4. *Gentle breezes* made a *mixture* of soft sounds.
5. His father would often *warn* him about the *dangers* to which he exposed himself in stock car races.
6. The team which takes the *"yes side"* of the debate would not *reveal* its sources of secret information.

7. Trying to conceal his *deceit,* the boy *pleaded with* his father to *delay* the search for the missing pies.

8. *Compelling* the boys to *break to pieces* their hide-out broke up their gang.

9. The constable *pointed out* a room in which the *mechanical man* could be installed.

10. When the child was found, he was on the *border* of collapse. He had been lost in a *maze* of back streets.

11. John spent the *intervening time* selling the *remaining scraps* of his property.

12. With *keen delight,* he studied the *outline* of the hills.

THIRD PRACTICE SET

Copy the *italicized* words. Beside each, write the letter of the word or group of words which is closest in meaning.

1. *Adaptable* persons: (a) easy going (b) suitable (c) readily adjustable (d) inclined to say yes (e) tactful

2. *Admonitory* glance: (a) anxious (b) reluctant (c) fatherly (d) imploring (e) warning

3. The *zephyr*-like music: (a) windy (b) full of fun (c) western (d) gentle, breezy (e) good-natured

4. The *demolition* crew: (a) demon-like (b) wrecking (c) bulldozer (d) landing ships (e) hook-and-ladder

5. *Labyrinthine* forests: (a) very dense (b) pathless (c) maze-like (d) threadlike (e) man-made

6. Demonstrated *guile*: (a) guilt (b) innocence (c) slipperiness (d) deceit (e) lack of frankness

7. To *defer* his departure: (a) disregard (b) delay (c) accept (d) regret (e) permit

8. The *argot* of gangsters: (a) plotting (b) evil thoughts (c) slang (d) pay-off or swag (e) ugly speech

9. To *deplore* slum conditions: (a) plead against (b) work to improve (c) criticize (d) bewail (e) write about

10. To *avouch* one's faith: (a) mention (b) give proof of (c) declare (d) explain (e) plead for

ANTONYMS

Which word comes nearest to being exactly **opposite** in meaning to the *italicized* word?

1. *Acquire* wealth: (a) waste   (b) expend   (c) worship   (d) accumulate   (e) be greedy for

2. A *rapturous* feeling: (a) downcast   (b) bored   (c) stifled   (d) delighted   (e) determined

3. *Labyrinthine* thoughts: (a) stupid   (b) matter of fact   (c) intricate   (d) uncomplicated   (e) free from secrets

4. *Guileless* as a small child: (a) innocent   (b) gentle   (c) obedient   (d) deceitful   (e) faithless

5. *Divulge* one's age: (a) conceal   (b) admit   (c) falsify   (d) apologize for   (e) vouch for

6. *Demolish* an argument: (a) affirm   (b) undermine   (c) construct   (d) strengthen   (e) review

7. *Curtail* expenses: (a) report accurately   (b) adjust   (c) reduce drastically   (d) explain   (e) increase

8. *Defer to* the coach's judgment: (a) turn to   (b) yield to   (c) postpone   (d) dislike   (e) defy

9. Use *jargon:* (a) truth   (b) clarity   (c) eloquence   (d) ordinary speech   (e) fairness

10. *Remnants* of a meal: (a) left-overs   (b) main part   (c) dishes   (d) recipes   (e) ingredients

UNIT TWO

Which of the words at the right offers the best answer to each question?

1. Which word expresses the most respect?

2. Which word recovers lost treasure?

3. Which buys back or makes amends?

4. Which consists of advice?

5. Find a word which often involves courts or the police.

6. Find the word that horrifies.

7. According to the Biblical account, for what did Noah prepare?

8. Find the word that haunts a person.

9. Which word denotes great damage?

10. Which word expresses affection as well as respect?

11. Which word describes a scene of great disorder and confusion?

12. Which word tells how a policeman twists a gun from a captured thief's grasp?

appall
wrest
counsel
guerdon
custody
cherish
deluge
brevity
salvage
obsess
redeem
havoc
esteem
chaos

• Word List—VERBS

1. **APPALL** (ă·pôl′) . . . . horrify, overcome with fear

   It appalls one to read about the slaughter that took place at Buchenwald.
   ► The wrecked car with the bodies near it was an appalling spectacle.

   > *Appall* comes from a French verb meaning "grow pale."
   > Fear Verbs: *scare, alarm, frighten, terrify, horrify*

2. **DISCERN** (dĭ·zûrn′) . . . . see clearly, perceive

   Nancy could discern her father's figure in the distance.
   ► The difference between the two drawings was scarcely discernible.
   ▣ A statesman needs to be a man of great discernment.

   > When you discern an object, you are able to detect it and separate it from its surroundings.
   > When you **perceive** an object, you are able to see it clearly enough to identify it. The word *perceive* also carries the meaning of "have insight" or "understand": It was not hard to perceive his reasons for leaving.

3. **ERR** (ûr) . . . . make a mistake; do wrong

   "To err is human; to forgive, divine."
   ► Your answer is erroneous (mistaken).
   ▪ At the front of the edition, the publishers inserted a list of errata (printing mistakes).

   > *Err* once meant "to wander." A **knight-errant** was a roving knight.
   > An **erratic** person is unpredictable; that is, you can never tell what he is going to do or say next.

4. **ESTEEM** (ĕs·tēm′) . . . . value highly; regard

   Fathers esteem the confidence their children show.
   The boy esteems it a privilege to confide in his father.
   ▪ Do your parents rise in your esteem (regard) as you grow older?

▷ He is a person of estimable courage (deserving respect).

To **appreciate** something is to value it sufficiently or recognize its value.
To **cherish** something is to have affection for it, as well as respect.

5. FEIGN (fān) . . . . **pretend**

"Feign a virtue if you have it not."
Father feigned fright when Junior rushed at him with a toy pistol.

A fighter will often make a **feint** or pretended blow to mislead his opponent and thus gain an advantage.

6. LOITER (loi'tēr) . . . . . . **move idly or aimlessly; dawdle**

Go directly to school and do not loiter on the way.
■ The police arrested a loiterer whom they found near the burning building.

To **dawdle** is to fritter away time, usually over trifles.
To **dally** is to waste time, often because one does not have a serious purpose.

7. MEDITATE (mĕd'ĭ·tāt) . . . . **think, reflect; intend**

Father meditates on family problems while he shaves.
■ In these moments of meditation, he solves many problems.
Early in the war, the man began to meditate treason.

Think Words: To **ponder** an idea is to weigh it thoughtfully. *Cf. ponderous*, which means "heavy."
To **contemplate** is to consider or intend, usually a situation or something definite: She contemplates marriage.
To **muse** is to meditate, probably in a whimsical or aimless manner.
To **ruminate** originally meant "chew the cud," as a cow does. It thus means "ponder" or "go over and over."

8. OBSESS (ŏb·sĕs') . . . . **beset; haunt**

Do not let fears of failure obsess you.
■ Cleanliness can become an obsession or mania.
▷ Even minor failures had an obsessive effect, keeping him awake at night.

See *harass* (hăr'ăs, hȧ·răs'), which means "disturb persistently" or "torment."

9.   REDEEM (rĕ·dēm′) . . . . buy back; make amends for

When my uncle could not pay on the mortgage, Father offered to redeem it (buy it back by paying it off).
The ex-convict worked hard to redeem himself in the eyes of his neighbors.

▶ Government bonds are redeemable as they mature.

■ Redemption of society is the act or process of saving it from sin, bondage, or evil.

■ "I know that my Redeemer lives" (one who will atone or make amends for me).

Redeem also means "deliver from wrongdoing and its penalties" by making amends.
Cf. salvage, ransom

10.   REGALE (rĕ·gāl′) . . . . entertain, delight

The hunter will regale us with his adventures in Africa.

■ Such regalement will make the evening more enjoyable.

11.   RELENT (rĕ·lĕnt′) . . . . . . become less severe, soften

The next day, his fury began to relent. At first, he refused to allow us to swim in his pool, but later he relented.
Having decided to execute his visitors, the king would not relent.

▶ John's relentless (unrelenting) efforts to master algebra were finally rewarded.

12.   SALVAGE (săl′vĭj) . . . . save; restore; recover the value of

Rescuers were able to salvage only part of the cargo before the ship sank.

▶ The ship itself proved salvagable, however.

▶ The salvage value of a car is the value of the materials that can be recovered and used again.

13.   WREST (rĕst) . . . . twist; pull away

A Communist group tried to wrest control of the labor union from the present officers by electing its own candidates.

Cf. wrestle, extort, usurp

▪ Word List—NOUNS

1. **BREVITY** (brĕv'ĭ·tĭ) . . . . shortness, conciseness

   Reporters like to interview the senator because of the brevity and clarity of his remarks.
   "Brevity is the soul of wit."

   To **abbreviate** is to shorten. What do **breviary** and **breve** mean?
   Review *curtail* (I, 1).

2. **CENSURE** (sĕn'shēr) . . . . . strong criticism, condemnation

   The assembly passed a vote of censure.
   ● Men censure Benedict Arnold for his treachery.

   A **censorious** person is a faultfinding person.

3. **CHAOS** (kā'ŏs) . . . . great confusion, disorder

   Her room was in chaos after the pillow fight.
   ▶ Life was chaotic in the bombed-out city.

   Bedlam, meaning "uproar" or "noisy confusion," comes from the name of an insane asylum in London, the Hospital of St. Mary of Bethlehem.
   Cf. pandemonium

4. **CITADEL** (sĭt'á·dĕl) . . . . fortress or stronghold

   The Alcazar was a famous citadel in Spain.
   Gibraltar has long been a citadel of British power.

   An **arsenal** is a factory or storage place for war material.

5. **CONSENSUS** (kŏn·sĕn'sŭs) . . . general agreement or opinion

   The consensus is against calling a strike.

6. **COUNSEL** (koun'sel) . . . . advice

   Unjustly accused of theft, Thomas needed counsel.
   ● He went to Mr. Snyder, who counsels freshmen boys.

   Counsel means "legal adviser," as well as "legal advice." One who gives advice is a **counselor.**
   The word *council* refers to a group which decides what to do. Its members are **councilors.**

7. CUSTODY (kŭs'tô·dĭ) . . . . . keeping, care; imprisonment

The court gave Mrs. Whitman custody of her child.
Police took the man into custody (imprisonment).
Mr. Eppling is the new custodian (caretaker) of city hall.

8. DELUGE (dĕl'ûj) . . . . . . great downpour or flood

Noah built his ark just before history's greatest deluge.
● My sister would like to be deluged with invitations.

The Nile River **inundates** (floods) its banks every spring.
Antediluvian means "before the Deluge," or just very ancient:
Brother's antediluvian vehicle is really only ten years old.

9. DEMEANOR (dê·mēn'ẽr) . . . . conduct, behavior; manner

Mary of Scotland's demeanor was calm as she faced death.

Mien (mēn) has the same meaning and perhaps the same origin as
demeanor: Uncas was an Indian of proud and silent mien.
Deportment is another word for one's behavior or bearing.

10. EPOCH (ĕp'ŏk) . . . . era, period of time

The depression of 1929 began an epoch of low wages.
▸ The invention of the telegraph was an epochal event.

An event that is **epochal** or **epoch-making** is distinctive or outstanding enough to mark the beginning or end of an era.
Era is often used to refer to a period of time reckoned from a particular date, as, for example, "the Christian era."
An **aeon** (ē'ŏn) is a very long period of time: thousands of years.

11. GUERDON (gûr'dŭn) . . . . reward

"What if I perish? The guerdon is gained, and the lady is
saved!" cried the knight.

Reward Words: *award, premium, recompense, requital*

12. HAVOC (hăv'ŭk) . . . . . . devastation, destruction

Hardly a dozen houses were left standing, so great was the
havoc wrought by the tornado.

In the Middle Ages, "Cry havoc!" was the call permitting an army to
pillage and plunder.

FIRST PRACTICE SET

Copy the *italicized* words. Beside each, write an appropriate definition.

1. It is now easy to *discern* the motives which made him *err* in his youth.

2. Mother would not *relent* and she did not *loiter* when she went to look for me.

3. Mr. Horton's dignified *demeanor* hardly changed as he swam out to *salvage* his hat.

4. The editor will *meditate* a long time before he dares to write an editorial of *censure* about the City Council.

5. The *deluge* made *chaos* of the telephone system.

6. My *counsel* is that you cultivate *brevity* in writing.

7. Mr. Livingston tried to *wrest* his child from his wife's *custody*.

8. The *consensus* is that she will *feign* illness in order to avoid having to leave.

9. We all *esteem* the banker because he tried to *redeem* himself when the bank failed.

10. He likes to *regale* his friends with the dreams that *obsess* him at night.

11. The *havoc* which bombs caused in the *citadel* will *appall* the new troops.

12. In earlier *epochs,* a fine sword was often given to a hero as *guerdon*.

SECOND PRACTICE SET

Which base word from this unit best replaces each *italicized* word or group of words?

1. The *general agreement* seems to be that *shortness* is preferable in the ribbon-cutting ceremony.

2. The *flood* of mail which the singer gets shows how his hearers *highly value* him.

3. An F.B.I. agent will *move about aimlessly* near the hide-out and *pretend* loss of memory.

4. Try to *see clearly* the difference between courage and rashness. Do not let false hopes *beset* you.

5. The *great confusion* in the gymnasium will *dismay* you.

6. A boy *makes a mistake* if he does not seek wise *advice* in planning his future.

7. The *distinctive era* of widespread *devastation* was an inevitable result of the war.

8. Claudius deserves *strong criticism* because he managed to *take by force* the throne from his brother.

9. Let us *reflect* on what the *reward* should be for saving the *fortress*.

10. After tripping on the curb, Mr. Bumble tried to *restore* his usually calm *behavior*.

11. By *entertaining* him with stories, she tried to make the Sultan *become less severe*.

12. The painter is in police *imprisonment* because he could not *buy back* the notes he signed.

THIRD PRACTICE SET

On a separate sheet of paper, write the numbers of the *italicized* words. Beside each, write the number of the matching word or group of words from the second column.

1. Father's *discernment*
2. Hours of *meditation*
3. An act of *redemption*
4. Financial *obsession*
5. *Bedlam* in the nursery
6. A gangsters' *arsenal*
7. The *era* of plastics
8. Bashful *mien*
9. *Inundation* of gifts
10. A *feint* at the enemy

1. pretended blow or strike
2. something that besets one
3. purchase or acquisition
4. behavior, bearing
5. deliverance
6. weapons or ammunition
7. flood
8. reflection
9. period of time
10. uproar
11. concentration
12. perception

1. *Antediluvian* relics
2. The *epochal* discovery
3. *Obsessive* dislikes
4. *Redeemable* coupons
5. *Relentless* pursuit
6. *Salvagable* metal
7. An *estimable* gentleman
8. *Ponderous* equipment
9. *Discernible* imperfections
10. *Erroneous* counsel

1. worthy of respect
2. eligible to be bought back
3. dating from before the Great Flood
4. never letting up
5. capable of being seen
6. capable of being saved
7. distinctive, outstanding
8. mistaken
9. deceptive
10. crazy or half insane
11. haunting
12. heavy

A WORD FOR IT

What word from the unit best replaces each *italicized* word or group of words?

1. A dog probably cannot *see differences in* colors.

2. Good music is the one thing Ray does not *value sufficiently.*

3. Who is the most *faultfinding* person you know?

4. When he is supposed to be studying, Frank often *fritters away his time with trifles.*

5. An important decision must be *weighed thoughtfully* for some time.

6. A *pretended move* fooled the other team.

7. The right to vote is a privilege to *value with affection.*

8. She began to *think in a whimsical manner* about her plans.

9. What *reward* might a faithful knight expect?

10. It is foolish to *waste time because one does not have a serious purpose* and neglect one's opportunities.

SHIPWRECKED

Write a paragraph on this topic. If you describe a large ship with a valuable cargo and if your imagination is adequate, you will find that you can use more than half the words in this unit.

If you prefer, write a description of an earthquake or a tornado. This will also give you an adventure with many words in the unit.

_____

Which of the choices best matches the *italicized* word?

1. A *dour* look: (a) sour, bitter (b) stern, gloomy (c) ugly, spiteful (d) sick or sickly

2. A *plaintive* note: (a) easy to understand (b) broad and flat (c) legal (d) mournful

3. *Lucid* thoughts: (a) free-flowing (b) honest (c) clear (to the mind) (d) beautiful

4. A *pensive* mood: (a) thoughtful (b) tired (c) heavy (d) grief-stricken

5. A *candid* reply: (a) sweet (b) misleading (c) confident (d) frank

6. *Plausible* schemes: (a) reasonable-appearing (b) dishonest (c) fair (d) vexatious

7. *Furtive* actions: (a) clever (b) stealthy (c) quick, jerky (d) dishonest

8. *Droll* behavior: (a) ducklike (b) oddly amusing (c) unusual (d) playful

9. *Nebulous* plans: (a) hazy (b) treacherous (c) ambitious (d) explicit

31

▸ Word List—ADJECTIVES

1. **BRUSQUE** (brŭsk) . . . . **abrupt; blunt**

   The officer was quite brusque. "Watch where you're going," he bellowed.
   - "I'm not deaf," she answered brusquely.
   - The officer was angered by her brusqueness.

2. **CANDID** (kăn'dĭd) . . . . **frank, honest**

   The boy was very candid about his low grades.
   - The doctor told her to answer each question candidly or he could not help her.
   - A bracing candor (frankness) was one of the main charms of her very vital personality.

   The Latin root means "white, whiteness."

3. **CANINE** (kā'nīn) . . . . **of a dog, doglike**

   Doctors often learn about human sickness from a study of canine disease.

   Canis (kā'nĭs) Major is the Great Dog Constellation, a group of stars which includes Sirius, the Dog Star.

4. **DOUR** (do͞or) . . . . **sullen, gloomy**

   The wearing hardships of a mountain existence made the pair dour.
   - Dourness hindered them in making friends.
   - The old man turned away dourly.

5. **DROLL** (drōl) . . . . **oddly comical or amusing**

   We all enjoyed the pet duck's droll antics.
   - The clown's drolleries (jesting) amused the children.

   Droll comes from a Dutch word meaning "short, stout fellow."
   Laugh Words: ***mirth, jest, jollity, glee, hilarity***
   Hilarity is noisier than mirth, funnier than jollity or glee. (See II, 10.)

6.   FURTIVE (fûr′tĭv) . . . . sly, stealthy

The man kept darting furtive glances at the door.

■ When we found out what he had stolen, we could understand his furtiveness.

Furtive comes from the Latin *furtivus*, meaning "stolen."
Surreptitious is a synonym, implying a sense of guilt.

7.   GHASTLY (gȧst′lĭ) . . . . horrible; pale

"What a ghastly crime!" the lady exclaimed.
She looked aghast (terrified) when she saw the corpse.

Ghastly comes from the Old English word *gast*, meaning "spirit or ghost." It is thus a variant form of **ghostly** which has acquired its own special meaning.
Cf. grisly, gruesome, grotesque, macabre

8.   HOARY (hōr′ĭ) . . . . white or gray with age; ancient

The hoary-headed gentleman is ninety years old.
The ground was covered with hoar frost.

Hoary is so often used in describing elderly people that it has acquired the additional meaning of "old."
Whitish Words: **bleach, blanched, dapple-gray, ashen, argent, ceruse**

9.   LUCID (lū′sĭd) . . . . clear in (or to) the mind

During a lucid moment, the dying man asked for his son.
■ The lucidity of the argument made it convincing.

Lucid also means "shining, glowing, transparent," although this meaning is not commonly used today.
Lucifer, a name for Satan, means "light-bearer." (See dictionary.)
Lucite is a plastic used in making reflectors for light.
A **pellucid** pond lets light through and is, therefore, **translucent.**

10.   MATURE (mȧ·tūr′) . . . . ripe; fully developed

The corn was mature in August.
He was very intelligent, but some of his attitudes were immature (not grown-up, not adult).
A proposal in 1910 to build superhighways would have been premature (occurring before the proper time).
■ Plans for the celebration reached maturity in the fall.

11. **MOTLEY** (mŏt′lĭ) . . . . . varied in colors, kinds, elements

A motley flock of chickens flapped and squawked in the barnyard.

A motley crowd gathered around the prison as the hour for the execution approached.

In medieval times, *motley* referred to the parti-colored garment of a court jester.

12. **MUTE** (mūt) . . . . silent, speechless

The man stood mute before his accusers.

▪ Sudden danger often produces momentary muteness.

► The muted (muffled) tones of a bass horn could be heard.

Mute also means "incapable of speech," as in the case of a deaf mute or a person literally dumb.

13. **PENSIVE** (pĕn′sĭv) . . . . deeply thoughtful; wistful

There was a pensive look in her eyes as she thought about the places she had visited and the people she had met.

▪ Her pensiveness was one of her most attractive qualities.

Wistfulness is sadder than **pensiveness.**
Reverie is a state of pensiveness but is more of a daydream. It comes from *rêver*, a French word meaning "to dream."

14. **PLACID** (plăs′ĭd) . . . . calm, serene

The Swiss are placid people who get along well with all of their neighbors.

▪ Do the high altitudes at which they live foster placidity?

- "I always like to read," he answered placidly.

Synonyms: *peaceful, tranquil, quiet, unruffled*

15. **PLAINTIVE** (plān′tĭv) . . . . sad, mournful

The plaintive note of an owl broke the stillness of the placid evening.

▪ Do you like the plaintiveness of cowboy songs such as "The Last Roundup"?

▪ The plaintiff in the accident case sued for $10,000 damages.

The **plaintiff** at law is the one who complains.

16. PLAUSIBLE (plô′zĭ·b′l) . . . . appearing true or reasonable

The ghost story was a plausible yarn.

■ The author has a knack of giving plausibility to the most improbable tales.

Opposites: *implausible, incredible*

17. POTENT (pō′tĕnt) . . . . powerful; very effective

The Postmaster General was a potent influence in politics.

■ The potency of the drug makes it dangerous.

■ A tribal head is a minor potentate (monarch).

► The boy's potential (possible) capacity for leadership began to show as soon as he entered school .

18. PUNGENT (pŭn′jĕnt) . . . . sharp, stinging, keen

The pungent odor of ammonia filled the laboratory.

■ The pungency of Mr. Mason's wit was widely admired.

To **pique** (pēk) one's curiosity is to arouse it sharply.
Piquant remarks are sharp, tart, pungent.

19. RIGOROUS (rĭg′ĕr·ŭs) . . . . . . rigidly severe, exacting

The training of a jet pilot is long and rigorous.

■ Northern states feel the rigors of winter.

– Football players must train rigorously.

A **rigid** schedule is stiff, unbending.
Stringent laws bind one tightly or closely.
Inclement weather is merely unfavorable.
An **austere** person is harsh, stern, severe, serious, as in discipline.

20. RUEFUL (roo′fool) . . . . sorrowful; pitiable

A rueful expression appeared on her face when she saw the low grade on her paper.

■ The ruefulness of his tone made us sympathize immediately.

● He will rue (regret) it if he eats a whole pie.

21. VAGUE (vāg) . . . . indefinite; hazy

We saw the vague outline of a mountain through the mist.
Vague plans are always hard to carry out.

■ The vagueness of the man's answers about where he had been made the police suspicious.

> **Nebulous** means "hazy, indistinct, confused." It comes from the Latin *nebula*, "a mist."
> An **obscure** answer is not clear or plain.
> An **ambiguous** statement is unclear because it can be understood in more than one way.
> Opposites: *clear, explicit, definite*

22. WANTON (wŏn′tŭn) . . . . . senseless; malicious; reckless

The soldiers showed a wanton disregard for property as they spread out through enemy country.
A wanton wind whisked the leaves back and forth.
■ The windstorm flattened houses with the wantonness of a child sweeping away a toy village.

> Poetically, *wanton* may mean "playful" or "luxurious." It may also mean "loose morally." The word was created out of two Old English words. The earliest meaning was "undisciplined."

23. WARY (wâr′ĭ) . . . . cautious; watchful

Pedestrians who are wary in traffic live longer.
■ With catlike wariness, the Indian crawled toward the fort.

> To be wary is to be cautious in facing danger.
> To be **chary** is to be frugal or cautious in giving: Teachers are often chary of praise.

24. WEIRD (wērd) . . . . unearthly, eerie

Weird cracking noises made the house seem haunted.
‐ The music is weirdly beautiful.
■ Its weirdness has the Oriental quality of the "Danse Chinoise."

> *Weird* comes from the Old English word for fate or destiny.

25. WILY (wīl′ĭ) . . . . crafty, cunning, sly

Wily traders took advantage of the African natives, exchanging gaudy trinkets for valuable tusks.
■ It was the fighter's wiliness rather than the power of his punches that made him dangerous.
■ Samson was a victim of Delilah's wiles (tricks, cunning).

FIRST PRACTICE SET

Copy the *italicized* words. Beside each, write an appropriate definition.

1. "Looking *rueful* won't help!" was her *dour* comment.
2. He prefers to be *candid* even at the risk of seeming *brusque*.
3. The victim was *mute* and *ghastly* in the *weird* light.
4. *Furtive canine* eyes followed the *wary* creature.
5. *Mature* individuals are sometimes *pensive* or *plaintive*.
6. A *motley* gang of boys watched the *wily* tailback run.
7. The idea that *potent* enemies had brought about the manager's dismissal was *plausible*.
8. The man's *hoary* hair and gentle smile gave little hint of his *wanton* cruelty.
9. The teacher's deportment is *placid* and his thoughts, *lucid*.
10. The boy is known for his *droll* actions and *pungent* quips.

SECOND PRACTICE SET

Which base word from this unit best replaces each *italicized* word or group of words?

My friend Tom has an *oddly comical* sense of humor. Usually, he is quite *serene* and *deeply thoughtful,* but I have known him to be quite *blunt* in his efforts to be *honest.* His talk is very *clear to the mind,* and his suggestions are seldom *hazy.* Naturally *cautious in facing danger,* he seems *stealthy* only because he is shy.

His friendliness is a *doglike* kind of devotion, and it is a *horrible* mistake to accuse him of a *reckless* crime like poisoning a *gloomy* miser. The charge is not *reasonable,* and he does not belong with a *varied* assortment of jailbirds.

The *exacting* questioning of the police left him *sorrowful* and *unable to speak.* His voice grew *mournful* under the *stinging* accusations of a *white-haired* detective who tried to link him with the *eerie* activities of a powerful South Side gang. He has a *fully developed* mind and good character, however, and could never belong to a group of *crafty* criminals.

THIRD PRACTICE SET

Write the numbers of the *italicized* words. Beside each, write the number of the matching word from the second column.

1.	A *plausible* theory	1.	keen
2.	A *candid* criticism	2.	fully developed
3.	*Wanton* mischief	3.	cheerful, pleasant
4.	A *furtive* search	4.	exacting
5.	*Mute* confession	5.	reasonable-appearing
6.	*Pungent* quips	6.	calm, serene
7.	*Lucid* explanation	7.	reckless
8.	*Mature* plans	8.	speechless
9.	*Rigorous* control	9.	frank, truthful
10.	*Placid* as a cow	10.	sly, stealthy
		11.	angry, irritable
		12.	clear (to the mind)

WRITE A PARAGRAPH

Invent a short tale about a conqueror, a criminal, or a countess, using as many of the words in this unit as you can slip in without overloading the story. Bring in two or three words from earlier units if you can. Underline each word taken from a unit.

UNIT FOUR

Which of the choices best matches the *italicized* word?

1. *Purge* one's tongue: (a) cleanse (b) remove (c) burn (d) twist

2. The old *derelict*: (a) tired sailor (b) widow (c) kind of car (d) outcast

3. *Cite* the guide book: (a) examine carefully (b) disregard (c) refer to as proof (d) hunt it up

4. *Satiate* one's appetite: (a) whet (b) satisfy to excess (c) share with another (d) overcome

5. A magic *potion*: (a) charm or spell (b) ability (c) liquid dose (d) cavern

6. A *harbinger* of joy: (a) messenger (b) symbol (c) embodiment (d) haven

7. A clever *epithet*: (a) disguise (b) performance (c) token or gift (d) descriptive title

8. A small *aperture*: (a) change (b) opening (c) tool (d) camera

9. An effective *anecdote*: (a) remedy (b) long paragraph (c) proverb (d) brief story

• Word List—VERBS

1.   ABATE (*à·bāt'*) . . . . . . ○ . . . . . lessen, decrease

Nothing could abate the zeal and perseverance with which Edison worked at a problem.

The epidemic of smallpox began to abate in the fall.

■ Its abatement brought relief and rejoicing.

> Ebb Words: Crime began to **decrease** (grow less).
> The number of criminals began to **diminish.**
> The wave of excitement will **subside** (quiet down).
> Tides **ebb.**
> "The long day **wanes**" (fades, dies down).
> Antonym: The moon **waxes** before it wanes.

2.   ABET (*à·bĕt'*) . . encourage or help (usually in mischief or crime)

His brother was eager to abet him in the joke he wanted to play on their sister.

■ The gunwoman became a famous abettor of crime.

> To **sanction** an act is to aid by giving approval, both to good acts and bad.

3.   CITE (*sīt*) . . quote; mention or refer to (as a proof or example)

Can you cite an instance in which a dog saved a child's life? Corporal Billman was cited for bravery after he cleaned out a machine gun nest.

■ It took citations (references to passages) from the encyclopedia to convince her that Texas is the largest state.

> In law, to cite a man is to summon him to appear in court.

4.   ENTICE (*ĕn·tīs'*) . . . . allure; inveigle

The kidnaper offered candy to entice the little girl into his car.

■ Yielding to the enticement of spring, we went for a walk along the brook.

▶ Dora looked enticing in her new dress.

Entice sometimes means "tempt": "If sinners entice thee, consent
thou not."
Cf. decoy, beguile, seduce

5. **FRUSTRATE (frŭs'trāt)** . . . . thwart; defeat

The villain in a story always tries to frustrate the hero.
■ Her failure to win left her with a feeling of frustration.

Hinder Words: You **foil** a criminal by throwing him off his course.
You **balk** a plan by setting up obstacles.
You **circumvent** a scheme by getting around it somehow.

6. **LAMENT (lå·měnt')** . . . . feel sorrow for; bewail

You did not lament the loss of your milk teeth.
■ No word of lament escaped his lips after the funeral.
■ The lamentations of hired mourners helped make a Roman
funeral successful.
▶ The accident that broke the man's back was a lamentable
(regrettable) consequence of carelessness.

Accent *lamentable* on the first syllable.
Review *rue, rueful, plaintive* (I, 3).

7. **MANIFEST (măn'ĭ·fĕst)** . . . . . . show plainly, reveal

The salesman manifested great enthusiasm for older-model
cars.
■ Christmas always brings a manifestation (display) of Aunt
Susan's lack of skill in selecting neckties.
▶ The boy's fondness for chess was manifest (clear, plain).

A **manifesto** is a formal declaration.

8. **PERVADE (pĕr·vād')** . . . . . . spread through, permeate

Every year on Mother's Day, the aroma of roses pervades
the house.
■ The student from India was impressed by the pervasiveness
of the Christmas spirit in America.
▶ George's pervasive sense of humor finds something amusing
in every incident, including household catastrophes.

Synonyms: *permeate, saturate*

9. **PULVERIZE** (pŭl′vẽr·īz) . . . . reduce to powder

    Pulverize each pill and dissolve it in water.
    ▪ The machine is used for the pulverization of limestone.

    Pulvis is Latin for "dust."

10. **PURGE** (pûrj) . . . . cleanse; clear

    He will purge the house of pests by fumigating it.
    The party's membership will be purged of those who are
    disloyal.
    ▪ Purgation of the infected area took a long time.
    ▪ The medicine is a purgative.

    Purge may also mean "clear a person of guilt" or "wipe out an
    offense legally." Consult a dictionary for other meanings.
    To **expurgate** a book is to remove what is considered offensive.
    Purgatory is a place for purifying one's soul by purging away sins.

11. **REPROACH** (rḕ·prōch′) . . . . blame; upbraid

    Do not reproach him for failing if he did his best.
    ▪ Reproach is especially hard for a proud person to bear.
    ▶ She rebuked him with a reproachful look.
    ▶ Lincoln's life was almost irreproachable, and Robert E. Lee
    was a man equally reproachless (faultless).

    Blame Words: *chide, upbraid, rebuke, reprove, reprimand, cen-
    sure* (I, 2), *recriminate*

12. **RESENT** (rḕ·zĕnt′) . . . . take offense at

    The foreman resents any kind of interference.
    ▪ Martha felt resentment when anyone criticized her.
    ▪ She did not show her resentfulness, but her friends sensed it.

13. **SATIATE** (sā′shĭ·āt) . . . . satisfy to excess

    There was enough food to satiate a thousand, and every-
    body ate all he could.
    ▪ Only a few did not reach the point of satiety (sȧ·tī′ĕ·tĭ).

    To **sate** one's appetite for fun is to satisfy it to the full.
    To **glut** the market is to flood it. What is a **glutton?**
    A **surfeit** (III, 3) is an excess of something.
    Cloying sweetness is excessive sweetness that no longer pleases.

■ Word List— NOUNS

1. ABYSS (á·bĭs') . . . . deep or bottomless chasm

   The climber slipped and fell into an abyss a thousand feet
   deep.
   Hundreds of nations have been lost in the abyss of time.
   ▶ The savage's ignorance of American life is abysmal (immeasurable or unfathomable).

   An abyss is anything profound or immeasurable. The Greek root
   means "without bottom."
   A **fissure** is merely a narrow opening or cleft.

2. ANECDOTE (ăn'ĕk·dōt) . . . . . . brief story or incident

   Mr. Coe's wife did not like anecdotes about pretty women.
   ▶ The address was wholly anecdotal and most of the inci-
   dents came from the speaker's own experience.

   Query: What do we mean when we say that a man is in his "anec-
   dotage?" (See dictionary.) Look up **dotage** also.
   What is the word for something to offset the effect of poison?

3. APERTURE (ăp'ẽr·tûr) . . . . an opening

   The apertures in the castle wall admitted little light.
   The cameraman adjusted the aperture in his camera for a
   snow scene.

   The aperture in a camera is the opening that lets in light.

4. AROMA (á·rō'má) . . . . odor, fragrance

   She liked the aroma of new-mown hay.
   ▶ The cabinet was filled with aromatic (spicy, pungent)
   herbs, such as sage and basil.

5. DERELICT (dĕr'ĕ·lĭkt) . . . . an abandoned ship; an outcast

   The derelict stayed afloat until it was sunk in a storm.
   The hobo is a human derelict who has no home, no job, and
   very little to live for.

▣ His wanton act of dereliction almost cost him his life.

To be **remiss, slack,** or **negligent,** as in guarding a base, is to be careless and neglectful.
To be **derelict** is to disregard or abandon one's duty shamefully. The Latin root means "utterly forsaken."

6. **EPITHET** (ĕp′ĭ·thĕt) . . . . descriptive title

"Carrot-top" is an epithet for a redhead.

An epithet often functions as an adjective, as in "Ivan the Terrible." An **appellation** is a name or title: Mr. Cruncher's appellation was "Jerry."

7. **FIEND** (fēnd) . . . . demon, monster

Only a fiend could have sent so many human beings to the gas chambers and concentration camps.
▶ The fighter attacked with fiendish energy.

A dope fiend is a demon about dope. A chemistry "fiend" is especially fond of chemistry, but this use of the word is not acceptable in formal writing.

8. **HARBINGER** (här′bĭn·jēr) . . . . . . forerunner, herald

Dawn was, in this case, the harbinger of victory.
Sorrow is often a harbinger of joy.

Synonym: ***precursor***

9. **OMEN** (ō′mĕn) . . . . portent, foretoken

The howling of a dog was once thought to be an omen of death.
▶ Ominous (threatening) sounds came from the lions' den.

A **portentous** (III, 4) event is one that **augurs** or foretells very good or very bad fortune.
A **fateful** day is one which will decide somebody's fate.
A **foreboding** or **presentiment** is a knowing or feeling beforehand that something disastrous or marvelous is going to happen.

10. **PESTILENCE** (pĕs′tĭ·lĕnz) . . . . . . a widespread disease

The Black Death was a pestilence that once destroyed one third of the people in Europe.

▻ The old man's head is full of pestilent (harmful) ideas.

A pestilence may be either a disease or the epidemic it causes.
A **pest** is a nuisance of some kind, or a harmful insect or animal.
Cf. pester, pestiferous, pernicious (II, 9)

11. POTION (pō'shŭn) . . . . a liquid dose; a drink

Socrates drank the deadly potion without hesitation.
▻ Potable water is fit to drink.

Both *potion* and **potable** come from the Latin verb *potare*, meaning "to drink."

12. SEVERITY (sė·vĕr'ĭ·tĭ) . . rigor, sternness; plainness (of outline)

Recruits often dislike the severity of military discipline.
The severity of the modernistic cathedral is impressive.
▻ The winters in Minnesota are very severe.

Synonym: The **austerity** (hardships) of frontier life fostered fine qualities of character.

FIRST PRACTICE SET

Copy the *italicized* words. Beside each, write an appropriate definition.

1. When Sam stops *abetting* the mischief, the trouble will *abate*.
2. The pilot *cited* three *omens* of good luck.
3. The mysterious *potion* did not *entice* us.
4. He *laments*, and his wife *resents*, every attempt to *frustrate* his business ventures.
5. The *anecdote* was about a huge meteorite which created quite an *abyss* when it struck the earth.
6. Only a *fiend* would spread the germs of a *pestilence*.
7. *Pulverize* moth balls and their *aroma* will soon *pervade* the house.
8. Do not *reproach* the bees for their *severity* in *purging* the hive of its drones.
9. The *derelict* in the sea proved to be the *harbinger* of trouble.
10. George *manifests* no surprise at the *epithet*.

SECOND PRACTICE SET

Which base word best replaces the *italicized* word or words?

1. The king will *encourage* the plot to push the enemy knight into the *deep chasm.*
2. *Inveigled* by a favorable *foretoken,* the general would not wait.
3. By his *sternness,* the man tried to *thwart* the boy's courage.
4. Did the *monster* at any time *reveal* fear?
5. The *widespread disease* made many *feel sorrow for* their sins.
6. Can you *mention* several *brief stories* which teach that it is unwise to *take offense at* fancied injuries?
7. The *fragrance* of the finest food becomes unpleasant to those who *satisfy to excess* themselves.
8. The *outcast* was *cleared* from the accusation of dishonesty.
9. The *descriptive title* "Pandora" was intended to *upbraid* Mary for being too curious.
10. The bird which he could see through the *opening* in the tent was a *forerunner* of defeat.

THIRD PRACTICE SET

Write the numbers of the *italicized* words. Beside each, write the number of the matching word or words from the second column.

1. *Ominous* rumblings	1.	distasteful
2. *Fiendish* glee	2.	fit to drink
3. *Anecdotal* writing	3.	harmful
4. *Cloying* music	4.	sorrowful
5. *Aromatic* plants	5.	immeasurably deep
6. *Negligent* dishonesty	6.	demonic
7. *Pestilent* thoughts	7.	threatening
8. *Abysmal* despair	8.	filled with brief stories
9. *Severe* economy	9.	excessively sweet
10. *Potable* river water	10.	spicy-smelling
	11.	careless
	12.	rigorous

UNIT FIVE

In each case, which of the choices is most appropriate?

1. Warm weather plus soft varnish: You will (a) adhere (b) elude (c) emulate (d) intimate

2. Comic-book prank plus Dad: Dad will (a) disperse (b) chastise (c) assail (d) enhance

3. Bad man plus police: He will try to (a) adorn (b) assail (c) elude (d) disperse

4. One barn plus one careless hobo: Result is (a) apathy (b) discretion (c) accomplice (d) conflagration

5. One victory plus celebration: Result is (a) aggravation (b) torpor (c) elation (d) exertion

6. One surgeon plus accident victim: Surgeon needs (a) defiance (b) decorum (c) conjecture (d) dexterity

7. One hero plus a boy's admiration: The boy is sure to (a) enhance (b) emulate (c) evince (d) adhere

8. One miser, completely self-centered: Result is (a) castigation (b) avarice (c) defiance (d) stupor

• Word List—VERBS

1. ADHERE (ăd·hēr') . . . . stick fast, cling

Paint will not adhere readily to a polished metal surface.

■ The Christian religion has about seven hundred million adherents (followers) in the world.

■ The company's adherence to its agreement not to hire non-union labor proved rather costly.

■ Adhesion of two internal organs caused Napoleon much pain.

► Adhesive tape adheres to the skin.

2. ADORN (à·dôrn') . . . . decorate, add beauty

Tapestries adorn the walls of the palace.

■ Excessive personal adornment shows bad taste.

Cf. beautify, embellish, bedeck

3. ALTER (ôl'tēr) . . . . change, modify

"A cry of 'Shame! shame!' . . . induced Prince John to alter his ungenerous purpose."

■ Alteration of the new suit is necessary to make it fit better.

► The determination of Columbus to reach the Indies by sailing west was not alterable.

An **alter ego** is a close friend or another self. It is an expression unchanged from Latin which means, literally, "another I."
Cf. unalterable

4. ASSAIL (ă·sāl') . . . . attack

This article assails the chief of police for failing to catch the thugs who robbed the Central Bank twice.

She sat fortifying her mind "against those treacherous feelings which assailed her from within."

■ The injured man could not identify his assailant.

An **assault** is almost always a violent or bodily attack of some kind: The assault on the city failed. (See dictionary for legal definition.)

5. **AUGMENT** (ôg·měnt′) . . . increase; make or become larger

Father works nights to augment his income.
"As the fire augmented, symptoms of it became soon apparent in the chamber where Ivanhoe was watched and tended by Rebecca."
- The governor recommended augmentation of the National Guard from 50,000 to 75,000 men.

6. **CHASTISE** (chǎs·tīz′) . . . . punish

"We are . . . rather to lament than chastise his backsliding."
- Junior deserved the chastisement he got for tormenting his brother.

   To chastise a person is usually to inflict bodily punishment.
   To **castigate** is to criticize or upbraid severely.
   To **chasten** is to purify or bring about moral improvement, chiefly through trials and suffering.

7. **DISPERSE** (dĭs·pûrs′) . . . . scatter; separate

The crowd did not disperse at once.
- "The Prince resumed his retreat from the lists, and the dispersion of the multitude became general."

8. **ELUDE** (ê·lūd′) . . . . escape; evade

The boy tried to elude his pursurers by hiding in a barrel.
"These knights, therefore, their aim being thus eluded, rushed from opposite sides . . ."
- That elusive (hard-to-catch or -hold) halfback slipped through the entire opposing team and made a touchdown.

9. **EMULATE** (ěm′ů·lāt) . . . . strive to equal or excel

Robert E. Lee was, in many ways, a man to emulate.
- A boy often shapes his life in emulation of the men he reads about in biographies.

10. **ENHANCE** (ěn·hàns′) . . . . . heighten; make greater

Trees enhance the value of the property.
"The impatience of Cedric had been enhanced by his confinement."

■ Her smile lent enhancement to all her other charms.

To enhance is to improve the quality of something and thus make it more attractive.
To **augment** is to increase the quantity or number: The troop was soon augmented by reinforcements from the rear.

11. EVINCE (ê·vĭns′) . . . . show, reveal

A "poker face" is an expressionless face which does not evince surprise.
"The antagonist of Grantmesnil . . . evinced awkwardness and want of management of the weapon and of the horse."

People evince and **manifest** (I, 4) qualities or feelings.
They **display** and **exhibit** things, such as jewels, cars, and hobbies.

12. EXTRICATE (ĕks′trĭ·kāt) . . . . disentangle

"To extricate himself from the stirrups and fallen steed was to the Templar scarce the work of a moment."
■ Extrication of the driver from the wreck took over an hour.

An **inextricable** mystery is one which cannot be disentangled. Accent *inextricable* on the second syllable.

13. INTIMATE (ĭn′tĭ·māt) . . . . hint; imply

Did you intimate that you would go to the carnival if you had the money?
■ Rowena "drew with dignity the veil around her face as an intimation that the determined freedom of his glance was disagreeable."

■ Word List—NOUNS

1. ACCOMPLICE (ă·kŏm′plĭs) . . . . . . partner in a crime

Without an accomplice he could not have obtained the combination to the safe.

A **confederate** is an ally, usually in something unlawful or at least mischievous.

2. **ANTAGONIST** (ăn·tăg′ŏ·nĭst) . . . . . opponent, adversary

"One of their antagonists was overthrown."

● His conceited manner antagonizes (renders unfriendly) those who might be his friends.

▶ Agnes has an antagonistic (unfriendly) attitude.

Antagonist refers to a rival but not necessarily to an adversary (in the sense of a hostile person or enemy).

3. **APATHY** (ăp′à·thĭ) . . . . . . lack of feeling; indifference

The apathy of Cedric's companion "served to defend him against everything save the inconvenience of the present moment."

▶ The boy's apathetic eyes were half closed with weariness.

Lethargy is drowsiness or sluggishness from some physical cause, such as overeating. The word comes from *Lethe*, the Greek name for the mythological river of forgetfulness.
Torpor is sluggishness from temporary loss of physical powers, as from cold.
A **stupor** is a deadened condition, especially of the mind, as from drugs.

4. **AVARICE** (ăv′à·rĭs) . . . . . . greed for money, cupidity

"'Do not thou interrupt me with thine ill-timed avarice,' said the outlaw."

▶ The old miser grew more avaricious as the years went on.

Greed Words: ***stingy, covetous, miserly, niggardly, parsimonious***

5. **CONFLAGRATION** (kŏn′flà·grā′shŭn) . . . . very large fire

"The maniac figure of the Saxon Ulrica was . . . tossing her arms abroad with wild exultation, as if she reigned empress of the conflagration which she had raised."

The fire bombs caused appalling conflagrations in London.

6. **CONJECTURE** (kŏn·jĕk′tûr) . . . . guess, inference

"On his retiring to his tent, many who had lingered in the lists, to look upon and form conjectures . . . also dispersed."

▶ The conjectural nature of football predictions makes them highly unreliable.

7. DECORUM (dē·kō'rŭm) . . . . proper behavior

The prime minister is very naturally a model of decorum.

▶ With a decorous gesture, he waved me into the car.

■ The millionaire found decorousness in dress easier to achieve than decorousness in conversation.

Behavior Words: *mien, demeanor* (I, 2), *deportment, propriety* (III, 3)

8. DEFIANCE (dē·fī'ăns) . . . . . open disregard, challenge

"The music also of the challengers breathed from time to time wild outbursts expressive of triumph or defiance."

▶ There was a defiant look in the batter's eyes as he faced the pitcher.

● The secrets of life in the ocean still defy scientists.

9. DEXTERITY (dĕks·tĕr'ĭ·tĭ) . . . . skill, adroitness

A surgeon must possess great digital (finger) dexterity.
"The champions a second time . . . closed in the center of the lists, with the same speed, the same dexterity . . . "

– "See how dexterously they avail themselves of every cover which a tree or bush affords."

Dexterity comes from the Latin root *dexter* meaning "right" or "to the right," and is sometimes used to mean "right-handedness."

10. DISCRETION (dĭs·krĕsh'ŭn) . . . . . prudence, judiciousness

Martha could invite her friends to the house at her own discretion if she told her mother in time.

▶ George was discreet enough to wait until his father was in a more amiable mood before asking for the family car.

Discretion often means "the freedom to make one's own decisions."

11. ELATION (ē·lā'shŭn) . . . . . . exultant gladness or pride

Elation over his success in the contest made him jubilant.

● His success elated his parents.

12. EXERTION (ĕg·zûr'shŭn) . . . . vigorous effort

"Athelstane had a disposition too inert and unambitious to make the exertions which Cedric seemed to expect . . ."

● The doctor will exert himself to save the victim's life.

Cf. endeavor, meaning "an attempt or sustained effort"

FIRST PRACTICE SET

Copy the *italicized* words. Beside each, write an appropriate definition.

1. Gum seldom *adorns* anything to which it *adheres*.
2. The team tried to *alter* its offensive and *assail* its opponents through the line.
3. Bob threatened to *chastise* the boys if they did not *disperse*.
4. The opportunity to *augment* his income *eluded* his grasp.
5. Tom *evinced* no surprise when advised to *emulate* his uncle.
6. His burly *antagonist intimated* that the boy was a coward.
7. The man's *apathy* about giving money was due to *avarice*.
8. The enemy met with *defiance* our *conjecture* about victory.
9. The archer had *discretion* and did not boast of his *dexterity*.
10. All *exertions* to check the *conflagration* were useless.

SECOND PRACTICE SET

Which base word from this unit best replaces each *italicized* word or group of words?

1. Our *exultant gladness* was *heightened* by the knowledge that the judges would *cling* strictly to the rules.
2. "Smiles *add beauty to* a face but frowns don't," she *implied*.
3. "A mere *guess* does not *modify* my attitude," she said.
4. His *opponent attacked* him from the side.
5. The firebug's *partner in crime* watched the *very large fire* with complete *lack of feeling*.
6. Father decided to *punish* William for his lack of *proper behavior* at his sister's party.
7. She liked to watch football players *disentangle* themselves from each other and *scatter*.
8. You will *increase* your output perceptibly if you *strive to equal* a master workman's *skill*.
9. He had the *judiciousness* to realize that he could not *escape* the police much longer.
10. His *open disregard* of society increased along with his *greed for money*.

THIRD PRACTICE SET

On a separate sheet of paper, write the numbers of the *italicized* words. Beside each, write the number of the matching word or group of words from the second column.

1. *Extrication* from difficulty	1. increase in quantity
2. The Pimpernel's *elusiveness*	2. striving to be the equal
3. An *assault* on his honesty	3. increasing dislike
4. *Torpor* because of the heat	4. scattering
5. Gentle *chastisement*	5. stinginess
6. The *intimation* of treachery	6. modification
7. *Adherence* to a building code	7. heightening
8. *Dispersion* of snowflakes	8. disentanglement
9. *Augmentation* of one's resources	9. attacker
10. *Emulation* of heroes	10. punishment
11. *Adornment* of the new building	11. slow wasting away
12. The *avariciousness* of Mr. Brown	12. attack
13. *Alteration* of a road plan	13. act of sticking to
14. *Enhancement* of opportunities	14. being hard to catch
15. The mayor's *assailant*	15. sluggishness (temporary)
	16. hint or implication
	17. decoration

1. *Apathetic* attitudes	1. unfriendly
2. *Unalterable* reluctance	2. drowsy
3. Her *discreet* praise	3. skillful
4. *Antagonistic* remarks	4. prudent, judicious
5. The *elusive* enemy	5. challenging
6. A *lethargic* expression	6. exultant
7. *Dexterous* movements	7. indirect
8. *Defiant* gestures	8. purified by suffering
9. An *elated* grandfather	9. unchangeable
10. A *chastened* look	10. distressed
	11. without feeling, indifferent
	12. hard-to-catch

UNIT SIX

What is the best response to each question?

1. Which is luminous? (a) a mine shaft (b) a firefly (c) an electric blanket (d) an eyeshade

2. Which is lurid? (a) city dump on fire (b) lights on football field (c) living room at night (d) harvest moon

3. Which makes one languid? (a) coffee (b) a good movie (c) a spanking (d) a hot afternoon

4. What makes one's breath humid? (a) diet (b) moisture (c) bad odor (d) running

5. Are domestic tastes (a) dull (b) those of a servant (c) home-centered (d) homely?

6. Where would a nomadic person live? (a) in the slums (b) in a trailer (c) in a castle (d) in a lighthouse

7. Would nocturnal habits be (a) musical (b) shady (c) adventurous (d) practiced at night?

8. Would copious supplies be (a) plentiful (b) defective (c) scanty (d) well-arranged?

▶ Word List—ADJECTIVES

1. COPIOUS (kō'pĭ·ŭs) . . . . abundant, plentiful

Copious showers made the cisterns overflow.

■ The copiousness of the harvests brought prices down.

> Plenty Words: **Ample** appreciation is more than sufficient.
> **Bountiful** appreciation is abundant, in the sense of generous.
> **Profuse** appreciation is poured forth to excess.
> What does **cornucopia** mean?

2. DOMESTIC (dŏ·mĕs'tĭk) . . . . . of home life or homeland

Skill in cooking is a domestic virtue, and domestic happiness is one of the conditions of a happy marriage.

Domestic cheese is cheese made in one's homeland.

Domestic animals are tame animals trained to live with man.

● It is difficult to domesticate a tiger because it is big, wild, and dangerous.

3. EMINENT (ĕm'ĭ·nĕnt) . . . . . . outstanding, prominent

Dr. Straus, an eminent Austrian surgeon, is in this country.

■ The eminence of the author helped the sale of his book.

■ From an eminence (elevation or hill), Napoleon watched the battle.

> Query: What is the right of **eminent domain?** How has it been used in your community?
> Fame Words: *renowned, celebrated, distinguished, illustrious, notorious.* Which one is unfavorable?

4. FRUGAL (froo'găl) . . . . economical; sparing; thrifty

Frugal habits enabled them to save a thousand dollars a year.

■ Is frugality always a virtue? It verges on miserliness.

> **Prodigal** (lavish) and **prodigality** are opposites of *frugal* and *frugality.*
> Cf. *wasteful, extravagant*

5. HOMELY (hōm′lĭ) . . . . **plain, unpretentious**

Homely pleasures and homely food never quite lose their appeal.

One might sing, "Be it ever so homely, there's no place like home."

Though homely, the Taft girl is not ugly.

■ Her homeliness is no handicap.

6. HOSTILE (hŏs′tĭl) . . . . **unfriendly, warlike**

The hostile glances of the braves showed their enmity.

■ The hostility of the natives made it unsafe to land.

Synonyms: *adverse, averse, inimical, antagonistic* (I, 5)

7. HUMID (hū′mĭd) . . . . **damp, moist**

One feels warmer in the humid air of New Orleans than in the dry air of Arizona.

■ The tropical humidity of the jungle was oppressive.

Query: What is a **humidifier**? Does your home have one?

8. LANGUID (lăng′gwĭd) . . . . **drooping; listless**

Hot, sticky July days make one feel languid and spiritless.

■ On such days, a delicious languor steals over one toward evening.

► August is a languorous month, too, especially at the seashore.

● The flowers will languish for lack of water.

To **languish** is to droop or pine away, as one might from grief or imprisonment.
Lassitude is weariness or languor, whether it comes from work, weather, or some other cause.

9. LAUDABLE (lôd′á·b′l) . . . . . **praiseworthy, commendable**

Jim made a laudable effort to win the tennis match.

● We laud those who gave their lives in a noble cause.

► The paper contains a laudatory editorial about a teacher who is retiring.

"Laus Deo" means "Praise (be) to God."

10. LENIENT (lē′nǐ·ĕnt) . . . . mild, merciful

The warden is very lenient with the convicts whom he has found trustworthy.

■ The prison board approves of leniency (lenience) where it is justifiable.

Lenity has almost the same meaning as *leniency.*

11. LUMINOUS (lū′mǐ·nŭs) . . . . . . glowing, giving off light

Neon signs are luminous and numerous.

■ The luminousness (luminosity) of an October moon is the crowning glory of autumn.

■ Jupiter is the brightest luminary among the planets.

A **luminary** is a celestial body or, figuratively, a celebrity on earth who gives off considerable light. In the same way, a glowing mind is said to be luminous.
Cf. lucid (I, 3), *lumen, luminescence, luminiferous, illuminate, illumination*

12. LURID (lū′rǐd) . . . . . shining with a fiery glare; horrible

A halo of lurid light hovered over the blast furnace.

The paper carried a lurid account of the airplane disaster.

Lurid may mean "wild, unnatural, sensational, terrifying, ghastly" (I, 3): A lurid crime is one marked by violent passion.

13. NOCTURNAL (nŏk·tûr′năl) . . . . . . occurring at night

During his nocturnal wanderings, the soldier got lost in a labyrinth of alleys.

Nocturnal flowers bloom at night, and many wild animals engage in nocturnal hunting.

■ The next piano number was a nocturne.

A **nocturne** is a dreamy, romantic musical composition, often dealing with or referring to night. It may also be a painting of a night scene.

14. NOMADIC (nŏ·măd′ĭk) . . . wandering, having no fixed home

Hobos live a nomadic life.

The Bedouins are nomadic Arabs.

■ They live in a manner typical of desert nomads.

Nomad goes back to a Greek word meaning "pasturing, roaming about for pasture."

15. OBLIQUE (ŏb·lēk') . . . . slanting; indirect

The oblique lines in the shaded area of the drawing indicate the concrete foundation.

The lawyer's questioning was oblique because he wanted to trap the witness.

− The spy approached the fort obliquely.

Oblique behavior is behavior that is indirect and thus underhanded or tricky.

An oblique line is neither parallel to, nor at a right angle with, a given line. An oblique angle is any angle except a right angle.

An **obtuse** angle is wider than a right angle. An obtuse person is "dense" or thick-headed.

16. OBNOXIOUS (ŏb·nŏk'shŭs) . . . . . . offensive, hateful

Television advertising is often obnoxious because it lasts too long or repeats itself too much.

▪ Its obnoxiousness does not keep people from watching favorite programs, however.

Noxious means "harmful": Carbon monoxide is a noxious gas.
Cf. odious

17. OFFICIOUS (ŏ·fĭsh'ŭs) . . . . . . forward, meddlesome

It was very officious of Mr. Popple to come to the meeting uninvited and attempt to tell the officers how to run the business.

▪ His officiousness made us dislike him.

Cf. intrusive, obtrusive

18. PERPETUAL (pēr·pĕt'ṵ·ăl) . . . . . unending, lasting forever

At that period, Mexico was in a state of perpetual unrest.

The peak of Mt. Everest is covered by perpetual snows.

● This monument will perpetuate the memory of Albert Einstein.

▪ We hold the land in perpetuity (pûr'pė·tū'ĭ·tĭ); i.e. forever.

Anything perpetual extends only as far as one can foresee. Perpetual care as provided with the purchase of a cemetery lot is not really eternal care.

Anything **incessant** or **interminable** is often annoying as well as unceasing.

Anything **everlasting** or **eternal** reaches to the limits of time.

19. **REGAL** (rē′găl) . . . . royal, fit for a king

The Bidwells live in a home furnished with regal splendor.
- They entertain guests regally.
▪ Mr. Bidwell carries himself with an air intended to suggest regality.

The word ***regalia*** originally referred to the emblems and decorations of royalty. Today it is applied to the emblems of any organization.

20. **ROGUISH** (rō′gĭsh) . . . . knavish; mischievous

Putting the wormy apples at the bottom of the basket was a roguish trick.
Ben's roguish disguises amused everybody at the party.
▪ His roguishness is always clever and yet harmless.

What is the "rogues' gallery" in the post office?

21. **VEHEMENT** (vē′ĕ·mĕnt) . . . . violent; passionate

A congressman from Michigan made a vehement speech against the banking bill.
▪ Elijah's vehemence against the priests of Baal terrified his listeners.

22. **VINDICTIVE** (vĭn·dĭk′tĭv) . . . . . vengeful, seeking revenge

He was in a very vindictive mood because he had been unfairly accused.
▪ The boy tore up his sister's comic books in sheer vindictiveness because she had taken his skates.

23. **VOCIFEROUS** (vō·sĭf′ĕr·ŭs) . . . . clamorous, loudly insistent

Several vociferous boys disturb the neighborhood on their way home.
▪ Their vociferousness wakes up children who are taking naps.
● The boys in the swimming pool vociferate their displeasure when the water is cold.

Clamorous outcries are urgently noisy.
An **obstreperous** crowd is noisy in an unruly sense.
A **blatant** outburst has a coarse, bellowing quality.

24.   **VULNERABLE** (vŭl'nĕr·à·b'l) .   .   . susceptible to injury or attack

People who live in glass houses should not throw stones because the houses are vulnerable to vindictive assailants.

■ The vulnerability of Achilles' heel cost him his life.

General Wing thought his forces were invulnerable to attack.

25.   **ZEALOUS** (zĕl'ŭs) .   .   .   .   .   . very active; eager; devoted

Doctors were very zealous in testing the Salk vaccine before it was released for wide use.

■ Florence Nightingale was a zealot in the true sense of the word.

A **zealot** is a person who is deeply and even vehemently zealous in working for a cause.

A **fanatic** is over-zealous. **Fanaticism** consists in redoubling your effort when you have forgotten your aim, according to Santayana's famous definition.

A **bigot** is zealous in a blind and intolerant manner, particularly in behalf of a cherished belief.

FIRST PRACTICE SET

Copy the *italicized* words. Beside each, write an appropriate definition.

1. The air was *humid* and the sky was *luminous*.

2. *Copious* use of soap is a good *domestic* habit.

3. *Frugal* housewives are *hostile* to waste, and so they plan their meals carefully.

4. He could not be *lenient* in punishing so *obnoxious* a misdeed.

5. She carried herself with *regal* dignity and her eyes expressed *perpetual* wonder.

6. With *roguish* glee, the baby pulled the *officious* lady's hair.

7. The man was as *vindictive* toward his enemies as he was *vehement* about his beliefs.

8. Her son's *laudable* achievements made her *vociferous*.

9. Years of *zealous* research made him an *eminent* inventor.

10. Since the *lurid* gossip was not true, his reputation was not *vulnerable*.

SECOND PRACTICE SET

Which base word best replaces the *italicized* word or words?

1. Uncle Herman grew *passionate* at the *mischievous* reminder.

2. *Horrible* accounts of injuries to children are *hateful* to mothers.

3. *Unending* success made her *glowing*.

4. Fleeing criminals lead a *wandering* life that is also largely *restricted to night*.

5. "Pug" was an *unpretentious* dog who liked *abundant* food.

6. The *damp* air of the tropics fosters *listless* enjoyment.

7. Most mothers are *unfriendly* to dirt and *very active* in the use of soap.

8. Is a *merciful* judge always *praiseworthy?*

9. The *prominent* scientist was very *sparing* in his eating habits.

10. Her new evening gown is *fit-for-a-queen* even though the silk is a *homeland* product.

THIRD PRACTICE SET

Write the number of the *italicized* words. Beside each, write the number of the matching word or words from the second column.

1. *Luminousness* of the firelight
2. *Frugality* in buying
3. *Zealot* for peace
4. The invalid's *lassitude*
5. *Vehemence* of the attack
6. The candidate's *homeliness*
7. The writer's *eminence*
8. A criminal's *vindictiveness*
9. *Humidity* in Florida
10. *Obliqueness* of the rain

1. great violence
2. weariness
3. moistness of the air
4. deeply devoted worker
5. slanting quality
6. glowingness
7. fiery glow
8. vengefulness
9. listlessness
10. thrift
11. plainness of face
12. prominence

1. *Nomads* of Arabia
2. The guard's *officiousness*
3. Sign showing a *cornucopia*
4. The player's *vulnerability*
5. *Zealousness* in politics
6. A child's *roguishness*
7. *Regalia* of a general
8. A father's *leniency*
9. The boy's *obnoxiousness*
10. Hidden *hostility*

1. horn of plenty
2. odiousness
3. unfriendliness
4. emblems, rights, decorations
5. mercifulness
6. meddlesomeness
7. formality
8. mischievousness
9. susceptibility to injury
10. commendation
11. men without fixed homes
12. devoted activity

RATHER PERSONAL

Think of a classmate, acquaintance, or celebrity to whom one or more of the adjectives in this unit may be applied. Write a short description of this person.

ANTONYMS

On a separate sheet, write the number of the word which is most
nearly the **opposite** of the *italicized* word.

1. *Humid* weather	1. friendly
2. *Vindictive* spirit	2. pleasing
3. A *lenient* teacher	3. blameworthy
4. *Copious* weeping	4. forgiving
5. *Laudable* motives	5. lavish
6. *Obnoxious* mosquitoes	6. gentle
7. *Vociferous* ducks	7. dry
8. *Hostile* newspapers	8. strict
9. *Frugal* with words	9. ugly
10. *Vehement* objections	10. scanty
	11. untruthful
	12. quiet

A POSTSCRIPT IN VERBS

What verb from the unit will best replace each *italicized* word or
group of words?

1. In folktales, princesses always *pine away* in towers.

2. The device will *add moisture to* the air.

3. A wild horse is difficult to *train for farm (or home) duties*.

4. We *make to last forever* the memory of George Washington.

5. The boys *make noise* gaily on the playground.

UNIT SEVEN

Which is the best answer to each question?

1. Which does one find in a grave? (a) incognito (b) rendez-vous (c) repose (d) succor

2. What, most of all, made Adolf Hitler terrible? (a) tyranny (b) visage (c) insolence (d) retinue

3. What does the Red Cross furnish chiefly? (a) rendezvous (b) repose (c) obeisance (d) succor

4. Which form of anger is the most justifiable? (a) ire (b) wrath (c) indignation (d) rage

5. Which word refers to the point in the sky directly overhead? (a) acme (b) summit (c) apex (d) zenith

6. Which word best describes senseless chatter? (a) incessant (b) infernal (c) inane (d) errant

7. Which word best describes a house only fifteen feet from yours? (a) adjoining (b) adjacent (c) abutting (d) contiguous

8. What kind of sorrow lasts the longest? (a) continual (b) perpetual (c) continuous (d) incessant

9. Which word best describes a dog's faith in his master? (a) implicit (b) inane (c) inferior (d) agile

65

► Word List—ADJECTIVES

1. **ACUTE** (á·kūt′) . . . . **sharp, severe**
   The point of the spear was acute and highly polished.
   There is an acute shortage of persons trained in mathematics.
   ■ The acuteness of the pain doubled him up in agony.

   Sharp Words: *keen, discerning* (I, 2), *astute, perspicacious* (III, 3)

2. **ADJACENT** (á·jā′sĕnt) . . . . **neighboring, near**
   The adjacent forest abounded with outlaws.
   ■ The adjacency of the playground makes the location a noisy one.

   Near Words: Adjacent lots do not necessarily touch each other, but **adjoining, abutting** and **contiguous** lots do. What is a bridge abutment? Are England and France adjacent or contiguous countries?

3. **AGILE** (ăj′ĭl) . . . . **nimble, quick-moving**
   Monkeys are remarkably agile animals.
   ■ A circus acrobat must display great agility.

   Nimble Words: A **nimble** person is quick and deft of body or mind. A **lithe** or **supple** body or mind is **pliant, limber, flexible,** bending readily.

4. **ERRANT** (ĕr′ănt) . . . . **roving, wandering**
   Gurth was worried at the thought of the "errant knights and errant squires . . ." who might rob him.

   A **knight-errant** was a wandering knight in search of noble adventures. Scott wrote stories of knight-errantry.
   Cf. nomadic (I, 6), *itinerant*

5. **EXORBITANT** (ĕg·zôr′bĭ·tănt) . . . . **excessive**
   "Said Isaac, 'I cannot make the choice, because I have not the means of satisfying your exorbitant demand.'"
   ■ The exorbitance of the prices kept customers away.

   Cf. extravagant, unreasonable, inordinate, unconscionable

6. **EXULTANT** (ĕg·zŭl'tănt) . . . . joyful, jubilant

The downfall of Bois-Guilbert made Rebecca exultant because Bois-Guilbert was her father's enemy.

● Readers today exult over Ivanhoe's prowess as a knight.

■ Cries of exultation greeted Ivanhoe's triumphs at the tournament.

To **jubilate** is to rejoice wholeheartedly.
A **jubilation** or **jubilee** is a celebration. See dictionary for religious meanings of *jubilee.*

7. **IMPLICIT** (ĭm·plĭs'ĭt) . . . . unquestioning; implied

"They promised implicit obedience and departed with alacrity on their differing errands."

Dad gave his implicit approval by not refusing to let Tom drive to the game.

■ The implicitness (absoluteness) of Ted's faith in the coach was justified.

8. **INANE** (ĭn·ān') . . . . senseless, empty

Mrs. Potter made several inane remarks about how big the children were getting.

■ The rescue party reported that the survivors were in a state of inanition (exhaustion) but were otherwise all right.

■ "Do we not while away moments of inanity . . . by repeating some trivial movement or sound?"

Pronounce the *a* in *inanity* as in *tan.*

9. **INCESSANT** (ĭn·sĕs'ănt) . . . . ceaseless, continual

Incessant attacks on the fortress finally made victory possible.

– Lucy is the one who talks incessantly.

Ceaseless Words: A **continual** noise is one which keeps occurring at frequent intervals.
A **continuous** noise is a steady noise which does not let up until something is done about it.
A **perpetual** noise is one which lasts indefinitely and probably cannot be stopped.
An **eternal** noise is literally one which lasts forever. *Perpetual* and *eternal* may be used interchangeably. See *perpetual* (I, 6).

10. **INCOGNITO** (ĭn·kŏg'nĭ·tō) . . . . in disguise

Since the King wished to be incognito during his visit, he gave his name as Mr. Rex.

- Celebrities sometimes travel incognito to escape reporters.

11. **INERT** (ĭn·ûrt') . . . . inactive

Neon, an inert gas, will not combine chemically with anything.

The lifeguard laid the child's inert form on the beach.

■ A state of inertia (sluggishness, lack of activity) prevailed.

A **passive** person is unwilling to take the lead in anything.
An **indolent** (II, 8) or **slothful** person is lazy.
A **dormant** condition is literally a sleeping condition.
A **listless** manner is indifferent and uninterested.
Cf. apathy, lethargy, torpor, stupor (I, 5)

12. **INFERIOR** (ĭn·fêr'ĭ·ẽr) . . . . . low(er) in place or quality

This year's crop of oranges is inferior to last year's.

■ Almost every one has a feeling of inferiority in some field.

Ersatz material is a substitute, usually inferior.

13. **INFERNAL** (ĭn·fûr'năl) . . . . hellish, fiendish

"Would I were out of the shade of these infernal bushes!" said Gurth in *Ivanhoe*.

The infernal plotting of the rebels kept the city in turmoil.

Hades was the underworld or infernal region of Greek mythology.
An **inferno** is a hell or a scene so horrible as to resemble hell: Soon the factory was a flaming inferno.
Cf. diabolical, devilish, satanic, demoniac

■ **Word List—NOUNS**

1. **FUGITIVE** (fū'jĭ·tĭv) . . . . . . one who flees; a runaway

The fugitive was a bank robber, who later shot himself.

▶ Fugitive sunbeams are fleeting or temporary.

A **refugee** is one who, for safety, flees from his home or homeland.

2. INDIGNATION (ĭn'dĭg·nā'shŭn) . . . . . justifiable **anger**

"The Prince rolled his eyes in indignation."

▸ "The indignant swineherd resumed his sullen silence."

Indignation is a rather dignified word for anger about something wrong or unfair.
Wrath may refer to punishment or revenge as well as anger.
Ire is a poetic or a newspaper word for anger.
Cf. fury, rage, resentment (I, 4), *exasperation* (II, 6)

3. INSOLENCE (ĭn'sŏ·lĕns) . . . . . insulting behavior; **impudence**

"Woe betide him unless his skill should prove some apology for his insolence!"

▸ "I have a debt to pay to that insolent peasant who yesterday insulted our person."

▸ The man lost his job because, in an insolent moment, he called the boss a "dope."

4. OBEISANCE (ō·bā'săns) . . . . . . a bow or curtsy; **respect**

The Palmer, "after a low obeisance, tasted a few drops."
The referee at least did obeisance to the football rules.

Obeisance comes from the same root as *obey.*
See *deference* and *homage* (III, 1), which are forms of *respect.*

5. RECOMPENSE (rĕk'ŏm·pĕns) . . . . . compensation; **reward**

" 'An evil recompense,' said Rebecca, 'for the surrender of the rights which are dearest to humanity.' "
Years of hard work finally brought their recompense in public esteem.

● Locksley directed Cedric to recompense his followers with half the spoil.

6. RENDEZVOUS (rän'dĕ·vōō) . . . appointment; **meeting place**

"I have a rendezvous with death," wrote Alan Seeger.
Gurth believed "both that the gang was strong in numbers and they kept regular guards around their place of rendezvous."

● The two companies will rendezvous at midnight on Omaha Beach.

7. **REPOSE** (rĕ·pōz') . . . . rest; quiet

    "The looks of Wamba . . . indicated . . . a sort of vacant
    curiosity, and fidgety impatience of any posture of repose."
    * "The travellers paused . . . to repose their horses."

8. **RETINUE** (rĕt'ĭ·nū) . . . . train of attendants

    "A grand flourish of trumpets announced Prince John and
    his retinue."
    The bride's retinue included a flower girl and a ring bearer.

    A **cortège** is a procession, as at a funeral.
    Cf. escort

9. **SUCCOR** (sŭk'ẽr) . . . . aid, help

    She entreated her father "not to leave the oppressed and
    endangered without counsel and succor."
    * Wamba "made a brave though ineffectual attempt to
    succor his master."

10. **TYRANNY** (tĭr'ă·nĭ) . . . . . oppressive, unjust government

    "A circumstance . . . tended to enhance the tyranny of the
    nobility and the sufferings of the inferior classes."
    ▶ "Tell your tyrannical master, I do only beseech him to
    dismiss the Lady Rowena in honor and safety."
    ▪ Some of his enemies called Lincoln a tyrant (despot).

    Tyrannize means "rule oppressively."
    Cf. despotism

11. **VISAGE** (vĭz'ĭj) . . . . face, countenance

    The ugly visage of the creature haunted him in his dreams.
    * The boy envisaged (pictured) himself as a second Babe
    Ruth.

12. **ZENITH** (zē'nĭth) . . . . highest point

    The actress was at the zenith of her career when she died.
    Saturn will soon be at its zenith in the night skies.
    The zenith is the point in the sky directly overhead.

    Peak Words: ***pinnacle, summit, peak, apex, acme***

FIRST PRACTICE SET

Copy the *italicized* words. Beside each, write an appropriate definition.

1. *Acute* famine stalked the *adjacent* towns.
2. The *agile* acrobat charges *exorbitant* prices for a single performance.
3. The *incessant* cheering sounded rather *inane* to people who were not interested in the game.
4. *Errant* minstrels warned the *exultant* king that his popularity was at its *zenith*.
5. Mentally *inert* herself, she had *implicit* confidence in her husband's judgment.
6. *Inferior* coal causes *infernal* inconvenience.
7. The *fugitive* was traveling *incognito*.
8. The man's *insolence* aroused her *indignation,* and his sinister *visage* alarmed her.
9. The knight accepted his *recompense* with a deep *obeisance*.
10. The *rendezvous* in the woods provided a place for *repose*.

SECOND PRACTICE SET

Which base word best replaces the *italicized* word or words?

1. The *runaway* hid in the *nearby* building.
2. The knights set out in *disguise,* dressed as *wandering* priests.
3. The man's *justifiable anger* was great when *aid* did not come.
4. The *jubilant* duke's *insulting behavior* enraged the king.
5. The *reward* for an active campaign was a well-deserved *rest*.
6. The *quick-moving* scout soon found the *appointed meeting place.*
7. Being jealous, she made *senseless* remarks about the bride's *train of attendants.*
8. The king's *oppressive government* brought *excessive* prices.
9. After the *continual* use of artificial respiration, the *inactive* swimmer showed signs of recovery.
10. *Unquestioning* faith reached its *highest point* in Sarah's confidence that her father would win the election.

THIRD PRACTICE SET

On a separate sheet, write the numbers of the *italicized* words. Beside each, write the number of the matching word or group of words from the second column.

1.	The *agility* of a panther	1.	inactivity
2.	Military *inferiority*	2.	jubilation
3.	*Exorbitance* of his demands	3.	exhaustion
4.	*Inertness* of a turtle	4.	sharpness
5.	*Implicitness* of a child's faith	5.	nagging fear
6.	Songs of *exultation*	6.	excessiveness
7.	*Inanity* of his existence	7.	nimbleness
8.	*Inanition* from weariness	8.	roving adventuresomeness
9.	Mental *acuteness*	9.	animal energy
10.	Modern *knight-errantry*	10.	lower quality
		11.	absolute trustfulness
		12.	emptiness, senselessness

1.	*Tyrannical* habits	1.	disguised
2.	His *passive* attitude	2.	quick-moving, deft
3.	*Fugitive* thoughts	3.	oppressive
4.	*Indignant* fathers	4.	impudent
5.	*Abutting* timbers	5.	careful, cautious
6.	Performing *incognito*	6.	fleeting, short-lived
7.	A *supple* body	7.	justifiably angry
8.	*Contiguous* spheres of action	8.	not active
9.	An *insolent* remark	9.	bending readily, lithe
10.	"Jack, be *nimble!*"	10.	supporting (and thus touching)
		11.	catching, tending to adhere
		12.	touching or bordering

UNIT EIGHT

Which is the best answer to each question?

1. What kind of music is played at parades? (a) sinister (b) martial (c) menial (d) intricate

2. What must every soldier be? (a) valiant (b) obstinate (c) predatory (d) massive

3. What do we do to the enemy? (a) liberate (b) remonstrate (c) traverse (d) vanquish

4. When an attack comes, we must (a) terminate it (b) requite it (c) relinquish it (d) traverse it.

5. A sentry had to be shot because he was (a) sinister (b) precarious (c) negligent (d) menial.

6. What did we do when we could not hold the hill? (a) surmount it (b) relinquish it (c) traverse it (d) remonstrate with it

7. The work of cleaning up the mess hall is (a) massive (b) intricate (c) sinister (d) menial.

8. You would describe a fifty-ton tank as (a) massive (b) insurmountable (c) negligible (d) predatory.

9. A man unjustly accused of neglecting his duty should (a) terminate (b) relinquish (c) remonstrate (d) vilify.

73

• Word List— VERBS

1. **LIBERATE** (lĭb'ēr·āt) . . . . set free, release

   "To liberate a suitor preferred by the Lady Rowena was a pitch far above . . . De Bracy's generosity."

   ■ "The inventive genius of Wamba had procured liberation for himself and his companion in adversity."

   A **liberator** is one who sets you free.
   A **libertine** (lĭb'ēr·tēn) is one who is too free in his moral behavior.

2. **RELINQUISH** (rē·lĭng'kwĭsh) . . . . give up; let go

   The daughter would not relinquish her claim to her mother's property.

   ■ Relinquishment of the Philippine Islands by the United States liberated them and gave them independence.

   Give-Up Words: *yield, cede, waive, forego, surrender, resign, renounce, abdicate*

3. **REMONSTRATE** (rē·mŏn'strāt) . . . . . protest; expostulate

   "The Saxon, indeed, had remonstrated strongly with his friend upon the injudicious choice."

   ■ "Unheeding this remonstrance, . . . Brian de Bois-Guilbert kept his eyes riveted on the Saxon beauty."

4. **REQUITE** (rē·kwīt') . . . . repay; reward

   "May God requite you for your kindness," the little old lady exclaimed.

   ■ Old age brought requital for the sufferings of earlier years.

   Pay Words: **Requital** may be either retaliation or reward.
   To make **reparation** is to repair or pay for a damage done.
   To make **restitution** is to restore what has been taken wrongfully or to compensate for it.
   To **rectify** a mistake or a wrong condition is to correct it.
   To deserve **redress** for a wrong or injustice is to deserve amends.
   Cf. reimburse, indemnify, recompense (I, 7)

5. **RETARD** (rê·tärd′) . . . . delay; hinder

    "But think not, and speak not, now, of aught that may retard thy recovery."
    ■ The late spring that year caused retardation of crops.

    In music, *retard* means "slow down."

6. **SEGREGATE** (sĕg′rê·gāt) . . . . . . separate, set apart

    The Supreme Court decided that schools must no longer segregate Negro children from white children.
    ■ In a hospital, segregation of contagious cases is necessary.

7. **SURMOUNT** (sûr·mount′) . . . . . . overcome, rise above

    A spire surmounts the tower of the new church.
    "Not even the prospect of reward . . . could surmount this apprehension."
    ▶ He found as he got older that obstacles were surmountable if he faced them intelligently.

    Surmount means, literally, "mount upon": The troops tried to surmount the hill.

8. **TERMINATE** (tûr′mĭ·nāt) . . . . end, finish

    "Few augured the possibility that the encounter could terminate well for the Disinherited Knight."
    ▶ After what seemed an interminable delay, she was ready.
    ■ The company announced the termination of its contract.

    To **exterminate** something is to put an end to it: This powder will exterminate ants.
    The **terminus** or **terminal** is the end or final point: New York City is the terminus of numerous railroads.

9. **TRAVERSE** (trăv′ērs) . . . . pass or move across

    Experienced woodsmen traverse the forest without a compass.
    "The scoutmaster arrived after a brief delay, during which John traversed the apartment with unequal and disordered steps."

    Traverse has other meanings including "thwart," "contradict," and "deny." (See dictionary.)

10. **VANQUISH** (văng′kwĭsh) . . . . conquer, defeat

The Syrians were able to vanquish their foes.

▶ The Normans "were jealous of permitting to the vanquished Saxons the possession or the use of swords and spears."

Defeat Words: *subdue, quell, subjugate, surmount*

11. **VAUNT** (vônt) . . . . boast of, brag

"I conjure thee . . . by the knighthood thou dost vaunt . . . are these things true?"

▪ The Knight makes it his vaunt that no one can catch him.

▶ Slaying the mouse was another instance of Father's unvaunted heroism.

12. **VILIFY** (vĭl′ĭ·fi) . . . . speak evil of

Mr. Nye vilified his opponent by calling him a scoundrel.

▪ This campaign of vilification proved unwise.

● The opponent would not revile Mr. Nye no matter what the accusations were.

To **revile** is to abuse, assail, defame. It originally meant "treat or regard as vile."
Cf. upbraid, berate, vituperate

▶ Word List—ADJECTIVES

1. **INQUISITIVE** (ĭn·kwĭz′ĭ·tĭv) . . . . curious, prying

Girls are often very inquisitive.

▪ The newspaperman's inquisitiveness was not gratified.

An **inquisition** is an investigation, especially to punish people whose religious beliefs are considered false.
An **inquest** is an official inquiry into the cause of death where there may have been a crime.

2. **INTRICATE** (ĭn′trĭ·kĭt) . . . . complicated, complex

A bombsight is an exceedingly intricate mechanism.

▪ The intricacy of the forest paths made it easy to get lost.

3.   MARTIAL (mär'shăl) . . . . warlike, military

"All that was beautiful and graceful in the martial array had disappeared."

- The old lady couldn't remember whether her nephew wrote about a field marshal or a court-martial.

Martial law is military rule. For the armed forces, **courts-martial** take the place of civil courts. When a soldier is court-martialed, he is put on trial for an offense and judged by a military tribunal.

4.   MASSIVE (măs'ĭv) . . . . huge, solid, heavy

Three of the massive pillars are still standing.

- The massiveness of the Great Pyramid is awe-inspiring.

5.   MENIAL (mē'nĭ·ăl) . . . . servile; proper to slaves

Menial work, such as scrubbing floors or washing dishes, is unpleasant, everyday drudgery.

- In a medieval castle, the menials were often mistreated.

To be **servile** is to be slavishly humble and cringing.
To be **subservient** is to be readily submissive to someone else's domination.
Cf. obsequious

6.   NEGLIGENT (nĕg'lĭ·jĕnt) . . . . . . careless, neglectful

The driver was put in prison for being criminally negligent.

- The Templar and De Bracy expected the besiegers "to avail themselves of every negligence which might take place in the defense elsewhere."

Negligible details are small enough to disregard or treat carelessly.
A **negligee** is a woman's loose dressing gown.

7.   OBSTINATE (ŏb'stĭ·nĭt) . . . . stubborn, dogged

Why did the coach have to be obstinate about letting Joe go into the game today?

- "The followers of Front-de-Boeuf and his allies showed an obstinacy in defense proportioned to the fury of the attack."

Obdurate means "hard-hearted, hardened," especially against moral influence.
Cf. intractable, pertinacious (III, 8)

8. **PRECARIOUS** (prė·kâr′ĭ·ŭs) . . . . . . insecure, uncertain

"The situation of the inferior gentry was unusually precarious."

■ The precariousness of Bob's position on the roof alarmed his mother.

‑ Mountain climbers cling precariously to the sides of cliffs.

Precarious means "uncertain," in the sense of being subject to persons and conditions beyond one's control.

9. **PREDATORY** (prĕd′ȧ·tō′rĭ) . . . . . . plundering, robbing

Wolves are predatory beasts.

► The lion, too, is a predacious animal, which destroys other animals for food.

10. **REQUISITE** (rĕk′wĭ·zĭt) . . . . . . necessary; indispensable

A sense of humor is requisite to success in teaching.

■ In most careers, perseverance is a requisite.

● The boss will requisition a hundred pairs of overalls.

Need Words: *necessary, needful, essential, indispensable*

11. **SINISTER** (sĭn′ĭs·tēr) . . . . ill-boding, evil

The dark, sinister figure was waiting on the corner.

Sinister may also mean "on the left-hand side," especially in heraldry: The coat of arms had a bar sinister of red.
Something **ominous** is itself threatening (I, 4): An ominous rumbling began to come from the volcano.
Portentous applies to something foreshadowing evil or an amazing event (III, 4).

12. **SUNDRY** (sŭn′drĭ) . . . . various

The path along the cliff has given way in sundry places.

■ Drugstores and ten-cent stores are well stocked with sundries (various minor articles too numerous to list).

To **sunder** old ties is to break them **asunder** or apart.

13. **VALIANT** (văl′yănt) . . . . brave, courageous

"The valiant never taste of death but once."

■ Ivanhoe was admired for his gallantry and valor.

FIRST PRACTICE SET

Copy the *italicized* words. Beside each, write an appropriate definition.

1. Police *liberated* the suspects they had *segregated.*
2. The man was glad to *relinquish* his *menial* duties.
3. I *remonstrate* because you *requite* me badly for the service I did you.
4. Nothing could *retard* him in his desire to *surmount* the *massive* debts that confronted him.
5. The chase did not *terminate* until he had *traversed* two counties.
6. Our players *vaunt* their ability to *vanquish* the other team.
7. The lad was too *inquisitive* about the *intricate* machine.
8. *Martial* music stirred the tribe's *predatory* instincts.
9. It is *requisite* that you prove he was *negligent.*
10. In *sundry* ways, he liked to *vilify* the boss.

SECOND PRACTICE SET

Which base word best replaces the *italicized* word or words?

1. He asked *prying* questions about my *servile* chores.
2. *Complicated* plans were made to *release* the captive.
3. The gobbler struts with a *military* air and seems to *boast* his superiority.
4. Dad *expostulated* with the boys because of their *plundering* raids on the family refrigerator.
5. The sickness began to spread through the town in spite of *stubborn* efforts to *set apart* all people who were ill.
6. Our old rivals failed to *conquer* us because they were *neglectful* about training rules.
7. If you *speak evil of* him, your friendship with him will become very *insecure.*
8. It is *indispensable* that we find a way to *reward* the heroism that cost him a long illness.
9. The spy had to *give up* the pass which permitted him to *go across* enemy territory.
10. The false alarm was an *ill-boding* attempt to *delay* the work.

THIRD PRACTICE SET

On a separate sheet, write the numbers of the *italicized* words.
Beside each, write the number of the matching word or group of
words from the second column.

1. Tardy *relinquishment*	1. bravery
2. Well supplied with *sundries*	2. act of delaying
3. *Retardation* of pay raises	3. release
4. A lion's *valor*	4. uncertainty
5. *Subjugation* of pagan tribes	5. giving up
6. A pig's *obstinacy*	6. repayment
7. Life's *precariousness*	7. reluctance
8. *Requital* of services	8. revilement
9. *Liberation* of energy	9. miscellaneous articles
10. Newspaper *vilification*	10. act of bringing under control
11. *Termination* of a treaty	11. obtuseness
12. Demand for an *inquest*	12. stubbornness
13. A grim *remonstrance*	13. expostulation
14. A reporter's *inquisitiveness*	14. act of putting an end to
15. "Poor *vaunt* of life indeed"	15. boast
	16. official inquiry
	17. curiosity

REDSKIN RELUCTANCE

Indians make a good creative topic for this unit. You might
describe a battle in which the Indians defend their territory against
incoming white settlers. A powwow would also be a good subject
and would serve to illustrate just as many of the words—more, in
fact, because the chiefs can always talk about fighting.

If you want to play fair, remember that the Indians kept
treaties better than the white men did.

THE JACKPOT UNITS

How would you like to have a master key that will help you unlock the meanings of dozens of long words and scores of "hard" words? The Jackpot Units in this book will provide you with such a key. Among its values are these:

1. By using this key, you can increase your understanding of many words, both familiar and new. For example, you will discover that the word *suspicious* carries the meaning of "looking under" the surface of things.

2. With the help of this key, you will be able to work out the meaning of a long word like *circumlocution,* from the prefix *circum-,* which means "round," and the root *locu,* which means "talk or speak."

3. This key will also help you remember the difference in meaning between two words which look somewhat alike; for example, *inhale* and *exhale,* or *introvert* and *extrovert.*

4. The key can help to solve some of your spelling problems by giving you, for example, the reason for the double *s* in *misspell* and the double *c* and double *m* in *accommodate.*

THE KEY

Many words have three parts:

1. A prefix or beginning
2. A root or stem: the middle, base part, or "chassis"
3. A suffix or ending

A knowledge of these three parts is the master key.[1]

---

[1] The prefix, root, and suffix forms which you will study in the Jackpot Units will appear in their most common English spellings.

In order to see how the master key works, you might try it on the following words: *retraction, prearrangement,* and *super-fluity*. The result, as shown in this chart, is a number of parts, each with its own meaning.

Prefixes		*Roots*		*Suffixes*	
re-	back, again	*-tract-*	draw, pull	*-ion*	act of
pre-	before, ahead of time	*-arrange-*	arrange[2]	*-ment*	act or fact
super-	over, above	*-flu-*	flowing	*-ity*	state or condition of

Once you know the meaning of each part, you can arrive at the meaning of the total word.

retraction: act of drawing back, especially something that has been said

prearrangement: act of arranging something ahead of time

superfluity: state of flowing over and above; i.e., an unnecessary quantity of something

Here are the same words used in sentences:

The newspaper printed his **retraction** of the charge that government funds were being spent unwisely.

As if by **prearrangement,** all the congressmen arrived at the same instant.

In his speech before the government committee, he avoided a **superfluity** of words.

---

[2] This root really consists of a smaller root (*-range-*) plus a prefix (*ar-*). It means "put in order." The two parts have grown together so fully that they may be considered a single unit.

The three prefixes will help unlock such words as these:

react	superfine
reform	superheat
readjust	rewrite
reunite	reaffirm
prepay	traction
premeditate	fluid
preagreement	superior

In the Jackpot Units, you will learn how prefixes and roots make up words. In the Appendix, you will learn about suffixes. Your study of these forms will win you a rich award: dozens of new words.

Prefixes and roots are obviously very important. Some of them are used hundred of times in all sorts of words and in all kinds of combinations. If you learn only a few dozen of the most common prefixes and roots, you will automatically acquire a vast number of new words.

Once you have learned a root, you can usually recognize it when you meet it in a new word. This is not always the case with a prefix. Some prefixes undergo a change in spelling when added to certain words or roots. For instance, when the prefix *in-* is added to the root *-mov-*, the *n* changes to *m*, as in *immovable*.

This change in spelling reflects a change in pronunciation. When you add a prefix to a root, you sometimes put side by side two consonants which are difficult to pronounce together. The last consonant of the prefix and the first consonant of the root may form a hard combination. This was the case when the prefix *in-* (not) was first attached to the root *-mov-*. It is not easy for English-speaking people to pronounce an *n* and an *m* together. These sounds are combined in some other languages but rarely in English. If you try to say *inmovable* you will see why. A change or simplification is certainly needed.

When such a difficult combination occurs, the neighboring sounds usually influence each other in one of two ways: either one of the consonants is dropped, or a different consonant is substituted in its place. The easy-to-pronounce modern word *immovable* shows the influence of the strong *m* of the root on the *n* of the prefix. The result is the substitution of a different consonant in the prefix.

Whenever you find a prefix which has changed in spelling before a certain consonant, you will have discovered an example of this process of simplification.

Suffixes do not always attract as much attention as prefixes, perhaps because they come at the end of a word. They must not be dismissed as unimportant, however. Observe what they can do:

child	(noun)
child*ish*	(adjective, unfavorable in tone)
child*like*	(adjective)
child*hood*	(noun)

Suffixes show the part of speech and may also show the user's attitude. If the root is the chassis of a word, the suffixes may be thought of as different body styles.

The study of suffixes will be taken up later. The prefixes and roots must come first. One doesn't begin the study of an animal's anatomy with the tail.

UNIT NINE

What is the meaning of the *italicized* prefix or root in each of the sentences below? Choose the correct meaning from among those listed in the right-hand column. Remember that the same meaning may be expressed by more than one prefix or root.

1. *Non*essentials are __?__ important.

2. To *mis*apply a statement is to apply it __?__.

3. To *ob*viate a difficulty is to make headway __?__ it.

4. He concealed his *anti*pathy for us (feeling __?__ us).

5. To *se*clude oneself is to __?__ oneself __?__.

6. *Contra*band goods are goods imported __?__ the law.

7. An *ab*erration is a wandering __?__ the truth.

from, away from
shut
toward
away (apart)
hang
not
down (from)
against
make
wrong(ly)

This is the first of the four JACKPOT UNITS in Part One. Other Jackpot Units are included at the end of Part Two.

Study List— PREFIXES

AGAINST GROUP

1. ANTI- . . . . against, opposing; opposed to

An antidote is a remedy which acts *against* the effects of a poison.

An antonym is a word whose meaning is *opposite* to that of another word.

Antipathy is a feeling *against* someone.

An antiseptic acts *against* the bacteria which cause blood poisoning.

Cf. antislavery, anti-war

2. COUNTER- . . . CONTRA- . . . against, opposing; opposed to

A counterclaim is an *opposite* or *opposing* claim.

A counterbalance is an *opposing* force or weight.

To contrive a counterplot is to contrive an *opposing* plot.

An antidote will counteract or act *in opposition* to a poison.

When you contradict someone, you say the *opposite* of what he has said.

A piece of contraband merchandise is something smuggled in *against* the law.

Cf. counterfeit, counterirritant, counterproposal

3. OB- . . . . against, opposing; opposed to

An objection is an idea hurled *against* something.

To obstruct a plan originally meant to build *against* it.

Anything which oppresses, pushes or presses *against*.

The prefix *ob-* has other meanings as well. The *b* sometimes changes to the letter with which the root begins.

Notty Group

4.   IN- . . . . **not**

One who is ineligible is *not* eligible.

A person incapable of doing something is *not* capable.

Inconsistent behavior is *not* uniform or harmonious.

> The prefix *in-* becomes *im-* before *m* and *p; il-* before *l; ir-* before
> *r: immovable, impossible, illogical, irreligious,* etc.
> Sometimes this prefix means "against," as in *indict.*
> Another equally important meaning will be taken up in the next unit.

5.   NON- . . . . **not**

A nonconductor is *not* a conductor of electricity.

Wit which is nonpareil is *not* equaled and is thus unsur-
passed.

Nonviolent resistance is resistance which is *not* violent.

> For more words using this prefix, see your dictionary.
> *Cf. nonresident, nonsense, nonunion*

6.   UN- . . . . **not**

Unfeigned surprise is *not* pretended.

An unsophisticated person is *not* experienced in worldly
matters.

An unwarranted statement can*not* be proved or justified.

> This prefix comes from Old English.
> Sometimes *un-* expresses the idea of reversing, as in *untwist, untangle,*
> and *undress,* but this meaning is not so common as the meaning of
> "not."
> *Cf. unconfirmed, ungenerous, ungovernable, unattached, unbearable,*
> *unceasing, uncompromising, unmanageable*

Miss Wrongly

7.   MIS- . . . . wrong(ly), incorrect(ly)

One who misbehaves behaves *wrongly.*

To miscalculate is to calculate *incorrectly.*

A mischance is a piece of ill fortune or bad luck; i.e., something which has gone *wrong*.

Misconduct is *wrong* conduct.

Down's, Out's, and From's

8. AB- . . . . from, away; down from

Absence is being *away from* someone or something.

An abrupt departure breaks *away* too quickly.

To abdicate is to declare one's separation *from* a throne or some such responsibility.

To abduct is to lead *away from* home or to kidnap.

When you abhor something, you shrink *from* it.

Sometimes *s* is added, as in *absent*, from *ab* and *esse*, "be away." The *b* is omitted before *v*, as in *avert*, "turn away."

9. DE- . . . . from, down from, down

If you depopulate a town, you remove the inhabitants *from* it.

To depress a lever is to push or press it *down*.

When one descends, he goes *down*.

To despise a person is to look *down* upon him.

To deter a thief is to frighten him *from* the crime (III, 1).

10. DIS- . . . . away, away from

To dismiss a class is to send the students *away*.

You disarm a bandit by putting or taking *away* his weapon(s).

A disaster is an unforeseen calamity. (The word originally expressed a separation from the protection of one's guiding star.)

Cf. disarrange, disapprove, discharge, discolor, discomfort, disconnect

11. EX- . . . . out, from, forth

An excerpt is something plucked *out from* a book, record,
or speech.

To excommunicate a person is to exclude him *from* membership in a church.

An ex-president is a person who has gone *from* or *out from*
the office and is, therefore, a former president.

The prefix *ex-* is reduced to *e* before *d, g, l, m, n, r, v,* and, in rare
instances, before *b* and one or two other consonants: *edict, educate,
egress, elude, elect, emit, enervate, erupt,* and *evaporate.*
Ex- becomes *ef-* before *f.* It also sometimes becomes *es-* or *ec-:
efface, effect, escape, escort, ecstasy,* and *eccentric.*
See also *excoriate, exhume, ex libris, extant, extradite,* and *exodus* if
you wish to *ex*tract (draw out) a few more word secrets.

12. SE- . . . . away, apart

South Carolina was the first state to secede or go *apart* from
the union.

To select a partner is to choose or set him *apart.*

If you seclude yourself, you shut yourself *apart.*

In *sedition,* the *se-* becomes *sed-.* Can you suggest a reason? See dictionary for the root. What is the first letter of the root? How might
this influence the prefix?

13. SUB- . . . . under, beneath

A subcellar is *under* a cellar.

A subagent works *under* an agent.

A subcontract is an *under*-contract or one used in carrying
out a more extensive contract.

Anything subhuman is *beneath* the human level.

To support a person is to carry him from *beneath.*

The *b* sometimes changes to agree with the first letter of the root
to which the prefix is attached, as in *supposition,* a basic assumption
or belief lying *beneath* one's thinking.

Study List— ROOTS AND STEMS

1.   -CLUDE-, -CLUS- . . . . shut, close

To exclude a person is to *shut* him out or inflict exclusion.
To preclude an accident is to *shut* it out beforehand or prevent it.
Upper and lower teeth occlude or *shut* together.
This *shutting* together is known as occlusion.
What do dentists mean when they speak of malocclusion?

2.   -FACT-, -FECT- . . . . **-FICT-** . . . . make; do

A factory is a building where things are *made*, usually by machine.
To manufacture originally meant to *make* by hand.
The effect of something is the result; i.e., the way it has "*made* out."
A fictitious excuse is *made* up, not real.

3.   -JECT-, -JACULAT- . . . . cast, hurl

A projectile is an object to *hurl* forward or forth.
An abject person is literally *cast* away. Therefore, like a castaway, he feels downhearted, lacking in self-respect, and even contemptible.
A dejected person is merely *downcast* or discouraged.
To eject or evict tenants from a building is to force them out; i.e., to *cast* them out.
"Get out!" he ejaculated fiercely (*hurled* forth or exclaimed).

Cf. object(ion), subject(ion)

4. **-LUDE-, -LUS-** . . . . play (in sense of lead or run)

To delude a person is to *lead* him from what is true.

A delusion is a *misleading* or false idea.

If one eludes a pursuer, he succeeds in *running* away.

An elusive thief is usually a wily one.

His elusiveness makes him hard to catch.

Cf. prelude, postlude, interlude

5. **-MIT-, -MISS-** . . . . send, sent

To emit a yell is to *send* it out or forth.

Emission of energy from the sun furnishes power for use on earth.

When you dismiss a person, you *send* him away.

A request for early dismissal was not granted.

A diplomatic mission may be the errand of a group *sent* abroad by the government or it may be the group itself.

An emissary is a person *sent* out or forth, as a messenger or representative.

Coming in the next unit: *admit, commit, permit, remit, transmit,* and their variant forms.

6. **-MOVE-, -MOTE-, -MOB-** . . . . move

To remove something is to *move* or take it away.

It is not possible to *move* an immovable object.

To demote a man is to *move* him down to a less important job or rank.

A motive is that which *moves* one to act.

Emotion is a *moving* forth of feeling.

A mobile face is one which changes expressions; i.e., *moves* readily.

Cf. motion, motor, motivation; mobility, immobile

7.   -PEND-, -PENSE- . . . . hang; weigh

To ex<u>pend</u> money originally meant to *weigh* it out.

Why is the ap<u>pend</u>ix of a book so called?

An im<u>pend</u>ing storm is *hanging* over or likely to come soon.

To dis<u>pense</u> justice is to put it in force; i.e., to *weigh* it out.

A sus<u>pension</u> bridge has its roadway *hanging* from cables.

Cf. suspend, suspense; pensive, pensiveness; dispense, dispensation; compensate, recompense (I, 7), *propensity* (III, 3)

8.   -PON- . . . . -POSE-, -POSIT- . . . . place, put

Your op<u>pon</u>ent is a person who *places* himself on the opposite side.

An ex<u>pon</u>ent of art is one who *places* or sets it forth by expounding, interpreting, and encouraging it.

To de<u>pose</u> a king is to *put* him down from the throne.

To ex<u>pose</u> a film or a crime is literally to *put* it forth.

A de<u>posit</u>ion is the act of *putting* down or removing a person from office, or putting down testimony under oath for a court.

The *Pon* Words come from the Latin verb *ponere,* meaning "set, place, put": *component, proponent, postpone,* and others.
The *Pose* Words come from the Latin verb *pausare* by way of the French verb *poser,* "put down": *compose, propose,* and others.
Forms and meanings of *-pon-* and *-pos-* have become confused so that, for practical purposes, they are best presented together.

9.   -SOLVE-, -SOLU- . . . . disunite; loosen; free

To dis<u>solve</u> a partnership is to *disunite* it.

A <u>solve</u>nt is a liquid which will *loosen* or dissolve a solid.

A person who is <u>solve</u>nt is able to pay his debts and is thus *loosened* or *freed* from them.

To grant ab<u>solut</u>ion is to *free* a person from sin or guilt.

Cf. solve, solution, soluble, insoluble; resolve, resolution

10. **-TORT-, -TORQU-** . . . . twist

> To distort the facts is to *twist* them away from the truth.
>
> Extortion is *twisting* or squeezing money out of someone dishonestly.
>
> Torque is force that creates a *twisting* or rotating motion, as in the driveshaft of a car.

11. **-TRACT-** . . . . draw, drag, pull

> To distract someone's attention is to *draw* it away.
>
> Noise is often a distraction.
>
> To abstract material from a book is to *draw* ideas from it and summarize them in a brief statement.
>
> A fit of abstraction is a state in which you are mentally *withdrawn*.
>
> To extract material from a book is to *draw* out direct quotations.
>
> Extraction of a tooth without an anaesthetic would be quite painful.
>
> *Cf. tractor, traction, tractable, intractable*

12. **-VOLVE-, -VOLU-** . . . . roll, turn

> If a duty devolves upon you, it literally *rolls* down on you.
>
> To evolve an idea is to develop it or to *roll* it forth gradually.
>
> The theory of evolution attempts to explain how all living things developed or "*rolled* forward" from a few simple forms of life.
>
> A voluble person talks smoothly and glibly; i.e., *rolls* words easily.

Note: Most of the prefixes and roots presented in this unit come from the Latin language.

FIRST PRACTICE SET

What is the meaning of *italicized* prefixes or roots in the following sentences?

1. A *sub*cellar is a cellar __?__ a cellar.

2. An *ob*trusive person is one who thrusts himself __?__ the wishes of others.

3. A *non*assessable policy is one which is __?__ assessable.

4. A *counter*plot is a scheme __?__ a plot.

5. *Anti*-aircraft guns are directed __?__ aircraft.

6. __?__-the-beginning inhabitants are called *ab*origines.

7. A *mis*demeanor is one form of __?__ conduct.

8. *Il*limitable stretches of desert are expanses which are __?__ limited.

9. A con*ject*ure is a __?__ at the truth.

10. *Mot*ive power is what __?__ a car.

11. An *in*accessible spot is one __?__ easy to approach.

12. *Dissolu*tion sometimes means the __?__ of the body __?__ from its physical life.

13. A *pend*ulum is a weight to __?__ from a ceiling or clock.

14. A *tract*able person is easy to __?__ along with you.

15. To *dis*miss a person is to __?__ him __?__.

16. *De*fection from duty is __?__ an escape __?__ it.

17. To *elude* the hounds is to __?__ __?__ from them.

18. To *distort* the truth is to __?__ it __?__ the facts.

19. Re*volv*ing mirrors are so called because they __?__.

20. Com*pon*ents are parts you __?__ together.

SECOND PRACTICE SET

What one word made with roots and prefixes of this unit, may be used in place of each of the following *italicized* words or groups of words?

1. A spy who spies *against* spies: __?__

2. Resistance which is *not* violent: __?__

3. Sentiment or *feeling against* something proposed: __?__

4. Disaster that *hangs* over or *against* one: __?__

5. That which *moves* one to act: __?__

6. A person who *weighs* his thoughts very carefully: __?__

7. To *loosen away* a solid substance by a liquid: __?__

8. The movement *opposed to* war: __?__*war*

9. Writing which can*not* be read: __?__*legible*

10. Act of *shutting* one *out* from something: __?__

11. To calculate *incorrectly*: __?__

12. *Twisting* or squeezing (money) *out of* a person: __?__

13. Noises or actions *pulling* one *away from* what he is doing: __?__

14. *Setting apart* the items one wants, such as clothes in a store: __?__

15. A bridge *hung under* its supports: __?__

16. A person *sent forth* to carry out a mission: __?__

17. A belief *placed under* one's thinking and therefore the belief on which it rests: __?__

18. State of being *cast down*: __?__

19. A form of *make-believe*: __?__

20. A false idea *playing down from* the truth: __?__

THIRD PRACTICE SET

What is the meaning of the *italicized* prefix or root in each of the sentences below?

1. *Im*mature corn is __?__ ripe.
2. To *sub*merge is to dip __?__.
3. To *ex*hale is to breathe __?__.
4. *Un*disguised dislike is __?__ concealed.
5. A *counter*claim in a damage suit is a claim __?__ the one who is suing.
6. A *fict*itious account is one you __?__ up.
7. To *eject* a person is to __?__ him __?__.
8. A de*positi*on is the act of __?__ down evidence under oath for a court.
9. A *miss*ive is something you are __?__, usually a letter.
10. *Demot*ion is __?__ a person __?__ to a less important job.

ANTONYMS

By adding or substituting one of the prefixes in this unit, write the opposite of:

1. connect
2. logical
3. septic (poisonous)
4. approval
5. behavior
6. include
7. proposal
8. metal
9. inject
10. religious

FOR EXTRA CREDIT

1. With the help of your dictionary, compile a list of *dis-* words and their positive forms.
2. List words in which the prefix *un-* adds the meaning of "reversing."

UNIT TEN

Which word from the list at the right best expresses the meaning of each *italicized* prefix or root in the sentences below?

1. To *ap*pend a footnote is literally to hang it __?__ the article.

2. An *inter*regnum is a period __?__ reigns.

3. An odor which *per*meates a room is spread __?__ the air.

4. An organ *pre*lude is a playing __?__ the service.

5. The *post*erior end is __?__.

6. A *port*age makes it necessary to __?__ a canoe.

7. A *scribe* is one who can __?__.

8. Sopori*fer*ous atmosphere is sleep-__?__

9. *Verte*brae are parts of the spine which are so-called because they __?__.

10. A *spir*ometer measures __?__.

through
out, forth
to, onto
before
behind
between
write
carry
turn
look
bearing
breath

This is a JACKPOT UNIT

Study List— PREFIXES

Direction

1. AD- . . . . to, toward; against

To adhere to an idea is to stick *to* it.

An adverse opinion is one turned *against* something.

To attract attention is to draw it *toward* oneself.

This prefix often changes its *d* to the first letter of the root to which it is joined. Sometimes the *d* is dropped before *s*.
Cf. *affection, affix, affront, aggregate, allude, astringent*

2. CIRCUM- . . . **PERI-** . . . . around, about

To circumnavigate the earth is to sail *around* it.

Circumlocution is talking *around* a topic, or using round-about expressions.

The pericardium is the membrane or sac *around* the heart.

In ancient Greece, the peripatetics were teachers who walked *about* while they taught.

The perimeter of a rectangle is the measure or distance *around* it.

3. IN- . . . . to, toward; into

To inject fuel is to "hurl" or force it *into* an engine.

To become involved in a crime is to be drawn *into* it.

An immigrant is one who migrates *into* a country.

One who imbibes sunshine is one who "drinks" it *in*.

Examples of *in-* meaning "not" are given in I, 9.
Cf. *indwell, inflame, influx, ingraft, ingrain, ingrown, illuminate*
The prefixes **intra-, intro-** mean "within": Intramural sports are games within the walls of one's own school.
An intravenous injection is injection of food or medicine within a vein.

4. PER- . . . . **through**

A p<u>er</u>ceptive person sees *through* your actions readily.

To p<u>er</u>colate coffee is to filter hot water *through* it.

When smoke p<u>er</u>meates the room, it spreads *through(out)*.

5. PRO- . . . . **for; forward; before; favoring**

A p<u>ro</u>clivity for heavy eating is a natural tendency *for* or toward it.

P<u>ro</u>crastinating is putting *forward* until tomorrow what ought to be done today.

In drama, a p<u>ro</u>logue is a speech or short scene *before* the main part of the play.

A p<u>ro</u>-Russian envoy to the UN is one *favoring* Russia.

In such words as *pronoun* and *proconsul, pro-* means "in place of."

6. RE- . . . . **back(ward), again**

To r<u>e</u>tract a statement is to take it *back*.

When you r<u>e</u>iterate a question, you ask it *again*.

Cf. *react, readjust, reform, regain, refresh, revolve, remake, retort*

7. TRANS- . . . . **across, beyond**

To tr<u>ans</u>mit a message to Europe is to send it *across* the ocean.

Tr<u>ans</u>verse paths turn *across* each other, forming a criss-cross.

When you tr<u>ans</u>cend a difficulty, you "climb" *across* or beyond it.

Julius Caesar wrote a famous report on tr<u>ans</u>alpine Gaul, a region *beyond* the Alps.

Cf. *transport, transatlantic, translate* (carry across), *transference*

Time

8. **POST-** . . . . after

A <u>post</u>dated check is dated *after* or later than the date
when it is written.

To leave something to <u>post</u>erity is to leave it to future generations, to those who will come *after* us.

Cf. postgraduate, postpone, postscript

9. **PRE-** . . . **ANTE-** . . . . before, ahead of time

To <u>pre</u>clude an encounter with an enemy is to shut it out
or prevent it *before* it can happen.

A <u>pre</u>meditated killing is one planned *ahead of time*.

A <u>pre</u>monition is a warning *before* a catastrophe occurs, a
sense of foreboding.

Antemeridian means "occurring *before* noon."

An <u>ante</u>type is an *earlier* form or prototype from which a
later form has developed.

Cf. preplan, preheat, pre-exist; anteroom, antechamber, antecedent

Relationship

10. **CON-** . . . **SYN-** . . . . together, with

A <u>con</u>vention is a coming *together*.

To <u>col</u>laborate is to work *together* on a project (III, 1).

A <u>com</u>motion is a noisy or violent moving about, as when
many people move *together*.

A <u>com</u>pendium is a book which gathers or "hangs" *together*
all the essential information on one subject.

<u>Syn</u>thesis is the process of placing *together* separate ele-
ments to create something new or different.

<u>Sym</u>pathy is feeling *with* someone.

A symposium is a conference in which one topic is discussed and different opinions about it are placed *together*.

Under the influence of the first consonant of the root, the prefix *con-* may appear as *com-, col-, co-,* and *cor-. Syn-* may become *sym-.*
Cf. concord, collect, cooperate, corroborate, correlate; synonym, symphony, symptom

11.   INTER- . . . . between, among

An interjection is an exclamation, sometimes thrust *between* other words in a sentence or conversation.

An intermission comes *between* the acts of a play.

Cf. interchange, interscholastic, intercom(munication), interfere

Study List— LATIN ROOTS

1.   -CEDE-, -CEED-, -CESS- . . . -GRESS . . . . . go, move

An antecedent is the word or phrase that *goes* before a pronoun and to which the pronoun refers.
To exceed the limit is to *go* out of or beyond it.
A recession is a business setback; i.e., a *moving* backward.
To progress is to *go* forward. To regress is to go backward.
An egress is an exit.
A speaker who digresses *goes* away from his main subject.
An aggressive attitude is a *going*-toward or pushing attitude. (III, 5)

2.   -DUCE-, -DUCAT-, -DUCT . . . . lead

To induce a boy to go is to *lead* him toward going.
A good education *leads* to knowledge.
A ductile metal is easily "*led*" or shaped.

Cf. reduce, reduction; deduce, deduction; abduct, abduction; conduct, conducive; adduce, traduce, duct, educate

3.   -FER- . . . . -LATE- . . . .   carry, bear; bring

A soporiferous drug is sleep-*bringing*.

An odoriferous cheese is an odor-*laden* kind.

To collate texts is to *bring* them together and examine them critically; to translate is to *carry* into another language.

Fer Words: *differ, infer, confer, refer, prefer, transfer, offer, suffer* Words like *interfere* come from a different root, a Latin word meaning "to strike."
Cf. ablative, prelate, relate, dilate (**II, 1**)

-PORT-, -PORTAT- . . . .   carry, bring

To portage a canoe is to *carry* it overland.

To comport oneself wisely is to behave wisely.

The importation of cars from abroad is the act of *bringing* them into the United States.

Cf. deport, deportation; transport, transportation; disport, purport

4.   -FUSE- . . . .   pour

To interfuse kindness is to *pour* it among other acts.

The tonic will infuse (*pour* in) new energy into his body.

Effusive emotion is feeling which *pours* forth without restraint.

Cf. confuse, confusion; suffuse, suffusion; diffuse, diffusion, profuse, profusion; refuse, refusal

5.   -PEL-, -PULSE- . . . .   drive; push

To dispel gloom is to *drive* it away.

To repel an enemy is to *drive* him back.

An impulse is a sudden *push* toward action of some sort.

Impulsiveness is a trait of those who often yield to impulses.

Cf. compel, compulsion, compulsory; repel, repellent, repulse; propel

6. **-SCRIBE-, -SCRIPT-** . . . . write, **written**

To inscribe a name on a plaque is to *write* or engrave it on.

One who subscribes to a program *underwrites* it.

To transcribe a recipe is to make another copy; i.e., *write* it across.

Before the invention of printing, there were many scribes: men whose occupation was *writing*.

A scriptorium is the *writing* room in a monastery.

Cf. ascribe, ascription; describe, description; prescribe, prescription; circumscribe, proscribe; scrip, script, scripture

7. **-SERVE-** . . . . keep; **save**

Do you conserve your energy?

Did he reserve the tickets? A reservation is important.

A subservient person is one who is slavishly polite and easy to *keep* under.

Cf. preservation, preservative; conservation, conservative; deserve, subserve

8. **-SON-** . . . . **sound**

The twins answered their mother's question in unison; i.e., with one *sound*.

Because the cave was resonant, our footsteps filled it with *sound*.

Other *Son* Words: *assonance, dissonance; consonant; sonorous*

9. **-SPEC-, -SPECT-, -SPIC-** . . . . look (at), **see**

To speculate about the future is to meditate on it; i.e., to *see* it mentally.

Introspection is *looking* within oneself in order to examine one's thoughts and feelings.

A circumspect person is one who always *looks* around him and is, therefore, discreet and prudent.

A suspicious person is distrustful and always *looking* under the surface of things.

Cf. expect, inspect, respect, and their kin; also *spectator, spectacle, spectacular; specter* (ghost); *spectrum; conspicuous*

-VIDE-, -VIS- . . . . see

To provide is to *see* ahead or plan for the future.

To visualize something is to *see* it with your mind's eye.

A vista is a *sight* or view. (The word comes from Italian.)

The Greek root **scope,** meaning "sight," is found in a dozen or more names given to such "looking" devices as the microscope, spectroscope, kaleidoscope, periscope, telescope, stereoscope, and iconoscope. *Cf. vision, revision, visible, invisible, visual; visit, visitor; advise*

10. **-SPIRE- . . . . -HALE-** . . . . breathe

If someone aspires to be a great musician, he longs for or strives toward this goal; i.e., he *breathes* toward it.

When someone expires, he dies; i.e., he *breathes* his last.

To inhale is to *breathe* in; to exhale is to *breathe* out.

Halitosis is bad or offensive *breath.*

Other *Spire* Words: *conspire, conspiracy; inspire, inspiration; respire, transpire; aspirant*
Cf. spirit, spiritual, inspirit, spirited, despirited; inhalation, exhalation

11. **-TAIN-, -TEN-** . . . . hold

A dish that retains heat *holds* it.

A retentive memory *holds* facts well.

Tenets are beliefs or doctrines *held* as true, especially by a church or other organization.

Cf. detain, detention; attain, attainment; contain, containment, content(s); tenable, tenement

12. -VENE-, -VENT- . . . . **come, a coming**

> When members of an organization con<u>vene</u>, they *come* together.
>
> The Elks' con<u>vent</u>ion (*coming* together) takes place soon.
>
> Will the government inter<u>vene</u> (*come* between) in the labor dispute?
>
> Inter<u>vent</u>ion may prevent a strike.

> Cf. *event, eventuate; advent, circumvent, prevent, invent*

13. -VERT-, -VERSE- . . . . **turn**

> He a<u>vert</u>ed his eyes from the wreck.
>
> Can you di<u>vert</u> (*turn* away) her attention?
>
> To in<u>vert</u> a fraction is to *turn* it upside down.
>
> To re<u>vert</u> to earlier habits is to *turn* back to them.
>
> <u>Vert</u>igo is dizziness, a state in which everything seems to be *turning* around you.
>
> When you ad<u>vert</u>ise a product, you try to *turn* public attention toward it.
>
> To re<u>verse</u> your steps is to *turn* back.

> Other *Vert* Words: *introvert, extrovert; convert, conversion; aversion*
> Cf. *advertisement, perverseness*

14. -VOKE-, -VOCAT- . . . . **call**

> To re<u>voke</u> a permit is to *call* it back.
>
> One's <u>voc</u>ation is his *calling* or occupation.
>
> A con<u>voc</u>ation is a *calling* together or assembly.
>
> The in<u>voc</u>ation in church is a prayer at the beginning of the service *calling* upon God for His presence.

> Cf. *invoke, evoke; provoke, provocation; revocation*

Note: The prefixes and roots presented in this unit are all from Latin, except for the Greek *peri-, syn-,* and *-scope. Pro-* occurs in both Greek and Latin. In both languages, it has the same meaning.

FIRST PRACTICE SET

Give the meaning of the following *italicized* roots and prefixes.

1. *Conspir*ators literally __?__ __?__.

2. To speak in uni*son* is to speak with __?__ __?__.

3. In a day or two he will *proceed*: __?__ __?__.

4. To *sym*pathize is to feel __?__ a person.

5. He did not *advocate* a new tax: __?__ __?__.

6. The teacher is very *circumspect* in her behavior: She __?__ __?__ carefully.

7. A *peri*scope is a device for looking __?__ something.

8. To *induct* a new member is to __?__ him __?__ the club.

9. Who will *intercede* __?__ __?__ for Ralph in his dispute with the coach?

10. A *congress* of workers is a __?__ __?__.

11. When a doctor *prescribes*, he __?__ __?__ what the patient is to take.

12. To *transfuse* blood is to __?__ it __?__.

13. An insect *repellent* __?__ the insect __?__.

14. A *post*-mortem takes place __?__ death.

15. He could not *reserve* a seat: __?__ __?__.

16. To *confer* about arrangements is to __?__ __?__ the ideas of each conferee.

17. To *import* wool is to __?__ it __?__ the country.

18. A *transgression* is a __?__ __?__ the boundaries between right and wrong.

19. A *diversion* is a __?__ away and a di*gression* is a __?__ away from an intended course of action.

20. The *ante*chamber lies __?__ the main room.

SECOND PRACTICE SET

Supply a word formed from the roots and prefixes of this unit to fit each definition in parentheses.

1. It was necessary to __?__ Junior's activities. (limit by "writing around")

2. A sieve won't __?__ water. (hold together)

3. "__?__ to high ideals," he urged. (breathe or work toward)

4. We must __?__ new life into the club. (pour in)

5. The girl should __?__ the boy through a doorway. (go before)

6. The __?__ for winning the pennant is good. (view forward)

7. The remark does not __?__ to you. (hold through)

8. An __?__ orchestra will be organized. (between schools)

9. The __?__ was clogged. (tube to "lead" air in)

10. He told about the canoe __?__. (act of carrying)

11. The boy is quite __?__. (easy to keep under)

12. George could __?__ the entire scene. (see in his mind's eye)

13. A __?__ will be held in May. (a calling together)

14. Can you __?__ English into French? (carry across)

15. He is too much inclined to __?__ and brooding. (looking within)

16. Her cheerfulness will help to __?__ the gloom. (drive away)

17. The shore line began to __?__ as the ship moved away from the land. (go back)

18. The usual means of __?__ from the castle was cut off by the fire. (going out from)

19. Spinach is a vegetable for which some children have a great __?__. (turning away from)

20. A salesman has to be quite __?__ in a gracious kind of way. (going toward or pushing)

THIRD PRACTICE SET

On a separate sheet, write the numbers of the *italicized* words.
Beside each, write the number of the matching word or group of
words from the second column.

1. *Circumvent* a foe	1. hold back or onto
2. *Divert* attention	2. pull against
3. *Retain* one's hope	3. work together
4. *Interject* a word	4. turn away
5. *Accede* to a request	5. spread through
6. *Invoke* the law	6. come or get around
7. *Produce* new evidence	7. lean back
8. *Collaborate* on a book	8. go back
9. Eyes *regress* often	9. call into action
10. Ideas *permeate*	10. hurl in between
	11. lead forth (forward)
	12. go toward, grant

THE RIGHT WORD

What one word from this unit may best be substituted for each
italicized group of words in the following sentences?

1. They held a *placing-together* of different ideas on the subject of
   taxes: __?__

2. When the jury brought in a verdict of murder in the first degree,
   there was quite a *noisy moving together* in the courtroom:
   __?__

3. The manager found that his new assistant had a tendency to
   put-forward-until-tomorrow: __?__

4. Every effort to *shut off beforehand* useless arguments failed:
   __?__

5. The *man who serves in place of the consul* represented his
   country at the ceremonies: __?__

UNIT ELEVEN

Select the word from the list at the right which provides the best answer for each of the following:

1. Something for a patient about to have an operation

2. Something to contract the tissues and stop persistent bleeding

3. An investigation to determine why the patient died

4. A word for upright living

5. A word to use when orders or instructions cancel earlier orders

6. A place of sorrow for a crime one has committed

7. A word for "a view of death"

8. Something the doctor gives a patient merely to please him and not for medical reasons

9. The worship of the dead or undue reverence for them

10. Needed for the diagnosis of heart trouble

post-mortem
anaesthetic
penitentiary
necrolatry
astringent
thanatopsis
cardiogram
rectitude
placebo
excision
invictus
countermand

Study List—ROOTS AND STEMS

1.   -AQUA-, -AQUE- . . . . **water**

He has a new aquarium, a glass tank for fish and plants that live in *water.*

Aquaplaning over the surface of the *water* is great fun.

It is one of the more difficult aquatic sports.

An aquamarine dress is the color of sea *water.*

Subaqueous life is life under *water.*

An aqueduct is a conduit for *water.*

2.   -AUDI-, -AUDIT- . . . . **hear, listen to**

An audible sigh is loud enough to be *heard.*

An audience is a group of *listeners.*

An auditorium is primarily a place for *hearing* a program.

Cf. inaudible; audition, auditory; audit

3.   -CIDE-, -CIS- . . . . **-SECT-** . . . . **cut**

To decide a matter is to *cut* it off from further consideration.

When a surgeon makes an incision, he *cuts* into a tissue or organ.

Incisors are teeth adapted for *cutting* into food.

To dissect a frog is to *cut* it apart.

A sect, a section, and a sector are all *cuts* or parts from a larger whole.

The root *-cide-* often adds the meaning of "a deadly cut" or "killing," as in *homicide,* killing a person, *regicide,* killing a king, and *suicide,* killing oneself.
The word *coincide* comes from a different root, meaning "to fall."

4.   -CORD- . . . . -CARDI- . . . . heart

Concord is harmony and agreement; i.e., *hearts* together or in accord.

A written record of a conversation can later call it to *heart* or to mind again.

A cardiac ailment affects the *heart*.

A cardiogram is a record of the action of the *heart*.

5.   -CUR- . . . -CURS-, -COURSE- . . . . run(ning)

To incur dislike is to *run* into it.

A cursory reading is a *running* or hasty reading.

A discursive speech has a tendency to ramble or *run* away in various directions.

The concourse of two rivers is the place where they *run* together.

A courier was originally a runner, but today may be a special messenger or attendant.
Current originally meant "running"; *course* originally meant "a running"; *excursion* originally meant "a running forth."
See also *concur, recur.*

6.   -DICT- . . . . say, command
-LOQU-, -LOCU- . . . . talk, speak

A dictator has complete *say* in his country.

He will issue many edicts *(commands)*.

A dictaphone is a mechanical ear which records what a person *says* or dictates into it.

A loquacious person is *talkative*.

A colloquy is a *talking* together or conversation.

An interlocutor is someone who takes part in a dialogue; i.e., a *talker*, questioner, or interpreter.

Cf. indicate, addict, dictate, contradict, predict; indict (II, 5); *also eloquent, elocution; circumlocution*

7. -FID-, -FIDE- . . . . faith, trust

Fidelity is *faithfulness.*

In the Middle Ages, the Crusaders considered their enemies to be infidels, men without *faith* in God.

Perfidy is disloyalty or breach of *faith.*

A diffident person lacks *faith* in himself and is, as a result, hesitant and often shy.

To confide in someone is to put *trust* in him.

8. -FLAGR- . . . -PYR- . . . . flame, fire

A flagrant abuse is one that is glaring or *flaming.*

A conflagration is a very large or destructive *fire.* (See I, 5.)

The dead chieftain's body was laid on a funeral pyre (heap of wood for *burning* corpses).

Pyrotechnics is the making or use of *fireworks.*

The root *-ard-*, "burning," is discussed in II, 10.

9. -FLECT-, -FLEX- . . . . bend

To reflect the sun's rays is to *bend* them back.

To deflect a blow is to turn or *bend* it away.

A circumflex accent is a curved line over a letter; i.e., one *bent* around it.

Cf. *inflect; flexible, inflexible; reflex*

10. -FRACT- . . . -RUPT- . . . . break, burst

To fracture one's arm is to *break* it.

An infraction of the rules is a *breaking* of them.

When a volcano erupts, molten lava *bursts* forth.

A rupture is a *breaking* through.

To disrupt a meeting is to *break* or *burst* it apart.

Cf. *fraction, diffraction, refract, refractory*

11. **-HERE-, -HES-** . . . . stick, cling

Gum will ad<u>here</u> or *stick* to a desk.

Particles of sand and cement co<u>here</u> or *cling* together to form concrete.

In<u>here</u>nt qualities are those which *cling* to a person because they are inborn.

Ad<u>hes</u>ive tape *sticks* to the skin. (See I, 5.)

Inherit and *heredity* do not come from this root. They come from the Latin *heres,* meaning "heir."

12. **-LUC- . . . . -LUMEN-, -LUMIN- . . . . -PHOTO-** . . . . . light

A <u>luc</u>id discussion is as clear as day*light*. (See I, 3.)

A trans<u>luc</u>ent pane allows *light* to pass through but is not transparent.

A <u>lumen</u> is a unit for measuring *light*.

A <u>lumin</u>ous dial gives forth *light*.

To il<u>lumin</u>ate a street is to *light* it up.

A <u>photo</u>graph is a picture made by the action of *light* on film.

<u>Photo</u>synthesis is the formation of carbohydrates in the chlorophyll-containing tissues of a plant exposed to *light*.

13. **-MAND-** . . . . order, command

If you counter<u>mand</u> an order, you give a *command* against carrying it out.

When a Senator says that he has <u>mand</u>ate from the people, he means that they have *ordered* him to act in a certain way or to take a particular stand.

To re<u>mand</u> a suspect is to *order* him back to prison to await further investigation.

If you de<u>mand</u> an answer to your question, you *order* some-one to reply.

14.   -MERGE-, -MERSE- . **dip, plunge; sink**

When a submarine submerges, it *plunges* under the surface.

To merge a company is to cause it to be absorbed; i.e., *sink* its identity by combination with another company.

To immerse a casting is to *sink* it into a liquid such as paint.

15.   -MORT- . . . THANA- . . . . **death**

A mortal wound is one that causes *death*. (See III, 3.)

The mortality rate is the *death* rate.

A post-mortem is a medical examination conducted after someone's *death* in order to find the cause of death.

"Thanatopsis," the title of a poem by William Cullen Bryant, means a "view of *death*."

Euthanasia is mercy killing or the putting to *death* of persons considered incurably ill.

Necro- means "dead body." A necrology is a list of those who have died during the year. A necropolis is a city of the dead; i.e., a cemetery. A person who practices necromancy believes that he can make predictions by communicating with the dead.

16.   -NOUNCE-, -NUNCI- . . . -SERT- . . . . **declare**

To denounce graft is to *declare* yourself against it.

To renounce the throne is to *declare* no further claims to it. Giotto's painting, "The Annunciation," depicts the angel's *declaration* to Mary, the mother of Jesus.

To assert the truth is to *declare* it positively.

17.   -NOV- . . . . **new**

A novice is a person who is *new* in a job or who has newly joined a group.

An innovation is a *new* way of doing something.

Note: **Neo-** in II, 12 is a Greek prefix meaning "new."

18. **-PEN- . . . -PENIT-** . . . . . . punish(ment); sorrow for sin

A penalty is a *punishment*.

A penal colony is a place of *punishment*.

Penitence is *sorrow* for wrongdoing.

A penitentiary is a prison; i.e., a place of *sorrow* for crime.

Penalty comes from the Latin *poena*, "punishment."
Penitence derives from *poenitere*, "to be sorry."

19. **-PLAC-** . . . . please
-PLACA- . . . . appease

A placid lake *pleases* because it is calm.

A placebo (plȧ·sē′bō) is a medicine, especially an inactive one, given simply to *please* or satisfy the patient.

One can sometimes placate (plā′kāt) or *appease* an enemy.

An implacable enemy is one you cannot *appease*.

20. **-PRESS-** . . . . squeeze, press

To depress a person is to sadden him; i.e., to *press* down his spirits.

When you repress a laugh, you *squeeze* it back.

Cf. suppress, impress, express, oppress, and their variant forms.

21. **-RECT-** . . . . right

To rectify a mistake is to make it *right*.

An erect person is one who stands *upright*.

Rectitude is righteousness or moral *uprightness*.

22. **-SANCT-** . . . . holy, sacred

To sanctify a place or a life is to make it *holy*.

A sanctimonious air is one of pretended *holiness*.

Cf. sanction (under *abet* in I, 4), *sanctuary, sacrosanct, sanctity* (saintliness)

23.   -SENT- . . . . -PATH- . . . . feel

Dissent is disagreement; i.e., a *feeling* away from something.

Sentiment is *feeling*.

Overdone or insincere *feeling* is sentimentality.

If you have sympathy for someone, you share his *feelings*; i.e., *feel* with him.

Antipathy is a strong *feeling* against something.

Apathy is a state of indifference or a lack of *feeling*.

Pathos is the quality in writing, music, or a situation that arouses a *feeling* of pity.

The root -*path*- originally meant "suffering." Today it often means "disease," in such words as *psychopathy* and *pathology*.

24.   -STRINGE-, -STRICT- . . . . . . draw together, tighten

Stringent laws are *tight* laws.

An astringent is a substance that contracts or *draws together* the tissues of the body.

To restrict one's privileges is to limit them; i.e., to *draw* them back.

A stricture of the intestine is a *drawing together* of the walls.

25.   -VINCE-, -VICT- . . . . conquer, overcome

To convince a person is to *overcome* his objections.

When one evinces surprise, he shows it. (The word once meant "overcome.")

When a landlord evicts tenants, he puts them out and thus recovers or *reconquers* his own property.

The victor is one who *conquers*; he is invincible.

Note: The roots presented in this unit are Latin, except for -*cardi*-, -*photo*,- *thana*-, -*necro*-, and -*path*-, which are of Greek derivation.

FIRST PRACTICE SET

What is the meaning of each *italicized* prefix or root in the following sentences?

1. An *aud*itor is one who __?__.

2. To con*fide* in a person is to __?__ that person.

3. *Aqua*marine is the color of sea __?__.

4. To pro*nounce* a word is to __?__ it correctly.

5. A con*strict*ion in an artery is a __?__ing together of its walls.

6. Co*hes*ion is what makes particles __?__ together.

7. A *rect*angle has a __?__ angle at each corner.

8. The peri*cardi*um is a membrane surrounding the __?__.

9. Infanti*cide* is the __?__ of a baby.

10. To contra*dict* a statement is to __?__ the opposite.

11. E*locut*ion is the art of __?__ing forth.

12. A *penit*ent is __?__ that he did wrong.

13. Dis*sent* is __?__ away from someone else's view.

14. A *pyr*omaniac has a fondness for starting __?__s.

15. To re*mand* a person to prison is to __?__ him back.

16. An in*vinc*ible army is impossible to __?__.

17. To e*luc*idate a problem is to throw __?__ on it.

18. When one dis*rupt*s a gang, he __?__s it apart.

19. A *merge*r is a __?__ing together of two or more companies.

20. A *nov*a is a star that suddenly exhibits __?__ brilliance and then fades rather rapidly.

21. A *lumen* is a unit to measure the flow of __?__.

22. A *sanct*uary is a __?__ place.

SECOND PRACTICE SET

Which word from this unit best replaces each *italicized* word or group of words?

1. After a *hasty* reading, he signed a paper *declaring against* all *new ways of doing things* in government.

2. *Breakings* of the traffic code tend to increase the *death* rate from accidents.

3. Benedict Arnold's *breach of faith* aroused *strong against-feeling* throughout the country.

4. A medical student learns surgery by *cutting apart* dead bodies and by making *cuts into tissues or organs.*

5. The doctor found that his patient had a *heart* disorder and a *break* in the abdominal wall.

6. *Faithfulness* is one of the *clinging within* qualities that is most admirable.

7. The sentence for *person-killing* is ten to twenty years in a *place of sorrow for wrongs committed.*

8. We expected that anyone with a face so *light-giving* would have a *shared feeling* for our plight.

9. Unless you *plunge* the phosphorus *in* water, it will start a *large fire.*

10. We tried to *appease* the *conqueror* with a large gift.

11. A life that is *full-of-pretended-holiness* is easier than a life of genuine *moral uprightness.*

12. *Pleasingly calm* weather helps people who feel *pressed down.*

THIRD PRACTICE SET

On a separate sheet, write the numbers of the *italicized* words. Beside each, write the number of the matching word or group of words from the second column. A few are either variant forms of words covered in this unit or words which you should understand after studying the unit.

1. A *flagrant* insult
2. A *pathetic* mistake
3. *Translucent* plastic
4. *Subaqueous* foliage
5. Sincere *sentiment*
6. A *penitent* brother
7. *Mandatory* participation
8. *Inflexible* discipline
9. A *diffident* cousin
10. A *cohesive* family

1. self-distrustful; hence, hesitant
2. ordered, required
3. unintentional
4. unbending
5. inclined to cling together
6. very sympathetic
7. glaring or blazing
8. under the water
9. letting light through
10. sorry for wrongdoing
11. arousing feelings of pity
12. feeling, emotion

1. *Fidelity* in marriage
2. Experience in *necromancy*
3. A brief *colloquy*
4. *Rectification* of old errors
5. Legality of *euthanasia*
6. *Diffraction* of light
7. A delayed *audition*
8. Missing *incisor*
9. *Compression* of ideas
10. A long *novitiate*

1. squeezing together
2. mercy killing
3. a hearing
4. breaking apart into components
5. period of newness, apprenticeship
6. tooth for cutting
7. confirmation
8. faithfulness
9. prediction by communication with the dead
10. a talking together
11. act of making right
12. statement or declaration of intention

THE RIGHT WORD

1. Streets *intersect*	1. push lightly aside
2. Malaria will *recur*	2. bend or turn away
3. *Confide* in a parent	3. press under
4. *Deflect* the attack	4. throw light upon
5. *Disrupt* arrangements	5. dip under or sink
6. *Adhere* to the contract	6. cut between or across
7. *Elucidate* a theory	7. talk down forcefully
8. Watch it *submerge*	8. make holy or sacred
9. *Suppress* a yawn	9. trust with (secrets)
10. *Sanctify* a life	10. break or burst apart
	11. run or come back
	12. stick, cling to

EXTRA EXPERIENCE

1. Make a list of fifty adverbs that may be formed from words
   in this unit. Use as many of the "root words" as you can.
2. Using the master key, work out the meaning of each of the
   following words: *concordat, immortalize, sentimentalize, invincible, disinherit,* and *neuropathology.*

·MCMLVII·

UNIT TWELVE

What is the meaning of the *italicized* prefix in each sentence? In each case, it will be a number.

1. To *bis*ect an angle is to cut it in __?__ parts.

2. A *cent*ime is one —?—th of a franc.

3. A *non*agenarian has reached the age of __?__ty.

4. An *oct*ogenarian has reached the age of __?__ty.

5. *Mono*theism is belief in __?__ God.

6. A *tetr*ahedron is a solid having __?__ surfaces.

7. A *cent*enarian is __?__ years old or more.

8. A *sex*tant is one __?__th of a circle.

9. Nebraska has a *uni*cameral legislature: __?__-chambered.

10. A *sept*ennial is the __?__th anniversary.

11. *Hept*archy means government by __?__ rulers.

Study List—PREFIXES*

NUMBERS

1. UNI- . . . MONO- . . . . **one**

> To unite two people in marriage is to make them *one*.
>
> A unicellular animal has only *one* cell.
>
> He raised his monocle, his *one* eye-glass.
>
> In a monologue, one person does all the talking.
>
> A monopoly exists when *one* person or company controls the sale or use of a product. (See also *cartel* in II, 5.)

2. DU- . . . BI- . . . . **two**

> A duet is a musical composition for *two* performers.
>
> When duplicate prizes are awarded, similar prizes are given to *two* persons.
>
> A bimonthly payment may be required either every two months or *twice* a month. Let the payer beware!
>
> Man is a biped or *two*-footed creature.
>
> The prefix *di-* means "two" in words like *dicotyledon,* a plant having two seed leaves. Do not confuse with *dia-* meaning "through, between, across," as in *dialect, diameter, diaper, diapason, diocese.*

3. TRI- . . . . **three**

> Triplets require *three* bassinets.
>
> If you type a list in triplicate, you make *three* copies.
>
> A triennial event occurs every *three* years.
>
> To trisect an angle is to cut it into *three* parts.
>
> The prefix *tri-* occurs in both Latin and Greek words.
> *Cf. triumvirate* (government by three rulers)

---

* Note: When both Latin and Greek prefixes are given, the Latin is given first, sometimes in two forms.

4. QUADR- . . . TETR- . . . . **four**

> A quadrant is one *fourth* of a circle.
>
> A quadrangle is a *four*-cornered court or lawn with a border of buildings, especially on a college campus.
>
> Among the officials of the Roman Empire were the tetrarchs (tē'trärks), each of whom ruled *one four*th of a province.
>
> Lead tetraethyl (*four* ethyls) is used in gasoline.
>
> *Cf. quadruplex, quadruplicate; tetralogy*

5. QUIN- . . . PENT- . . . . **five**

> The *five* Dionnes were the most famous quintuplets to be born in recent times.
>
> All *five* boys of our basketball quintet are good athletes.
>
> A pentastyle is a building with *five* columns in front.
>
> Pentecost comes the *fiftieth* day after the second day of the Passover.
>
> How did the Pentagon Building in Washington, D. C., get its name?

6. SEX- . . . HEX- . . . . **six**

> A sextet is a group of *six*, usually musicians.
>
> A sexagenarian is a person in his *sixties*.
>
> A hexagon is a *six*-sided figure.
>
> Hexameter is poetry which has *six* feet to a line.

7. SEPT- . . . HEPT- . . . . **seven**

> September was the *seventh* month of the old Roman year, the first month being March.
>
> A septuagenarian is a person in his *seventies*.
>
> A heptagon has *seven* sides.
>
> It is heptangular because it has *seven* angles.

8. OCT- . . . . **eight**

> An octagon is a figure having *eight* sides.
>
> An octet is a group of *eight* or music for *eight* instruments.
>
> October was the *eighth* month in the Roman calendar.
>
> The prefix *oct-* occurs in both Latin and Greek words.

9. NON- . . . NOV- . . . ENNEA- . . . . **nine**

> A nonagon is a *nine*-sided figure.
>
> A nonagenarian is a person in his *nineties.*
>
> November was the *ninth* month in the Roman calendar.
>
> An ennead is a group of *nine,* especially nine gods.
>
> The root *-nov-*, meaning "new" (listed in I, 11), should not be con-
> fused with the prefix *nov-*.
> The form *ennea* is found in only a few words, and the entry is in-
> cluded merely for the sake of completeness.

10. DEC-, DECI- . . . . **ten**

> A decade is a *ten*-year period.
>
> The Ten Commandments comprise the Decalog(ue).
>
> To decimate an army originally meant to kill every *tenth*
> man; today it means to destroy a large part of the army.
>
> The form *deci-* is used with the meaning of "a tenth," as in *decimal*
> and *decimeter.*
> *Cf. decemvir, decasyllable, decathlon*

11. CENT- . . . HECT- . . . . **one hundred**

> A century is a period of *one hundred* years.
>
> A centimeter is *one hundredth* of a meter.
>
> A hectograph is a duplicating machine which can make a
> *hundred* copies of a manuscript.
>
> A hectometer is *one hundred* meters.
>
> In the metric system, *cent-* is used with the meaning of "one hun-
> dredth"; *hect-* with the meaning of "one hundred." An alternate form
> of *hect-* is *hecat-*.

12.   MILL-, MILLI- . . . KILO- . . . . one thousand

A millenium, literally a period of a *thousand* years, is now thought of as a period of general happiness in the indefinite future.

A milligram is one *thousandth* of a gram.

A kilogram is a *thousand* grams.

The *thousand* prefixes occur chiefly in units of the metric system, where *milli-* is used with the meaning of "one thousandth," and *kilo-* with the meaning of "one thousand."

QUANTITIES

13.   EQU- . . . . equal

The two towns are equidistant from the Mississippi River.

An equable climate does not vary much.

Equanimity is calmness and evenness of temper.

Cf. equilateral, equation, equipoise, equilibrium

14.   MULTI- . . . POLY- . . . . many; several

A multigraph machine makes *many* copies.

Multifarious schemes are of *many* kinds.

A polygon is a *many*-sided figure.

A polyglot is a person who knows *several* languages.

Polytheism is belief in *many* gods.

Cf. multimillionaire, multicellular, multitude; also *polygamy* and *polytechnic,* in which both the prefix and the roots are of Greek origin.

15.   SEMI- . . . DEMI- . . . HEMI- . . . . half

A semiannual event occurs every *half* year.

A demigod is a *half* god.

A hemisphere is a *half* sphere.

The prefix *hemi-* is Greek, *demi-* is French-Latin, and the Latin *semi-* is related to *hemi-*.

16. SUPER- . . . ULTRA- . . . HYPER- . beyond, excessive; exceeding

Superabundance is *exceeding* abundance.

Supernal beauty is *beyond* ordinary loveliness.

An ultracritical person is *excessively* critical.

Hyperacidity is *excessive* acidity.

A hypercritical person is *excessively* critical.

The prefix *hyper-* is Greek; both *super-* and *ultra-* are Latin.
Cf. *superheat, supercharger, superior; ultramodern; hypersensitive*

Study List— NUMBER-LINKED ROOTS

1. -ANNU-, -ENNI- . . . . year(s)

A semiannual meeting occurs every six months or half *year*.

An annual flower has to be planted each *year*.

A perennial plant blossoms *through the years* or at least for several years without replanting.

A biannual convention meets twice a *year*.

A biennial celebration takes place every two *years*.

A quadrennial convention comes every four *years*.

Cf. *centennial, millennium*

2. ARCH- . . . -ARCH- . . . . chief, principal; ruler

An archangel is a *chief* angel.

A patriarch is the father and *ruler* of a large family or tribe.

Anarchy is a state of society without *rulers* or laws.

The form *-arch-* may be a prefix or a suffix, as well as a root. It is related to the Greek *archos,* "ruler" and carries an additional meaning of "the earliest or oldest."
The form **archeo-** means "ancient": The expression, "methinks," is archaic.
Archaeology is the study of life in ancient times, generally by means of examining ruins and long-buried relics.

3. -GAMY- . . . . marriage

Bi<u>gamy</u> is *marriage* to two persons at the same time.

Poly<u>gamy</u> is *marriage* to several or many women.

The root *-gamy-* is Greek, from *gamos,* "marriage."
The roots **-nub-** and **-nupt-** are Latin: Connubial bliss is the happiness of marriage, and nuptial vows are marriage vows. (See *nuptial* in II, 1.)

4. -GON- . . . . angle

A penta<u>gon</u> is a figure with five *angles* or sides.

An octa<u>gon</u> has eight *angles*.

5. -LATER- . . . . side

A <u>later</u>al pass in football is a *side*wise pass as opposed to a forward pass.

A bi<u>later</u>al agreement affects two *sides* or two countries.

Uni<u>later</u>al action is one-*sided*.

The Greek root **-hedron-** also means "side," usually of a solid figure, as in *tetrahedron.*

6. -LOGUE- . . . . **-LOGY-** . . . . speech; science

The pro<u>logue</u> to *Romeo and Juliet* is a *speech* given before the play begins.

A dia<u>logue</u> is conversation or *speech* between two persons.

A eu<u>logy</u> is a rather formal *speech* or writing in praise of someone.

Bio<u>logy</u> is the *science* of living things. It has many branches, such as physio<u>logy</u> and zoo<u>logy</u>.

Psycho<u>logy</u> is the *science* of the mind.

The Greek root *logos* means "word," somewhat in the sense of "spoken knowledge." It also means "a collection," in such a word as *trilogy,* which refers to a group of three related operas, plays, or novels. *Cf.* -locu- (I, 11)

7. **-METER-** . . . . measure, measurer

The perimeter of that field (the *measure* around it) is almost a mile.

A speedometer is a speed *measurer*.

Cf. kilometer, cyclometer, pentameter

8. **-PED-, -PEDE-, -POD-** . . . . foot

A biped is an animal which has two *feet*.

To impede progress is to hinder or obstruct it; i.e., to put one's *foot* against it.

A chiropodist treats one's *foot* or feet.

Cf. pedal, pedometer, pedestal, impediment; podiatry, podium

9. **-PLI-, -PLIC-** . . . . fold

A pliable person is easily influenced; i.e., *folded*.

To implicate someone in a crime is to involve him or to *fold* him into it.

Cf. supplicate, duplicate, triplicate, quadruplicate; multiplication

---

Note: In this unit, the roots *-arch-, -gamy-, -gon-, -meter, -pod-,* and *-hedron* are Greek. The others are Latin.

Counting Off

Study these carefully. Then test yourself on them or have a friend quiz you by giving you a word and asking, "How many?"

Sides	*Marriage*
unilateral—having *one* side	monogamy—*one* wife
bilateral	bigamy
trilateral	polygamy
quadrilateral	

Births	**Feet**	**Music**
baby	monopode	solo
twins	biped	duet
triplets	tripod	trio
quadruplets	quadruped	quartet
quintuplets	octopus	quintet
sextuplets	decapod (lobster)	sextet
septuplets	centipede	septet
octuplets	millipede	octet

Elderly Persons		**Transportation**	**Radio and Television Tubes**
sexagenarian	60-69	unicycle	diode—*two* elements
septuagenarian	70-79	bicycle	triode—*three* elements
octogenarian	80-89	tricycle	pentode—*five* elements
nonagenarian	90-99		
centenarian	100 plus		

Celebrations		**Multiplication**
annual (every year)		single
biennial (every *two* years)		double
triennial		triple
quadrennial		quadruple
quinquennial		quintuple
sexennial		sextuple
septennial		septuple
octennial		octuple
decennial		decuple
centennial		centuple
sesquicentennial	(150 years)	
tercentennial	(300 years)	
millennial	(1000 years)	

Parts	*Ships*
tripartite—having *three* parts	unireme—*one* row of oars
quadripartite	bireme
quinquepartite	trireme
sexpartite	quinquereme

Poetry

Every line of English poetry contains a certain number of *feet* or *measures*, each of which ordinarily has one accented syllable.

1. monometer (mȯ·nŏm'ė·tēr) Away'!
2. dimeter (dĭm'ė·tēr) Away' we go'!
3. trimeter (trĭm'ė·tēr) Away' we go' to school'!
4. tetrameter (tė·trăm'ė·tēr) Away' we go' to school' each day'!
5. pentameter (pĕn·tăm'ė·tēr) We al'ways take' our books' to school' each day'. Who says' we al'ways go' to school' to play'?
6. hexameter (hĕx·ăm'ė·tēr) This' is the for'est prime'val, the mur'muring pines' and the hem'locks.
7. heptameter (hĕp·tăm'ė·tēr) I hope' to go' abroad' when school' is out' in June' this year'!
8. octameter We plan' to spend' the sum'mer, when' it comes', near San' Francis'co Bay'. (Just double No. 4.)

Look up *triad* and *triolet*.

Numbers

million—a thousand thousand	1,000,000—	6 ciphers
billion	1,000,000,000—	9 ciphers
trillion	1,000,000,000,000—	12 ciphers
quadrillion	1,000,000,000,000,000—	15 ciphers
quintillion	1,000,000,000,000,000,000—	18 ciphers
sextillion	1,000,000,000,000,000,000,000—	21 ciphers
septillion	1,000,000,000,000,000,000,000,000—	24 ciphers
octillion . . .	1,000,000,000,000,000,000,000,000,000—	27 ciphers
nonillion . .	1,000,000,000,000,000,000,000,000,000,000—	30 ciphers
decillion	1,000,000,000,000,000,000,000,000,000,000,000—	33 ciphers

Metric System

You will have to learn the metric system if you take many science courses. Remember that *cent-* gives the meaning of $\frac{1}{100}$, whereas *hecto-* gives the meaning of 100. *Milli-* gives the meaning of $\frac{1}{1000}$ and *kilo-*, that of 1000. From the meaning of the prefix, determine which fraction or number should go in each blank.

1 meter	= 39.37 inches	1 gram	= .0353 ounce
1 hectometer	= __?__ meters	1 hectogram	= __?__ grams
1 kilometer	= __?__ meters	1 kilogram	= __?__ grams
1 centimeter	= __?__ meter	1 centigram	= __?__ gram
1 millimeter	= __?__ meter	1 milligram	= __?__ gram

FIRST PRACTICE SET

What is the meaning of each *italicized* prefix or root?

1. A *sept*et is a group of __?__ performers.

2. An *octo*syllable is a word of __?__ syllables.

3. Disease *deci*mated the army (destroyed one __?__th of the men).

4. An *arch*bishop is the __?__ bishop.

5. To *quint*uple a figure, multiply it by __?__.

6. *Du*plex means __?__ fold.

7. *Poly*andry is a social system in which a woman has __?__ husbands.

8. A *tetra*logy is a set of __?__ related plays.

9. A *mono*tonous voice is one which stays on __?__ tone most of the time.

10. *Octa*vo is the size of a book made by folding large sheets of paper three times to form __?__ leaves or sixteen pages.

SECOND PRACTICE SET

What is the meaning of each *italicized* prefix or root?

1. A *hex*archy is a group of __?__ friendly or allied rulers.

2. A *quinque*partite arrangement has __?__ parts.

3. *Mono*gamy is __?__ to __?__ person.

4. A *sept*enary celebration occurs once in __?__ years.

5. A *penta*hedron has __?__ surfaces.

6. A *quad*rennial event occurs once in __?__ years.

7. *Hepta*meter has __?__ __?__ in a line.

8. *Quad*ruplex telegraphy involves __?__ messages over one wire at the same time.

9. A *tetr*arch ruled one __?__*th* of a province.

10. An *oct*angular figure has __?__ angles.

11. A *deca*syllable is a line of __?__ syllables.

12. The *centi*grade thermometer has __?__ degrees or steps.

13. A *heca*tomb was the public sacrifice of __?__ oxen.

14. At the time of the *equi*nox, the days and nights are of __?__ length.

15. A *polygon* has __?__ __?__.

16. *Ped*ate is a term in zoology which means "__?__-like."

17. An *archi*tect is literally a __?__ builder.

18. Icthy*ology* is the __?__ of fishes.

19. A *multilater*al contract would have __?__ __?__.

20. Com*plic*ity in a revolt means being __?__ into it.

THIRD PRACTICE SET

What word from this unit best replaces the *italicized* word or group of words?

1. One does not often meet a *person one hundred years old:* __?__

2. A square is always *equal-sided:* __?__

3. The design on the window is a *nine-sided figure:* __?__

4. The heavyweight champion is a *half-god* to many boys: __?__

5. *Five-measure-verse* is used in English poetry more than any other kind: __?__

6. Moses presented the *Ten Commandments* to the children of Israel: __?__

7. Every school needs a *machine to make one hundred copies:* __?__

8. Written history goes back only a few *thousand-year periods:* __?__

9. *Marriage to many women* was once quite a common custom for *father-rulers:* __?__; __?__

10. The salesman claimed that the addition of a new chemical had made the hose more *easily bent:* __?__

11. A college in Ohio will soon celebrate its *150-year-ago-founding:* __?__

12. One must distinguish a *half-circle* from a *half-sphere:* __?__; __?__

13. A *many-sided figure* belongs to plane geometry, but a *figure with many faces* to solid geometry: __?__; __?__

14. From its name, one would expect __?__ to be the ninth month of the year.

15. Ulcers are often produced in the stomach by *acidity beyond normal:* __?__

WHAT IS IT?

1. A quadrangle
2. An ennead
3. Hexameter
4. A centimeter
5. Polytheism
6. The Trinity
7. A duplex house
8. A unique drawing
9. A tercentennial
10. A tetrahedron

11. A decathlon
12. An ultra-loyal citizen
13. A multicellular plant
14. A pentagon
15. A superabundance
16. A lateral gesture
17. Annular rings
18. A multiplicity of plans
19. A millipede
20. A demitasse of coffee
    (tasse = cup)

CONSTRUCTIVE PROJECTS

1. Compile an *-ology* list. You may find it helpful to consult a college catalog. This could be an individual or a group project.
2. Look up the article on books in any good encyclopedia. Prepare a report for the class explaining how the sections or "signatures" are printed, folded, and bound. Demonstrate folio, quarto, octavo, and sixteenmo.

CREATIVE EXERCISE

New words are continually being invented. Many of these words are constructed from familiar prefixes and roots.

Write down what you would expect each of the following words to mean:

trigamy	a trilogue	polyarchy
a centagon	decuplets	octoplicate

Which may be found in an unabridged dictionary? How do the actual meanings compare with anticipated meanings?

Could a *hemigon* exist? A *sesquigenarian?* A *polymonocle?* Can you see any objection to the creation of a word like *multigon* or *tetralateral?*

FINAL TESTS

From the base words of the unit, write the word which best replaces each *italicized* word or group of words.

UNIT 1

1. A few *gentle breezes* slipped over the *edge* of the hill.

2. As long as germs can *make (themselves) suitable by changing* themselves, the new drugs will not *do away with* disease.

3. The treasurer *declares* his desire to *reduce* expenses.

4. General Spotts will *name* someone to wipe out the *remainders* of enemy resistance.

5. If the draft board will *postpone* his induction, he will have time to sell the car he *obtained* about a year ago.

6. In the *maze* of Los Angeles freeways, the traffic *risks* are less than one would imagine.

7. The *confusing lingo* of an auctioneer fills the *intervening time* between programs.

8. Mr. Forbes promised not to *disclose* his son's *deceit* to his mother.

9. It was useless to *reprove* a *mechanical "man"* about crossing the street, but one might influence the operator.

10. We *entreat* all who love their country to salute the flag with *keen delight*, realizing what it represents.

UNIT 2

1. It is hard to *see clearly* the beginning of an *era* of prosperity.

2. His quiet *conduct* may indicate that he likes to *think*.

3. A sudden *downpour* produced *great disorder* at the picnic.

4. It is the fear of betrayal by someone within the *stronghold* that *haunts* its defenders.

5. Because he followed wise *advice,* he did not *make a mistake*.

6. It was hard for the man to *save* much of his self-respect after the *strong criticism* he received in public.

7. She tried to *pretend* surprise when the officers took her into *imprisonment*.

8. Is there a way to *make amends for* the *devastation* caused by the fire?

9. It would *horrify* the painter to know how little his neighbors *value highly* any work of art.

10. The teacher will *entertain* us with the story of how Delilah managed to *pull away* the secret of Samson's strength from him.

UNIT 3

1. The hobo's voice was *mournful* and his manner *stealthy*.

2. The *calm* lake looked *unearthly* in the moonlight.

3. A *deeply thoughtful* look appeared in her eyes when we told her how *rigidly severe* the training was.

4. The assortment was *varied in kinds* but the thief took it all with *reckless* haste.

5. A *crafty* chess player left me in *sorrowful* defeat.

6. *Sharp* criticisms will make him more *sullen* than he is now.

7. He remained conscious and *clear-minded* for almost an hour after the *horrible* accident.

8. The puppets are *oddly amusing* creatures with their cracked, *doglike* voices.

9. It is easier for a *fully developed* mind to be *honest* with itself.

10. Illness is a *reasonable,* as well as a *very effective,* excuse for staying home.

UNIT 4

1. The *widespread disease* will *decrease* when fall comes.

2. The lumps must be *reduced to powder* before you mix the *liquid dose.*

3. The *monster,* blinded by the storm, fell into the *very deep chasm* in the mountains.

4. The *descriptive title* "Marshmallow" was intended to *blame* him for his lack of firmness.

5. The *brief story* was about a human *outcast* who reformed.

6. The coach will *take offense at* any attempt to *encourage* the captain in his big-headedness.

7. A four-leaf clover might be *referred to* in a discussion of *portents* of good luck.

8. Why *bewail* the effort to *cleanse* the organization of deadwood?

9. How could one fail to *reveal* an interest in science when it *spreads through* our world in so many ways?

10. He let luxuries he could not afford *allure* him, and it was this weakness which *defeated* him as an artist.

UNIT 5

1. Amid shouts of *challenge,* the knights *attacked* the castle.

2. Because of their *adroitness,* no one could *escape* them.

3. With admirable *prudence,* the defenders *scattered.*

4. Some of their *adversaries* were unable to *disentangle* themselves from their armor.

5. The shields of those who *clung* to the lord of the castle were *decorated* with crescents.

6. The defenders tried to *strive to equal* the *vigorous efforts* of their leader.

7. The arrival of another band of knights *made larger* the forces of the attackers and heightened their *exultant gladness*.

8. Their motions *implied* that they wanted to *modify* the plan of attack.

9. It would *heighten* their chance of winning, according to their *guesses*, if they could toss a firebrand through an aperture in the wall.

10. This was done with the help of *partners* on the inside. A *very large fire* was started which drove the defenders outside.

UNIT 6

1. The *glowing* face of the clock seemed *unfriendly* to the refugee as it announced the hour.

2. In the *fiery, glaring* light of the burning city, the stranger looked doubly *vengeful*.

3. The gipsy was a *listless* person who led a *wandering* life.

4. War, with its *abundant* bloodshed, becomes more and more *hateful* to the human race.

5. He lives in *unending* distress because he is *plain-featured*.

6. The *outstanding* singer carries herself with *royal* grace.

7. Though *mischievous* among friends, he is sometimes *forward* among strangers.

8. The coach is likely to be *violent* at first but he will be rather *mild* when he calms down.

9. The President's *for-the-homeland* program is truly *praise-worthy*.

10. Rodney is a *very active and devoted* worker, but he sometimes becomes *clamorous* at a party.

UNIT 7

1. Her *justifiable anger* because of the affront was *severe*.

2. The farms *neighboring* to the highway are *of low quality*.

3. *Jubilantly*, the *runaways* fled from the prison camp.

4. *Roving* rats made up the Pied Piper's *train of attendants*.

5. The *insulting behavior* of a farmer irritated a banker who was traveling *in disguise*.

6. His *countenance* grew more menacing as the *ceaseless* questioning continued.

7. The merchants proved *nimble* in marking up prices that were already *excessive*.

8. Our faith in the old man's wisdom grew less *unquestioning* when the *aid* he had promised did not arrive.

9. Night brought no *quiet*, and *hellish* monsters haunted his dreams.

10. The scout's body lay *inactive*, and he could not keep his *appointment*.

UNIT 8

1. The prince was *set free* on the condition that he would *give up* his claim to the throne.

2. Still in *warlike* formation, the troops spread out so as to *separate* the nearest enemy units.

3. She has a right to *protest* when *plundering* boys raid the yard.

4. The army *boasts of* its ability to hold the *insecure* position indefinitely.

5. *Repaying* good for evil *hinders* enmity.

6. The scientist must be *prying* enough to *overcome* the obstacles that beset him in his search for new knowledge.

7. The hunt for the *huge* culprit, an elephant, *ended* in a barn.

8. He must try to *conquer* this attitude because it is *proper-only-for-slaves.*

9. It is hard to tell whether a bull is *brave* or merely *stubborn.*

10. The clerk was too *neglectful* to handle the *complex* details of his office properly.

U N I T 9

Write the word, formed from the roots and prefixes of this unit, which may be used in place of each of the following groups of words.

1. Loosening someone from his guilt: __?__

2. The drawing out or forth of a tooth: __?__

3. The twisting of facts away from the truth: __?__

4. The moving out or forth of feeling: __?__

5. The process of rolling or bringing something forth, especially animals from very simple beginnings: __?__

6. The act of putting a king out of, or down from, the kingship: __?__

7. The act of shutting a person apart: __?__

8. Someone whose opinions are placed against yours: __?__

9. The act of sending someone away: __?__

10. A word that describes a face which moves or changes expression readily: __?__

UNIT 10

Write the word from this unit which best replaces the *italicized* word or words in each sentence.

1. Heavy soot *poured among* the fresh breezes of the bay.

2. Gasoline *drives* a car *forward*.

3. The business of the company is to *carry* cars from England *into* the United States.

4. Scientists study the *carrying across* of thoughts from one mind to another.

5. Newspapers will *bring back* the results of the election.

6. The *writing* upon the monument is badly chipped.

7. The report showed no progress—nothing but *backward going*.

8. It is a *device for seeing around something*.

9. *Looking around carefully before one acts* is a trait of a wise person.

10. He works toward *(breathes toward)* a high goal.

UNIT 11

1. He showed *insincere, excessive feeling* but not *lack of feeling*.

2. He feels deep *sorrow for wrongdoing*, and he *declares to* (all) that he will never do such a thing again.

3. It was hard to *press under* a laugh when he slipped into the pool with his clothes on, even though I tried to *feel with him*.

4. Two people tried to *break apart* the harmony of the meeting. A sense of *feeling together* did not exist.

5. *Faithfulness* to duty is a quality which, in this family, is *clinging-within*.

6. The trout hid under a rock but often made *runnings forth* among the *underwater* plants.

7. The monk led a life of *saintliness* and *moral uprightness*.

8. The *death* rate from *heart* ailments is very high.

9. Nero *had the say* about everything and seemed *unconquerable* at first.

10. Gordon would like to have *very tight* laws to silence people who are too *talkative*.

UNIT 12

1. The insect which has literally *a thousand feet*

2. A state of society in which there is just *one ruler*

3. A figure having *eight sides or angles*

4. Something that occurs *every four years*

5. A distance of *one hundred meters*

6. An old man in his *nineties*

7. The *science of life*

8. The condition of a triangle having *equal sides*

9. A person easily *folded or bent* to your will

10. *Marriage to two* persons at the same time

DIVISION TESTS

Write the numbers of the *italicized* words. Beside each, write the number of the matching word or words from the other column.

UNITS 1, 2, 3

SECTION 1

1. *Curtail* expenses
2. *Feign* disgust
3. *Acquire* property
4. Dreams *obsess*
5. Citizens *esteem* him
6. Crimes *appall*
7. Fathers *admonish*
8. Committees *defer* action
9. Men *err*
10. Laws *abolish*

1. get, procure
2. warn, reprove
3. do away with
4. frighten
5. cut down, reduce
6. delay, postpone
7. horrify, overcome with fear
8. pretend
9. convince
10. make mistakes
11. beset or haunt
12. value highly

SECTION 2

1. In the *interim*
2. Legal *counsel*
3. Clever *ambush*
4. Solemn *demeanor*
5. Police *custody*
6. Road *hazard*
7. Childish *jargon*
8. *Guerdon* of praise
9. Building's *contour*
10. Newspaper *censure*

1. impatience
2. outline, profile
3. intervening time
4. a lying in wait
5. advice
6. confusing lingo
7. distrust
8. risk or danger
9. keeping, care
10. conduct, behavior
11. a reward
12. strong criticism

143

Section 3

1. *Pensive* moments
2. A *lucid* explanation
3. *Candid* remarks
4. *Droll* behavior
5. A *mature* mind
6. *Potent* friends
7. A *plausible* reason
8. A *dour* face
9. A *motley* group
10. A *hoary* grandfather

1. powerful, very effective
2. deeply thoughtful, wistful
3. ripe, fully developed
4. clear in or to the mind
5. sullen, gloomy
6. oddly comical, amusing
7. white or gray with age
8. pleasant, airy
9. varied in colors, kinds
10. appearing true or reasonable
11. frank, honest
12. witty, resourceful

UNITS 4, 5, 6

Section 4

1. *Manifest* a willingness
2. *Reproach* one's father
3. *Satiate* one's thirst
4. *Entice* a customer
5. *Chastise* a team
6. *Emulate* a saint
7. *Pulverize* a rock
8. *Augment* one's knowledge
9. *Extricate* a dog
10. *Enhance* one's skill

1. allure, inveigle
2. weaken
3. blame, upbraid
4. reduce to powder
5. show plainly
6. satisfy to excess
7. increase, to make larger
8. punish
9. heighten or make greater
10. strive to equal or excel
11. disentangle
12. explain clearly

Section 5

1. Court *decorum*
2. Vague *aroma*
3. Scornful *fiend*
4. Appalling *conflagration*
5. Great *discretion*
6. Devastating *pestilence*
7. Fierce *avarice*
8. Wine-colored *potion*
9. Phantom *derelict*
10. Rude *antagonist*

1. opponent, adversary
2. very large fire
3. prudence, judiciousness
4. proper behavior
5. greed for money
6. odor
7. vague suspicion
8. abandoned ship
9. demon, monster
10. widespread disease
11. ghost, spirit
12. liquid dose or drink

Section 6

1. A *lurid* tale
2. *Oblique* route
3. *Vindictive* sailor
4. *Luminous* sky
5. A *zealous* worker
6. An *eminent* writer
7. A *languid* air
8. *Roguish* joy
9. *Vehement* rage
10. *Officious* helpfulness

1. outstanding, pre-eminent
2. vigorous, powerful
3. glowing, giving off light
4. shining with fiery glare
5. slanting, indirect
6. forward, meddlesome
7. violent, passionate
8. vengeful, seeking revenge
9. very active and devoted
10. knavish, mischievous
11. drooping, listless
12. quiet, thoughtful

UNITS 7, 8, 9

SECTION 7

1. To give *succor*
2. Accidental *exclusion*
3. Stately *retinue*
4. Full *absolution*
5. Courtly *obeisance*
6. Old *delusion*
7. Fair *recompense*
8. Shameless *extortion*
9. Extreme *dejection*
10. Life's *zenith*

1. a bow or curtsey
2. compensation, reward
3. aid, help
4. highest point
5. train of attendants
6. shutting out
7. state of being downcast
8. forceful denial
9. false idea
10. "loosening" from guilt, forgiveness
11. act of twisting something from
12. release from debt

SECTION 8

1. *Inert* ingredient
2. *Intricate* calculations
3. A *predatory* cat
4. *Agile* arms
5. A *sinister* look
6. The *errant* stranger
7. A *valiant* doctor
8. *Menial* submissiveness
9. *Infernal* remorse
10. *Implicit* hope

1. nimble, quick moving
2. undisciplined
3. unquestioning or implied
4. inactive
5. treacherous
6. hellish, fiendish
7. roving, wandering
8. complicated, complex
9. servile, proper to servants
10. plundering, robbing
11. brave, courageous
12. ill-boding, evil

Section 9

1. *Surmount* a problem
2. *Vilify* a good man
3. *Emit* a squeak
4. *Traverse* a field
5. *Abstract* an article
6. *Evolve* a plan
7. Players *remonstrate*
8. *Eject* a cartridge
9. *Demote* a foreman
10. *Requite* a compliment

1. protest, expostulate
2. repay, reward
3. overcome, rise above
4. pass or move across
5. speak evil of, revile
6. untangle
7. cast out or forth
8. send forth
9. roll forth gradually
10. draw the main ideas from
11. work lose
12. move down to lower position

UNITS 10, 11, 12

Section 10

1. *React* violently
2. *Transcend* the limits
3. *Erupt* unexpectedly
4. *Remand* a prisoner
5. *Adhere* to rules
6. *Compress* a report
7. *Disrupt* a scheme
8. *Reflect* light rays
9. *Incur* hatred
10. *Imbibe* willingly

1. act backward or in response to
2. drink (in)
3. stick to
4. climb across
5. order back
6. bend back
7. descend slowly
8. burst forth
9. squeeze together
10. think loosely
11. run into
12. break apart or burst

Section 11

1. A *mobile* defense
2. *Intramural* sports
3. A *perceptive* mind
4. *Ductile* material
5. *Cursory* preparation
6. *Soporiferous* atmosphere
7. *Loquacious* beggar
8. *Aggressive* playing
9. *Refractory* actions
10. *Sanctimonious* manner

1. seeing through things readily
2. easily "led" or shaped
3. sleep-bringing
4. brave, courageous
5. moves or changes readily
6. within the walls
7. running, hasty
8. talkative
9. pretending goodness
10. tending to break away (from rules)
11. going toward, pushing
12. imaginative

Section 12

1. The factor of *torque*
2. Public *symposium*
3. Exemplary *deportment*
4. Tallest *aspirant*
5. Noble *motive*
6. Hospital *cardiogram*
7. Veritable *necropolis*
8. Vigorous *impulse*
9. Lively *sexagenarian*
10. Weekly *convocation*

1. unwillingness
2. that which moves on (to act)
3. twisting or rotating motion
4. placing together of ideas on some topic
5. carriage or behavior
6. city of dead bodies, cemetery
7. person in his sixties
8. six-year study of heart trouble
9. sudden push toward action
10. one who breathes or strives toward something
11. record of heart action
12. a calling together or assembly

PART **II**

ROAD SIGNS

When you see one of these symbols in front of an illustrative sentence, watch for the part of speech it denotes:

- ● a **verb** form of the base word
- – an **adverb** form of the base word
- ■ a **noun** form of the base word
- ► an **adjective** form of the base word

For Pronouncing Key, see page 406.

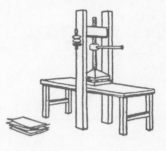

UNIT ONE

Which word from the list at the right gives the best answer to each question?

1. Before you buy a business, what must you do about the reports of its income and profits?
2. If the seller seems over-eager, what attitude should you take?
3. After a time, what happens to new equipment?
4. What must you do when you buy merchandise?
5. What will your secretary be expected to do if you ask her to stay late?
6. After work, what should you do with your worries?
7. What kind of attitude toward employees is too lenient?
8. How are you likely to look if a terrifying crisis comes?
9. How will an excitable wife act if the business fails?
10. What will friends do if you fail?

overt
acquiesce
indulgent
corroborate
discriminate
livid
console
hysterical
dubious
dilate
banish
depreciate

• Word List—VERBS

1. **ABRIDGE (à·brĭj)** . . . . shorten, condense

    The program was so long that each speaker had to abridge his remarks.

    ▪ The magazine prints abridgments of current books.

    Query: What is an unabridged dictionary?
    Summary Words: *epitome, compendium, abstract, digest, synopsis,* and *syllabus.* How is each one used?

2. **ACQUIESCE (ăk'wĭ·ĕs')** . . . . assent, agree quietly

    I am sure the children will acquiesce in any plans we make for a trip this summer.

    ▪ He "gave no other answer than a gruff sound of acquiescence."

    Other Yes Words: *assent* (I, 11), *accede, concur* (I, 11)
    Cf. quiescent (calm), *tranquil, inactive, inert* (I, 7)

3. **ALLUDE (à·lūd')** . . . . mention, refer to casually

    When you talk to her, do not mention or even allude to the accident because she is very sensitive about it.

    ▪ The "Rime of the Ancient Mariner" contains numerous allusions to sailing and the sea.

    ▶ This allusive quality adds to the poem's beauty and shows Coleridge's knowledge of the sea.

    See also *cite* (I, 4), meaning "mention or refer to as example."

4. **BANISH (băn'ĭsh)** . . . . drive, send, or put away

    The king decided to banish his quarrelsome nephew for three years.

    ▪ In vain, the nephew protested the decree of banishment which made him an exile.

    Life would be happier if we could banish fear and selfishness.

5. **CONSOLE** (kŏn·sōl') . . . . comfort, solace

When her brother was killed, her parents tried to console her.

■ Her friends tried to bring consolation, too, but nothing seemed to lessen her grief.

► For weeks, she remained inconsolable.

To **comfort** a person is to ease his grief over some situation.
To console a person is to make him understand and accept a situation that is grieving him.
The word *console* (kŏn'sōl), meaning "cabinet" (as for a radio, a television set, or an organ), is not derived from the same root.

6. **CONSTITUTE** (kŏn'stĭ·tūt) . . . . form, make up

The judge had trouble deciding whether refusal to sign a contract constituted, in itself, a violation of the labor laws.

■ The Senator received telegrams from many of his constituents (voters who make up his district).

■ His constituency as a whole sanctioned his action.

Constituent is also an adjective meaning "component, serving to make up" something: A mild acid is one of the constituent parts of honey.

7. **CONTRIVE** (kŏn·trīv') . . . . . . devise; bring about; plot

Mother will contrive a way to get my sister out of the house before the surprise party.

Sam contrived to keep the car going until he could get it to a garage.

■ The contrivance consisted of a little strip of tin in the distributor.

8. **CORROBORATE** (kŏ·rŏb'ŏ·rāt) . . . . . . verify, confirm

The police could not corroborate the suspect's claim that he had been out of town the night of the hold-up.

► There was corroborative evidence that he had been out of town the preceding night.

■ However, there was corroboration also for the neighbor's report that he had seen burglar tools in the trunk of the suspect's car.

9. **CULMINATE** (kŭl′mĭ·nāt) . . . . . . reach the highest point

The winter festivities culminate in the celebration of Christmas and New Year's Day.

■ In Christian churches, Easter is the culmination of the year's religious observances.

Culminate derives from a Latin word meaning "top."
Climax Words: **summit, acme, crown, zenith** (I, 7)

10. **DEPRECIATE** (dė·prē′shĭ·āt) . . . . . . decrease in value

During the first year, a new car will depreciate in value as much as a fourth or a third.

■ The depreciation on a new house is slight, however. It may even appreciate (increase) in value.
Why depreciate honest effort, even if it proves futile?

■ Such depreciation does no good.

Depreciate also means "belittle, speak slightingly of."
Cf. *disparage* (III, 1)

11. **DILATE** (dī·lāt′) . . . . enlarge upon; expand

The pupils of one's eyes will dilate in the dark.
The veteran likes to dilate upon his war experiences.

Dilate comes from the Latin *dis-*, "apart," and *latus,* "borne, carried." (See I, 10.)
Cf. *expatiate*
Dilatory (dĭl′à·tō′rĭ) comes from a Latin word meaning "delay":
Dilatory behavior is dawdling or delaying behavior.

12. **DISCRIMINATE** (dĭs·krĭm′ĭ·nāt) . . . observe differences; make a distinction (for or against)

Can you discriminate between these two shades of blue?
Some Americans still discriminate against persons of a different race.

■ Her excellent discrimination in women's clothing makes her a good buyer.

► The newspaper accused the senator of having made discriminatory remarks about farmers in his latest television speech.

► Word List—ADJECTIVES

1. ARID (ăr′ĭd) . . . . **extremely dry**

Arizona has an arid climate.

■ Its aridity (aridness) makes irrigation necessary.

An uninteresting book or a barren personality may be described as arid.
Antonyms of *arid* are *wet* and *humid*: Florida has a humid climate.

2. CHRONIC (krŏn′ĭk) . . . . . **constant; habitual; recurring**

Chronic sinusitis is a fairly common ailment.

Her brother is a chronic complainer.

- He seems chronically unable to hold a job.

3. DUBIOUS (dū′bĭ·ŭs) . . . . **doubtful, causing doubt**

A dubious look appeared on her face when the magician beckoned her to the stage.

■ The dubiousness of the weather discouraged us from taking the trip.

- He is indubitably (undoubtedly) the better tennis player.

Other Doubt Words: **Dubiety** (dṵ·bī′ĕ·tĭ) is doubtfulness.
A **dubitable** proposal is one to be doubted; an **indubitable** proposal, one not to be doubted.

4. FEROCIOUS (fė·rō′shŭs) . . . . **fierce, savage**

The fire was as ferocious as a tiger.

■ The ferocity of the police dog kept prowlers away.

Cf. truculent (trŭk′ṵ·lĕnt), *truculence* (III, 5)

5. HYSTERICAL (hĭs·tĕr′ĭ·kăl) . . . . **wildly emotional, frenzied**

The mother of the children became hysterical when she found that the house was on fire.

The house party culminated in an almost hysterical outburst of laughter.

■ A fit of hysteria seized the girls.

6. **INDULGENT** (ĭn·dŭl′jĕnt) . . . . **yielding, lenient**

Mr. Haines was very indulgent with his daughter, letting her have almost anything she wanted.

* When she was small, he let her indulge (gratify) her fondness for candy.

▪ The wealthier families lived a life of luxury and self-indulgence.

An indulgent person may be almost too kind and lenient.

7. **INTERNAL** (ĭn·tûr′năl) . . . **inside, within (the body or country)**

He died from an internal injury, probably a ruptured liver.
England's internal or domestic affairs were in good order.

▪ A liquid prepared for external use only must not be used internally.

An **intern** is a doctor, often one who is in training or who serves as an assistant within a hospital.
What is an internal combustion engine?
Why is the Bureau of Internal Revenue so named?

8. **LETHAL** (lē′thăl) . . . . **deadly**

One drop of the poison constitutes a lethal dose.
Beyond certain limits, exposure to radioactivity is lethal.

Lethal comes from one of the Latin words for death.

9. **LIVID** (lĭv′ĭd) . . . . . . **pale; lead-colored, grayish blue**

Long illness and confinement had made the man's face livid.

▪ It had the lividness of a clouded sky.

Livid may mean "black-and-blue" or "discolored" when describing a bruise or scar.

10. **NUPTIAL** (nŭp′shăl) . . . . **of marriage or a wedding**

October 4 was to be the nuptial day for the heiress and her titled English fiancé.
The royal nuptials will take place in the spring.

The word *nuptials* refers to the associated social events, as well as to the wedding itself. The word is now used chiefly in newspaper society columns.

11. **OVERT** (ō′vûrt) . . . . **open, unconcealed**

The attack on Pearl Harbor was an act of overt hostility following months of secret preparation.
- The man's threat was made overtly, not merely hinted at in his letter.

12. **SENILE** (sē′nīl) . . . . **of old age**

Loss of memory is a common trait of senile behavior.
- Thinking only of the past is another mark of senility.

Senility often refers to the physical or mental weakness of extreme old age.

13. **VIRTUAL** (vûr′tṳ·ăl) . . . **being something in effect although not in actual fact**

The president of that country claims to be democratic but he is a virtual dictator.
- The general manager's secretary is virtually the general manager.

FIRST PRACTICE SET

Copy the *italicized* words. Beside each, write an appropriate definition.

1. The manager tried to *contrive* a better way to *discriminate* between genuine and counterfeit bills.

2. Jewels do not *depreciate,* but the banker is *dubious* about mining stocks.

3. Doctors *corroborate* the statement that the pupils of the eye *dilate* when the new medicine is used.

4. The woman whose husband had been killed was *hysterical* with grief when the policeman tried to *console* her.

5. Her parents must *acquiesce* in the *nuptial* arrangements before any plans can be announced.

6. Medicine has found ways to *banish* several of the *chronic* ailments of mankind.

7. An *internal* upheaval brought to the throne a *ferocious* general who made Spain a *virtual* fortress.

8. The mayor was too *indulgent* toward certain of his friends to *abridge* their part in the centennial ceremonies.

9. The judge did not *allude* to the company's *overt* defiance of the government.

10. Long years in a cave had made the hermit *livid* in appearance and *senile* in actions.

SECOND PRACTICE SET

Which base word from the unit best replaces each *italicized* word or phrase?

1. The newspaper account of the crime *refers casually* to the way the storekeeper tried to *devise* a trap for the burglar.

2. Friends tried to *comfort* Ben when the coach had him *sent away* from the football squad.

3. The skull and crossbones on the label helps one *make a distinction* between *deadly* chemicals and harmless ones.

4. *Old-age* disorders left the man *lead-colored*.

5. She has a *recurring* tendency toward *wildly emotional* behavior when she gets too excited.

6. The Senator was glad to *assent* because the plan was, *not really but in its effect*, a great inspiration.

7. If he would agree to *condense* his long speech, it would not *decrease in value*.

8. The child saw the *yielding* look in his mother's eyes and continued to *enlarge* upon his reasons for skipping piano-lessons.

9. Neighbors *confirm* the *savage* behavior of the Boynton dog.

10. The wedding *reached its highest point* when the *marriage* vows were spoken.

THIRD PRACTICE SET

Which of the lettered items is most nearly **opposite** in meaning to the word printed in capital letters?

1. ACQUIESCE: (a) consent (b) dissent (c) resent (d) incense (e) present

2. LETHAL: (a) gas-dispelling (b) memory-restoring (c) life-giving (d) slow-acting (e) having an antidote

3. DILATE: (a) grow narrow (b) amplify (c) intensify (d) move fast (e) explain

4. LIVID: (a) calm (b) clean (c) ruddy (d) bruised (e) well-healed

5. VIRTUAL: (a) seeming (b) actual (c) wicked (d) benevolent (e) intentional

6. INDULGENT: (a) lovable (b) lenient (c) low in social rank (d) unyielding (e) ambitious

7. ARID: (a) flat (b) humid (c) mountainous (d) pale (e) well-populated

8. DEPRECIATE: (a) deteriorate (b) increase in value (c) display (d) admire (e) sell wisely

9. OVERT: (a) unwarlike (b) hostile (c) tricky (d) hidden (e) slavish

10. SENILE: (a) intelligent (b) doubtful (c) youthful (d) rich (e) emotional

THE RIGHT WORD

On a separate sheet, write the numbers of the *italicized* words. Beside each, write the number of the matching word or words from the second column.

1. Tardy *consolation*
2. Shameless *dilatoriness*
3. Awkward *contrivance*
4. Moon's *aridity*
5. Growing *dubiety*
6. Accidental *corroboration*
7. Near the *culmination*
8. Prolonged *banishment*
9. Mass *hysteria*
10. *Synopsis* of the story

1. extreme dryness
2. highest point
3. exile
4. summary
5. frenzy
6. display
7. slowness
8. solace
9. device
10. hesitation
11. verification
12. doubtfulness

1. *Allusive* lines
2. A *quiescent* mood
3. *External* pressure
4. *Inconsolable* mothers
5. *Dilatory* progress
6. *Truculent* manners
7. *Discriminating* taste
8. A *constituent* item
9. *Chronic* disability
10. *Indulgent* coach

1. lenient
2. component
3. permanent
4. troublesome
5. referring to something
6. impossible to comfort
7. dawdling
8. calm
9. indefinite
10. ferocious
11. able to observe differences
12. from the outside

1
2
3
4
98765 1

UNIT TWO

Which word from the list at the right fits best in each blank?

1. We arrived at the party late because the car would not __?__ properly.

2. One of the contests required everyone to __?__ verses to popular tunes.

3. In another contest, Bill had to __?__ seasickness.

4. One game involved __?__s. For example, Vera's card had "as lovely as" on it, and the card she drew said "sour milk."

5. Helen, who likes to __?__, said the party was like opening night at the circus.

6. "I'm so exhausted I'll never __?__," she exclaimed once.

7. "Won't somebody please __?__ me?"

8. Tom pretended that he wanted to __?__ her and suggested calling a doctor.

9. Helen started to __?__ by asking him why he didn't behave better, but someone interrupted.

promulgate
humiliate
simile
exaggerate
jeopardize
accelerate
metaphor
recuperate
simulate
impale
retaliate
improvise
resuscitate

• Word List—VERBS

1. **ACCELERATE** (ăk·sĕl′ēr·āt) . . . . speed up

   Unfilled orders for the new model made it necessary to accelerate production.

   ■ This acceleration created three hundred new jobs.

   > *Celerity* means "swiftness." Why is the foot accelerator on a car so named?
   > *Accelerando* is a musical term meaning "gradually faster."
   > *Decelerate* means "slow down."

2. **COMPENSATE** (kŏm′pĕn·sāt) . . make up for; pay, remunerate

   Her high grades in English and history compensate to some degree for her low marks in mathematics and science.

   ■ A workman's compensation program makes up in money for injury or accidental death.

   > Synonyms: *recompense* (I, 7), *counterbalance, reimburse, recoup, indemnify, make reparation*
   > For other *Pens* Words, see I, 9.

3. **EXAGGERATE** (ĕg·zăj′ēr·āt) . . . . overstate, magnify

   Early reports usually exaggerate the number killed in a major catastrophe.

   ■ Such exaggeration grows out of haste and excitement.

4. **HUMILIATE** (hů·mĭl′ĭ·āt) . . . lower the self-respect of, mortify

   Failure to win the trophy did not humiliate Roger because he had done his best.

   ■ The defeat brought a sense of humiliation to the team.

   ■ People liked him as a leader because he had the humility (lack of pride) to seek good advice.

   > Like *humiliate*, the word *humility* goes back to the Latin *humus*, meaning "earth, ground." A person who has humility is free of false pride; i.e., is humble and close to the earth.
   > Synonyms: *shame, degrade, disgrace, dishonor, debase, abase*
   > Antonyms: *exalt, honor, glorify*

5. IMPALE (ĭm·pāl′) . . . . pierce, thrust through

Bobby likes to impale a fresh worm on the hook and cast in his line.

■ The savages followed the impalement and burning of their captive with a wild dance.

● Impaled by his own admissions, the suspect was convicted.

Impale originally meant "fix upon a stake or anything sharp by thrusting it up through the body."
Transfix is a synonym: She stood transfixed (as if pierced) at the horrible sight.

6. IMPROVISE (ĭm′prŏ·vīz) . . . . . compose offhand, arrange a makeshift (of)

Minstrels could improvise poetry as they sang.

By putting his coat on inside out, Scotty improvised a Chinese costume.

■ The pianist played an improvisation on a theme from one of Grieg's compositions.

See also *improvident,* "lacking foresight."

7. JEOPARDIZE (jĕp′ẽr·dīz) . . . . endanger

Fast driving jeopardizes many lives.

■ It is seldom necessary to put one's life in such jeopardy.

The word *jeopardy* comes from *jeu parti,* a French expression meaning "a divided game," one with even chances. The Latin roots are *jocus,* "a joke or play," and *partire,* "divide."

8. PERPETRATE (pûr′pĕ·trāt) . . . . perform, carry out

It took two to perpetrate the bank robbery.

■ One perpetrator was soon caught, but the other escaped.

■ The perpetration of the crime required much planning.

Perpetrate is used chiefly of pranks, blunders, or evil deeds.

9. PROMULGATE (prŏ·mŭl′gāt) . . . . . make known, publish

The king promulgated a decree making the day a holiday.

■ One function of the Department of Agriculture is the promulgation of crop reports.

To **disseminate** information is to spread it abroad as one sows seed.

10. **RECUPERATE** (rė·kū'pēr·āt) . . . . . regain strength, recover

A storage battery will recuperate slightly after a heavy drain.

◁ Recuperation is slow after a long illness.

▸ Youth has great recuperative power.

To recuperate from one's losses on the stock market is to recover what one has lost.
To **recoup** is to make up for losses or to repay. For the legal meaning, see dictionary.

11. **RESUSCITATE** (rė·sŭs'ĭ·tāt) . . . . revive, bring back to life

Every Scout learns to resuscitate a victim of drowning.

▣ Fluttering eyelids are one sign that resuscitation is progressing.

Ancient customs and practices can be resuscitated, too.

12. **RETALIATE** (rė·tăl'ĭ·āt) . give like for like (especially evil for evil)

A vindictive person watches for a chance to retaliate for an injury he once received.

▪ The Christian code opposes retaliation.

▸ Executing its prisoners is one of the retaliative measures an enemy may take.

See also *reprisal*, especially as used in wartime.

13. **SIMULATE** (sĭm'ů·lāt) . . . . feign, pretend; imitate

The toy engine simulates the noise and smoke of a real engine.

He simulates a humility which is not part of his real character.

▸ A simulated enemy attack was part of the war games.

▣ Doctors say her condition is a simulation of a nervous breakdown and not the real thing.

Feign Words: To simulate a quality is to assume the appearance by the way one talks and acts.
To **affect** or **feign** courage is to pretend to have it, usually without such careful efforts as simulation suggests.
Counterfeit courage looks like real courage but is only an imitation.
Cf. feign (I, 2)

▪ Word List—NOUNS

1. METAPHOR (mĕt′á·fēr) . . . . implied comparison

"All the world's a stage" is a metaphor from Shakespeare.
▶ Metaphorical language compares two things not of the same class or kind.

A **mixed metaphor** is a combination of comparisons which results in a confusing and often ridiculous picture. In the following example, the moon is simultaneously compared to a chariot and a face: The moon, a silver chariot, took one last look around and then rolled away.

2. MORON (mō′rŏn) . . . . . . person of low intelligence

A moron can wreck a car more readily than he can build one.
▶ Making faces at the teacher is moronic behavior.

Psychologists recognize various degrees of mental deficiency. A moron is brighter than an imbecile or an idiot (the lowest degree) and is able to learn a simple trade or craft. In ordinary usage, however, the word is applied to anyone who acts in a dull or foolish manner.

3. NONENTITY (nŏn·ĕn′tĭ·tĭ) . . person or thing of no importance

Before she went to Hollywood, she was a complete nonentity.
The thirty-year-old trade treaty has become a nonentity.

4. PARITY (păr′ĭ·tĭ) . . . . equality, equivalence

The new treaty between the two countries provides for parity in arms.
Between baboons and men there is a very great disparity (inequality) in strength as well as intelligence.
▶ Although the par value of the stock was 100, he sold it at 115.

The par value of a stock is the original or the legally established price. The par value of money is the established value of the money of one country in terms of that of another using the same metal as the standard of value.

5.   **QUORUM** (kwō'rŭm) .   .   . number needed to transact business

According to the by-laws, we cannot vote a loan until we have a quorum present.
The constitution of the club defines a quorum as one third of the paid-up members.

In Latin, *quorum* meant "of whom."

6.   **ROSTRUM** (rŏs'trŭm) .   .   .   . a platform for public speaking

The four debaters sat together on the rostrum.
A hush settled over the audience as the President approached the rostrum.

In Latin, the word *rostrum* meant "beak," especially the beak or prow of a ship. It also came to mean "platform." The speakers' platform in the Roman Forum was decorated with the beaks of captured warships and hence was often called "the beak." The word was later applied to any platform where people made speeches.
A **dais** is a platform, usually at one end of a room, which is generally used for a throne, a speaker's table, or a lecture stand.

7.   **SATELLITE** (săt'ĕ·lĭt) .   .   .   .   . small planet revolving around
a larger planet

The planet Jupiter has many satellites.
Several of the countries in eastern Europe have, of necessity, become Russian satellites because of their economic and military dependence on Russia.

8.   **SCROLL** (skrōl) .   .   .   .   .   . ancient rolled manuscript

The first Dead Sea Scrolls were discovered in 1947.
"It matters not how strait the gate,
     How charged with punishments the scroll . . ."

Scroll has come to mean, metaphorically, a list or schedule, as used in the above quotation from the poem "Invictus," by William Ernest Henley. The word may also refer to an ornament resembling a partly unrolled manuscript.

SIMILE (sĭm'ĭ·lē) .   expressed comparison (usually with *like* or *as*)

"My love is like a red, red rose" is a familiar simile from literature. Robert Burns used it in one of his best-known poems.

Bunyan's *Pilgrim's Progress* is told in the similitude (like-ness) of a dream.

It is easy to confuse similes with **metaphors.** In a metaphor, the comparison is implied. In a simile, it is stated outright. For example:
Excitement like a bonfire (simile)
Excitement blazed and crackled (metaphor)

When you want to describe something, the first simile that comes to mind is usually a *cliché,* an expression that has become trite or stereotyped because it has been used so many times; for example, "strong as an ox," "dead as a doornail." In speech and writing, try to use similes that are fresh and vivid.

Verisimiltude means "the appearance of truth or reality": Stories that seem true to life are said to have verisimilitude.

10. SOVEREIGN (sŏv′ĕr·ĭn) . . . . supreme ruler, monarch

The British sovereign is the titular head of the English Church.
▶ In the United States, the sovereign power belongs to the people.
■ If a world government were set up, each nation would have to surrender part of its sovereignty (supreme power).

Sovereign comes from French but goes back to the Latin *super,* "above." (I, 12.)

11. STRATUM (strā′tŭm) . . . . layer or level

He is a writer who came from the lowest stratum of society.
▶ In a gorge or glen, one may see stratified rock.

Strata is the plural form: A geology class studies rock strata.

12. TENACITY (tĕ·năs′ĭ·tĭ) . . . . unyielding firmness

Bulldogs are famous for their tenacity.
– We tried to change his mind but he clung tenaciously to his original idea.

Firm Words: *Tenacity* stresses courage and resolution in doing something. (See *Tain* Words in I, 10.)
Perseverance emphasizes steadfastness in doing something, often in spite of obstacles.
Persistence suggests repetition to a degree that may be annoying.
Obstinacy refers to the kind of stubbornness which is often unintelligent.
Pertinacity, which means "stubborn perseverance," sometimes has unfavorable implications (III, 8).

FIRST PRACTICE SET

Copy the *italicized* words. Beside each, write an appropriate definition.

1. Doctors quickly *resuscitated* the unconscious captain, but it took a month for him to *recuperate* from his injuries.
2. The *tenacity* of our team was enough to *compensate* for its lack of brilliance in strategy.
3. Tom's assignment was to *simulate* a man trying to *improvise* music on a trombone.
4. The veteran *exaggerates* the extent to which he *jeopardized* his life in the war.
5. The car was *impaled* on a fence-post after skidding off the highway. Police called the driver a *moron*.
6. A bare *quorum* was present when the plan was approved, and it was necessary to *promulgate* the details to the entire membership.
7. Why should it *humiliate* a man to discover that his car will not *accelerate* as fast as his neighbor's car?
8. To call your school years "the seedtime of life" is to use a *metaphor;* to say that teaching is "like planting seed" is to use a *simile.*
9. In composition, the two limestone *strata* are about on a *parity.*
10. "Whose little *satellite* are you?" said the speaker when a lost two-year-old came toddling up to the *rostrum.*

SECOND PRACTICE SET

Which base word from this unit best replaces each *italicized* word or group of words?

1. Three boys *carried out* a fake drowning to see whether the lifeguard knew how to *revive* a person. (He did.)
2. The guard decided to *give like for like* for this attempt to *mortify* him.

3. He determined to *pretend* anger and, waving an oar, threatened to *thrust through* the boys.

4. They replied that they would *arrange off-hand* some sort of trap in the sand to *remunerate* him for such cruelty.

5. The guard declared that each of them was a *person of no importance* as well as a *person of low intelligence.*

6. "I like your *implied comparison,*" one of the boys laughed. "You have *equality* with George III: he was insane."

7. "You *magnify* the extent to which you *endanger* me," the lifeguard said.

8. "The *unyielding firmness* with which you annoy me is amazing," he continued. "Please *speed up* your departure.

9. "One is a *number needed to transact business,* and, as I am *supreme ruler* here, I banish you from the beach this week.

10. "You come from the lowest *layer* of Hillville society, and I will *make known* your mischievousness everywhere."

THIRD PRACTICE SET

On a separate sheet, write the numbers of the *italicized* words. Beside each, write the number of the matching word or group of words from the second column.

1.	Fiendish *reprisals*	1.	thrusting through
2.	Slow *recuperation*	2.	imitation
3.	Unexpected *jeopardy*	3.	carrying out
4.	Striking *similitude*	4.	entanglement
5.	*Impalement* with spears	5.	supreme control
6.	Skillful *simulation*	6.	acts of retaliation
7.	Needed *dais*	7.	disputation
8.	Disputed *sovereignty*	8.	swiftness
9.	Amazing *celerity*	9.	resemblance
10.	*Perpetration* of fraud	10.	danger
		11.	platform
		12.	recovery of strength

ANTONYMS

Which of the lettered items is most nearly **opposite** in meaning to the capitalized word?

1. EXAGGERATE: (a) tell the truth   (b) explode   (c) distort   (d) minimize   (e) reconsider

2. HUMILIATE: (a) exalt   (b) abase   (c) inflate   (d) resolve   (e) laud

3. ACCELERATE: (a) impel   (b) retard   (c) protect   (d) examine   (e) exhilarate

4. NONENTITY: (a) good-for-nothing person   (b) saint   (c) celebrity   (d) coward   (e) philanthropist

5. PARITY: (a) inequality   (b) farm losses   (c) price shift   (d) deflation   (e) inflation

6. SOVEREIGN: (a) poverty   (b) misrule   (c) loss of throne   (d) humility   (e) subject

7. PROMULGATE: (a) discuss   (b) suppress   (c) file away   (d) verify   (e) censor

8. MORONIC: (a) imbecilic   (b) very witty   (c) talkative   (d) highly intelligent   (e) treacherous

9. METAPHORICAL: (a) comparable   (b) fantastic   (c) literal   (d) imaginary   (e) moronic

10. IMPROVIDENT: (a) wasteful   (b) irreverent   (c) exercising foresight   (d) ambitious   (e) God-fearing

VARIETY

Write a paragraph describing an illness, an accident, a game, a prank, or a poem. Use as many words from this unit as possible.

black

UNIT THREE

Which is the best answer for each question?

1. Would an effigy be: (a) a ghost? (b) a monster? (c) a cartoon character? (d) an image?

2. Would a hybrid be: (a) a bird? (b) a crossbred plant? (a) a pedigreed animal? (d) a kind of fish?

3. Would a despot be: (a) a servant? (b) a dullard? (c) a tyrant? (d) a kind of worker?

4. Would an affinity for hoboes be: (a) a fondness? (b) a dislike? (c) a distrust? (d) an understanding?

5. Would opulence be: (a) poor eyesight? (b) abundance? (c) weariness? (d) fullness from overeating?

6. Miniver Cheevy missed "the medieval grace of iron clothing." Was the clothing: (a) dignified? (b) fantastic? (c) belonging to knighthood? (d) belonging to the Middle Ages?

7. Would a spontaneous outburst be: (a) fiery? (b) self-generated? (c) wild? (d) carefree?

8. Would an impromptu impersonation be: (a) rehearsed? (b) unprepared? (c) well acted? (d) poorly acted?

▪ Word List— NOUNS

1. **AFFINITY** (ă·fĭn'ĭ·tĭ) . . . . attraction, kinship

   George's affinity for horses was a trait he probably acquired from his father.

   Disease and filth have a marked affinity for each other.

   Affinity also means "readiness to combine with," especially in chemistry: Oxygen has an affinity for hydrogen.

2. **DENIZEN** (dĕn'ĭ·zĕn) . . . . inhabitant

   Frogs are denizens of swamp land.

   The English sparrow, imported from abroad to destroy a pest, has become a denizen of the American countryside.

   The word *denizen* is also used to refer to a foreign word, plant, or animal that has been accepted or naturalized.

3. **DESPOT** (dĕs'pŏt) . . . . . ruler with absolute power, tyrant

   Hitler became a dangerous despot after Hindenburg died.

   The despotism of Alexander the Great did not last.

   ▶ Julius Caesar had despotic dreams, but he retained the outward forms of the Roman republic.

   Cf. tyranny (I, 7)

4. **EFFIGY** (ĕf'ĭ·jĭ) . . . . image, likeness

   For the carnival, the students made a huge effigy of Comus, mythological god of festivals, and carried it in the parade.

   The mob burned an effigy of the despot.

   An effigy is usually the image of a person who is the object of hatred or laughter.

5. **HYBRID** (hī'brĭd) . . . . a cross between two varieties

   The corn that most farmers plant is a hybrid.

   ● The way to get new varieties of a plant or animal is to hybridize.

► Tom's car is a hybrid (crossbred) variety. The body is of one make, the chassis of another.

Hybrid is a scientific term applied to crossbred plants or animals.
Mongrel is a rather scornful word which is applied to a dog or other animal of mixed breed.

6. **ILLUSION** (ĭ·lū′zhŭn) . **something deceptive or unreal; a deception**

The pools of water which seemed to lie across the pavement ahead were an illusion. This illusion is one form of mirage.

● To disillusion a child about Santa Claus is to take away from him an unreal but very charming belief.

► Some kinds of pain and sickness are very illusory (imaginary, unreal).

A **delusion** is a false idea about something, such as believing that you can buy friendship or impress people by boasting.
A **mirage** is an optical illusion caused by atmospheric conditions.
An **hallucination** is an illusion in which a person sees or hears something that does not exist except in his own mind.

7. **IMPUNITY** (ĭm·pū′nĭ·tĭ) . . . **freedom from punishment or loss**

One cannot steal with impunity.

A despot can murder his enemies with impunity, under the guise of purging his party or his army of disloyal elements.

► When the police take punitive action, they act to punish someone.

Immunity is lack of susceptibility to a disease or some other widespread evil.
Exemption is release from some obligation or duty, such as paying taxes.
Remission is forgiveness, which frees one from the guilt which results from a wrong doing.

8. **OPULENCE** (ŏp′ū·lĕns) . . . . **wealth, abundance**

The opulence of Croesus, king of the ancient land of Lydia in the sixth century B.C., is proverbial.

Nature's opulence is not spread uniformly over the earth.

► The Nizam of Hyderabad is one of the most opulent men who ever lived.

An **affluent** person is a rich person, especially one who gets and spends money freely.

9. **POSTERITY** (pŏs·tĕr′ĭ·tĭ) . . . . future generations collectively

   Posterity will long remember Lindbergh's flight to Paris.

   ▸ The stinger of the bee, wasp, and other insects is located in the posterior (back, rear) section of the body.

   The Latin root means "after, subsequent, following."

10. **PRECISION** (prė·sĭzh′ŭn) . . . . exactness

    The teacher's mind operates with precision.

    ▸ She is very precise about following the pattern when she cuts out a dress.

    – A football was precisely what he wanted for Christmas.

11. **PROXIMITY** (prŏks·ĭm′ĭ·tĭ) . . . . nearness

    The proximity of the well made our insurance rate lower than is usual in the country.

    Propinquity (prŏ·pĭng′kwĭ·tĭ) means "nearness" in blood relationship, time, or place: The law forbids people to marry if a propinquity of kinship exists.
    Approximate and *proximate* mean "next" or "very near" in quantity, quality, or position.
    An **approximation** is a near or close estimate.

12. **REMINISCENCE** (rĕm′ĭ·nĭs′ĕns) . . . . recollection

    Since the two mothers had gone to high school together, they enjoyed sharing reminiscences.

    ● It is fun to reminisce because the unpleasant is readily forgotten.

    ▸ When Grandfather was in a reminiscent mood, he told of his adventures in World War I.

13. **VENGEANCE** (vĕn′jăns) . . . . infliction of injury or suffering
    as a recompense

    As an act of vengeance, the Indians killed the white man after he had shot one of their braves.

    ▸ A vengeful person is one who is eager for revenge.

    Vengeance is usually more terrible than punishment.
    Retaliation is hitting back, especially in return for harm. (See II, 2.)
    Acts of **reprisal** are acts of retaliation, injuries in return for injuries, especially those committed by nations at war.

▸ Word List—ADJECTIVES

1. **ADROIT** (*à·droit'*) . . . . skillful, clever

    Philip is very adroit in managing to get spending money from his sister when he needs it.
    ■ Delicate surgery requires great adroitness.

    > *Adroit* comes from the French *à droit*, "to the right."
    > **Dexterous** (I, 6), means "clever and skillful," particularly in using the hands. See *deft*.
    > Antonyms: **clumsy, awkward, inept, maladroit**

2. **FACILE** (*făs'ĭl*) . . . . smooth-working, easily done

    The juggler performs with facile grace.
    ■ She speaks French with unusual facility (ease).
    ● An electric mixer facilitates cake making.

    > A **facility** is anything which makes life easier or more convenient: The factory has a good cafeteria, an air conditioned lounge, and many other facilities for the workers.

3. **FELINE** (*fē'līn*) . . . . catlike; sly

    With feline stealth, he waited behind the curtain like a cat watching for a mouse.
    ■ The larger felines, such as tigers and lions, are often dangerous creatures.

    > A feline is an animal of the cat family.

4. **IMPROMPTU** (*ĭm·prŏmp'tū*) . . . . . on the spur of the moment

    At the first meeting of the convention, Mayor Hatfield made an impromptu speech of welcome.
    Robert can always give an impromptu dramatization at a party.
    ■ Marilyn played a Chopin impromptu on the piano.

    > To speak **extempore** (*ĕks·tĕm'pô·rē*) is to speak impromptu, or with little or no preparation.
    > *Cf. improvise* (I, 2)

5. **MEDIEVAL** (mē'dĭ·ē'văl) . . (characteristic) of the Middle Ages

A castle was a medieval fortress.

Medieval life was rather dreary in winter because even the castles were gloomy and cold.

6. **MEDIOCRE** (mē·dĭ·ō'kēr) . . . . . . average, commonplace

A mediocre player is neither very good nor very bad.

- The pamphlet implied that Americans admire mediocrity and that democracy encourages it.

7. **PRODIGIOUS** (prō·dĭj'ŭs) . . . . . enormous, marvelous

Paul Bunyan's muscular feats were prodigious.

- The prodigiousness of American productive capacities is hard for some people to grasp.
- Mozart, a skilled pianist at the age of four, is an outstanding example of a child prodigy.

8. **PROSAIC** (prŏ·zā'ĭk) . . . . dull, uninteresting

Although his trip abroad must have been exciting, his letters home were prosaic and boring.

- More authors write in prose than in poetry.

The term **prose** refers to all writing or speech which is not poetry or verse. *Prosaic* may, therefore, also mean "of the nature of prose." A **prosy** account is especially wearisome prose.

9. **SPONTANEOUS** (spŏn·tā'nė·ŭs) . . . . . arising from within; natural; impulsive

Spontaneous applause greeted every song.

- Jane's spontaneousness (spontaneity) was refreshing.

Can you explain how spontaneous combustion occurs in fresh hay or oily rags?
An **impulsive** action is sudden and unexpected, but may not be as spirited or exuberant as spontaneous action.

10. **SUBTLE** (sŭt''l) . . . . . . delicate; artful; requiring acuteness

Do you like the subtle flavor of this cream sauce?

The principal is a man of subtle wit.

■ Few grasped the subtlety of the argument that the meek do inherit the earth after the violent have destroyed themselves.

- The witness subtly betrayed his comrade.

Subtle poisons are very **insidious** (II, 9).

11. **TRANSIENT** (trăn'shĕnt) . . . . fleeting, short-lived

Transient beams of sunlight filtered through the broken clouds.

■ The transience of a child's delight is matched by the transience of a child's sorrow.

▶ Poets and clergymen like to point out that life itself is very transitory.

An **ephemeral** idea lasts but a day: Most newspaper writing is highly ephemeral.
An **evanescent** smile is one which fades quickly.
A **transitory** joy is short-lived.
What is the meaning of *sic transit gloria mundi?*

12. **VIRILE** (vĭr'ĭl) . . . . manly, masculine, vigorous

The novel was written in a direct and virile style.

■ Dr. Williams has a vitality and virility that always inspires confidence.

FIRST PRACTICE SET

Copy the *italicized* words. Beside each, write an appropriate definition.

1. *Medieval* men little dreamed of the scientific wonders that *posterity* would achieve.
2. Uncle Ben gave a *facile reminiscence* about shooting at an *effigy* of Hitler.
3. The *proximity* of the coach accounted for the *precision* with which the plays were executed.
4. The lynx is a *feline* creature which is a *denizen* of the forests of Canada and the United States.

5. At first, he was dazzled by the seeming *opulence* of the room, but then he saw that the furnishings, though colorful, were really very *mediocre.*

6. *Illusions* of *impunity* prevented the bully from feeling any fear of *vengeance.*

7. Her acting was *subtle,* her dancing *adroit,* and her tantrums *transient.*

8. Do the *hybrid* sunflowers have as much *affinity* for sunshine as older varieties?

9. The *impromptu* speech about potatoes was *spontaneous* enough but very *prosaic.*

10. The *virile despot* has *prodigious* energy.

SECOND PRACTICE SET

Which base word from this unit best replaces each *italicized* word or group of words below?

1. The new *cross between two varieties* is too *commonplace* to sell well.

2. Is the apparent *attraction* of plants for moonlight just *something deceptive?*

3. The *image* is that of a fighter who is a *manly* brute but not a very *artful* speaker.

4. *Future generations collectively* will remember the *great wealth* of the Rockefellers.

5. One cannot wreak *infliction of injury as a recompense* with complete *freedom from loss.*

6. The *nearness* of the lake prompted Mrs. Meek to tell us a *recollection* about her narrow escape from drowning.

7. The *absolute ruler* lived in a house whose style was *out-of-the-Middle Ages.*

8. The diplomat's speech was both *skillful* and *smoothly done.*

9. The *inhabitants* of that region lead rather *uninteresting* lives.

10. He spoke with *enormous* power even though his speech was *on-the-spur-of-the-moment.*

THIRD PRACTICE SET

Which word or expression is most nearly **opposite** in meaning to the word in capital letters?

1. OPULENCE: (a) fullness (b) poverty (c) weakness (d) energy (e) luxury

2. AFFINITY: (a) endlessness (b) great depth (c) close relationship (d) repulsion (e) mysteriousness

3. ILLUSION: (a) reality (b) dreamlessness (c) playfulness (d) disregard (e) fantasy

4. PROXIMITY: (a) a kind of fuse (b) boundary (c) remoteness (d) disuse (e) precision

5. VENGEANCE: (a) fury (b) kindness (c) forgiveness (d) peaceableness (e) revival

6. POSTERITY: (a) being ahead of time (b) lifelikeness (c) adroitness (d) medieval life (e) ancestors

7. IMPUNITY: (a) with punishment (b) virtue (c) responsibility (d) bigness (e) with fondness

8. PRECISION: (a) promptness (b) watch-making skill (c) bulldozer quality (d) lack of skill (e) inexactness

9. VIRILITY: (a) strength (b) devilishness (c) femininity (d) fancifulness (e) lack of solidity

10. ADROITNESS: (a) lack of subtlety (b) acuteness (c) inaccuracy (d) ineptness (e) bad manners

THE RIGHT WORD

On a separate sheet of paper, write the numbers of the *italicized* words. Beside each, write the number of the matching word or group of words from the second column.

1. Disappointing *mediocrity*
2. A very large *effigy*
3. *Subtlety* of color
4. Acts of *reprisal*
5. *Prodigy* of learning
6. *Hallucinations* at night
7. *Delusions* of wealth
8. Delightful *spontaneity*
9. Exciting *reminiscence*
10. *Transience* of sunbeams

1. fleetingness
2. spirited naturalness
3. mystery
4. commonplaceness
5. persistent quality
6. deceptions not visible to another
7. marvel
8. false ideas
9. delicacy
10. likeness
11. recollection
12. retaliation, especially in war

1. *Ephemeral* fame
2. *Feline* gentleness
3. *Illusory* gains
4. *Medieval* travel
5. *Hybrid* rabbits
6. *Facile* charm
7. *Extempore* discussion
8. *Despotic* madness
9. *Approximate* perfection
10. *Punitive* action

1. providing punishment
2. easy, smooth
3. uninteresting, commonplace
4. tyrannical
5. near or approaching
6. unprepared, spontaneous
7. lasting but for a day
8. of the Middle Ages
9. imaginary
10. catlike
11. crossbred
12. irregular

UNIT FOUR

Which word or phrase best completes the sentence?

1. A querulous housekeeper is (a) queer   (b) quiet   (c) quick to complain   (d) quaintly curious.

2. A plebeian custom is (a) luxurious   (b) commonplace   (c) laughable   (d) embarrassing.

3. Stringent regulations are (a) severe   (b) involved in red tape   (c) tiresome   (d) strenuous.

4. An inscrutable expression is one that is (a) happy   (b) unchanging   (c) sad   (d) mysterious and hard to read.

5. Capricious behavior is (a) given to dancing   (b) fond of fun   (c) subject to whims   (d) hard to discourage.

6. Morbid details are (a) sad   (b) horrible   (c) vivid   (d) related to death.

7. A lugubrious death scene is (a) dismal   (b) shocking   (c) terrifying   (d) bloody.

8. An inveterate dislike is (a) gained in wartime   (b) of animal origin   (c) firmly established   (d) unreasoning.

► Word List—ADJECTIVES

1. AUSTERE (ŏs·tẽr′) . . . . . . stern, strict; severely simple

Life was rather austere for the Pilgrims in New England.
- Austerity marked the life of most frontier settlements.
- The mountain people have simple tastes and live austerely.

> *Austere* comes from a Greek verb meaning "parch."
> To be austere is to lack color, warmth, liveliness, or adornment.
> To be **sober** is to be serious, restrained, and temperate—perhaps even solemn and grave in bearing.
> To be **severe** is to be uncompromising or exacting.
> To be **stern** or **rigid** is to be inflexible and unalterable.
> An **ascetic** life is one of self-denial, avoiding pleasure and, perhaps, finding virtue in painful acts of self-discipline.
> *Cf. rigorous* (I, 3)

2. AVID (ăv′ĭd) . . . . eager, greedy

Joe is avid about stamp collecting.
- He orders first-day covers with great avidity.

> *Avid* comes from a Latin verb meaning "long for."

3. CAPRICIOUS (kȧ·prĭsh′ŭs) . . . subject to whims, changeable

She is so capricious that you never can predict where she will go or what she will do.
- One of her recent caprices was to take up fencing.

> A **caprice** is a change of mind without apparent motive.
> A **whimsical** person is given to odd notions of a quaint or comical nature.
> See also *erratic*, under *errant* (I, 7).

4. COMPETENT (kŏm′pė·tĕnt) . . . capable; adequately qualified

A competent secretary, who can type and take dictation well, earns good pay.
- Competence in meeting people and in handling office routine is important, too.

The previous secretary was incompetent.

5. **DEFICIENT** (dĕ·fĭsh′ĕnt) . . . lacking in some respect; defective

Pancakes are quite deficient in vitamins.

■ A deficiency of protein in their feed kept the hens from laying eggs.

■ Some years ago, deficiency of iodine in drinking water was recognized as a cause of goiter.

Deficient sometimes means "insufficient." What is the cure for deficient courage?
A **deficit** is the amount of money which is lacking to make up a required amount. (See II, 5.)

6. **DEMURE** (dĕ·mūr′) . . . . modest and sedate

Carolyn has bright eyes and a demure smile.

■ Her demureness is well-mannered and somewhat prim, but it is not simulated.

Modest Modes: A **sedate** person is often more dignified and serious than a demure one.
A **modest** person has poise and ability but does not push himself forward. He is unassuming.
A **bashful** person shows his shyness in self-consciousness.
A **diffident** person is timid because he does not trust himself.

7. **DIMINUTIVE** (dĭ·mĭn′ů·tĭv) . . . . undersized, small

A dwarf is a diminutive human being.

■ Morning brought diminution of our hopes of finding the lost girl alive.

● The supply of iron ore in the United States will continue to diminish (grow less).

To **diminish** the paint supply is to reduce the quantity.
To **dilute** the paint supply is to thin it out with a solvent and thus reduce the quality.

8. **EXPLICIT** (ĕks·plĭs′ĭt) . . . . definite, clearly stated

Father's instructions for back seat drivers are very explicit: "Keep quiet!"

■ Everybody likes our teacher's explicitness about the way to write a composition.

Implicit instructions are implied and not stated directly (I, 7).
See *Plic* Words (I, 12).

9.   FORMIDABLE (fôr′mĭ·dà·b′l) . . . hard to overcome; menacing

   East High has a formidable team this year. It has lost only
   one game.

   Solid geometry is a formidable subject for students who try
   to memorize the theorems.

   - The boxer tried to scare his opponent by glaring formida-
   bly at him.

10.   INEXORABLE (ĭn·ĕk′sô·rà·b′l) . . . . unyielding, unrelenting

   The union was inexorable in its demand for shorter hours.

   - The management was inexorably opposed to granting the
   demand.

   ■ The inexorableness of the law of gravitation makes it necessary to be careful about climbing high peaks.

   The Stiff Family: *inflexible* (I, 11), **rigid, unalterable** (I, 5),
   obstinate (I, 8), *obdurate, implacable*
   Cf. *stern* (listed under *austere* in this unit)

11.   INSCRUTABLE (ĭn·skrōō′tà·b′l) . . . mysterious, unfathomable,
                                                                beyond comprehension

   "In any of the burial-places of this city through which I pass
   is there a sleeper more inscrutable than its busy inhabitants are?"

   ■ Houdini had the inscrutability (inscrutableness) of the
   master magician. Many of his feats have never been explained or duplicated.

12.   INVETERATE (ĭn·vĕt′ẽr·ĭt) . . . . habitual, firmly established

   Americans are inveterate coffee drinkers.

   ■ It was the inveteracy of Dr. Manette's prison habits which
   made them reassert themselves later on when he was over-
   wrought.

   Query: Can you find a connection between *inveterate* and **veteran?**
   Cf. *chronic* (II, 1)

13.   LUGUBRIOUS (lŏ·gū′brĭ·ŭs) . . . . . . mournful, doleful

   "The Song of the Shirt" by Thomas Hood is a lugubrious
   poem.

- "I haven't a friend in the world," she wailed lugubriously.
- Travelers enjoyed the lugubriousness of the witch dance.

Lugubrious grief is sometimes excessive to the point of being funny.

14.   MELANCHOLY (mĕl′ăn·kŏl′ĭ) . . . . . gloomy, depressing; soberly thoughtful

Much personal suffering and the many problems resulting from the War Between the States made Lincoln's life one of the most melancholy in American history.
- He may have been on the verge of melancholia at one time.

Melancholy is lingering, lasting sadness.
Melancholia is a mental condition marked by extreme depression and gloom.
Wistfulness is mild sadness.
Dejection is downcast sadness.
Cf. dour (I, 3), *despondent* (III, 2)

15.   METICULOUS (mê·tĭk′ū·lŭs) . . . . . scrupulous about details

She is very meticulous in measuring out exactly the right amount of each ingredient.
- Mr. Tilton's meticulousness in adjusting each string on the piano until it is exactly right makes him a good piano tuner.

16.   MORBID (môr′bĭd) . . . . unwholesomely horrible, gruesome

Many parents think that horror-comics are too morbid and should be banned.

An execution is too morbid a spectacle to be held in public.
- Readers find considerable morbidity in some of Poe's short stories.

Morbid comes from the Latin word *morbus*, "disease." The word may be applied to diseased tissues and parts of the body, as well as to unhealthful scenes.

17.   MUNIFICENT (mū·nĭf′ĭ·sĕnt) . . . . . very generous, lavish

The trip to Europe was a munificent reward for a rather small service.
- The munificence of the floral displays made the exhibition one of the best in the world.

Cf. opulence (II, 3)

18.   OPPORTUNE (ŏp′ŏr·tūn′) . . . . timely, seasonable

Because of Christmas bills, January is not an opportune month to ask your parents for a new television set.

- Senator Wiggins is too much of an opportunist. He waits to see what people want and then advocates it vehemently.
- Can an opportunism which thus sacrifices conscience and principles ever succeed?

19.   PLEBEIAN (plē·bē′yăn) . . . . . . common, ordinary, low-class

As long as Sam enjoys only popular music his tastes will remain plebeian.

The dictator thought he could control the plebeian element of the population by threats.

- A plebescite is a vote by the people on a specific issue, especially on a choice of sovereignty.
- Freshmen at Annapolis and West Point are jokingly called "plebes" (inferior people).

In ancient Rome, a member of the lower class—the *plebs*—was called a **plebeian.** A member of the upper class, a full-fledged citizen, was called a **patrician.** Today, the word *patrician* refers to any person who is very well-bred and cultivated.

Gentleman originally meant "well-born." *Gentle* goes back to the Latin *gentilis*, meaning "of the same tribe."

Aristocrat, a Greek word, originally referred to a member of the ruling class. Today it is also applied to anyone who is superior to other people. (See II, 12)

Cf. mediocre (II, 3)

20.   PRECIPITOUS (prē·sĭp′ĭ·tŭs) . . . . very steep

The car plunged straight down a precipitous mountainside.

It was very precipitate of him to ask for a date before he had been introduced.

His precipitant demand for the man's arrest got him into trouble which he could have avoided by keeping calm.

- The champion's knockout blow precipitated the challenger onto the ropes.

The adjectives ***precipitate*** (prē·sĭp′ĭ·tât) and ***precipitant*** mean "sudden, rash, overhasty."

The verb ***precipitate*** (prē·sĭp′ĭ·tāt), means "hurl headlong" or "bring to a crisis."

21. PRECOCIOUS (prĕ·kō′shŭs) . . . . . ahead in development, especially mental

Sally is a precocious child: she is in the fifth grade but could easily do ninth grade work.

■ Sally's mother likes to talk about her daughter's precocity (precociousness).

Precocity (prĕ·kŏs′ĭ·tĭ) is used especially of the mental development of children. In botany, it is applied to plants which flower, fruit, or ripen early.
Cf. dementia praecox

22. PUGNACIOUS (pŭg·nā′shŭs) . . . inclined to fight, quarrelsome

The boy's pugnacious attitude got him into needless trouble.

■ The state chairman's political pugnacity over appointments disrupted the party and caused it to lose control of the state.

Fond-of-Fight Words: *combative, contentious, pugilistic, bellicose, belligerent* (II, 9)

23. PUNCTILIOUS (pŭngk·tĭl′ĭ·ŭs) . . . . . exact in observance

The lawyer is very punctilious in matters of court etiquette.

■ The initiation ceremony was conducted with great punctilio (punctiliousness).

A punctilious person is strict about matters of form, ceremony, and conduct.
A **punctual** person is exact about being on time.
A **scrupulous** person is exact in matters of belief and conscience.
A **meticulous** person is exact and painstaking about minute details, almost to excess.

24. QUERULOUS (kwĕr′ů·lŭs) . . . . . . fretful, complaining

Having too much of too many things had made her querulous and difficult to please.

■ Her friends found it hard to endure her querulousness.

Cf. petulant, peevish, captious (III, 5)

25. STRINGENT (strĭn′jĕnt) . . . . strict, severe; tight

In most states, stringent laws govern the sale of guns.

■ The stringency of stock market regulations is intended to help prevent disastrous inflation.

FIRST PRACTICE SET

Copy the *italicized* words. Beside each, write an appropriate definition.

1. Oddly enough, the *diminutive* jockey is *avid* about art and is a gifted landscape painter.

2. The monks lived an *austere* life with a *formidable* discipline, spending many hours in silent meditation.

3. The *opportune* arrival of police led to the burglar's arrest, and the judge was *inexorable* in sentencing him for the maximum term because the man was a third offender.

4. The doctor explained to Mrs. Johnson that her husband's *melancholy* mood had produced his morbid thoughts and *querulous* talk; there was nothing physically wrong with him.

5. A *competent* supervisor will be *explicit* in giving directions about how to do the work.

6. At home, Father is an *inveterate* tease; at work, he is a *meticulous* mechanic with *stringent* standards.

7. My *demure* sister is *precocious* in school and quite *capricious* about choosing her friends.

8. Joe gasped when he saw the *precipitous* slope he had to climb, but he was not *deficient* in courage.

9. Einstein's *inscrutable* intelligence did not keep him from being *punctilious* toward visitors; indeed, he was a man of great kindliness and courtesy.

10. Perhaps it is his *plebeian* upbringing which makes Ralph so *pugnacious* at a party.

SECOND PRACTICE SET

On a separate sheet, write the numbers of the *italicized* words. Beside each, write the number of the matching word or group of words from the second column.

1. *Whimsical* remarks
2. A *dejected* champion
3. A *pugnacious* hobo
4. A *diffident* person
5. *Lugubrious* scenes
6. *Melancholy* truth
7. *Inflexible* habits
8. *Querulous* anxiety
9. *Wistful* eagerness
10. A *modest* smile

1. mildly sad
2. competent but not pushing oneself
3. doleful
4. rigid, unbending
5. petulant
6. full of fear
7. self-distrusting
8. bellicose
9. depressing
10. quaintly different
11. reluctant
12. sad (in downcast sense)

1. A long-awaited *plebescite*
2. *Morbidity* of the story
3. Inexcusable *deficiency*
4. Spinster's *meticulousness*
5. *Inscrutability* of genius
6. Unexpected *competence*
7. Military *punctiliousness*
8. *Inveteracy* of one's hopes
9. *Diminution* of reserves
10. Unusual *precocity*

1. incomprehensibility
2. reduction
3. capability
4. deep-seatedness
5. evasion or escape
6. being ahead in development
7. horribleness
8. shortage or lack
9. careful attention to details
10. lack of ability
11. ballot or vote
12. exactness in observances

THIRD PRACTICE SET

Which word in each group is most nearly **opposite** in meaning to the word in capital letters?

1. MELANCHOLY: (a) gloomy (b) ugly (c) happy (d) disappointed (e) laughable

2. CAPRICIOUS: (a) severe (b) constant (c) confident (d) demure (e) low-class

3. INEXORABLE: (a) loose (b) yielding (c) changeable (d) tight (e) indistinct

4. MUNIFICENT: (a) unfortified (b) half-crazy (c) cautious (d) stingy (e) inclined to worry

5. DIMINUTIVE: (a) generous (b) oversized (c) fractional (d) abundant (e) musical

6. AUSTERE: (a) gay (b) healthy (c) undignified (d) capricious (e) incompetent

7. EXPLICIT: (a) vague (b) empty (c) vain (d) soft (e) lucid

8. OPPORTUNE: (a) appropriate (b) unpleasant (c) upright (d) ill-timed (e) unresponsive

9. LUGUBRIOUS: (a) horrible (b) inspiring (c) cheery (d) easy to explain (e) witty

10. FORMIDABLE: (a) friendly (b) easy to overcome (c) enormous (d) easy going (e) cowardly

UNIT FIVE

Which is the best answer for each question?

1. If you disburse a thousand dollars, do you (a) steal it? (b) eye it in disgust? (c) pay it out? (d) refuse it?

2. If you incriminate someone, do you (a) exonerate him? (b) implicate him? (c) condemn him? (d) accuse someone else?

3. If you perjure yourself, do you (a) tell a lie? (b) serve on a jury? (c) lose your temper? (d) tell the truth?

4. If you infringe, do you (a) elaborate? (b) embroider? (c) spread out? (d) encroach?

5. Is a cartel (a) a ticket? (b) a permit? (c) a combination? (d) a European card game?

6. Is a lucrative occupation (a) profitable? (b) dishonest? (c) easy? (d) temporary?

7. Do actuarial statistics have to do chiefly with (a) bankers? (b) real estate? (c) insurance? (d) manufacturing?

•Word List— TEN VERBS OF BUSINESS AND LAW

1.   ACQUIT (ă·kwĭt′)   .   .   .   .   . release or clear (from a charge,
                                                                crime, obligation)

An anxious wife watched the jury acquit her husband of
the murder charge.
■ The acquittal made her very happy.
● No matter what emergency may arise, he will acquit (behave) himself well.

To *absolve* a person is to release him from a sin, charge, duty, or
penalty. (See -*solv*- in I, 9.)
Cf. *exonerate, exculpate* (III, 2)

2.   ALLEGE (ă·lĕj′)   .   .   .   . declare, assert

The defense alleges that the prisoner is insane.
■ These allegations are supported by the testimony of three
psychiatrists.

Synonyms: *state, affirm* (I, 1), *asseverate, aver*
Antonyms: *deny, contradict*

3.   BEQUEATH (bē·kwēth′)   .   .   .   . give in one's will

Mr. Arnold decided to bequeath his stocks to his son.
■ This bequest will be worth $150,000 after taxes.

4.   DISBURSE (dĭs·bûrs′)   .   .   .   .   .   . pay out, expend (money)

The primary duty of the treasurer is to disburse funds.
■ This disbursement is subject to stringent regulations.

The word *disburse* is more technical than **expend** and more formal
than **pay.**
To **reimburse** a friend who paid a bill for you is to pay him back
again.
The **Bourse** in Paris is the stock exchange.
The **bursar** of a college is the treasurer.
Burse-words came from the Latin word *bursa*, "a purse," which in
turn came from a Greek word meaning "hide of an animal." Can
you think of an explanation for this shift in meaning?

5. EMBEZZLE (ĕm·bĕz″l) . . . take by fraud (money or property entrusted to one's care)

For years Mrs. Osborne, a lady cashier, managed to embezzle small sums by falsifying accounts.

■ When her embezzlement was discovered, the total amounted to $30,000.

■ She was tried as an embezzler and convicted.

6. INCRIMINATE (ĭn·crĭm′ĭ·nāt) . . involve or implicate in a crime

A pair of blood-stained gloves served to incriminate him.

■ To avoid self-incrimination, he refused to make any statement.

To **discriminate** between flavors is to be able to detect differences between them. (See II, 1.)
To **recriminate** is to reply to an accusation by accusing the accuser: Recriminations in a trial are useless.

7. INDICT (ĭn·dīt′) . . . . charge, accuse

The grand jury will probably indict him for theft.
The first step in prosecuting Mrs. Osborne was for the county grand jury to indict her for embezzlement.

■ Many newspapers joined in an indictment of the President's foreign policy.

8. INFRINGE (ĭn·frĭnj′) . . . . encroach upon, violate

Keeping chickens in a town infringes upon the rights of neighbors to the enjoyment of pure air and quiet.
The air-pressure device infringes upon another inventor's patent.

■ All infringements of the new bicycle law will be punished.

Infringe originally meant "break in upon." It belongs to the *Fract* Words (I, 11).

9. PERJURE (pûr′jẽr) . . . . testify falsely

No bribe could induce the witness to perjure himself.

▶ Perjured testimony is false testimony under oath in court.

■ "At lovers' perjuries, they say, Jove laughs." (*Romeo and Juliet*)

10. **PROSECUTE** (prŏs′ė·kūt) .   . instigate legal proceedings against

The District Attorney decided to prosecute Mrs. Osborne
for embezzlement and also on two charges of forgery.

▪ He had gathered considerable evidence for use in the prose-
cution of the case.

▪ It was his duty as prosecutor to present the case against
Mrs. Osborne.

Prosecute belongs to the *Sequ* Words (II, 12). See also *pro-* (I, 10).
What is the literal meaning of *prosecute?*
Cf. persecute

▪ Word List— FIVE NOUNS OF BUSINESS AND LAW

1. **CARTEL** (kär·tĕl′) .   .   .   . an international combine to control
output and prices

A Swiss cartel sells watches and watch movements in many
countries.

Cartel is the European word for a trust.
A **trust** is a combination of firms to gain a monopoly and control
prices.
A **monopoly** in business is the exclusive control of the manufacture
or sale of a product. This control may involve the manipulation of
prices.
A **syndicate** is a combination of bankers or other businessmen organized to finance a special project. The word is also applied to an agency
which supplies stories and articles to newspapers.

2. **DEFICIT** (dĕf′ĭ·sĭt) .   . amount by which a sum of money falls short

The treasurer reports a deficit of $2,500 in the fund for
repairs to the plant.

▷ Spending more than one takes in is deficit spending.

In Latin, *deficit* means "it is lacking."

3. **DOCKET** (dŏk′ĕt) .   .   .   . list of cases for trial; court schedule

After the holiday, the police-court docket was unusually
crowded.

4.   LIBEL (lī'běl) . . . . written or printed defamation

An atomic scientist sued the newspaper for libel because it published a cartoon of him holding a hammer and sickle.

▶ The article about Mr. Harper is libelous because it implies that he once accepted a bribe. Even if he had, the statement gives a false impression of his character, and he may be able to collect damages.

See dictionary or encyclopedia for other meanings of *libel*. Ordinarily a damaging statement has to be circulated rather widely to be libelous. The **libellant** or victim has to prove that he has suffered damage which can be expressed in terms of money.

Defamation consists of false and malicious attacks on someone's reputation.

Slander is spoken defamation or false report.

5.   LITIGATION (lĭt'ĭ·gā'shŭn) . . . lawsuit or process of carrying on a lawsuit

The litigation over the will lasted for months.

One of the litigants, an heir, tried to break the will and another died before the estate was settled.

Litigious men are inclined to carry on lawsuits whenever **litigable** problems arise.

▶ **Word List—FIVE ADJECTIVES OF BUSINESS**

1.   ACTUARIAL (ăk'tû·âr'ĭ·ăl) . . . . having to do with insurance risks and rates

Actuarial studies show that people live longer now on the average than they did fifty years ago.

■ As an actuary, who computes risks and rates, he is skillful in compiling and analyzing statistics.

Actuary goes back to the Latin *actus,* "an act," and originally meant "copyist or clerk"; i.e., one whose professional acts were writing and copying.

Act Words: To **actuate** a pump is to put it into motion.

To **actualize** a plan or dream is to carry it out.

To **activate** a camp is to put it into operation.

To **counteract** a poison is to act against it.

2. **FISCAL** (fĭs'kăl) . . . **financial; having to do with public funds**

The president of the company is quite concerned about fiscal problems connected with the new tax law.

The Secretary of the Treasury is an authority on fiscal matters.

The fiscal year is the legal or financial year of the Government or a large corporation.

Money Words: *Fiscal* comes from the Latin word for a basket of rushes, which came to mean "a money basket" or "public chest." A **pecuniary** consideration is one involving money. The word comes from the Latin word *pecus*, "cattle." Can you see any connection? *Cf. mercenary* and *lucrative*, which follow, and *disburse* above.

3. **LEGITIMATE** (lĕ·jĭt'ĭ·mĭt) . . . . **lawful; permissible**

Shooting an assailant in self-defense is legitimate homicide.

Illness at home is a legitimate excuse for being absent from school.

■ A court questioned the legitimacy of the actor's first marriage.

• A few states have legitimized slot machines.

Legitimate drama is the term applied to drama written for the stage, rather than for the movies, radio, or television. See dictionary for other meanings of *legitimate*. *Cf. illegitimate, illegitimacy*

4. **LUCRATIVE** (lū'krá·tĭv) . . . . . . **profitable, remunerative**

Buying houses when prices were low and selling them for three times what he had paid proved to be very lucrative.

■ The lucrativeness of the fur business made it possible for my uncle to retire when he was forty-five.

Lucrative means "money-making" and comes from the Latin *lucrum*, "gain."

5. **MERCENARY** (mûr'sĕ·nĕr'ĭ) . . . **acting from desire for money**

The real estate men have mercenary reasons for wanting the new highway to go through the center of the town.

■ Mercenaries are soldiers hired by a government which is not their own.

▪ Word List—FUNERAL WORDS

1. **BEREAVEMENT** (bê·rēv′měnt) . desolation, loss (especially by death)

   When the boy's parents were killed in an accident, it took years for him to get over his bereavement.
   - As a result of the epidemic, the Browns were bereaved (deprived) of their son.
   ▸ Bereft of hope, the man could work no longer.

   The Old English ancestor of *bereave* meant "rob."
   Bereft implies the loss of abstract qualities such as confidence or hope; *bereaved*, the loss of persons.

2. **CONDOLENCE** (kŏn·dō′lĕns) . . formal expression of sympathy

   When a neighbor's child died, my mother wrote a note of condolence.
   - Mary condoled with her sister when their father was killed.

   Compassion implies pity and, often, mercy or charity.
   Commiseration usually implies pity that is outwardly expressed. It may also refer to the attitude of a person who sees the misery of others but cannot help.

3. **DIRGE** (dûrj) . . . . funeral song or tune

   The natives chanted a weird dirge when the chief died.

   A **requiem** is a musical church service for the dead, usually a Requiem Mass.
   An **obituary** is a printed notice of someone's death.

4. **EPITAPH** (ĕp′ĭ·tàf) . . . . tombstone inscription

   Collecting epitaphs in old cemeteries is an unusual hobby.
   A collector of epitaphs is called an epitaphist.

   Tomb Words: A **mausoleum** is a large tomb built above ground.
   A **sepulcher** is a tomb somewhat less imposing than a mausoleum.
   A **cenotaph,** meaning "empty tomb," is a monument in honor of a person who is buried elsewhere.
   A **sarcophagus** is a stone coffin, especially one with a carving or inscription on it.

5. INTERMENT (ĭn·tûr′mĕnt) . . . . burial

The interment of the dead pilot took place the day after the crash.

● "The evil that men do lives after them,
     The good is oft interred with their bones."

(*Julius Caesar*)

To **disinter** or **exhume** a body is to dig it up after burial. These words may be used metaphorically when speaking of taking out any object that has been put away for some time.

———

FIRST PRACTICE SET

Copy the *italicized* words. Beside each, write the appropriate definition.

1. The grand jury will *indict* the brother too because he helped *embezzle* the money.

2. The state will *allege* that the treasurer refused to *disburse* the funds set aside for charities by the directors.

3. Why *infringe* on a neighbor's rights and *perjure* yourself by denying you knew that the old man would *bequeath* his estate to you?

4. The jury will have to *acquit* him if he does not *incriminate* himself.

5. The *fiscal* policies of an insurance company involve *actuarial* tables.

6. The *cartel* operated with a *deficit* for a year or two.

7. The manufacturer will *prosecute* the author of the article on a charge of *libel*.

8. *Bereavement* led the two fathers to exchange expressions of *condolence*.

9. Writing *epitaphs* is a *legitimate* but not a *lucrative* occupation.

10. The native *dirge* accompanied the *interment* of the pilot who crashed in Africa.

SECOND PRACTICE SET

On a separate sheet, write the numbers of the *italicized* words. Beside each, write the number of the matching word or group of words from the second column.

1. Severe *indictment*	1. business deal
2. Danger of oil *monopoly*	2. claim or statement
3. Detailed *obituary*	3. misfortune
4. Unusual *bequest*	4. taking money by fraud
5. Patent *infringement*	5. deep sympathy
6. Unexpected *acquittal*	6. death notice
7. Egyptian *sarcophagus*	7. exclusive control
8. A libelous *allegation*	8. something given in a will
9. Unwanted *commiseration*	9. inscribed stone coffin
10. Clever *embezzlement*	10. accusation
	11. encroachment
	12. release from charges

1. *Discriminate* shades of color	1. pay back again
2. Likely to *recriminate*	2. defame by something written
3. Motives that *actuate*	3. make lawful
4. *Bereave* of a father	4. exhume, dig up
5. *Reimburse* a friend	5. follow up
6. A demand to *disinter*	6. free from blame
7. *Libel* a Congressman	7. injure seriously
8. *Absolve* the driver	8. cause action
9. *Legitimize* gambling	9. accuse the accuser
10. *Prosecute* a mission	10. recognize
	11. deprive
	12. frighten

THIRD PRACTICE SET

Which of the lettered items is most nearly **opposite** in meaning to the word in capital letters?

1. DEFICIT: (a) sell-out (b) surplus (c) new supply (d) falsification of accounts (e) overdraft

2. ACQUIT: (a) behave (b) accept (c) convict (d) persevere (e) release

3. ALLEGE: (a) deny (b) keep in suspense (c) falsify (d) divide (e) raise a question

4. PERJURE: (a) reimburse (b) allege (c) absolve (d) declare love (e) testify truthfully

5. INCRIMINATE: (a) excuse (b) counteract (c) exonerate (d) misjudge (e) repeat a crime

6. LUCRATIVE: (a) made by a cartel (b) unremunerative (c) disbursing too much (d) unmercenary (e) stingy

7. INTER: (a) prevent burial (b) exhume (c) place in sepulcher (d) commiserate with (e) burn to ashes

8. LEGITIMATE: (a) undramatic (b) accidental (c) illegal (d) infringing (e) lucrative

9. DISBURSE: (a) have no funds (b) pay unwillingly (c) discourage payment (d) economize (e) accumulate

10. MERCENARY: (a) without thought of reward (b) unmilitary (c) generous (d) spontaneous (e) insincere

UNIT SIX

Which word or phrase best completes each statement?

1. A stiffening of the body is (a) cajolery (b) clairvoyance (c) catalepsy (d) emaciation.

2. A strange figure floating in mid-air is (a) an apparition (b) a clairvoyant (c) an alien (d) a façade.

3. Deceptive behavior is (a) reconnaissance (b) alienation (c) duplicity (d) dissipation.

4. A stranger in a country is (a) a confederate (b) an apparition (c) an abstainer (d) an alien.

5. A person with strange seeing power is (a) a deprecator (b) a dissipater (c) a confederate (d) a clairvoyant.

6. A half-joking way of getting cooperation is (a) exasperation (b) cajolery (c) condescension (d) domination.

7. A somewhat violent way of getting information is to (a) elicit it (b) educe it (c) evoke it (d) extort it.

8. Refraining from something is (a) abstinence (b) ascertainment (c) elicitation (d) anguish.

• Word List—VERBS

1. **ABSTAIN** (ăb·stān') . . . . refrain; hold (oneself) back

    The senator says that he will abstain from voting on the
    new tax law.
    ■ His abstention may permit the law to pass.
    ■ During Lent, some practice abstinence (self-restraint),
    going without alcoholic beverages, tobacco, or meat.
    ► He is an abstemious person who eats sparingly. His ab-
    stinent habits contribute to his good health.

    > See other *Tain* Words (I, 10).
    > Synonyms: *forbear, desist*
    > Antonym: *indulge* (II, 1)

2. **APPREHEND** (ăp'rė·hĕnd') . . . . arrest; grasp; fear

    The police planned to apprehend the smuggler at the
    southern border.
    The townspeople did not apprehend the meaning of the
    message from the king.
    ■ The woman's apprehensions about burglars were ground-
    less; however, she still took every conceivable precaution
    against being robbed.

    > Other words from the Latin *prehendere*, meaning "seize":
    > To **comprehend** is to understand; i.e., to seize or put together the
    > meaning of something.
    > To **reprehend** is to rebuke or blame, and a reprehensible act is a
    > blameworthy one.
    > *Cf. misapprehend*

3. **ASCERTAIN** (ăs'ēr·tān') . . . . find out

    Bob tried to ascertain the cause of the mysterious noise he
    heard during the night.
    ► The scientist knew how much was ascertainable about life
    at the bottom of the sea.

    > Military **reconnaissance** is a survey or examination of a territory to
    > ascertain the position of enemy troops or to gather other information.

4.   **CAJOLE** (kȧ·jōl') . . . . coax, wheedle; persuade by flattery

Dunstan planned to cajole Silas Marner into lending him the money he needed.

▪ The little girl often won her own way by combining tears and cajolery.

5.   **CONCEDE** (kŏn·sēd') . . . . admit; yield, grant

The union did not want to concede the employer's right too close the plant.

I concede your claim to the purse because you found it.

▪ Labor leaders sought new concessions from employers in the form of shorter hours and a guaranteed annual wage.

The word *though* has **concessive** force. It admits something: Though I hate you, I will help you.
What was the original meaning of *concede?* (See *Cede* Words in I, 10.)
See also **concession** and **concessionaire,** as they refer to a carnival or fair.

6.   **CONDESCEND** (kŏn'dė·sĕnd') . . . . come down to another's level, deign

She would not condescend to notice him when they passed on the street.

"The squire condescended to preside in the parlor of the Rainbow rather than under the shadow of his own dark wainscot."

▪ The scout leader's air of condescension irritated the boys.

Cf. **patronize,** in the sense of *condescend.*

7.   **DEPRECATE** (dĕp'rė·kāt) . . . . disapprove; protest against

He found it easy to deprecate modern art until he began to understand it.

▪ In the same way, he approached classical music with deprecation.

▹ The butler hesitated at the door and gave a deprecatory (apologetic) cough before interrupting the conversation.

Originally, *deprecate* meant "avert by prayer"; i.e., to pray something away.
Cf. **imprecation, imprecatory**

8. **DISSIPATE** (dĭs'ĭ·pāt) . . . . squander; dispel

She was inclined to dissipate too much energy on useless activities.

It took all morning for the sun to dissipate the mist.

Books like *Ben Hur* show how the energies of wealthy Romans were dissipated by indulgence in extravagant and immoral pleasure.

■ The emperors joined in the dissipation (excessive indulgence in pleasure).

Cf. dissolute

9. **DOMINATE** (dŏm'ĭ·nāt) . . . . . . control, tower above

Mrs. Drumb dominates her husband shamelessly.

The Washington Monument dominates Potomac Park.

■ The rebels fought against Russian domination of their country.

To **domineer** is to rule in an overbearing way.
To have **dominion** is to have the ruling power over an area. The Dominion of Canada is now a self-governing member of the British Commonwealth, but it was originally ruled by the British Crown.
Dominus is the Latin for "Our Lord." What does **Anno Domini** mean?

10. **ELICIT** (ê·lĭs'ĭt) . . . . draw forth

The army interpreter tried to elicit information from the captured soldier.

■ The elicitation of facts about plans, numbers of troops, and so on would be useful.

To **extort** a reply is to draw it forth by force or trickery.
To **evoke** a reply is to call it forth by making the person want to speak.
To **educe** a reply is to lead forth some information that has been hidden.

11. **EMACIATE** (ê·mā'shĭ·āt) . . . . make very lean

An extended hunger strike will emaciate a man rapidly, as Mahatma Gandhi discovered when he was the dominant spiritual leader of India.

▶ Molly was "a young woman, but emaciated, with long black hair."

■ Famine and disease bring emaciation to their victims.

12. **EXASPERATE** (ĕg·zăs′pēr·āt) . . . irritate thoroughly, infuriate

Bob's carelessness about following instructions was enough to exasperate any employer.
- "Nancy was so exasperatingly quiet and firm."
- Godfrey's exasperation over the loss of his horse, Wildfire, scarcely exceeded that of Dunstan, who had caused the horse's death.

Cf. tease, vex, inflame, incense

13. **EXHORT** (ĕg·zôrt′) . . . . urge; advise earnestly

Between halves, the coach is sure to exhort us to do better.
"Williams exhorted his friend to confess, and not to hide his sin any longer."
- The exhortations of Mr. Crackenthorp had little effect on Silas.

▪Word List— NOUNS

1. **ALIBI** (ăl′ĭ·bī) . . . . . the claim of having been elsewhere when an offense was committed

The police checked each suspect's alibi with great care.
Godfrey's "imagination constantly created an alibi for Dunstan."

In everyday speech, *alibi* means "an excuse."

2. **ALIEN** (āl′yĕn) . . . unnaturalized foreigner; stranger, outsider

Linen weavers "were to the last regarded as aliens by their rustic neighbors."
- Bad manners will alienate (make strangers of) one's closest friends.
- American citizens have certain inalienable privileges, including freedom of speech and religion.
- The idea of a state church is alien (hostile) to American beliefs.

3. **ALTERCATION** (ôl'tēr·kā'shŭn) . . . . angry dispute, quarrel

    The altercation between the truck driver and the cab driver
    was conducted in a loud tone of voice.

    The arrival of a policeman put an end to the altercation.

4. **ANGUISH** (ăng'gwĭsh) . . . . intense suffering

    "He must have made the effort at a moment when all his
    energies were turned into the anguish of disappointed
    faith."

    ▶ She was pinned under the wrecked car, and no one heard
    her anguished screams.

5. **APPARITION** (ăp'à·rĭsh'ŭn) . . . . . . specter, phantom

    Every man present . . . "had an impression that he saw, not
    Silas Marner in the flesh, but an apparition."

    In the middle of the night, he saw an apparition which
    looked like his father.

    Cf. hallucination and *illusion* (II, 3)

6. **BARRAGE** (bà·räzh') . . . . . . barrier of artillery fire;
                                       heavy onslaught (of words, blows, etc.)

    At dawn, the enemy laid down a heavy barrage to keep our
    forces from advancing.

    A barrage of rotten apples convinced the cow that small
    boys are cruel and treacherous.

    The barrage of traffic noises put an end to our conversation.

    The military meaning of *barrage* is the key to its metaphorical meaning.
    Cf. salvo, fusillade

7. **CATALEPSY** (kăt'à·lĕp'sĭ) . . . . . a stiffening of the body with
                                          loss of consciousness

    The man on the flying trapeze was undoubtedly not subject
    to catalepsy.

    ▶ "It was at this point in their history that Silas's cataleptic
    fit occurred during the prayer meeting."

    Epilepsy is a disease of the nervous system producing convulsions and,
    sometimes, cataleptic seizures.

8. **CLAIRVOYANT** (klâr·voi′ănt) . . . one who has preternatural
insight or discernment

The clairvoyant used a crystal ball and a zodiac chart.
Scientific experiments in clairvoyance have been in progress
for years.

Clairvoyance is the ability to discern what is beyond the normal range
of the senses; for example, what is going on in the mind of another
person. The word comes from a French term meaning "see clearly."
Preternatural powers are beyond the natural or normal.

9. **CONFEDERATE** (kŏn·fĕd′ēr·ĭt) . . . . . an ally, accomplice

The thief's confederate helped him escape from prison.
- Six Indian tribes formed a confederacy to resist the en-
croachments of white men.
▶ Jefferson Davis was president of the Confederate States of
America.
- This confederation lasted from 1861-1865.

10. **CUPIDITY** (kṳ·pĭd′ĭ·tĭ) . . . excessive desire for wealth; greed

Silas's cupidity, which made him a miser after he went to
Raveloe, was a result of having no interests except money.
American income taxes do not foster cupidity.

Cupidity comes from a Latin word meaning "desire." From the same
root comes the name Cupid.
Cf. greed, covetousness, avarice (I, 5)

11. **DUPLICITY** (dṳ·plĭs′ĭ·tĭ) . . . . . double-dealing, deception

Much has been written about the duplicity of Communists.
Godfrey was not "sufficiently aware that no sort of duplicity
can long flourish without the help of vocal falsehoods."

The Latin word from which *duplicity* descends meant "folded in two."
(See *Plic* Words in I, 12.)

12. **FAÇADE** (fá·säd′) . . . . front; face

The façade of the Supreme Court Building in Washington
is massive and august.
Behind a façade of wealth, the man lived a lonely, impoverished life, without interests or friends.

FIRST PRACTICE SET

Copy the *italicized* words. Beside each, write an appropriate definition.

1. He tried to *ascertain* why his competitor would not *concede* him the right to use the special process.
2. *Cajole* her with a compliment and she will *condescend* to smile at you.
3. He had a tendency to *deprecate* my suggestions because he felt I was trying to *dominate* the situation.
4. We tried to *elicit* the facts that would *dissipate* suspicion.
5. The embezzler fled to Mexico but was so worried that the police might *apprehend* him that he grew pale and *emaciated*.
6. Mother *exhorts* the boys daily not to *exasperate* the neighbors by their noise or their activity.
7. The suspect's *alibi* depended on the word of a neighbor with whom he had had an *altercation* the night before the burglary occurred.
8. The *alien* was in *anguish* over the loss of his passport.
9. The criminal believed that he had seen an *apparition* of his dead *confederate* and decided to confess his crime.
10. A machine gun *barrage* damaged the *façade* of the largest building in the capital city.

SECOND PRACTICE SET

Which base word from the unit best replaces each *italicized* word or phrase?

1. The lawyer *granted* the genuineness of the criminal's *claim of having been elsewhere.*
2. We *found out* that the man is an *unnaturalized foreigner.*
3. His attempts to *refrain* from smoking brought him *intense suffering* at first.
4. He made *disapproving* remarks about her belief in *specters.*

5. If you *coax* him, you can *draw forth* the secret.
6. A *heavy onslaught* of paper wads *thoroughly irritated* the teacher.
7. A lady *earnestly advised* the police to *arrest* her husband before he could harm her.
8. Madam Rosina, who is a *person with preternatural insight,* sometimes suffers from *a stiffening of the body with loss of consciousness.*
9. How could anyone *stoop* to such *deception?*
10. The *angry dispute* is a result of his trying to *control* his father.

THIRD PRACTICE SET

Which of the lettered items is most nearly **opposite** in meaning to the word printed in capital letters?

1. ALIEN: (a) tourist (b) hero (c) citizen (d) fiend (e) helper
2. DOMINATE: (a) play the game (b) work hard (c) submit (d) weaken (e) mislead
3. EMACIATE: (a) make healthy (b) strengthen (c) become manly (d) impoverish (e) fatten
4. DEPRECATE: (a) like (b) praise (c) enlarge (d) make happy (e) enlighten
5. EXHORT: (a) condemn (b) restrain (c) confuse (d) imply (e) distrust
6. ABSTAIN: (a) purify (b) destroy (c) promote (d) indulge (e) strive for
7. ANGUISH: (a) ecstasy (b) patience (c) failure (d) dislike (e) good humor
8. DUPLICITY: (a) guile (b) wisdom (c) straightforwardness (d) willingness (e) monotonousness
9. APPREHEND: (a) release (b) eject (c) confirm (d) deny (e) disarm
10. CONCEDE: (a) elicit (b) deny (c) deprecate (d) disenchant (e) exhort

THE RIGHT WORD

On a separate sheet, write the numbers of the *italicized* words. Beside each, write the number of the matching word or group of words from the second column.

1. A *concession* to labor
2. Justifiable *apprehension*
3. *Emaciation* from disease
4. For *reconnaissance* purposes
5. The spoiled young man's *dissipation*
6. Resorting to *cajolery*
7. A *confederacy* of city states
8. Scoutmaster's *exasperation*
9. *Elicitation* of grievances
10. Lordly *condescension*

1. ascertainment
2. indulgence in harmful pleasure
3. displeasure
4. coming down to another's level
5. extreme irritation
6. claim granted
7. drawing forth
8. fear or alarm
9. free disclosure
10. leanness
11. flattery
12. alliance

1. *Alienate* a friend
2. *Educe* a blessing
3. *Dominate* the committee
4. *Extort* a sum of money
5. *Comprehend* a virtue
6. *Exhort* men to believe
7. *Domineer* over one's sister
8. *Evoke* enthusiasm
9. *Reprehend* for bad manners
10. *Elicit* praise

1. draw out (twist) by force
2. understand
3. call forth
4. draw forth (with some effort)
5. advise earnestly
6. make a stranger of
7. compel by commanding
8. rebuke, blame
9. control
10. lead forth gently
11. draw out by trickery
12. rule in overbearing way

UNIT SEVEN

Which word fits each situation best?

1. A baby's attempts to talk: (a) monotonous   (b) vacillating   (c) inarticulate   (d) vicious

2. Flashes of lightning: (a) intermittent   (b) juvenile   (c) provident   (d) skeptical

3. A clergyman who is traditional in matters of doctrine: (a) learned   (b) godly   (c) devout   (d) orthodox

4. A radiant bride at her wedding: (a) reinstated   (b) scrutinized   (c) pallid   (d) transfigured

5. A really dangerous criminal: (a) skeptical   (b) vicious   (c) turbulent   (d) intolerant

6. An American citizen voluntarily living in Italy: (a) ostracized   (b) banished   (c) exiled   (d) expatriated

7. A girl unable to make up her mind: (a) juvenile   (b) vacillating   (c) vitiated   (d) tolerant

8. A teacher when he hears an excuse for lateness: (a) skeptical   (b) vitiated   (c) transfigured   (d) juvenile

• Word List—VERBS

1. **GALVANIZE** (găl′và·nīz) . . . . stimulate, excite

   Criticisms galvanize the manager into acting quickly.
   ► A galvanic (electric) thrill went through the stands as the fullback crossed the goal line.
   • Galvanism has to do with electric currents, especially those produced by chemical action.

   > The word *galvanize* comes from the name of Luigi Galvani, the first investigator who discovered that electricity can be produced by chemical action.
   > **Electrify** is a synonym. What else does *electrify* mean?

2. **GRATIFY** (grăt′i·fī) . . . . please, afford pleasure to

   A victory over the only unbeaten team in our league will really gratify the coach.
   ► The response to the Community Chest was gratifying.
   ■ Godfrey Cass wanted "to snatch the strange gratification of seeing Nancy," even though he was already married.

3. **ITERATE** (ĭt′ēr·āt) . . . . utter; repeat

   The lawyer liked to iterate his accusations.
   ■ Iteration served to impress the jury with his claims.
   ► Older people often become iterative in their comments and requests.

   > **Reiteration** has almost the same meaning as *iteration*: The reiteration of advertising slogans on television programs often proves exasperating.

4. **NURTURE** (nûr′tŭr) . . . . nourish; foster, rear

   He nurtures a belief that he can have a business of his own in a few years.
   ■ "The little child knows nothing of parental love, but only knows one face and one laugh toward which it stretches its arms for refuge and nurture."
   ► George Eliot speaks of pale-faced weavers as having "un-nurtured souls."

5. **OSTRACIZE** (ŏs'trá·sīz) . . . . banish, exclude

If respectable people ostracize an ex-convict, how can he re-establish himself in society?

▫ Ostracism condemns him to loneliness or the wrong kind of associates.

See also *banish* (II, 1), *exile, deport,* and *expatriate,* all of which denote separation from a country.
A man can be banished from a social group as well as from a country.
An expatriate is usually a voluntary exile.
The government deports an alien who misbehaves.

6. **PREVARICATE** (prĕ·văr'ĭ·kāt) . . . . evade the truth; quibble

Susan tried to prevaricate about the low grades on her report card.

▪ Godfrey "entangled himself still further in prevarication and deceit by trying to conceal his misdeeds."

Prevaricate comes from a Latin word meaning "walk crookedly."
Cf. equivocate (III, 6)

7. **REINSTATE** (rē'ĭn·stāt') . . . . . restore to a former position

The company offered to reinstate a foreman who had been discharged unjustly.

▪ Godfrey hoped for reinstatement in his father's good graces when he repented of his misdeeds.

8. **SCRUTINIZE** (skroō'tĭ·nīz) . . . . examine closely

The doctor scrutinized John's bruise very carefully.

▪ James escaped his mother's scrutiny that morning because she was still in bed when he left for school.

9. **TOLERATE** (tŏl'ēr·āt) . . . . allow; put up with; forbear

The teacher refused to tolerate bad manners.

▸ One learns to be tolerant of political and religious views that are different from one's own.

▪ Tolerance toward other people's beliefs is a good attitude to cultivate; intolerance is not.

To tolerate another's views is neither to reject nor accept them but rather to listen to, discuss, and respect them.
Cf. tolerable

10. TRANSFIGURE (trăns·fĭg'ùr) . . . . . . transform, glorify

Reforestation will transfigure the barren hills near the town. The presence of Eppie transfigured Silas Marner by giving him something to live for besides his money.

■ This transfiguration was a gradual process.

Transform Words: To transfigure usually means to change the outward appearance only.
To **transmute** something is to change it from one nature or form into another. Medieval alchemists hoped to transmute iron into gold.
To **metamorphose** is to change into quite a different form, as when a caterpillar becomes a butterfly.

11. VACILLATE (văs'ĭ·lāt) . . . . . . waver or be changeable

Mr. Evans did not vacillate between duty and enjoyment. He resolutely and regularly put duty first.

■ Because he did not have the courage to confess his wrongdoing, Godfrey "fell back on suspense and vacillation."

12. VENERATE (vĕn'ĕr·āt) . . . . regard with deep respect; revere

We venerate the signers of the Declaration of Independence because they were courageous and farsighted.

■ Our veneration is tinged with awe and reverence.

► For many years, Bernard Baruch, the "elder statesman of Lafayette Park," was a venerable figure in American life.

Venerable implies advanced age as well as reverence. An archdeacon in the Anglican Church is addressed as Venerable.
The word is also applied to the lowest of the three degrees of sanctity in the Roman Catholic Church, below canonized and beatified.
Venerate and *venerable* come from a Latin word that is related to the name of the goddess of love, Venus.
Cf. deference, reverence, adoration

13. VITIATE (vĭsh'ĭ·āt) . . . contaminate; debase, render worthless

He let selfishness and jealousy vitiate his character.
The fact that one of the parties was insane at the time vitiates the contract.

■ The despotism of a king almost led to vitiation of British freedom.

In legal use, *vitiate* means "make ineffective or invalid."
Cf. debauch, deprave, pervert (I, 10), *impair, invalidate*

▸ Word List—ADJECTIVES

1. IMMUNE (ĭ·mūn′) . . . . insusceptible; protected

No one is completely immune to criticism.
- Young babies have a natural immunity to certain diseases.
- Inoculation will immunize one to typhoid fever.

One is immune to harmful things such as disease or criticism.
One is **exempt** from duties such as taxpaying or military service.

2. INARTICULATE (ĭn′är·tĭk′ů·lǎt) . . . . . unintelligible; mute

The baby made inarticulate sounds of joy.
Awe made him inarticulate as he gazed into the star-studded sky.

Cf. articulate, articulation, inarticulateness

3. INTERMITTENT (ĭn′tēr·mĭt′ěnt) . . occurring at intervals; periodic

Intermittent flashes of lightning illuminated the landscape.
- The intermittence of the showers made it hard to tell when the rain was really over.

Intermission comes from the same root. (See *Mitt* Words in I, 9.)

4. JUVENILE (jōō′vě·nĭl) . . . . youthful; for children; immature

His reading was juvenile, his behavior was juvenile, and, being just twelve, he was truly juvenile.

Puerile (pū′ēr·ĭl) means "childish" in an uncomplimentary sense. It is often applied to adults who behave in a childish way: Jumping up and down with anger is very puerile.

5. MONOTONOUS (mȯ·nŏt′ȯ·nŭs) . . . . unvarying, unvaried

The monotonous noise of the rain made us gloomy.
- He found it hard to get used to the monotony of operating a punch machine all day.
- Mary wanted to join the school chorus, but since she sang in a monotone, she wasn't eligible.

What other *Mono* Words do you recall? (See I, 12.)

6. PALLID (păl'ĭd) . . . . **pale, wan**

Illness had made her pallid, but her color soon came back.

■ Pallidness or pallor may indicate ill health.

Cf. ashen, bloodless, ghastly (I, 3)

7. PIOUS (pī'ŭs) . . . . **outwardly religious; godly**

Our new neighbor has a pious face, but we don't know yet whether he is really religious or not.

■ The piety of St. Francis was simple and sincere.

A pious person is outwardly religious but may or may not be godly and devout.
A **godly** person is full of reverence and love of God.
A **devout** person is fervent and devoted to prayer.
An **orthodox** person is one who holds closely to the basic doctrines of his religion.

8. PROTUBERANT (prŏ·tū'bēr·ănt) . . . . **bulging, swelling out**

John had a protuberant nose and a wide mouth.

It was hard to believe that "those large, brown, protuberant eyes in Silas Marner's pale face really saw nothing very distinctly that was not close to them."

9. PROVIDENT (prŏv'ĭ·děnt) . . . . **exercising foresight; thrifty**

Mary has a provident father who plans carefully, buys wisely, and saves something each month.

▶ A providential (lucky) rain arrived just in time to stop the forest fire from spreading.

■ Was it some kind of providence that gave the United States so many of the mineral deposits that it needs?

Providence is often used as a synonym for *Deity*.

10. SKEPTICAL (skĕp'tĭ·kăl) . . . . **doubting, reluctant to believe**

The farmer was skeptical about the value of the new seed.

■ When he saw the fine crops it produced, however, his skepticism disappeared.

■ The policeman is a skeptic about human nature because he sees so much of human shortcomings.

Cf. dubious (II, 1), *credible* (II, 8)

11. **TURBULENT** (tûr′bů·lĕnt) . . . . . . disorderly, tumultuous

When the crowd grew turbulent, the police arrived.

■ The turbulence of the winds increased as the hurricane came nearer.

Turb Words, from Latin *turba,* "a tumult" or "a crowd": **Turbid** waves are muddy; turbid thoughts are muddled.
Perturb and *disturb* both carry the meaning of agitation or disorder of some kind.

12. **VICIOUS** (vĭsh′ŭs) . . . . evil; unruly; depraved

The dog is vicious and has bitten several people.

■ The viciousness of drug addiction is depicted in a magazine article.

An evil act may be *infamous, iniquitous, immoral, criminal, depraved, nefarious* (II, 9), *villainous,* or *diabolical.* Add to the list, using a dictionary or thesaurus.

FIRST PRACTICE SET

Copy the *italicized* words. Beside each, write an appropriate definition.

1. Misdeeds which father cannot *tolerate* will *galvanize* him into doing something.

2. She *nurtured* the child as if he were her very own and often *iterated* how much she loved him.

3. His tendency to *prevaricate* about his failures led the club to *ostracize* him.

4. Mr. Brown was *gratified* by the beautiful present his co-workers gave him and *scrutinized* it many times with obvious delight.

5. When Mary heard that she was going to Rome, she was *transfigured* with joy. She had always *venerated* the city.

6. A tendency to *vacillate* will surely *vitiate* character.

7. *Inarticulate* at first, she soon recovered enough to talk in *intermittent* bursts about the *turbulent* debates on war.

8. The new boy has a *pallid* face and *protuberant* eyes.

9. Mr. Holton is a *provident* manager, but he has a *vicious* temper.

10. Reporters were *skeptical* when promised that the match would probably *reinstate* the man who was heavyweight champion for five years.

SECOND PRACTICE SET

Which word from the unit best replaces each *italicized* word or group of words?

1. The baby *uttered again* its *unintelligible* protest.

2. The herd of cattle was *stimulated* into flight by the *periodic* flashes of lightning.

3. The *youthful* delinquent tried to *evade the truth* when he went before the judge.

4. In *unvaried* tones, he begged the president to *restore to his former position* the office boy.

5. *Tumultuous* seas soon *rendered worthless* his efforts to swim to shore.

6. The child's *wan* face was *transformed* by summer sunshine.

7. Her *outwardly religious* actions *afford pleasure* to her mother.

8. A big dog *inspected closely* the *bulging* tail lights on the car.

9. She is a *thrifty* housewife and *rears* her children with affection and understanding.

10. We had to *exclude* Joe because he proved *unsusceptible* to good-natured criticism.

THIRD PRACTICE SET

Which of the lettered items is most nearly **opposite** in meaning to the capitalized word?

1. MONOTONOUS: (a) turbulent (b) intermittent (c) articulate (d) marked by iteration (e) intoxicating

2. VITIATE: (a) enliven (b) make joyful (c) deaden (d) ennoble (e) nurture

3. GRATIFY: (a) exasperate (b) vitiate (c) ostracize (d) upheave (e) transfigure

4. VICIOUS: (a) benevolent (b) cooperative (c) thrifty (d) gratifying (e) virtuous

5. IMMUNE: (a) unfortified (b) without walls (c) free from germs (d) unhealthy (e) susceptible

6. PROVIDENT: (a) irreligious (b) happy-go-lucky (c) vacillating (d) tolerant (e) intermittent

7. PROTUBERANT: (a) deficient (b) pallid (c) hollowed out (d) projecting (e) convex

8. TURBULENT: (a) calm (b) set in one's ways (c) inclined to prevaricate (d) not needing police (e) inactive

9. TOLERATE: (a) dislike (b) overcome (c) ostracize (d) persecute (e) harmonize

10. SCRUTINIZE: (a) disregard (b) examine (c) reject (d) make an exception (e) disapprove

A TALL TALE

Prevaricate in a paragraph or two about an adventure, such as an imaginary trip around the world. Use as many words from this unit as you can.

THE RIGHT WORD

On a separate sheet, write the numbers of the *italicized* words.
Beside each, write the number of the matching word or group of
words from the second column.

1. *Reiteration* of slogans
2. *Transfiguration* of society
3. *Reinstatement* of Republicans
4. Gay *prevarication*
5. Astonishing *puerility*
6. *Turbulence* of Niagara
7. An editor's *skepticism*
8. Words of *veneration*
9. *Pallor* of an invalid
10. Professional *ostracism*

1. childishness
2. evasion of the truth
3. tumultuousness
4. lack of color
5. mild dislike
6. reluctance to believe
7. deep reverence
8. exclusion from fellowship
9. unexpected release
10. restoration to former position
11. constant repetition
12. glorifying transformation

REPLACEMENTS

Which word from the unit best replaces each *italicized* word or
phrase?
1. Gertrude Stein was an American *voluntary exile* in Paris.
2. Joan was a *fervent, devoted* Catholic.
3. *Muddy-looking* clouds boiled up in the east.
4. The *electric* effect of the sudden noise caused the horse to bolt.
5. The government will *ship him out of the country* as an undesirable alien.
6. Cinderella was *changed into quite a different form*.
7. A doctor would like to be *protected and free* from night calls.
8. Treason is a *depraved* crime.
9. *Refusal to respect the beliefs of others* is un-American.
10. Good thoughts will *compel to leave* all bad thoughts.

Año 1570

UNIT EIGHT

Which word from the list at the right fits best in each blank?

1. A quality for which George Washington is famous: __?__

2. A word that explains the growth of butter-flies: __?__

3. A word that contains fire in its root: __?__

4. A word that tells what you receive when you "get what you deserve": __?__

5. A common cause for failure: __?__

6. A word especially applicable to the weather: __?__

7. One reason why teams play well: __?__

8. A word applicable to one's regrets over missed opportunities: __?__

9. A word that means "polite in a rather formal way": __?__

10. A word for the sky and stars: __?__

ardent
celestial
indolence
metamorphosis
futility
fluctuation
morale
veracity
civil
credible
retribution
utility

▶ Word List—ADJECTIVES

1.   ALTERNATE (ôl′tẽr·nĭt)   .   .   .   .   .   . every other (one); each
following the other

The club meets on alternate Tuesdays.
- Laughter and tears alternate (follow each other).
▶ Alternating electric current pulsates back and forth very
rapidly. The usual house current reverses its direction 120
times a second in completing its 60 "cycles."

An **alternative** is a second possibility or choice: The alternative to
school is a job.

2.   ARDENT (är′dĕnt)   .   .   .   . fervent, zealous; burning

He makes fiery speeches and shows in other ways that he is
an ardent supporter of the campaign.
■ Cromwell's soldiers had a religious ardor seldom found in
armies.

An ardent desire is a fiery one, glowing with feeling.
A **fervent** desire is boiling or burning.
A **passionate** desire is overpoweringly emotional.
A **zealous** nature is burningly active or diligent.
Cf. zealous and *vehement* (I, 6)

3.   BENIGN (bẽ·nīn′)   .   .   .   . kindly; favorable

The benign influence of the clergyman made many of the
villagers more considerate.
The new school has a benignant principal who is firm but
treats even ninth graders graciously.
■ "The rude mind with difficulty associates the ideas of
power and benignity."

A benign growth or tumor is one that is not **malignant** (II, 9) or
cancerous.

4.   CELESTIAL (sẽ·lĕs′chăl)   .   .   .   .   .   . heavenly; of the sky

Angels are celestial beings.
The stars are celestial bodies.

Celestial navigation depends on observing the positions of such celestial bodies as the sun, moon, and stars.

5. **CIVIL** (sĭv′ĭl) . . . . of a citizen or state; polite

Civil liberties guaranteed by the Constitution include freedom of speech and the right to vote by secret ballot.
Civil defense is a part-time activity for many citizens in civilian life (not military).
Grace is always civil.

- She treats people she does not like with careful civility but not real friendliness.

Civil **service** is public service in the local, state, or federal government, exclusive of military service.
Civil **war** is internal war or war within a country.

6. **COMPLACENT** (kŏm·plā′sĕnt) . . . . pleased (especially with oneself), self-satisfied

He is never complacent even though he has a straight-A record.

- Teachers do not have to criticize him for complacency.

7. **CREDIBLE** (krĕd′ĭ·b′l) . . . . believable

The sailor's account of his escape from the sunken ship through a porthole is barely credible.

- The credibility of the lost-Atlantis story has not been fully established.
The word *miracle* is used to explain things otherwise incredible.

A **credulous** person is easily deceived and is too willing to believe.
Undue **credulity** is often a result of ignorance.

8. **CULPABLE** (kŭl′pà·b′l) . . . . blameworthy, deserving blame

The boy most culpable in the lunchroom accident was the one who started the shoving.

- Realizing his culpability, he stayed out of school the next day.
"If there is an angel who records the sorrows of men as well as their sins, he knows how many and deep are the

sorrows that spring from false ideas for which no man is culpable."

A **culprit** is an offender, someone to blame for a crime or fault.
To **exculpate** someone is to free him from blame or clear him of a charge.
Cf. acquit and related words (II, 5).

9. ECCENTRIC (ĕk·sĕn'trĭk) . . . . **odd, peculiar**

The fact that he keeps irregular hours and has a fondness for snakes may mark him as eccentric, but this does not prove he is a genius.

■ One of Susan's eccentricities is a fondness for June bugs.

Originally, *eccentric* meant "off center." How is an eccentric wheel or cog used in machinery?
Cf. erratic, under *errant* (I, 7)

10. FUTILE (fū'tĭl) . . . . **useless, ineffectual**

All efforts to find the missing plane proved futile.

■ The drama showed the futility of trying to live without working.

An **effectual** plan produces the desired results; an **ineffectual** plan does not.
Cf. abortive

11. INCIPIENT (ĭn·sĭp'ĭ·ĕnt) . . . . . . **in the beginning stages**

A medical examination of the earliest symptoms showed incipient tuberculosis.

■ Because of its incipiency, the disease was readily curable.

Cf. percipient

12. LIBERAL (lĭb'ēr·ăl) . . . . **favoring progress; generous; broad**

A liberal education is a broad, general education.

● Knowledge liberates the mind from error.

■ We supported the Community Chest with great liberality.

A **liberal** favors what he believes to be progress.
A **conservative** wants to conserve what he believes to be the best elements of the past.
The Latin *liber-* means "free."
See dictionary for other meanings of *liberal* and I, 8 for other forms.

▪ Word List—NOUNS

1. **FALLACY** (făl'á·sĭ) . . . . . mistaken idea; false reasoning

   His philosophy of life is based on the fallacy that money always brings happiness.

   ► Human beings are very fallible (liable to error).

   ▪ Their fallibility is a popular topic for writing and discussion.

   ► The idea that cleverness is more important that honesty proved fallacious (fă·lā'shŭs).

   Opposite: *infallible, infallibility*

2. **FLUCTUATION** (flŭk'tṳ·ā'shŭn) . . rise and fall; continual variation

   Silas noticed "that Sara's manner towards him began to exhibit a strange fluctuation."

   ● Prices of farm products fluctuate considerably from one season to another, depending on the supply.

   Waver Words: To **undulate** is to rise and fall evenly like waves, and **undulations** are wavelike motions.
   To **vacillate** is to waver in one's mind or opinion, to be irresolute. (See II, 7.)
   To **falter** is to weaken or waver in one's determination; also, to speak in hesitating words.

3. **INDOLENCE** (ĭn'dô·lĕns) . . . . . . love of ease; laziness

   Indolence keeps some promising high school students from going on to college.

   ► The hot weather makes people feel indolent.

   Cf. slothful, slothfulness

4. **INFERENCE** (ĭn'fẽr·ĕns) . . . . . . conclusion, deduction

   When he saw police with drawn guns around the house, his inference was that there must be a dangerous person inside.

   ● One would infer from what the sailor said that he knew something about the tropics.

   Cf. imply: The sailor implies or hints his knowledge by what he says.

5. METAMORPHOSIS (mĕt′ȧ·môr′fô·sĭs) . . transformation, change
of form

In the first stage of the metamorphosis of a butterfly, the
eggs become larvae.
Falling in love brought a kind of metamorphosis to the shy
young man. He became gay and confident.
● The stamens of plants metamorphose into petals.

Metamorphosis comes from the Greek *morph-,* meaning "form," and
meta, meaning "after or beyond."
Morph Words include *amorphous,* "having no form," and *morphology,*
"the science of form(s)."

6. MORALE (mô·rȧl′) . moral or mental conditions; spirit, willingness

School morale reached a new high when we won the game.
Ted's bravery in rescuing his friend improved the morale
of the company.

Esprit de corps is a French phrase which literally means "the spirit
of the group." The term implies enthusiasm for, and devotion to, a
group on the part of its members.

7. RESURRECTION (rĕz′ŭ·rĕk′shŭn) . coming or bringing to life again

The resurrection of the old law is an important part of the
conservative party's program.
As he faced the guillotine, Sydney Carton kept repeating
the words, "I am the Resurrection and the Life, saith the
Lord."

Resurrection also refers to the state of those who have risen from
the dead.
An **insurrection** is a rising against or revolt (III, 4).

8. RETRIBUTION (rĕt′rĭ·bū′shŭn) . . . . . requital, punishment

Quick retribution overtook the thief. He fell into the swimming pool behind the house and drowned.
▶ There was retributory justice in making the boy pay for
the damage he had done.

Retribution implies a punishment that is deserved and often imper-
sonal. It may also refer to a return for good done, as well as for evil.
Vengeance and *reprisal* (II, 3), like *revenge,* usually imply a more
personal requital for evil.

9. **SUBTERFUGE** (sŭb'tẽr·fūj) . . . trick or artifice used to escape something unpleasant

When their father came to investigate the noise, the boys pretended to be asleep. It was not a very effective subterfuge. Sally feigned illness as a subterfuge to avoid studying.

A subterfuge is chiefly a means of escaping something unpleasant.
A **maneuver** or **stratagem** is a trick to accomplish something, often to deceive someone. A maneuver may also be a planned movement of troops or a clever move in a game.
A **ruse** is a trick intended to give a false impression, to mislead.
A **feint** (I, 2) is literally the pretended thrust of a fencer or boxer, intended to confuse the opponent. It may also be any trick designed to distract attention from one's real purpose.

10. **TEMERITY** (tē·mĕr'ĭ·tĭ) . . . . . rashness, reckless boldness

Hitler had the temerity to attack Russia while he was fighting the Western powers.
▶ A temerarious aviator flew a jet plane too fast and met with a fatal accident.

Cf. audacity (III, 1), *effrontery*

11. **TRADITION** (trȧ·dĭsh'ŭn) . . customs, stories, beliefs handed down

Tradition gives us many of the practices we follow today, such as carrying a bride over the threshold or dressing as witches on Hallowe'en.
The traditions of numerous peoples tell of a great flood which once devastated the earth.
▶ Travelers in Palestine usually visit the traditional birthplace of Jesus.
▪ The islanders were extreme traditionalists.
▪ Ancestor worship is the ultimate in traditionalism.

See dictionary for legal and theological meanings of *tradition*.

12. **UTILITY** (û·tĭl'ĭ·tĭ) . . . . . . usefulness; something useful

My fondness for flowers has little to do with their utility except as they help my morale.
Clothes pins are a minor household utility. Electricity is a major or public utility.

- An efficient packing company claims that it utilizes every part of a pig but the squeal.
- ▶ The utilitarian (practical) values of an education are numerous.

    Cf. utilitarianism, inutility

13.   VERACITY (vĕ·răs′ĭ·tĭ) . . . . truthfulness

He is a chronic liar who has mixed fact with fancy so long that veracity is now impossible for him.

- ▶ Poe's stories often sound like veracious (vĕ·rā′shŭs) accounts of actual events.

    Cf. verity, verisimilitude

FIRST PRACTICE SET

Copy the *italicized* words. Beside each, write an appropriate definition.

1. Old Dr. Martin is *benign* to friends, *civil* to enemies, but quite *eccentric* about his diet.
2. His *ardent* enthusiasm and *credible* arguments won the debate.
3. If the boy were *culpable*, how could he be so *complacent?*
4. Attempts to cure cancer are seldom *futile* when begun during the *incipient* stages of the disease.
5. Working on *alternate* days had an adverse effect on the man's *morale*.
6. It was a *celestial* being who announced Christ's *resurrection*.
7. It is a *fallacy* to believe that the *fluctuation* of the tides is due to the tipping of the earth.
8. The only possible *inference* one can draw is that your low grades are the result of *indolence*.
9. By various *subterfuges*, the swindler sought to escape the *retribution* that was due him.
10. No one questioned the *veracity* of the inventor's claims about the *utility* of the new floor treatment.

SECOND PRACTICE SET

Which word from the unit best replaces each *italicized* word or phrase?

1. The *rising* in China led to *internal* warfare.

2. The Democratic candidate is a *tireless and enthusiastic* campaigner. His opponent is more the *boiling-burning* type.

3. Student feeling about the *old customs* of the school seems to *rise and fall*.

4. Do the speaker's *overpoweringly emotional* criticisms of the Republican proposal *hint* that he is a Democrat?

5. The sophomores thought of a *trick intended to mislead* which they used to expose the *rash boldness* of the freshman president.

THIRD PRACTICE SET

Which of the lettered items is most nearly **opposite** in meaning to the words printed in capital letters?

1. ARDENT: (a) slow (b) even-tempered (c) indifferent (d) darkened (e) ungenerous

2. COMPLACENT: (a) impolite (b) discontented (c) unselfish (d) clever (e) dishonest

3. FUTILE: (a) effectual (b) encouraging (c) resourceful (d) dominant (e) impressive

4. ECCENTRIC: (a) round (b) benign (c) civil (d) complacent (e) ordinary

5. INCIPIENT: (a) healthy (b) prominent (c) terminal (d) unnoticed (e) exhausted

6. LIBERAL: (a) awkward (b) distasteful (c) efficient (d) hopeless (e) ungenerous

7. INDOLENT: (a) virtuous (b) energetic (c) humble (d) quick (e) generous

8. VERACIOUS: (a) untruthful (b) incredible (c) credulous (d) exciting (e) dull

9. TEMERARIOUS: (a) timid (b) cautious (c) deliberate (d) sensible (e) intelligent

10. FALLACIOUS: (a) wrong (b) benign (c) discreet (d) correct (e) courageous

THE RIGHT WORD

Write the numbers of the *italicized* words. Beside each, write the number of the matching word or words from the second column.

1. Swift *retribution*	1. devotion to patterns handed down
2. Obvious *utility*	2. politeness
3. A clever *subterfuge*	3. self-satisfaction
4. Great *benignity*	4. deduction
5. Good *morale*	5. belief in justice
6. Illusions of *infallibility*	6. trick to escape something unpleasant
7. Irritating *complacency*	7. trick of logic
8. Blind *traditionalism*	8. kindliness
9. A justifiable *inference*	9. requital
10. Undue *civility*	10. mental condition
	11. usefulness
	12. inability to err

UNIT NINE

Which word from the list at the right fits best in each blank?

1. The peasants felt deep __?__ (hatred) because of the oppressive rule of the aristocrats.

2. The attitude of the Defarges and their friends was very __?__ (gloomy) as they watched the poverty and suffering around them.

3. In order to escape detection, it was necessary for the Jacqueries to be very __?__ (watchful) in taking precautions.

4. Meanwhile, Monseigneur and his kind were much too __?__ (hopeful) about their future.

5. The aristocrats clung obstinately to their old ways and this __?__ (misguided stubbornness) helped bring on the revolution.

6. The king did not realize what a __?__ (fighting) mood filled the hearts of the peasants.

7. Gradually, fear began to spread through the city like some __?__ (secretly evil) poison.

8. Today, __?__ (forgetfulness) has erased the names of many heroes of the French Revolution.

perversity
rancor
vigilant
militant
insidious
venial
sanguine
oblivion
morose
depravity

231

▶ Word List— NINE EVIL ADJECTIVES

1. **ATROCIOUS** (à·trō′shŭs) . . . . . extremely wicked or bad

   The wholesale tortures and murders in Nazi prison camps were among the most atrocious crimes in history.
   - Stories of atrocities flourish in every war.

   > *Atrocious* is one of the strongest adjectives for evil but may be used ironically of something that is merely in bad taste.
   > *Cf. heinous, monstrous, nefarious, iniquitous, outrageous*

2. **BELLIGERENT** (bĕ·lĭg′ĕr·ĕnt) . . . . . quarrelsome; warlike; engaged in warfare

   His belligerent attitude made him unpopular at school.
   - The belligerents in World War II did not include Sweden.

   > Warlike Words: The word *bellicose* is often applied to a person's state of mind and implies a readiness to stir up fights.
   > *Pugnacious* is another word which means "combative."
   > *Quarrelsome* is used of someone who is ready to quarrel, even without good cause.
   > The word *contentious* is applied to a person who is always arguing about something.

3. **INCORRIGIBLE** (ĭn·kŏr′ĭ·jĭ·b'l) . . . . . incapable of reform; unmanageable

   A convict who is considered incorrigible is not eligible for parole.
   - The prisoner's incorrigibility makes it necessary for him to serve his full term.

   > *Incorrigible* may mean "impervious to punishment" or, when applied to a habit, "deeply established": He has an incorrigible weakness for practical jokes.
   > *Cf. inveterate* (II, 4) and *chronic* (II, 1)

4. **INSIDIOUS** (ĭn·sĭd′ĭ·ŭs) . . . . . treacherous; stealthily injurious

   Carelessness is an insidious habit.
   Scientists slowly began to discover the insidious effects of continued exposure to X-ray radiation.

-   For years, her selfishness had been hardening insidiously, until she was unable to care about anyone except herself.

    Cf. infiltrate

5. MOROSE (mȯ·rōs′) . . . . austerely bitter, gloomy

Ill health made her quite morose.

■ Her moroseness increased as her health grew worse.

-   "What good did it do to study?" he said morosely when he failed the exam.

6. NEFARIOUS (nė·fâr′ĭ·ŭs) . . . . very evil

Kidnaping is a nefarious crime because of the anguish it inflicts.

-   He was so despicable that he nefariously robbed a blind beggar.

    The word *nefarious* comes from the Latin *nefas*, meaning "crime," which was formed of *ne-*, "not," and *fas*, "divine law." Thus the word suggests a total disregard of law and morality.
    Antonyms: **righteous, virtuous, saintly, upright**

7. PERNICIOUS (pēr·nĭsh′ŭs) . . . . . highly injurious, deadly

Heroin is a pernicious drug.

■ Incitation to crime is one of the ways in which its perniciousness appears.

    Harm Words: **Baneful** means "destructive" and is the adjective form of *bane*, "ruin or harm," which comes from the old English word *bana*, "a murderer."
    Noxious is used of something which is harmful to the health.
    Cf. obnoxious (I, 6)

8. VENIAL (vē′nĭ·ăl) . . . . pardonable, excusable

The supervisor considers persistent tardiness a pernicious habit, but occasional tardiness only a venial fault.

■ Its veniality is inversely proportional to its frequency.

    Do not confuse *venial*, which comes from a Latin word meaning "forgiveness," with *venal*, which comes from a Latin word meaning "a sale": A corrupt legislature or government is full of venality.
    In theology, a venial sin is opposed to a **mortal** or deadly sin. (See *gluttony* below.)

9. **VENOMOUS** (vĕn'ŭm·ŭs) . . . . . . poisonous; spiteful

The cobra is a highly venomous snake found in Asia and
Africa.

In his venomous hatred, the actor tried to drown the man
who had damaged his reputation.

■ The venomousness of his hatred appalled everyone.

■ Word List—SEVEN KINDS OF EVIL

1. **DEPRAVITY** (dĕ·prăv'ĭ·tĭ) . . . moral corruptness, debasement

An ex-convict told about the utter depravity of underworld
practices.

• She knew that evil companions would deprave her brother.

► The criminal is so depraved that he has no regard for
human life at all.

Immorality is a weaker, less comprehensive word, implying less of
excessive moral corruptness.

2. **GLUTTONY** (glŭt'n·ĭ) . indulgence to excess, especially in eating

Gluttony had built the man's weight to nearly three hundred pounds.

■ Henry VIII is remembered as the king who was also a
glutton.

► His gluttonous appetite was famous.

According to Roman Catholic teaching, gluttony is one of the Seven
Mortal or Deadly Sins. Consult your dictionary for a list of the others.

3. **HERESY** (hĕr'ĕ·sĭ) . . . opinion(s) differing from accepted view

The idea that germs cause disease was once a scientific
heresy.

In the British court of 1780, any praise for George Washington was disturbing heresy.

■ Religious heretics were once burned at the stake.

▶ The man was condemned for his heretical views.

A religious **heretic** is one who rejects a belief which is considered important by his church.
An **infidel** is a disbeliever. During the Middle Ages, the term was often applied to a non-Christian.
An **agnostic** is one who suspends belief because he does not know about the nature of God and of the universe.
An **atheist** is one who denies the existence of a Supreme Being.

4. HYPOCRISY (hĭ·pŏk′rĭ·sĭ) . . . . pretense of being what one is not; sham

He was full of hypocrisy: he pretended to love music but listened to it only when he had guests whom he wanted to impress.

▶ He was hypocritical about money matters, pretending to be well-off when he was actually quite poor.

A **hypocrite** is an impostor, a dissembler.
Insincerity is milder and less deliberate than hypocrisy.

5. MALIGNITY (má·lĭg′nĭ·tĭ) . . strong desire to inflict harm; ill will

Madame Defarge's malignity toward aristocrats was not a sudden growth.

▶ Her privations had made her feel malignant toward those who had caused them.

Malignity is stronger than malice, which is merely ill will.
Malevolence is a mood of hatred or resentment. See *Mal* Words (II, 11).
Cf. benignity (II, 8)

6. PERVERSITY (pĕr·vûr′sĭ·tĭ) . . willful persistence in nonconformity or wrong; obstinacy

It was hard to understand her perversity in spending money on new furniture when she scarcely had enough to eat.
In her perverseness, she refused to be reasonable.

● Judges who will accept bribes pervert justice (thwart it, turn it away from the right course).

■ Such perversions destroy respect for the office of judge.

▶ He was in such a perverse mood that nothing pleased him.

See *Vert* and *Verse* Words (I, 10).
Cf. refractory, froward, headstrong, wayward

7.   RANCOR (răng'kĕr) . . . . bitter hatred, ill will

Captain Ahab's rancor grew steadily against the white whale which had bitten off his leg, and he resolved to destroy it.

• The loss so rankled that it destroyed his sanity.

The word *rancid* is applied to butter and fats which taste spoiled. *Rankle* comes from a Latin word meaning "a sore," which in turn descended from an early word for "dragon."

▸ Word List—NINE GOOD ADJECTIVES

1.   INGENIOUS (ĭn·jēn'yŭs) . . . . showing clever construction; resourceful, inventive

The clothesline tightener is an ingenious gadget.
Jim is very ingenious in solving crossword puzzles.

■ He displays a remarkable ingenuity (ingeniousness) in fixing toys and appliances.

Do not confuse *ingenious* with *ingenuous* (III, 5).

2.   INTREPID (ĭn·trĕp'ĭd) . . . . fearless, dauntless

The pilot was an intrepid aviator, being one of the first to fly more than twelve hundred miles an hour.

■ Walter Reed's intrepidity in risking his life enabled him to discover the cause of yellow fever.

3.   LACONIC (lá·kŏn'ĭk) . . . . concise, terse, pithy

"A light frown and a laconic 'Yes,' were the answers."
The so-called "sayings of Confucius" are popular examples of laconic statement.

This word is derived from the name of the Laconians, or Spartans, who were trained from childhood to say everything in the briefest and most concise manner possible.

4.   MILITANT (mĭl'ĭ·tănt) . . . . . engaged in fighting; combative

The Senator was a militant crusader for his ideals.

• Poor eyesight militates (contends) against success in school.

5. **OBLIVIOUS** (ŏb·lĭv′ĭ·ŭs) . . . . . . unconscious; unmindful

   When George studies, he is oblivious to the confusion around him.

   ■ Obliviousness of this kind results from strong concentration.

   ■ Sleep provides temporary oblivion (state of forgetfulness or of being forgotten).

   > **Lettres de cachet** were "blank forms for the consignment of anyone to the oblivion of prison for any length of time." Such forms were often used during the French Revolution.

6. **OSTENSIBLE** (ŏs·tĕn′sĭ·b′l) . . . . . . apparent; pretended

   His ostensible reason for taking a walk was to get some fresh air, but actually he hoped to meet Margaret.

   - The old lady was ostensibly sending a package to friends in Poland, but actually she was helping the F.B.I. expose a Communist scheme.

7. **SANGUINE** (sǎng′gwĭn) . . . . . hopeful, confident; bloody

   A sanguine nature like Martha's seldom experiences despair. The Reign of Terror was a very sanguinary affair (accompanied by much bloodshed).

   ■ Consanguinity (blood relationship) does not exist among adopted children.

   > **Sanguine** comes from the Latin word *sanguineus,* meaning "bloody." Since it was often used in describing a ruddy face, *sanguine* acquired the additional meaning of "having a warm, cheerful nature."
   > *Cf. optimistic, buoyant*

8. **UBIQUITOUS** (ū·bĭk′wĭ·tŭs) . . . . . . everywhere present

   Fear was a ubiquitous and insidious foe which, more than enemy gunfire, demoralized the town.

   ■ The ubiquitousness of the police prevented escape.

   Cf. omnipresent

9. **VIGILANT** (vĭj′ĭ·lănt) . . . . . . alert to danger; watchful

   The dog kept a vigilant watch over the sleeping child.

   ■ Dr. Manette's "vigilance and skill in conducting ingenious experiments brought a moderate number of patients."

   ■ The vigil (period of wakeful watching) at the sick man's bedside lasted all night.
   Cf. wary (I, 3), *vigilante*

THE LAST ENEMY

Danger—in the air, on the desert, in a war, in an earth-quake—is a logical topic for a militant paragraph. Many of the words in this unit are suitable for such a topic.

FIRST PRACTICE SET

Copy the *italicized* words. Beside each, write an appropriate definition.

1. The young sentry was determined to be *vigilant,* but sleep crept *insidiously* over him until he was *oblivious* to everything.

2. My cousin is *morose* when he is tired and when he is not tired, he is rather *incorrigible* in his *perversity* about teasing people.

3. Dope peddling is an *atrocious* activity because of the *nefarious* crimes committed to obtain money to buy narcotics.

4. Jealousy is *venomous* and can have *pernicious* effects on one's health as well as one's character.

5. Sixty years ago the idea that women should vote was political *heresy,* but those who held it worked with *militant* zeal.

6. *Gluttony* is unwise and is often considered one of the major forms of human *depravity.*

7. Claudius concealed his *malignity* toward Hamlet by showing *ostensible* goodwill and friendship.

8. This friendliness was simply *hypocrisy,* which lasted until he could find an *ingenious* way to murder Hamlet.

9. Brutus was too *sanguine* about the success of the plot against Caesar, and Cassius was actuated too much by *rancor* and jealousy.

10. He is very *laconic* in his speech and this makes him seem rather *belligerent.*

SECOND PRACTICE SET

Which base word best replaces each *italicized* word or group of words?

1. His *resourceful* methods of selling worthless stock to trustful old ladies was one of the more *extremely wicked* crimes in his career of *moral corruptness*.

2. He proved especially *treacherous* because he looked so honest, and he promoted his *very evil* schemes with elaborate *sham*.

3. When the judge declared him *incapable of reform* and gave him the maximum sentence, he became *sullenly bitter*.

4. His face grew dark with *intense desire to inflict harm* and *bitter hatred*. He turned to the judge with a *warlike* gesture, and the guards were forced to restrain him.

5. "You *poisonous* viper!" he declared. "My misdeed is no worse than your *eating too much*."

6. "I weigh too much," the judge admitted, "and I am not *unconscious* of the fact, but I think my fault is a *pardonable* one. At least it is far less *deadly* than the *fearless* kind of fraud and robbery you have perpetrated.

7. "It would be *opinion-differing-from-the-accepted-view* even to think of reducing your sentence, and no honest judge who knows your case would be *hopeful* enough to suggest it.

8. "I admire you for not showing *pretended* remorse, but your *willful persistence* in wrongdoing is well established."

9. "You are too *combative*," was the culprit's *pithy* reply.

10. "Authorities are too watchful, and the police are *everywhere present*."

THIRD PRACTICE SET

Which of the lettered items is most nearly **opposite** in meaning to the words printed in capital letters.

1. INCORRIGIBLE: (a) tireless (b) capable of reform (c) resolute (d) sanguine (e) ambitious

2. MOROSE: (a) sharp (b) healthy (c) weak (d) good-natured (e) humble-acting

3. MALIGNITY: (a) distrust (b) pleasure (c) benevolence (d) directness (e) fairness

4. OBLIVIOUS: (a) forgetful (b) heedless (c) mindful (d) wide awake (e) vigilant

5. LACONIC: (a) concise (b) agreeable (c) frank (d) wordy (e) quite emotional

6. PERNICIOUS: (a) noxious (b) harmless (c) noisy (d) not a drug (e) unsuspecting

7. OSTENSIBLE: (a) actual (b) plain (c) hypocritical (d) unintentional (e) relaxed

8. VENIAL: (a) incorruptible (b) inexcusable (c) deliberate (d) devilish (e) morose

9. SANGUINE: (a) bloodless (b) easy going (c) despairing (d) lifeless (e) unpromising

10. VIGILANT: (a) cautious (b) unwary (c) slow-moving (d) sleepy (e) tiresome

UNIT TEN

Which word from the list at the right fits best in each blank?

1. A humorous take-off of a daily scene: __?__

2. Words of ridicule or scorn: __?__

3. Noisy gaiety: __?__

4. Coaxing and flattery: __?__

5. Light-mindedness, lack of proper seriousness: __?__

6. Laughable absurdity: __?__

7. Literary form based on witty mockery:
   __?__

8. Joking, playful humor: __?__

9. Rapid, witty interplay in a conversation:
   __?__

10. Anticlimax or descent from the lofty to the
    commonplace: __?__

derision
jocularity
facetiousness
burlesque
satire
repartee
cajolery
bathos
irony
hilarity
levity
ludicrousness

Note: The JACKPOT SECTION of Part II begins in this unit and continues
in the two following units.

▪ Word List—FOR RIDICULE

1. DERISION (dḗ·rĭzh′ŭn) . . . . ridicule, mockery

Robert Fulton's steamboat was called, in derision, "Fulton's Folly."

- There are always those who like to deride inventors.
- ▶ Women's hats offer a perennial target for derisive (scornful) remarks.

> *Risible,* "pertaining to laughter," and *risibilities,* a person's "sensibilities to what is laughable," come from the same Latin root as *derision.*

2. BATHOS (bā′thŏs) . . . . anticlimax, false **pathos**

The tourist's letter was full of bathos. "A splendid Greek pillar," he wrote, "stood like a Havana cigar against the sky." The actors were good, but the plot was a tear-jerker, full of sentimentality and bathos.

> *Bathos,* which comes from a Greek word meaning "depth," means "a descent from the sublime to the ridiculous" in speaking or writing. It may also refer to a falsely pathetic effect in a story or play.
> *Pathos* (I, 11), from a Greek word for "suffering," refers to the quality in a book, a play, or in music which arouses a feeling of pity or sadness.

3. BURLESQUE (bûr·lĕsk′) . . . . humorous take-off or imitation

The play was a burlesque of modern politics.

- ▶ It included a burlesque version of a campaign speech.

> A *burlesque* is usually a comic imitation of an elevated or impressive situation or event. The term is also applied to a form of theatrical entertainment, developed during the nineteenth century, which consists of songs, short sketches, comic interludes, and dancing.
> A **parody** is an imitation of a well-known literary or musical composition. Do you know the famous parody of *Hiawatha?* It describes Hiawatha's mittens: "He to get the warm side inside, put the inside skin side outside."
> A **travesty** is an imitation which makes something serious appear as ridiculous: Because both the judge and jury were prejudiced, the trial was a travesty of justice.
> A **caricature** is a picture or description which distorts the features of a person or thing in order to poke fun.

4. **IRONY** (ī′rō·nĭ) . . . . . . humor, words, or situation opposite
to what is expected

John, who liked irony, referred to his battered old car as
"The Limousine."

▶ People who did not realize that he was being ironical were
always startled when they first saw the car.

It had rained almost all summer but, by an irony of fate, the
rain stopped just at the beginning of the forest fire season.

Sarcasm is harsh, cutting derision in which irony is often used.

5. **SATIRE** (săt′īr) . . . . . witty attack for the purpose of ridicule

Gulliver's Travels is a famous satire which ridicules the
follies of mankind.

The author, Johnathan Swift, is a skillful satirist.

▶ Cassius makes a number of satirical (derisive) remarks in
Shakespeare's *Julius Caesar.*

In hopes of improving society, the satirist uses wit, irony, sarcasm,
and other devices to attack vices or follies.

Note: *Derision,* the key word for this group, quite properly appears first. Note
that *levity* is the key word for the next group.

Word List— FOR LIGHT-HEARTED USES

1. **LEVITY** (lĕv′ĭ·tĭ) . . . . light-mindedness, frivolity

Levity is out of place in a cathedral.

The party was the occasion for levity of various kinds.

Levity often implies a light-mindedness which is improper or unseemly.

2. **FACETIOUSNESS** (fȧ·sē′shŭs·nĕs) . . . . witty levity

Because Bob Witt likes facetiousness, his companions call
him Half-Witt.

– Mrs. Witt facetiously calls her kitchen range an altar of
burnt offerings.

▸ A facetious person lacks seriousness and is fond of joking.

A **spoonerism** is a slip of the tongue by which two sounds are interchanged, especially at the beginning of words: The Labor candidate said, "It is a pleasure this afternoon to address so many noble tons of soil." The word comes from the name of Rev. William A. Spooner (1844-1930) of Oxford, England, who was noted for such slips.

3.   **FLIPPANCY** (flĭp′ăn·sĭ) .   .   .   .   . pertness; lightly disrespectful
speech or manner

He had no respect for the past and spoke of old traditions with flippancy.

▸ The principal was annoyed by John's flippant remark about the graduation exercises.

Flippancy often implies an unseemly levity when speaking of serious or sacred matters.

4.   **HILARITY** (hĭ·lăr′ĭ·tĭ) .   .   .   . boisterous gaiety

The hilarity of the party lasted long after midnight.

▸ The girls were hilarious when two boys arrived dressed as clowns.

Merriment is used to describe a gaiety that is less boisterous than *hilarity*.
Mirth is often used of great amusement or cause for laughter.

5.   **JOCULARITY** (jŏk′ů·lăr′ĭ·tĭ) .   .   .   .   . joking, jolly manner

Uncle Franklin's jocularity reminded the children of Santa Claus.

▸ He made jocular remarks about how Bob and Ann had grown.

Joy Words: A **jovial** man is hearty and good-humored. The word comes from the name of the Roman god, Jove.
Jocose remarks are intended to cause laughter; **jocular** remarks are similar but perhaps more exuberant.
The word *jocund*, which means "cheerful, gay," is often used in poetry.

6.   **LUDICROUSNESS** (lū′dĭ·krŭs·něs) .   . laughableness, ridiculousness

The ludicrousness of the clown kept the children laughing.

▸ An armadillo is a ludicrous-looking animal.

A ludicrous spectacle is laughable, usually because it is absurd, incongruous, or out of proportion in some way.
Cf. incongruous (III, 6)

7. **REPARTEE** (rĕp'ĕr·tē') . . . . . rapid, witty reply or conversation

> The French writer is as quick and deft as a fencer in conversation. His skill at repartee made him a very witty conversationalist.

Word List—ROOTS

1. **-ANIM-, -ANIMATE-** . . . . life, spirit

> Animosity is a *spirit* of ill will.
>
> A pusillanimous person has a cowardly *spirit*.
>
> A magnanimous leader is large of *spirit*.
>
> An animated expression is gay and full of *life*.
>
> An animate object is *alive*, an inanimate object is not *alive*.
>
> *Animus*, from the Latin word for "mind," now means "a spirit of strong hostility or ill will."
> *Cf. animism*

2. **-CARN-** . . . . flesh

> Carnivorous animals are *flesh*-eating animals.
>
> The incarnation of loveliness is loveliness in the *flesh* or in bodily form.
>
> The carnation was so named because it was *flesh*-colored.
>
> The word *carnival* was originally applied only to a festival held before the beginning of Lent. The name comes from the medieval Latin *carne vale*, "farewell to meat."

3. **-CHRON-** . . . . time

> The chronological order of events is the *time* order.
>
> A chronometer measures *time* more accurately than a watch.
>
> A chronic disease continues for a long *time*. (II, 1)
>
> A chronicle is a record of events, usually in their *time* order.

4.   **-COGN- . . . -SCIEN-** . . . . know, knowledge

Recognizing a word is *knowing* it again.

To have cognizance of a matter is to have *knowledge* of it.

A cognomen is the name one is *known* by, his surname or a nickname.

Prescience is *knowing* beforehand about future events; foreknowledge.

The word *science* was originally applied to knowledge in general.
See also *incognito* (I, 7), *cogitate* (which has a different root), and *-logy* (I, 12).

5.   **-CORP-, -CORPOR-** . . . . body

A corpse is a dead *body*.

A person who is corpulent is overweight; i.e., has too much *body*.

Incorporeal spirits are not in *bodily* form.

To incorporate a business is to give it a legal *body*.

Corporal punishment is the *bodily* kind.

The name of the military rank, *corporal*, comes, by way of French and Italian, from the Latin *caput*, "head."

6.   **-FERV- . . . -ARD-** . . . . glowing, burning

A fervent or ardent hope of becoming a writer is a *glowing* or *burning* hope.

A fervid enthusiasm is somewhat more intense than a fervent enthusiasm.

A perfervid enthusiasm is even more *glowing*, perhaps excessive.

To play football with ardor is to play it with *burning* zeal.

Ardor tends to suggest more fire and less heat than *fervor*. The roots are *fevere*, "glow, boil, rage" and *ardens*, "burning."
Effervesce originally meant "boil." Today it means "fizz" (like soda water): An effervescent disposition is sparkling and lively.
Cf. *ardent* (II, 8); *scintillate*

7. -HELIO- . . . . sun

A heliograph is an apparatus for sending messages by means of the *sun's* rays thrown from a mirror.

Heliopolis, the name of an ancient city in Egypt, literally means "City of the *Sun*." What are heliotropes?

8. -PARL- . . . . talk, speak

The parlor was originally a place for entertaining and for *speaking* with visitors.

A parliament is a congress; i.e., place for lawmaking and *speaking* on public matters.

Legal parlance is the legal way of *speaking*.

A parley is a conference or discussion; i.e., a *talking*.

These words go back to Old French.

9. -PET- . . . . seek; attack

A petulant person is impatient or irritable; i.e., makes slight *attacks* on everything.

Impetus is the driving force or incentive to *seek* a goal.

An impetuous person is quick to *seek* or *attack* something with great force.

Appetite, petition, competition, and *repetition* also come from the Latin root *petere,* "seek, attack." Can you explain the force of the root and prefix in each?
Cf. impulsive

10. -PLEN-, -PLENT- . . . . full(ness)

To replenish the refrigerator is to make it *full* again.

The plenitude of one's blessings is the *full* supply.

A plenary session is a *full* or complete session of delegates.

A plenipotentiary is an ambassador with *full* power to act.

A plenteous or plentiful supply of food is an abundant or *full supply.*

11. -ROG- . . . . **ask, say, declare**

To interrogate a prisoner is to *ask* him questions.

To abrogate a charter is to *declare* it out of existence (III, 9).

A derogatory remark is an uncomplimentary one which disparages someone; i.e., *says* something against him.

A prerogative is a privilege or right that other people do not have: It is not a state's prerogative to coin money. The Latin root meant "ask before someone else does."

12. -THERM-, -THERMO- . . . . **heat**

A thermal reaction is one involving *heat*.

Thermite is a mixture of powdered metals which generates intense *heat* and is used in fire bombs.

A thermometer measures temperature; i.e., *heat* and cold.

A thermos bottle has an outer case that *heat* cannot pass through easily.

In a thermonuclear reaction, nuclear fission releases *heat* energy.

Cf. thermochemistry, thermodynamics, thermocouple

13. -VI-, -VIA- . . . . **road, (high)way**

A devious route is a roundabout route, one that goes away from the direct *road*.

An obvious fact is clear and plain; i.e., it is in the *way* and easily seen.

To obviate a difficulty is to dispose of it; i.e., to find a *way* around.

A trivial excuse is a trifling excuse.

Trivial goes back to the Latin *tri*, "three," and *via*, "road." The crossing where three roads met was a place for gossip and petty trade. *Trivial* thus came to mean "unimportant."
Cf. scuttlebut, a naval term which first meant "drinking fountain" and later, "gossip, rumor."

Note: In this group of roots, *-chron-, -helio-*, and *therm-* are of Greek origin.

FIRST PRACTICE SET

Copy the *italicized* words. Beside each, write an appropriate definition.

1. A mock election is a form of *levity* which holds up to *derision* common political customs and ideas.

2. It usually opens with a *burlesque* campaign speech full of *facetious* remarks and wild promises.

3. The speakers display great *jocularity,* but the speeches often end in *bathos.*

4. The candidates assume *ludicrous* names, which are announced amid cheers and general *hilarity.*

5. The platform of each party usually contains *satire* on actual political party platforms and includes *ironic* comments on current events.

6. The public is offered glowing promises and *cajolery,* while the opposition is denounced with *derogatory* remarks.

7. Sometimes two of the candidates appear together and engage in *repartee.* An *impetuous* speaker may demand *corporal* punishment for his opponent.

8. The mass meetings of a mock campaign are full of *animation,* reflecting the *ardor* and enthusiasm of the participants.

9. Party members may be called to a *plenary* session to debate *trivial* but often comical matters, such as the design of party buttons.

10. The *fervent* interest aroused by a mock election often extends to actual elections and militates against *chronic* indifference.

SECOND PRACTICE SET

Which word from this unit best replaces each *italicized* word or group of words?

1. After considerable *coaxing,* we managed to lead the pony on-stage, where his appearance produced great *boisterous amusement* in the audience.

2. One of the characters in a *humorous take-off* of school life was a backward student full of *burning zeal* for sports.

3. Miss Potter was famous for *rapid, witty conversation* and for her *sparkling* charm.

4. Mr. Thompson's good-natured *jolly manner* made him popular with everyone and his *witty levity* was widely admired.

5. We read a *work of ridicule* which described modern city life with great *mockery.*

6. For the camping trip, we bought a *heat-retaining* jug and a notebook in which to keep a *record-in-time-order.*

7. The article deals with *plants which turn toward the sun.*

8. The officer who is going to *ask questions of* the prisoners can do so without any *spirit of ill will.*

9. When John needed a loan, he did not *ask* his father directly but used a *roundabout* approach.

10. The new puppy seemed to be the spirit of gaiety *in bodily form.*

THIRD PRACTICE SET

Which of the lettered items is most nearly **opposite** in meaning to the word printed in capital letters?

1. SERIOUS-MINDEDNESS: (a) derision (b) irony (c) levity (d) cajolery (e) ludicrousness

2. GLOOM: (a) hilarity (b) repartee (c) bathos (d) irony (e) impetus

3. MOROSE: (a) satirical (b) jocular (c) ironic (d) ludicrous (e) bathetic

4. FERVOR: (a) enthusiasm (b) jocoseness (c) sarcasm (d) indifference (e) irreverence

5. PLENARY: (a) wicked (b) adequate (c) incomplete (d) impoverished (e) careless

6. DEVIOUS: (a) saintly (b) slow (c) hasty (d) unwise (e) direct

7. HELIOCENTRIC: (a) concentric (b) epicentric (c) egocentric (d) geocentric (e) eccentric

8. CORPOREAL: (a) slender (b) underweight (c) rewarding (d) absent-minded (e) spiritual

9. PUSILLANIMOUS: (a) reluctant (b) lifeless (c) sensible (d) brave (e) domestic

10. DEROGATORY: (a) unquestioning (b) uncertain (c) complimentary (d) cheerful (e) tactful

MATCHING WORDS

Write the number of the *italicized* words. Beside each, write the number of the matching group of words from the second column.

1. *Incorporate* a business
2. *Satirize* the mayor
3. *Obviate* a difficulty
4. *Abrogate* an agreement
5. *Effervesce* gaily
6. *Replenish* the oil supply
7. Eyes that *scintillate*
8. *Cogitate* carefully
9. *Reanimate* a club
10. *Burlesque* a formal tea

1. declare it out of existence
2. make it full again
3. add or ask for gaiety
4. ponder or meditate
5. give it a legal body
6. give a humorous imitation of
7. bring it to life again
8. ridicule the follies of
9. sparkle and fizz
10. enliven with laughter
11. find a way around
12. twinkle, give forth sparks

THE RIGHT WORD

What word goes in each blank?

1. *Heli*um got its name from the fact it was first observed in the atmosphere of the __?__.

2. An iso*therm* is a line connecting points on the earth having the same mean __?__.

3. A pre*rog*ative is a prior __?__ that amounts to a privilege.

4. A *pleni*potentiary has __?__ power to act for his country.

5. A wind-lashed sea is im*petu*ous in that it __?__ a person who is in a ship or on shore.

6. Pre*scien*ce is __?__ beforehand.

7. *Helio*therapy is treatment of disease by means of __?__.

8. A *parl*ey between captains is a __?__.

9. Clocks which have been sy*nchron*ized keep __?__ together.

10. A *distorted drawing* of a famous man is a __?__.

EXTRA

1. Write a parody of a well-known poem.

2. Read a part of *Gulliver's Travels* which you have not read before and make a list of the human follies Swift is satirizing.

3. Read *The Animal Farm* by George Orwell, *The Screwtape Letters* by C. S. Lewis, or some other twentieth century satire. Write a brief report discussing what the author is satirizing and whether or not you think the satire is effective.

UNIT ELEVEN

Can you tell from its *root* which word is the best answer to each question?

1. Which word refers to the *end-place* where trains or buses stop?

2. Which word refers to *motherhood?*

3. Which word describes a weakness one is *born with?*

4. Which word describes an ape that is *man-like?*

5. Find the word which refers to something one inherits from his *father.*

6. Which word describes something that *belongs to the earth?*

7. Which word means *walk?*

8. Find the word which pertains to the *sea.*

9. Which word describes an animal that *has life both* on land and in the water?

perambulate
anthropoid
maternity
terrestrial
maritime
terminus
congenital
gratuity
amphibious
patrimony
dominion

This is a JACKPOT UNIT

253

Study List—TWENTY-SOME ROOTS

1.   -ALTER- . . . -HETERO- . . . .   other, different

To alter a dress is to change it; i.e., make it *other* or *different*. (See I, 5.)

To alternate between two pairs of shoes is to wear one pair and then the *other pair*. (See II, 8.)

A heterogeneous collection is a miscellaneous collection; i.e., one which contains items *other* than or *different* from each other.

Heterodox opinion is contrary to, or *other* than, the accepted, orthodox opinion.

2.   -AMBUL- . . . .   walk

An ambulatory patient in a hospital is one who is able to *walk;* he is not confined to bed.

A somnambulist is one who *walks* in his sleep.

The word *amble,* meaning "walk at an easy pace," comes from an Old French word which, in turn, derives from this Latin root.

3.   -DEXTER- . . . . . .   skillful (especially with one's hands)

Aunt Margaret is a dexterous or *skillful* seamstress.

A telephone operator needs dexterity or *skill*.

In Latin, *dexter* meant "right (hand)," hence, "skillful." The root also occurs in certain chemical terms, where it means "to the right or clockwise." (See I, 6).

4.   -DOMIN- . . . -DOMIT- . . . .   rule, govern; control

To dominate a son is to *control* him by strength or power. (See II, 6.)

A dominant factor is one which *controls* a situation.

Indomitable eagerness cannot be *controlled*.

See also *arch-* (I, 12) which expresses the idea of ruling as first or chief of those whom one controls.

5. **-FLU-, -FLUX-** . . . . flowing

The confluence of two rivers is their *flowing* together or meeting. What does *effluence* mean?

Superfluous comments are unnecessary, *flowing* above or beyond what is called for.

Our town has an influx of visitors every summer.

6. **-FORT-** . . . . strong; strength

To fortify a city is to make it *strong* against attack.

Fortitude is the *strong* endurance of suffering or hardship.

If you comfort a frightened child, you offer *strength* and sympathy to him.

See also *forte*, a musical term meaning "strong" or "loud."

7. **-FRATER(N)-, -FRATRI-** . . . . brother

A fraternal feeling is a *brother*ly feeling

A fraternity is a *brother*hood.

Fratricide is the killing of a *brother*.

Soror(i)- "sister," appears in *sorority* and *sororicide*.

8. **-GRATI-** . . . . free
   -GRATU- . . . . pleasing, agreeable

We had to pay for the coffee but the doughnuts were gratis (free of charge).

When a composition gratifies the teacher, it is *pleasing*. (See II, 7.)

To congratulate your brother on winning a prize is to express your *pleasure* at his success.

A gratuity in a hotel is a tip given because you find the room service *pleasing*.

Most of these words come from the Latin *gratus,* which means "pleasing." What does *persona non grata* mean?
Gratis comes from *gratia,* "a favor," and describes something done as a favor, without expectation of payment.
Cf. grateful, gratitude, ingratiate, gratuitous

9.   -MARI-, -MARINE- . . . . **sea**

Maritime provinces are those lying along the *sea*.

A submarine is a boat that can go under the *sea*.

Marine biology is the study of the plant and animal life of the *sea*.

Aquamarine is the color of *sea* water.

10.   -MATER(N)-, -MATR- . . . -METRO- . . . . **mother**

Maternal instincts are those of a *mother*.

A woman who is described as matronly is *motherly* and, as a rule, not very young.

A matron is a married woman who is probably a *mother*.

Nero committed matricide: he killed his *mother*.

A metropolis is an important city; i.e., a *mother* city.

Matrimony means "marriage," but comes from the Latin *mater,* "mother."
Cf. matrix

11.   -MUTE- . . . . **change**

Alchemists tried to transmute baser metals into gold.

The governor may commute the man's sentence to life imprisonment.

An immutable decree is one that nothing can *change*. (See III, 8.)

A biological mutation is a sudden variation in a plant or animal which causes the offspring to differ from the parents.

The variation is due to changes within the chromosomes or genes.

The Latin root is *mutare* "to change." The word *mute* (I, 3), in the sense of "dumb," comes from the Latin *mutus,* "not speaking."

12. -NASC- . . . . -GEN- . . . . born, birth

A nascent culture is one which is *new-born* or just coming into being.

When a country experiences a renascence in art, there is a *rebirth* or revival of interest after a time of indifference.

The genesis of an idea is its *birth* or origin.

A congenital defect is one with which a person is *born.*

Cf. *genealogy, gene, genetic(s), genitive, genethliac*

13. -NAUT- . . . . sail(or), ship(s)

A Greek myth tells of the Argonauts (*sailors* of the ship Argo), who accompanied Jason on his quest for the Golden Fleece.

Nautical terms are those pertaining to *ships* and sailing.

14. -PATR(I)- . . . . father

A patrimony is an inheritance from one's *father.*

"Gloria Patri" means "Glory to the *Father.*"

To repatriate a person is to re-establish him in his *fatherland.*

Cf. *patriarch* (I, 12), *patriot, compatriot, expatriate* (II, 1 under *banish*)

15. -POLIT- . . . . -CIVI- . . . . citizen
    -URB- . . . . -POLI- . . . . city

The word politics originally meant "pertaining to *city* government."

Civic pride is the pride a *citizen* takes in his home town.

Suburban areas are near a *city.*

An urbane person is courteous and polished, acquainted with the manners of *city* society.

A cosmopolis is a cosmopolitan city, one which has citizens from all over the world *(kosmos)*.

Cf. Annapolis, Minneapolis, political, politician, interurban, civilian, civilize, civil (II, 8)

16. **-SCEND-** . . . . **climb**

It took several days to ascend or *climb* Mt. Everest.

The beauty of the Rocky Mountains transcends words.

17. **-SIST-** . . . . **-STIT-** . . . . **stand(ing), set**

If your behavior is consistent, your actions today are in harmony with your actions yesterday. Your actions *stand* together.

A persistent worker is one who continues even in the face of difficulties. (The word originally meant *"standing through."*)

Twelve months constitute a year. The months are *set* together to form a year.

A destitute person is one who is abandoned or in extreme want. He has been *set* down from what he needs.

To make restitution is to make good any loss or damage, to *set* things back again as they were.

18. **-TERMIN-** . . . . **-FINI-** . . . . **end, limit, boundary**

To terminate a contract is to *end* it. (See I, 8.)

An interminable speech appears to have no *end*.

Life is finite because it has a *limit* or boundary, but space appears to be infinite; i.e., without an *end*.

The definition of a term presents the *limits* or *boundaries* of its meaning.

19. -TERR-, -TERRA- . . . -GEO- . . . . land, earth

Much territory in the West is arid.

The country is famous for its cold winters and rugged terrain or *land*.

Geology is the study of the *earth* and its make-up.

The geocentric altitude of a star is the altitude as measured from the center of the *earth*.

Cf. terrace, terra firma, terrestrial; geodesy, geodetic, geomancy

20. -VIR- . . . -ANTHROPO- . . . . man

To speak with virile forcefulness is to speak in a *manly* and powerful way. (See II, 3.)

Anthropology is the science which studies the development, customs, and beliefs of *man*.

An anthropoid ape is a *manlike* ape.

Caution: Latin has several roots containing -vir-, all of which have different meanings. *Virtue* comes from the Latin *virtus*, "strength." The root -viri-, as in *viridity*, means "green," and *virulent* comes from *virus*, "a poison."
Cf. triumvirate (I, 12)

Note: The roots -hetero-, -metro-, -poli-, geo-, and -anthropo- come from Greek. The others are of Latin origin.

Study List—MORE PREFIXES

1. AMBI- . . . AMPHI- . . . . both

A person who is ambidextrous uses *both* hands with equal ease.

Amphibious life can exist *both* in water and on land.

Ambiguous, which seems to belong in this group, actually comes from the Latin *amb*, "around," and *agere*, "to drive": An ambiguous answer can be understood in at least two different ways.

2. **MAGNA-, MAGNI-** . . . . large, great, big

A <u>magna</u>te is a *big* or dominant figure in business, industry, or some other field.

A microscope will <u>magni</u>fy or *enlarge* a germ so that it can be seen.

The <u>magni</u>tude of a task is its *bigness*.

Cf. magnanimous, magniloquent, magnificent; Magna Charta

3. **MAL-** . . . . ill; evil, wrongful

<u>Mal</u>ice is *ill* will.

To <u>mal</u>ign someone is to speak *evil* of him. (See *malignity* in II, 9.)

A <u>mal</u>ady is an *illness;* a <u>mal</u>ingerer is one who pretends *illness* to escape his duty.

A <u>mal</u>evolent person is one who wishes *evil* to other people.

Cf. maladjustment, malpractice, malfeasance, malformation; malcontent; mal de mer

4. **MAN-** . . . **CHIRO-** . . . . hand

A <u>man</u>uscript was originally a book or paper written by *hand*.

A <u>man</u>ual is a *handbook*.

<u>Chiro</u>graphy is *hand* writing.

<u>Chiro</u>practic is a system of adjusting the joints by *hand* in an attempt to cure disease.

5. **RETRO-** . . . . backward, behind

To <u>retro</u>gress is to move *backward*.

A <u>retro</u>active decision extends *backward* to an earlier action.

The <u>retro</u>renal area of the body is *behind* the kidneys.

Cf. retrospect, retrocession, retrograde

Note: In this group, the roots *amphi-*, and *chiro-* are of Greek origin.

FIRST PRACTICE SET

What word goes in each blank? Where there are two in a sentence, one involves a root or prefix from an earlier unit.

1. A person convicted of *mal*practice has done something __?__.

2. To have *dom*inion over twenty tribes is to __?__ them.

3. An *interurban* bus operates __?__ two __?__.

4. To per*ambul*ate in the park is to __?__ through it.

5. A *mal*ignant disease is especially __?__.

6. A *patri*mony is an inheritance from one's __?__.

7. To in*grati*ate oneself with John's mother is to make oneself __?__ to her.

8. *Sororicide* is the __?__ of one's __?__.

9. *Geo*graphy is the science which describes the __?__.

10. If you are fond of *retrospecti*on, you like to __?__ __?__ at former periods in your life.

11. Railroad lines which are co*terminous* have their __?__ together.

12. When she conde*scends*, she __?__ down to your level.

13. To re*sist* is to __?__ against something or oppose it.

14. A *terra*ce is a raised area of __?__.

15. A mis*anthrope* is a person who dislikes __?__.

16. In wartime, does an *amphi*bious operation take place on land, at sea, or __?__?

17. If you have no *alter*native, you have no __?__ choice.

18. A wealthy person is said to be af*flu*ent because money __?__ to or toward him quite readily.

19. *Ambidexter*ity is skill with __?__ __?__.

20. *Chiro*mancy is fortune telling by a study of the __?__. It is better known as __?__.

SECOND PRACTICE SET

Which word from this unit best replaces each *italicized* word or group of words?

1. St. Louis is located at the *flowing together* of the Mississippi and Missouri Rivers.

2. The man had *uncontrollable* courage.

3. Are television and the movies bringing a *rebirth* of interest in Shakespeare's plays?

4. It sometimes takes *strong endurance* to resist temptation.

5. George's collection of hats was *miscellaneous and mixed*.

6. As a boy, Mark Twain learned many *sailing* terms.

7. The invention of the steam engine signaled the *birth* of the industrial age.

8. The laws of gravity appear *unchangeable*.

9. Few people can honestly say, as Lincoln was able to, that they have *ill will* toward none.

10. The new law will be *in effect back* to the first of the year.

11. The *bigness* of the national debt is hard to visualize.

12. Dolls and puppies appeal to a girl's *motherly* instincts.

13. Favorable comments about the book will *please* the author immensely.

14. Bad weather made the crossing seem *without an end*.

15. Cain was guilty of *killing a brother*.

16. The parchment was unrolled and proved to be a *handwritten selection* dating back to the Middle Ages.

17. Alaska, the *land area* we bought from Russia, is very thinly populated.

18. The politician's answer to the reporter's question was deliberately vague and *capable of being interpreted in different ways*.

19. The population of San Francisco is *made up of people from many foreign cities.*

20. Is it necessary to give the guide a *tip* after we have completed the tour?

THIRD PRACTICE SET

Which of the lettered items is most nearly **opposite** in meaning to the word in capital letters?

1. DEXTEROUS: (a) unwise (b) clumsy (c) crafty (d) serious (e) sour

2. EFFLUENCE: (a) poverty (b) humility (c) distress (d) self-denial (e) self-containment

3. DOMINATE: (a) submit (b) apologize (c) resent (d) become small (e) subvert

4. TERRESTRIAL: (a) unmagnetic (b) celestial (c) urbane (d) unexciting (e) unstable

5. INFINITE: (a) earthly (b) cautious (c) extensive (d) limited (e) difficult

6. CONSISTENT: (a) erratic (b) disrespectful (c) without standing (d) enduring (e) egotistical

7. MAGNATE: (a) without magnetism (b) left-handed (c) nonentity (d) failure (e) rogue

8. MUTABLE: (a) invariable (b) talkative (c) proud (d) irregular (e) smooth

9. NASCENT: (a) congenital (b) uncongenial (c) dexterous (d) ungrateful (e) dying out

10. URBANE: (a) beneficial (b) robust (c) unpolished (d) trustworthy (e) disagreeable

REPLACEMENTS

Which word from this unit best replaces each *italicized* word or group of words?

1. A receptionist should avoid conversation that is *flowing-beyond-what-is-necessary*.

2. Lady Macbeth was a *sleep walker*.

3. The ruins of old walls still show how the city was once *made strong* against enemy attacks.

4. Bob couldn't decide whether or not he wanted to join the *brotherhood*.

5. The foreign ambassador had to return to his own country when our government declared that he was *someone-not-pleasing-or-welcome*.

6. Unfailing friendliness will *change (the base metal of)* distrust into confidence.

7. Her new dress is *the color of sea water*.

8. The boy's deafness is *the kind he was born with*.

9. A business will *move backward* if it does not move forward.

10. Tom's father is writing a *handbook* for golfers.

BONUS

1. From the material in this unit, build as many adjective pairs as you can, such as *alterable* and *unalterable*.

2. Look up and report on the Argonauts, the Renaissance, and the Magna Charta.

ΑΒΓΔ
ΕΖΗΘ
ΙΚΛΜ
ΝΞΟΠ
ΡϹΤΥΦΧΨΩ

UNIT TWELVE

Find a word from the list to match each phrase:

1. Film that responds to light of all colors: __?__

2. A group made up of people having the same background and similar ways: __?__

3. A period in history when men had learned to use polished stone implements and make pottery but had not learned to use metal: __?__

4. One who seems to know everything: __?__

5. A record of the motions and duration of an earthquake: __?__

6. A person who enjoys being with a flock of other people: __?__

7. Something which lasts but for a day: __?__

8. A drowsy child: __?__

9. A shapeless mass of putty: __?__

seismographic
homogeneous
orthopedic
somnolent
neolithic
panchromatic
amorphous
infinitesimal
omniscient
gregarious
ephemeral
euphemistic

This is a JACKPOT UNIT

Word List—PREFIXES

1. AUTO- . . . . self

An autobiography is a biography about *oneself*.

An autonomous tribe is *self*-governing; i.e., has its own laws.

Cf. autogenous, autohypnosis, autosuggestion; autopsy; autograph

2. BENE- . . . **EU-** . . . . well or good

A benefactor is a person who does *good* deeds.

A beneficent impulse is an impulse for doing something *good*.

A euphemism is a *good* or pleasant phrase which expresses an idea that is considered unpleasant. For instance, "to pass away" is a euphemism for "die."

3. EPI- . . . . upon, above

The epidermis is the outer layer of the skin; i.e., the layer that is *upon* the dermis (sensitive inner layer).

An epithet is a title or name put *upon* someone.

An epitaph is an inscription *upon* a tombstone (II, 5).

The epicenter of an earthquake is the point on the earth's surface *above* the focus of the quake.

4. HOMO- . . . . same, similar

To homogenize milk is to make it all the *same* by breaking down and blending the fat particles.

The result is a homogeneous or uniform mixture in which the cream no longer becomes separated and rises to the surface.

A homonym is a word which has the *same* pronunciation as another word but a different meaning and often a different spelling: *hold,* "to grasp," and *hold,* "interior of a ship," are homonyms, as are *meet* and *meat.*

5. HYDR-, HYDRO- . . . . water

To dehydrate prunes is to take the *water* out of them.

A hydrant is an outlet through which *water* may be drawn from the waterworks.

A hydroelectric plant produces electricity from *water* power.

Cf. *hydrophobia, hydrotherapy, hydraulic*

6. MICRO- . . . . very or extremely small

Microfilm is used for keeping photographic records of printed material in very *small* space.

Microorganisms or bacteria are extremely *small.*

7. NEO- . . . . new

A neophyte is a *new* convert to religion or a beginner in any field.

A neologism is a *new* word, phrase, or way of speaking.

Neon was so called when it was discovered because it was a *new* gas.

The Neolithic stage in human history was the *New* Stone Age.

The root *-nov-,* which also means "new," is discussed in I, 11.
The root *-lith-* means "stone."
Cf. *monolithic, paleolithic, lithograph*

8. OMNI- . . . **PAN-** . . . . all, every

An omniscient person seems to know *everything.*

Omnipotent Deity is *All*-Powerful.

A carnivorous (II, 10) animal eats only meat, but an

omnivorous animal eats both meat and vegetables or plants.
An <u>omni</u>vorous reader is a person who is fond of *all* kinds of
reading—novels, poems, plays, and so on.

A <u>Pan</u>-American conference involves *all* of the American
nations.

<u>Pan</u>chromatic film is sensitive to light of *every* color.

A <u>pan</u>acea is a cure-*all* remedy.

A <u>pan</u>theistic religion is one which identifies the universe
with God, or one which sanctions the worship of many gods.

9. **ORTHO-** . . . . **correct, true; right; straight**

<u>Ortho</u>graphy is *correct* spelling.

An <u>ortho</u>gonal figure has *right* angles.

An <u>ortho</u>dontist makes teeth *straight*.

Cf. orthodox

10. **PRIM-** . . . . **first, early**

The <u>prim</u>ary grades are the *first* or early grades.

<u>Prim</u>itive dwellings were man's *first* or early homes—prob-
ably caves.

<u>Prim</u>ogeniture is the inheritance of an estate by the *first*-born
or oldest son.

11. **PSEUDO-** . . . . **false; seeming**

A <u>pseudo</u>-scientific explanation is an explanation which is
seemingly scientific but not actually so.

A <u>pseudo</u>-classic is a *seeming* classic; i.e., a work which
pretends to be, or is wrongly considered, a classic.

12. **TELE-** . . . . **at a distance, far away**

<u>Tele</u>vision enables you to see pictures of something that is
happening *far away*.

Telepathy is thought transference, the communication from one mind to another, perhaps at a *distance*.

Note: The roots *bene-, nov-, omni-, prim-* are from Latin. The other roots are Greek.

Word List— ROOTS, LARGELY GREEK

1. **-CRAT-, -CRACY- . . . . -POT-** . . . . . power(ful), strength

    An autocrat is a ruler who holds absolute *power* himself.

    Democracy is a form of government in which the *power* is retained by the people.

    A potent chemical is a *power*ful one (I, 3).

    The potential of a battery is its *power* in volts or in energy; a potential market for a product is a possible market which does not yet exist in reality.

2. **-DOC- . . . . -DOCTRIN- . . . . -DOX-** . . teacher, teaching, opinion

    A docile child is easily *taught*. He is also manageable and obedient.

    The doctrines of a church are its *teachings*.

    To indoctrinate is to *teach* or instruct in the principles of something. (The word is often used in an unfavorable sense to imply that such teaching is prejudiced or one-sided.)

    A belief is orthodox if it accords with what a church or other group holds is the right *opinion*. (The word has acquired the additional meaning of "conventional.")

    Cf. heterodox (II, 11), *ortho-* (II, 12)
    The word *pedagogue,* "teacher," comes from two Greek words meaning "boy" and "leader." A course in pedagogy deals with methods and principles of teaching.

3. -DIURN- . . . . -JOURN- . . . . -EPHEMER- . . . . . day, daily

The <u>diurn</u>al course of the sun is its *daily* route across the sky.

A <u>journ</u>al is a *daily* record of experiences and thoughts.

<u>Ephemer</u>al fame literally lasts but for a *day*.

Both *-diurn-* and *-journ-* come from the Latin *dies,* meaning "day": *Dies Irae,* Day of Wrath. *-Journ-* comes by way of French.
A journey was once a day's work or a day's travel.
A journeyman in the medieval guilds was so called because he was hired by the day.

4. -GRAPH- . . . . -GRAM- . . . . write, writing; record

Your auto<u>graph</u> is your signature; i.e., your name as you *write* it.

An epi<u>gram</u> was originally a pungent or witty bit of *writing* upon some topic. Today, it may be any clever thought tersely expressed, whether or not it is written down.

A tele<u>gram</u> is the *written* text of a message which has been sent by electricity, usually across a considerable distance.

Cf. dictograph, photograph, pantograph, orthography, pseudepigrapha, graphology

5. -GREG- . . . . forming a herd or flock

A <u>greg</u>arious person enjoys being in a group or *flock* of people. He is sociable.

To con<u>greg</u>ate is to *flock* together.

When a hospital se<u>greg</u>ates patients with contagious diseases, it separates them from other patients; i.e., sets them apart from the *flock*.

6. -JUNC- . . . . -JUG(A)- . . . . join

A <u>junc</u>tion of two roads is the place where they *join*.

To con<u>jug</u>ate a verb is to give in order its inflected forms; i.e., to *join* these forms in a complete paradigm.

Conjugal vows are those which *join* persons in marriage.

The root -*jug(a)*- goes back to the Latin *jugum*, "a yoke." Thus, to sub-jugate a defeated enemy originally meant to put him under a yoke.
Cf. conjunction, injunction

7. -JURIS- . . . . law, right, justice
    -JURE- . . . . swear

To have jurisdiction over a territory is to have the *right* to say what is done; i.e., to govern it.

Jurisprudence is the science of *law* or a system of laws.

To perjure oneself is to *swear* falsely (II, 5).

To abjure bad habits is to *swear* off or renounce them.

A juror is literally *one who takes an oath*, and a group of jurors is a jury.

In folklore, when a witch conjures up a spirit, she *swears* a sacred oath or invokes a magic name.

Justice comes from the Latin *justus*, "just."
Jurisdiction and *injure* are from *jus, juris*, "a law."
Judge, judgment, judicial, judicious and other *Jud* Words come from Latin *judex*, "a judge."
Cf. adjudicate

8. -LIBER- . . . . free

To liberate a prisoner is to set him *free* (I, 8).

A liberal education *frees* one from narrowness and ignorance about life (II, 8).

To liberalize a health plan is to make it *freer* in terms of benefits.

A libertine is a person *free* from moral restraints and there-fore dissolute.

These words come from the Latin adjective *liber*, meaning "free." The word *library* comes from the Latin noun *liber*, "a book," as does the word *libel*. (See II, 5.)
Cf. illiberal, libertarian

9.   -MIGR(A)- . . . .   move (from place to place), travel

The Pilgrims migrated to America.

Migratory workers *travel* from one region to another, harvesting crops.

Immigrants *travel* into a country, emigrants go forth to live in some other country.

Cf. migrants, transmigration

10.   -MORPH- . . . .   form, shape

Anthropomorphic art represents a deity in human *form* or gives human characteristics to something not human.

An amorphous mass has no definite *shape*.

Morphology is a branch of biology dealing with the *form* of plants and animals.

11.   -(O)NYM- . . . .   a name

A pseudonym is a false *name*—a pen name, not an alias.

An anonym is a person of unknown *name*.

An anonymous letter is unsigned, sent with no *name* attached—usually because the writer is afraid to disclose his name.

An acronym is a name composed of the first letters (literally, the tips) of a long title or phrase. Thus NATO is an acronym for North Atlantic Treaty Organization.

Cf. antonym, homonym, synonym, eponym

12.   -SEQU-, -SECUT- . . . .   follow

A sequence is a series of items which *follow* one another.

The consequences of a decision are the events which *follow* together as a result of it.

Consecutive events *follow* one another.

Cf. sequel, execute, persecute, inconsequential

13. **-SOMN- . . . . -DORM-** . . . . **sleep**

A somnolent audience is drowsy or *sleepy*.

Somniferous speeches or drugs are *sleep*-inducing.

Insomnia is *sleep*lessness.

A dormitory is literally a place for *sleep*.

A dormant bear in a log is *asleep* for the winter.

Cf. somnambulist (II, 11 under *-ambulo-*)

FIRST PRACTICE SET

What is the meaning of each *italicized* root or prefix?

1. The forest *prim*eval is the __?__ forest before men disturbed it.

2. A *micro*groove record has __?__ grooves.

3. The *epi*cardium is the inner layer (part) of the pericardium. It lies __?__ the heart.

4. The *bene*diction at the end of the service is the blessing, the act of saying __?__.

5. An *auto*mat is a restaurant which offers __?__ service.

6. To discuss exports in the ag*greg*ate is to __?__ them together or discuss them as a whole.

7. A seismo*graph* makes a __?__ record of an earthquake.

8. A *di*ary is a __?__-by-__?__ account of one's experiences.

9. A *tele*photo lens on a camera gives a large image of a __?__ object.

10. *Morph*ology deals with the __?__ and structure of plants and animals.

11. In*somn*ia is inability to __?__.

12. Con*secu*tive days are those which __?__ each other.

13. A pleni*poten*tiary is an ambassador given full __?__ to act.

14. A *neo*plasm is a __?__ growth of some kind.

15. An *ortho*pedic doctor makes children's deformities __?__.

16. A *pan*acea is a dose or plan which will cure __?__ ills or evils.

17. A pluto*crat* is one whose __?__ lies in his wealth.

18. *Eu*phoria is a state of feeling especially __?__.

19. A patro*nym*ic is a __?__ based on one's father's.

20. The theory of trans*migr*ation holds that the soul __?__s from one body to another.

21. A *hydro*plane is one which can land on __?__.

22. An *omni*present spirit is present __?__ at the same time.

23. A bachelor *juris* is a "bachelor" of __?__.

24. A con*junc*tion is a word which __?__s together two statements.

25. *Hom*onyms are words or names whose pronunciation is the __?__ but whose meanings differ.

SECOND PRACTICE SET

Which word from this unit best replaces each *italicized* word or group of words?

1. The inventor of the *instrument for seeing very small objects* was a *person who did good things* for all mankind.

2. The *point above the center* of the earthquake is near the *joining point* of two valleys.

3. Birds are *inclined to form flocks* during their *trips from one place to another*.

4. The hot sun *takes the water from* one's body when large areas of the *outer skin* are exposed too long.

5. *New-Stone-Age* men lived in dwellings which were *of a very early type* and small.

6. A new *man who straightens teeth* moved to town and Mary, who collects *signatures* of famous people, mistook him for an actor.

7. His plans for the future were vague and *shapeless,* and his enthusiasm was *likely to last only a day.*

8. The book is a *seeming classic,* written in the form of a *daily record.*

9. The Philippine Islands have been *self-governing* since the United States acted to *set free* this territory.

10. Someone sent the local police *unsigned* letters about illegal activities in areas where the local police have *the right to say what is done.*

11. The unruly children became quiet and *teachable* because they felt that the new principal was *all-powerful.*

12. Sheep are *fond of flocking together.* They are not *able to eat everything.*

THIRD PRACTICE SET

Which of the lettered units is most nearly **opposite** in meaning to the capitalized word?

1. BENEFICENT: (a) contemptible (b) impoverished (c) malicious (d) unresourceful (e) hot-tempered

2. CONGREGATE: (a) disperse (b) dismiss (c) make smaller (d) dissociate (e) undermine

3. SOMNOLENT: (a) hopeful (b) alert (c) oratorical (d) competent (e) sleepy

4. OMNISCIENT: (a) blind (b) obtuse (c) unimaginative (d) unscientific (e) crassly ignorant

5. SEGREGATE: (a) isolate (b) integrate (c) restore (d) announce (e) emancipate

6. POTENT: (a) fierce (b) slow (c) cautious (d) weak (e) idle

7. CONSEQUENTIAL: (a) trivial (b) simple (c) disconnected (d) reluctant (e) uncooperative

8. DEMOCRACY: (a) hierarchy (b) oligarchy (c) monarchy (d) plutocracy (e) matriarchy

9. ANTONYM: (a) homonym (b) pseudonym (c) synonym (d) anonym (e) acronym

10. DORMANT: (a) living in a dormitory (b) slow witted (c) reluctant (d) aggressive (e) active

MATCHING WORDS

On a separate sheet, write the numbers of the *italicized* words. Beside each, write the number of the matching word or group of words from the second column.

1. A terse *epigram*
2. A new *acronym*
3. *Sequel* to the accident
4. *Omnipotence* of an emperor
5. *Homogeneity* of a group of people
6. Victim of *primogeniture*
7. Persistent *insomnia*
8. Kindly *pedagogue*
9. Irregular *conjugation*
10. A scientific *neologism*

1. uniformity
2. teacher
3. term for a model husband
4. set of verb forms
5. new word or phrase
6. name from first letters of a group of words
7. inheritance by firstborn
8. witty sentence or remark
9. incident which follows
10. new sense of power
11. sleeplessness
12. unlimited power

FINAL TESTS

What base word from the unit best replaces each *italicized* word or group of words?

UNIT 1

1. She knows he will *devise* some way to *decrease in value* her claim to the property.
2. The man's behavior was *typical of old age* but does not *form* an adequate reason for setting aside his will.
3. An *extremely dry* climate may help cure *constant* sinusitis.
4. A teacher can quickly *observe the differences* between a *fierce* person and a really angry one.
5. Her eyes will really *widen* when she finds that her election is *in-effect-but-not-actually* a certainty.
6. An *open* act of violence led to other disturbances which were *within-the-country* but of world-wide importance.
7. The terrifying ordeal made her too *wildly emotional* to *assent* to anything.
8. Doctors are *doubtful* about prescribing even a very small dose of a *deadly* poison.
9. The lawyer did *refer casually* to his efforts to *verify* the neighbor's complaint.
10. She *drove away* her misgivings as the *marriage* day drew nearer.

UNIT 2

1. He is a *person of no importance,* but he is not *a person of low intelligence.*
2. In the skit, George had to *imitate* the majestic dignity of a *supreme ruler.*

3. "You *magnify* my eagerness to *give like for like* for the injury you did me," Mr. Howe explained.

4. The new law will *speed up* the admission of refugees and have less tendency to inflict on them any *treatment which would lower self-respect.*

5. The speaker had lost his notes, and as he walked toward the *speaker's platform,* he tried to *compose off-hand* some arguments against the legislation.

6. His *unyielding firmness* may *make up* for his lack of resourcefulness.

7. The king ordered a herald to *make known* his decision about education, using *an expressed comparison* which compared it with the sun.

8. The man-made *small body revolving around a planet* is hardly on *an equality* with the moon.

9. Attempts to *bring back to life* the ski club succeeded for a while, but, after the loss of its faculty sponsor, it never *regained strength.*

10. Failure to have a *number needed to transact business* will *endanger* the society's chances for deciding the matter at this meeting.

UNIT 3

1. Like many *inhabitants* of the ocean, the seal spends part of the time on land. In this respect he has a *relationship* with the walrus.

2. Dreams of great *wealth* proved to be only *deception.*

3. Modern skyscrapers may not seem *enormous* to *future generaations.*

4. Operations on the ear require special *exactness* because of its *nearness* to the brain.

5. A watchmaker is *skillful* in making adjustments, and he works with *catlike* delicacy.

6. His *smooth, easy* manner of speaking gave him an advantage when he had to give *spur-of-the-moment* talks.

7. The monthly meetings were *uninteresting* affairs, and the refreshments were *average*.

8. Among some primitive tribes, *infliction of injury as a recompense* for murder is the duty of the victim's nearest male relative. Such action is not *impulsive* but required by custom.

9. The painter's work is always *masculine*. Sometimes he uses only primary colors, but at other times, he uses *artful, delicate* shades.

10. The *recollections* were as *fleeting* as the adventures that gave rise to them.

UNIT 4

1. *Stern* behavior is often *lacking* in charm.

2. An *eager* chess player is capable of *unyielding* logic.

3. Any *adequately qualified* mechanic will give you *clearly stated* answers.

4. Jane is *modest and sedate,* but her sister is spoiled and *subject to whims.*

5. He asked, in a *complaining* tone, why the rules about smoking were so *strict*.

6. He was very *exact* about observing them, however, just as he is *scrupulous in details* about all of his personal habits.

7. Jack, who was always *ready for a fight,* protested when Bob accused him of being *low-class* in his tastes.

8. Life after death remains an *unfathomable* mystery but not a *doleful* subject.

9. His *firmly established* reading habits should keep him from being too *gloomy* about being an orphan.

10. The arrival of the supply ship was *timely* because the difficulties of our situation were *hard-to-overcome*.

UNIT 5

1. The *lawsuit* will extend into the next *financial* year.

2. *Insurance-risk* figures probably show that people in *lawful* kinds of business live longer.

3. The court agreed that he had been a victim of *written defamation*. His business was unusually *remunerative* but legal.

4. It will be necessary to *institute legal proceedings against* the engineer if he *testifies falsely* himself.

5. Due to the loss of the $50,000 which the bookkeeper *took by fraud,* there will be a *shortage of funds* at the end of the year.

6. The jury which *charged* him is not the one which later voted that his partner should be *released from the charge.*

7. The plaintiff *declares* that he never received the $10,000 which was *given in a will* to him by his late aunt.

8. As a result of new evidence, the treasurer may find himself *involved in a crime.* He obviously *paid out* funds without being authorized to do so.

9. The *tombstone inscription* expresses the mother's sense of *desolation and loss.*

10. After the *burial,* several more notes arrived containing *expressions of sympathy.*

UNIT 6

1. He must *hold himself back* from criticism until he can *draw forth* the facts.

2. Gwen would not *come down to the level of* such *double-dealing* as her sister proposed.

3. He could not *dispel* his fears and, as a result of sorrow and worry, he became *very lean.*

4. Friends *urged* him regularly to overcome his *abnormal desire for wealth.*

5. This desire *thoroughly irritates* them, and it will *control* him completely in time.

6. Newspaper editorials *protest against* the ugliness of the *front* of the War Memorial Building.

7. The gypsy, who claimed to be a *person with preternatural insight,* foretold an early end to the *angry dispute* between the two friends.

8. When the police *arrested* them, the fugitives looked like two *specters.*

9. The editor's refusal to *admit* that he had supported a dishonest candidate subjected him to a heavy *onslaught* of angry abuse.

10. The thief's *accomplice* is an *unnaturalized foreigner.*

UNIT 7

1. He *wavers* about taking this job, and his wife is *doubtful* about whether he will like it.

2. Her success will *please* her father and *justify* his confidence in her.

3. Mr. Moore is inclined to *evade the truth* about his big deals, and this trait *debases* my confidence in him.

4. Ralph will not *put up with* any interference, and yet he is not so *full of foresight* as he ought to be.

5. The boys in the downtown gang are *disorderly* and *depraved.*

6. The bee sting gave him a *bulging* nose in the middle of his *pale* face.

7. The *unvarying* noise of the riveting machines soon rendered us *mute.*

8. The club will *exclude* him if he keeps *repeating* his complaint about the refreshments served at meetings.

9. The spring rain, which was *only-at-intervals,* soon *transformed* the flower garden.

10. When someone offers you candy, do not *closely examine* the entire box before making up your mind. This is a *childish* practice.

UNIT 8

1. The influenza, which was *in the beginning stages,* made him feel miserable and lowered his *mental spirit.*
2. *Laziness* made it easy to accept the *mistaken idea* that hard work is useless.
3. The *rise and fall* of the barometer shows how rain and fair weather *follow each other by turn.*
4. *Fervent* tourists do not consider travel a *useless* pastime.
5. Her plan to acquire a *mind-freeing* education was really a *trick* to escape having to work in an office.
6. The boy's *peculiar* behavior revealed that he was *blame-worthy* in the loss of the money.
7. The doctor is a *kindly* but *self-satisfied* person.
8. Claims made for the importance of *nonmilitary* defense are quite *believable.*
9. According to *handed-down story,* insanity was the *punishment* that came to the Babylonian king.
10. A stranger in town had the *rashness* to question the editor's *truthfulness.*

UNIT 9

1. The bull appears *sullenly ill-humored* and *warlike.*
2. Brusqueness is a *pardonable* fault if it does not spring from *bitter ill will.*
3. He showed his *pretense of being what he was not* by claiming to be abstemious when his appearance accused him of *eating to excess.*
4. He is an *inventive* mechanic whose *terse* comments puzzle some of his customers.
5. The *fearless* police officer caught the *poisonous* cobra which had escaped.
6. It was *opinion differing from the accepted view* to comment aloud on the *moral corruptness* of Nero's court.
7. Some household cleaning fluids contain a very *treacherous* and, in sufficient quantities, a *highly injurious* poison.

8. Warned to be *alert to danger,* the guard searched even travelers whose *apparent* business appeared completely innocent.
9. It was difficult to be *hopeful* when the pestilence was apparently *present everywhere.*
10. We had a *combative* team, *unmindful of* hardships.

UNIT 10

1. Her *liveliness* added to the *boisterous gaiety* of the party.
2. Tom feared the coach's *mockery* if he failed more than he did the *light-mindedness* of his teammates.
3. Attendants in a state hospital find that *coaxing* and *a joking manner* help win cooperation from the patients.
4. The skit is a *humorous take-off* of a business executive and his *irritable-impatient* secretary.
5. *Rapid witty conversation* should be free from *a spirit of strong hostility.*
6. At a track meet, he runs like the wind *in human form,* and it is a strange *effect caused by contrast between appearance and actuality* that his name should be Ledd.
7. We had to name the first five Presidents in *time* order—the full name and not just the *name each was known by.*
8. *Bodily* punishment was the boy's retribution for the *uncomplimentary* remark he made to a guest.
9. Her talk is *trifling* nonsense rather than the kind of *joking levity* she intends.
10. The secret of *plants that turn toward the sun* may be some kind of *heat-sensitive* reaction.

UNIT 11

1. Doris married an expert in *sea* engineering, but she still cannot understand *sailing* terms.
2. A *handbook* might help if she would continue, or *stand through,* in her study until she mastered the subject.
3. Japan's need for more *land* is a problem of importance and *largeness.*

4. Those who do not go forward *move backward,* and those who do not *climb* toward a goal tend to slip back.
5. The patient in the next room, who is *able-to-walk,* is a member of the *brotherhood* to which I belong.
6. The convict was about to give away his very *miscellaneous* assortment of rocks and minerals when the governor *changed* his sentence to life imprisonment.
7. The girl's *illness* was not serious, and she went back to college, where she is majoring in *the science which studies mankind.*
8. The city council voted to *put an end to* its contract for the repair of streets in *near-the-city* areas.
9. The *rebirth* of interest in Egypt will *please* a neighbor whose hobby is Egyptology.
10. *Strong perseverance* is his *controlling* trait in emergencies.

UNIT 12

1. He keeps a *daily record* to provide material for his *self-biography* some day.
2. The hospital needs *people who do good* to help organize a *powerful* appeal for funds.
3. An *unsigned* letter accused the governor of behaving like a typical *person who holds the power himself.*
4. Beeswax is a rather *shapeless* substance, which is quite *uniform or the same all the way through.*
5. Dr. Hertz will *travel forth* to Europe to continue his research in *thought transference.*
6. Are you *all-knowing* enough to list the major battles of World War II in the correct order; i.e., *as-they-follow-one-another?*
7. A *cure-all remedy,* by its very impossibility, can have only *false-seeming* science as its basis.
8. "Snafu" was a *new word* of World War II, an *expression-made-of-the-first-letters-of-words* for "situation normal: all fouled up."
9. *The science of law* attracts many of the best minds, but it is difficult for a *new person* (beginner).
10. The bulbs are *with-the-water-taken-out* and *inactive ("asleep")* during the winter.

DIVISION TESTS

Write down the number of the definition that goes with each *italicized* word.

UNITS 1, 2, 3

SECTION 1

1. Cars *depreciate*
2. *Compensate* for lost time
3. He will *acquiesce*
4. *Impale* with a sharp glance
5. *Dilate* at length
6. Votes *constitute* a victory
7. *Promulgate* the news
8. *Corroborate* a claim
9. *Retaliate* promptly
10. *Simulate* sorrow

1. form or compose
2. enlarge upon or expand
3. claim as one's own
4. make up for, pay
5. reject reluctantly
6. assent, agree quietly
7. give like for like (especially evil)
8. feign, imitate, pretend
9. make known, publish
10. decrease in value
11. pierce or thrust through
12. verify or confirm

SECTION 2

1. *Facile* wits
2. *Dubious* praise
3. *Lethal* gas
4. *Mediocre* skill
5. *Senile* feebleness
6. *Prodigious* courage
7. *Overt* challenge
8. *Subtle* treachery
9. *Transient* thoughts
10. *Chronic* fears

1. open, unconcealed
2. delicate, artful
3. bold, daring
4. smooth working
5. deadly
6. average, commonplace
7. constant, habitual, recurring
8. fleeting, short lived
9. old age
10. doubtful, causing doubt
11. deliberate, intentional
12. enormous, marvelous

285

Section 3

1. An arresting *simile*
2. Middle *stratum*
3. Demonstrate *tenacity*
4. *Denizen* of the jungle
5. Plant a *hybrid*
6. A *nonentity* in business
7. Robbing with *impunity*
8. Fabulous *opulence*
9. Prices at *parity*
10. Quaint *reminiscence*

1. layer or level
2. freedom from punishment
3. recollection
4. cross between two varieties
5. inhabitant
6. equality, equivalence
7. person of no importance
8. deformity of mind
9. readiness to act
10. unyielding firmness
11. wealth, abundance
12. expressed comparison

UNITS 4, 5, 6

Section 4

1. *Avid* about science
2. *Munificent* praise
3. *Inexorable* will power
4. *Actuarial* factors
5. *Austere* temperament
6. *Querulous* words
7. *Meticulous* craftsmanship
8. *Lucrative* labor
9. *Lugubrious* tears
10. *Inscrutable* designs

1. unyielding, unrelenting
2. mournful, doleful
3. profitable, remunerative
4. scrupulous, painstaking
5. mysterious, unfathomable
6. very generous, lavish
7. confident, hopeful
8. stern, strict, or severely simple
9. eager, greedy
10. having to do with insurance rates and risks
11. fretful, complaining
12. wise, prudent, far-seeing

Section 5

1. Speakers *allege*
2. Mothers *cajole*
3. Deeds *incriminate*
4. Kings *condescend*
5. Liars *perjure*
6. *Dissipate* anger
7. *Disburse* one's pay
8. *Elicit* an admission
9. *Exhort* a convict
10. *Indict* a suspect

1. charge or accuse
2. come down to another's level
3. dispel
4. urge, advise earnestly
5. declare, assert
6. punish gently
7. attract under false pretenses
8. pay out, expend
9. draw forth
10. involve or implicate in a crime
11. coax, wheedle, or persuade by flattery
12. testify falsely

Section 6

1. Brief *altercation*
2. Mining *cartel*
3. Transient *apparition*
4. A full *docket*
5. Wily *confederate*
6. Ancient *dirge*
7. Shameless *cupidity*
8. Delayed *interment*
9. Austere *façade*
10. Criminal *libel*

1. funeral song or tune
2. complicated plan
3. international combine to control output and prices
4. abnormal desire for wealth
5. burial
6. firmness or solidity
7. angry dispute, quarrel
8. list of cases for trial
9. specter or phantom
10. front or face
11. ally or accomplice
12. written or printed defamation

UNITS 7, 8, 9

Section 7

1. *Inarticulate* sounds
2. *Ardent* phrases
3. *Pallid* landscape
4. *Benign* motives
5. *Protuberant* hills
6. *Celestial* beauty
7. *Provident* parents
8. *Culpable* accomplice
9. *Incipient* plans
10. *Turbulent* rioters

1. stirring awe, enthusiasm, or delight
2. unintelligible, mute
3. kindly, favorable
4. fervent, zealous, burning
5. heavenly, of the sky
6. pale or wan
7. bulging, swelling out
8. blameworthy, guilty, deserving reproach
9. disorderly, tumultuous
10. plain, unadorned, without ornamentation
11. in the beginning stages
12. exercising foresight, thrifty

Section 8

1. *Incorrigible* offender
2. *Insidious* scheme
3. *Intrepid* admiral
4. A *laconic* editor
5. *Nefarious* monster
6. *Sanguine* predictions
7. *Pernicious* nonsense
8. *Venial* blunder
9. *Ubiquitous* rainfall
10. *Venomous* dislike

1. very evil
2. pardonable, excusable
3. twisted, disordered, full of confusion
4. incapable of reform
5. poisonous, malignant
6. present everywhere
7. concise, terse, pithy
8. treacherous, stealthily injurious
9. disastrous, fatal
10. highly injurious, deadly
11. hopeful, confident
12. fearless, dauntless

Section 9

1. Useless *subterfuge*
2. Mild *depravity*
3. Scientific *heresy*
4. Costly *veracity*
5. Deep seated *rancor*
6. Tiresome *reiteration*
7. Continual *indolence*
8. Delayed *retribution*
9. Clever *prevarication*
10. Great *temerity*

1. love of ease, laziness
2. opinion differing from accepted view
3. danger of discovery
4. foolishness, folly
5. requital or punishment
6. bitter hatred or ill will
7. rashness, rash boldness
8. repetition
9. moral corruptness, vitiation
10. truthfulness
11. trick to escape something unpleasant
12. evasion of the truth, quibbling

UNITS 10, 11, 12

Section 10

1. Sudden *animation*
2. *Chronicle* of adventure
3. *Parliament* of Canada
4. Soothing *jocularity*
5. Victorian *parlor*
6. Evangelistic *fervor*
7. Sparkling *repartee*
8. Odd *cognomen*
9. Unintended *bathos*
10. Poetic *satire*

1. anticlimax, false pathos
2. rapid, witty reply or conversation
3. place for speaking on public matters
4. work of ridicule (especially literary)
5. liveliness and spirit
6. surname or nickname
7. enthusiastic talk
8. joking, playful manner
9. burning zeal
10. regret, disappointment
11. place for speaking with guests
12. record of events (usually in time order)

Section 11

1. *Incorporate* a town
2. *Effervesce* gaily
3. *Replenish* the freezer
4. *Interrogate* a visitor
5. *Amble* slowly
6. *Dominate* easily
7. *Fortify* oneself
8. *Transmute* sorrow
9. *Abjure* a prejudice
10. *Migrate* westward

1. refill
2. swear off or renounce
3. walk at an easy or gentle gait
4. strengthen
5. enlarge, make larger
6. glow, bubble, show exhilaration
7. control, govern
8. move, travel
9. give legal body to
10. change, transform
11. admire, hold in high regard
12. ask questions of

Section 12

1. Chronic *somnambulist*
2. *Confluence* of traffic
3. Small *patrimony*
4. New *territory*
5. Frequent *malingerer*
6. *Neophyte* in the field
7. Poor *orthography*
8. Means of *telepathy*
9. Religious *orthodoxy*
10. History of *jurisprudence*

1. one who can't stay awake
2. beginner
3. one who walks in his sleep
4. thought transference
5. land in rather large areas
6. science of laws
7. inheritance from one's father
8. right teachings, established views
9. one who pretends illness to escape his duty
10. flowing together, meeting
11. spelling
12. money or reward for doing right

PART **III**

ROAD SIGNS

When you see one of these symbols in front of an illustrative sentence, watch for the part of speech it denotes:

- a **verb** form of the base word
- an **adverb** form of the base word
- a **noun** form of the base word
- an **adjective** form of the base word

For Pronouncing Key, see page 406.

UNIT ONE

Which word fits best in each blank?

1. Both writers and scientists will __?__ on the project.

2. Political candidates __?__ their opponents.

3. The police decided to __?__ the body.

4. He was pleased when his plans came to __?__.

5. Nitroglycerin may __?__ unexpectedly.

6. The threat of capital punishment may not __?__ a potential murderer.

7. One pays __?__ to a superior mind.

8. There was no solution to the problem: the scientists had reached __?__.

9. An upright citizen became the victim of __?__.

10. A flood or tornado causes __?__ as the inhabitants realize its destructiveness.

deter
exhume
homage
demur
collaborate
calumny
consternation
disparage
condone
fruition
elixir
an impasse
detonate

• Word List—VERBS

1. CAVIL (kăv'ĭl) . . . . . quibble, find fault unnecessarily

Jane liked to cavil about her sister's clothes.

■ These cavils helped her feel superior.

Cf. carp, captious (III, 5)

2. COINCIDE (kō'ĭn·sīd') . . . . occupy the same place or time; occur simultaneously; agree exactly

John's arrival in New York coincided with mine.

His opinions of the city, however, did not coincide with mine.

■ It would be quite a coincidence to meet a college classmate in London.

A **coincidence** is a chance occurrence which matches some other event or circumstance: It would be a startling coincidence if two cars of the same make broke down for the same reason, at the same place and time, on a country road.

3. COLLABORATE (kŏ·lăb'ŏ·rāt) . . . work together, cooperate

Two authors collaborated in writing "The Valiant."

■ The collaboration of Gilbert and Sullivan produced a popular series of light operas.

■ Collaboration with the enemy was severely punished during the war.

Collaborator usually means "scientific or literary co-worker." After World War II, the word was applied to those in liberated countries who had co-operated with the enemy.

Collusion means "secret cooperation for a fraudulent purpose."

4. CONDONE (kŏn·dōn') . . . excuse by seeming to overlook

Employers do not condone carelessness.

Martha overlooks but does not condone bad manners.

Condone also means "forgive by pretending not to notice."

5. **CONSTRUE** (kŏn·strōō′) . . . . interpret, explain

Joyce construes her friend's bad manners as an affront.
A foreign boy might construe the phrase "in Dutch" to mean "in Holland."
The two lawyers construed the law differently.
► Excessive cleanliness is construable as indicating a sense of guilt, according to some psychologists.

6. **CONTEMPLATE** (kŏn′těm·plāt) . . . . . intend; meditate

We contemplate moving to the country in the spring.
■ He would sometimes spend an hour in quiet contemplation of the problems that faced him.
► A cow has a contemplative manner which is misleading.

7. **DEMUR** (dė·mûr′) . . . . take exception, object

John demurred at having to mow the lawn on the first day of the baseball season.
The manager will demur if there is a clause in the contract he does not like.

8. **DETER** (dė·tûr′) . . . . . restrain through fear; discourage

The fate of climbers who lost their lives on Mt. Everest did not deter Tensing and his companion from trying.
■ Is capital punishment an effective deterrent to murderers?
Cf. dissuade

9. **DETONATE** (dĕt′ȯ·nāt) . . . . explode loudly

Dynamite detonates with a roar.
■ The detonation of the atomic bomb was heard for miles.

10. **DISPARAGE** (dĭs·păr′ĭj) . . . . belittle, speak slightingly of

The coach is too wise to disparage a beginner's attempts to play basketball.
■ Disparagement might discourage a good prospect.

In Old French, *disparage* meant "marry unequally." What do the root and prefix mean?

11. EMANATE (ĕm′à·nāt) . . . . flow or issue forth

Sincere courtesy emanates from genuine good will.

The rumor emanated from Washington and was soon published by newspapers throughout the country.

■ The process uses the emanation of energy from the sun.

> Forth Words: A river is said to **rise,** as from springs in the hills.
> To **derive** is to arise from: That word derives from French. *Derive* also means "obtain": He derives great pleasure from his hi-fi set.
> To **issue** is to come forth: Words issue from one's lips. *Issue* also means "put forth": The school issues baseball uniforms to the team.
> To **emerge** is to come forth or appear—quietly, gently, and perhaps slowly: New shoots emerge from the ground in April.

12. EXEMPLIFY (ĕg·zĕm′plĭ·fī) . . . . . serve as an instance of; show by example

Napoleon served to exemplify the futility of trying to unite Europe by force.

■ The life of Jesus provided an exemplification of his teachings.

▶ Socrates was a man of exemplary humility.

> **Exemplary** behavior is model behavior, worthy of imitation.
> How is *exemplify* related to **example?** (See dictionary.)

13. EXHUME (ĕks·hūm′) . . . dig up (especially a body), disinter

The widow wanted to have her husband's body exhumed for an autopsy.

■ The court ordered the exhumation.

> *Exhume* comes from the Latin *ex-*, "out of," plus *humus*, "ground."
> **Posthumous** comes from a different root, the Latin *postumus*, meaning "the last": A posthumous book is one published after the author's death. A posthumous son is born after the father's death.

■ Word List— NOUNS

1. ALACRITY (à·lăk′rĭ·tĭ) . . . . liveliness, willingness

Badminton is a game demanding alacrity.

The new bellboy responds with alacrity.

2. **AUDACITY** (ô·dăs'ĭ·tĭ) . . . . . . boldness; impudence

It takes audacity to be a lion trainer.

The audaciousness of the gambler astonished everyone.

▶ Bob's audacious criticism of the umpire was unnecessary.

Cf. insolence (I, 7), *effrontery, temerity* (II, 8)

3. **CALUMNY** (kăl'ŭm·nĭ) . . slander; false and malicious statement

Senator Fisher's record refutes the calumnies of his unscrupulous opponent, who accused him of accepting bribes.

● The Communists attempted to calumniate the British representative by means of a whispering campaign.

Synonyms: ***defame, malign*** (II, 9), ***traduce, vilify*** (I, 8)

4. **CHAGRIN** (shà·grĭn') . . . shame, humiliation; disappointment

The player who had fumbled the ball on the one-yard line tried to hide his chagrin.

▶ Martha felt chagrined because she did not have a date.

Cf. mortification, discomfiture

5. **CONSTERNATION** (kŏn·stēr·nā'shŭn) . . . . . dismay, terror

The sudden appearance of a Roman army spread consternation in the city.

Agnes fled in consternation when her brother dangled a live snake in the air.

Antonym: ***equanimity***

6. **DILEMMA** (dĭ·lĕm'à) . . . . . difficult choice; predicament

Ralph was in a dilemma: should he take the dull job which paid well or the interesting job which paid poorly?

The dilemma of the Japanese is a crucial one. They must either reduce the birth rate or find space somewhere for their expanding population.

Dilemma comes from a Greek word meaning "two assumptions." It implies a situation demanding a difficult choice between equally unwelcome alternatives.

A **quandary** is a state of perplexity when the choice that confronts one is puzzling or confused.

7. **ELIXIR** (ê·lĭk′sēr) . . . . . magic potion; medicinal liquid

During the Middle Ages, people hoped to discover an elixir of life, a liquid which would prolong life indefinitely.

The doctor prescribed elixir of turpen hydrate for Joe's cough.

8. **ENIGMA** (ê·nĭg′má) . . . . a puzzle, source of perplexity

▶ Her disappearance is an enigma the police cannot solve.

No one understood the teacher's enigmatic remark about huge four-leaf clovers growing along the highways.

9. **EXUBERANCE** (ĕg·zū′bēr·ăns) . . abundance, overflowing supply

▶ May is a month of springtime exuberance.

One can't help feeling exuberant.

Exuberance usually refers to an abundance of good spirits.
Cf. copious (I, 6), *effusive, prolific, luxuriant*

10. **FRUITION** (froō·ĭsh′ŭn) . . . . . . fulfillment, enjoyment

After many years, his work and hopes came to fruition when he discovered the cure for polio.

Fruition has also come to mean "the state of bearing fruit," because of its similarity to the word *fruit.*

11. **HOMAGE** (hŏm′ĭj) . . . . respect, reverence

The boy's gift expressed the homage of a grateful son.

The heroism of men like Ensign Gay deserves our homage.

Homage implies respect that is shown by outward actions.
During the Middle Ages, homage was a ceremony by which a vassal acknowledged his allegiance to his feudal lord. The word derives from the Latin *homo*, meaning "a man" or "a vassal."

12. **IMPASSE** (ĭm·pás′) . . . . . a situation from which there is
no escape; a deadlock

His friends gone and his health broken, the man faced an impasse.

The strike has reached an impasse. Neither side will make any further concessions.

Impasse is a French word meaning, literally, "a blind alley."
Cf. dilemma

FIRST PRACTICE SET

Copy the *italicized* words. Beside each, write an appropriate definition.

1. Mr. Gordon refused to *condone* the easy-going complacency which had caused the *dilemma*.
2. We cannot *collaborate* if either of us is going to *cavil* about minor details.
3. The action I *contemplate* is one which an enemy might *construe* as cowardly, but it will *exemplify* my belief that "discretion is the better part of valor."
4. The mother *demurred* at the idea of *exhuming* her son's body.
5. The office girls often *disparaged* the manager's judgment. Rebukes failed to *deter* them.
6. The spark which *detonates* the dynamite *emanates* from a battery behind the boulder.
7. Bill's *alacrity* in offering to do the chores showed that he regretted his *audacity* in criticizing his parents.
8. *Consternation* over his father's will led to the *calumny* which a cousin had circulated.
9. The wizard admitted with *chagrin* that his magic *elixir* had failed.
10. The way the twins' tastes *coincide* is no *enigma*.

SECOND PRACTICE SET

Which base word in this unit best replaces the *italicized* word or group of words?

1. A *predicament demanding a choice between equally unwelcome alternatives* made it impossible for the two scientists to *work together*.
2. She had the *impudence* to try to *excuse* her sister's dishonesty.
3. A gentleman would not use *false and malicious statement* to *belittle* his bitterest enemy.

4. People cannot always be *restrained through fear* from a foolish act by the threat of possible *shame.*

5. One would hardly *interpret* the *acts of respect* he paid his employer as an indication of enmity.

6. June's *terror* at the thought of performing in an assembly caused her to *object* at first.

7. We do not *meditate* any need for a *medicinal liquid* which will prevent stage fright.

8. For many years, the *puzzle* of how to release atomic energy created for scientists a seeming *situation from which there is no escape.*

9. Why do you *find fault unnecessarily* when your sister acts with *overflowing supply of good spirits?*

10. The police decision to *dig up* the body kept a second plot from coming to *fulfillment.*

THIRD PRACTICE SET

On a separate sheet, write the numbers of the sentences. Beside each, write the letter (*a, b, c,* or *d*) of the pair of words which best complete the sentence.

1. __?__ and __?__ are two qualities that make a personality lively and attractive.

   (a) contemplation—emanation (b) alacrity—exuberance
   (c) homage—consternation   (d) audacity—calumniation

2. A writer and a composer may __?__ on a musical comedy if their interests __?__ to a sufficient degree.

   (a) exhume—exemplify   (b) detonate—emanate
   (c) condone—disparage (d) collaborate—coincide

3. Without surgery, the patient would die, but he was too weak to survive an operation: Such was the __?__ that __?__ the doctor.

   (a) consternation—demurred (b) dilemma—deterred
   (c) cavil—condoned   (d) chagrin—emanated from

4. Stories that might __?__ the candidate's ability were said to __?__ from the opposition headquarters.

    (a) calumniate—detonate   (b) cavil about—collaborate
    (c) disparage—emanate   (d) condone—exhume

5. Political __?__ __?__ the treacherousness of men who invent them.

    (a) calumnies—exemplify   (b) cavils—contemplate
    (c) dilemmas—deter   (d) enigmas—disparage

6. "I Taste a Liquor Never Brewed" describes an imaginary __?__ to which Emily Dickinson pays poetic __?__.

    (a) chagrin—fruition   (b) elixir—homage
    (c) alacrity—disparagement   (d) consternation—
                                              contemplation

7. She may __?__, but do not __?__ as indifference her reluctance to accept the gift.

    (a) cavil—condone   (b) deter—disparage
    (c) coincide—contemplate   (d) demur—construe

8. A teacher cannot __?__ laziness, however much he may sympathize with the __?__ it causes.

    (a) condone—chagrin   (b) contemplate—alacrity
    (c) collaborate—calumny   (d) exemplify—exuberance

9. The cause of the explosion was __?__, but the noise and smoke caused widespread __?__.

    (a) a dilemma—chagrin   (b) a deterrent—detonation
    (c) a cavil—coincidence   (d) an enigma—consternation

10. Hours of solitary __?__ help one __?__ the treasures of a well stored mind.

    (a) collaboration—construe   (b) emanation—detonate
    (c) contemplation—exhume   (d) fruition—condone

THE RIGHT WORD

Which word from this unit best replaces each *italicized* word or group of words?

1. The author advertised for a *cooperating person* to help him with a book on Africa, someone with a very *bold* imagination.

2. *Disinterment* showed that there had never been a corpse in the coffin and created a *state of puzzled bewilderment* for the district attorney's office.

3. The director's words of *belittling comment* discouraged and *shamed* the cast.

4. The Eagle Scout is a boy whose behavior is *worthy-of-serving-as-an-example* and one not susceptible to *slander*.

5. The study of *(rays) flowing forth* from radium helped scientists understand atoms long before the *explosion* of the first A-bomb.

OBITER DICTA

Assume that you are a judge, legislator, or editorial writer. Compose a paragraph on a recent murder, a political scandal, or a current issue. You will be able to use many of the words from this unit, such as, *disparagement, calumny, chagrin, coincidence,* and *cavil.*

UNIT TWO

Which verb from the list at the right is most often connected with each of the numbered items?

1. Slaves?

2. Two friends who make up after a quarrel?

3. Towns about to be destroyed in warfare?

4. Invitations and social affairs?

5. Burnable trash?

6. Misbehavior in public office?

7. A broken chair and the attic?

8. Government financial aid?

9. Mistaken or ill-judged statements?

10. Dictators, big and little?

subsidize
mediate
impeach
reciprocate
usurp
reconcile
emancipate
relegate
vindicate
repudiate
evacuate
incinerate

• Word List—VERBS

1. **EMANCIPATE** (ê·măn′sĭ·pāt) . . . . . . liberate, set free

   Electricity emancipates women from the most wearing forms of household drudgery.

   ■ Lincoln is called the Great Emancipator because of the part he played in the emancipation of the Negroes from slavery.

2. **EVACUATE** (ê·văk′ū·āt) . vacate; withdraw (troops, inhabitants)

   The British decided to evacuate the town, removing the inhabitants as well as the troops.

   ■ The evacuation was a disciplined and orderly retreat.

   ■ There were quite a few women and children among the evacuees.

   > Empty Words: **vacant, vacuum, vacuous, vacuity**
   > The root of these words is the Latin *vacuus,* "empty."

3. **IMPEACH** (ĭm·pēch′) . call in question, bring accusation against

   You cannot impeach the honesty of a man who was never known to accept even a small gift from anyone who was trying to influence him.

   ▸ Washington was a man of unimpeachable (irreproachable) honor.

   ■ The House of Representatives drew up articles of impeachment (accusation of misconduct in public office) against President Andrew Johnson, but he was not convicted.

4. **INCINERATE** (ĭn·sĭn′ēr·āt) . . . . . burn to ashes, cremate

   One way to dispose of garbage is to incinerate it.

   ■ Incineration is effected in an incinerator.

   > **Cremate** means the same as *incinerate,* but is applied to the burning of corpses. Have you read "The Cremation of Sam McGee" by Robert W. Service?

5. MEDIATE (mē′dǐ·āt) . . . . bring about as go-between, act as harmonizing agent in

A clergyman and a lawyer were asked to mediate a settlement in the bus strike.

■ They formed a mediation board, which worked out a compromise.

■ Actually, the clergyman served as mediator, and the lawyer as legal advisor.

> See *arbitrate,* meaning "give a decision" or "settle a dispute after hearing both sides."
> An **arbiter** is an umpire, a person chosen to settle a dispute, and has more authority than a mediator. Many strikes are settled by **arbitration.**
> *Cf. intercessor* under *Cede* Words (I, 10)

6. RECIPROCATE (rė·sǐp′rō·kāt) . . . pay back; exchange favors or courtesies

The old gentleman grew very fond of the widow next door, but she did not reciprocate his affection.

Since the Clarks have entertained us very often and it is time to reciprocate, we are inviting them for Thanksgiving dinner.

■ Courtesy often requires a reciprocation of favors. Sending a thank-you note or gift is a widespread custom.

■ Marriage demands a high degree of reciprocity (mutual exchange, give and take).

> Query: What are reciprocal trade agreements? What is reciprocity (rĕs′ǐ·prŏs′ǐ·tǐ) in trade?

7. RECONCILE (rĕk′ŏn·sīl) . . . bring to agreement, harmonize

Our attempt to reconcile father and son failed.

■ We did not give up until every hope of reconciliation was exhausted.

It was quite hard to reconcile the agent's words with his deeds.

► The two aspects remained irreconcilable.

> *Conciliate* means "placate or pacify": When the voters complained about his bill, Senator Snooks tried to conciliate them. They mistook his conciliatory manner for weakness, however.

8. **RELEGATE** (rĕl′ê·gāt) . . . consign to inferior status, banish

   We shall relegate "Spike" to the basement until he can let the cat alone.

   ▪ Relegation of old cars to junk yards makes highways safer.

   Cf. banish and related words (II, 1).

9. **REPUDIATE** (rê·pū′dĭ·āt) . . . . . disavow; disown, reject

   The company was quick to repudiate the statement of one of its salesmen that its nylon stockings would last ten years.

   ▪ Germany's repudiation of the Treaty of Versailles paved the way for World War II.

   One may repudiate a claim, a son, a belief, a charge or accusation, a debt.
   The Latin root, *pudere,* "feel shame," appears in **impudent,** "shameless," and **pudency,** "bashfulness," as well as in *repudiate.*

10. **SUBSIDIZE** (sŭb′sĭ·dīz) . . . . grant financial aid to

    The Federal Government subsidizes farmers by buying their surplus crops.

    ▪ The article said that American subsidies to foreign governments would help maintain world peace.

11. **TEMPORIZE** (tĕm′pô·rīz) . . . . . act evasively to gain time;
    yield temporarily to circumstances

    When asked for an opinion of a controversial topic, politicians often temporize by giving a cautious or ambiguous answer.

    ▪ Temporization may take the form of refusing to comment at all.
    Connie had to temporize by going out with both boys until she could decide which one she liked best.

12. **USURP** (û·zûrp′) . . . . seize (power or control) wrongfully

    A foreigner managed to usurp the throne of Persia.

    ▪ Like most usurpers, he made his usurpation legal.
    Jacob usurped Esau's birthright and blessing.

    One may usurp an office, a place, powers, or rights.

13. VINDICATE (vĭn′dĭ·kāt) . . . . . justify; clear of a charge or criticism; defend successfully

Police investigation failed to vindicate the driver, who had been accused of criminal negligence in the child's death.

The westward voyage of Columbus vindicated his belief that the earth was round.

■ The jury's verdict of "Not guilty" provided vindication for the barber's claim of innocence.

Cf. exculpate, exonerate, acquit (II, 5)

► Word List—ADJECTIVES

1. ALTRUISTIC (ăl′trŏō·ĭs′tĭk) . . . unselfishly concerned for others

A good teacher is usually altruistic and interested in his students.

■ Collections, benefits, and Christmas baskets serve to express the altruism of youth groups.

■ Mrs. Beaver is an active altruist in community affairs.

A **philanthropist,** or lover of mankind, is an altruist who gives large sums of money.
A **humanitarian** is an altruist interested chiefly in reducing human suffering and pain.
A **charitable** person is altruistic but on a somewhat smaller scale than a philanthropist.
A **benefactor** is an altruist who does good deeds of all kinds, big or little (II, 12).

2. AMICABLE (ăm′ĭ·ká·b′l) . . . . friendly, peaceable

Amicable relations prevail between the United States and Canada.

■ Disputes are settled amicably.

Amiable means "good-natured, friendly," as applied to persons and animals but not to nations: The man next door is always very amiable.
Amity means "friendship or harmony," especially between nations: A spirit of unwonted amity prevailed in the Security Council of the United Nations.
That which is **inimical** is hostile, unfriendly.

3. **AMOROUS** (ăm′ô·rŭs) . . . . loving, fond

The bride and groom exchanged amorous glances.

■ They did not try to conceal their amorousness.

Love Words: An **amative** nature is one disposed to loving.
To be **enamored** of an idea is to be charmed by it.
Inamorata is a rather literary word meaning "a woman loved."

4. **ASTUTE** (ăs·tūt′) . . . . shrewd, crafty; keen of mind

The quarterback was astute enough to sense the weaknesses of the other team.

■ The G-Man's astuteness led to the killer's capture.

Cf. adroit (II, 3), *wily* (I, 3), *cunning, discerning* (I, 2), *sagacious* (III, 3)

5. **AUTHENTIC** (ô·thĕn′tĭk) . . . genuine, entitled to acceptance

The will must be authentic because the signature has been verified.

■ The historical authenticity (correctness of the main events) in the novel makes it worth reading.

● We have affidavits to authenticate (prove the genuineness of) the letter from Hawthorne to his wife.

Cf. historicity

6. **DESPONDENT** (dĕ·spŏn′dĕnt) . . . . . dejected, despairing

The death of his wife made Poe despondent.

■ He found little relief from his despondency.

Cf. melancholy (II, 4)

7. **DIDACTIC** (dĭ·dăk′tĭk) . . . . morally instructive

Alexander Pope wrote didactic poetry.

■ Didacticism is a trait of his poetry.

Didactic sometimes means "teacherlike" in an unfavorable sense: The little boy was annoyed by his big sister's didactic manner.

8. **FELICITOUS** (fĕ·lĭs′ĭ·tŭs) . . . . appropriate; aptly-chosen; happily expressed

You came at a felicitous moment, for I've just been paid.

■ James Thurber expresses himself with rare felicitousness.

- Felicitate (congratulate) the groom but *not* the bride.
- Wish her great felicity instead.

   Felicity usually means "bliss" or "happiness," but may also mean "aptness in expression."

9. **HEINOUS** (hā′nŭs) . . . . **hateful, odious**

   How could two old ladies be guilty of such heinous murders as those in *Arsenic and Old Lace?*
   - The heinousness of the attack was heightened by the careful way in which it was planned.

   Cf. monstrous, nefarious, villainous, flagrant, atrocious (II, 9)

10. **IMPERIAL** (ĭm·pẽr′ĭ·ăl) . . . . **majestic, befitting an emperor**

   The leader of the procession walked with imperial dignity.
   - The small country accused its larger neighbor of imperialism; i.e., seeking to extend its control beyond its own borders.

     He had a right to order me off his property, but he did not need to be so imperious (overbearing) about it.
   - His imperiousness antagonizes the other neighbors too.

   The Latin root is *imperium*, "sovereignty," from which is also derived the word *empire.*
   Cf. regal (I, 6)

11. **INADVERTENT** (ĭn′ăd·vûr′tĕnt) . . . **unintentional, thoughtless**

   Bob worked the problem correctly but arrived at the wrong answer because of an inadvertent error in addition.
   - Mr. Andrews lost quite a few friends through inadvertence (negligence). He did not make it a point to remember their likes and dislikes.

   Cf. other *Vert* Words (I, 10), also *advert, advertent.*

12. **INNOCUOUS** (ĭ·nŏk′ů·ŭs) . . . . **harmless**

   Kittens are innocuous creatures before they get old enough to destroy birds.
   - The innocuousness of most American snakes makes hiking safer here than it is in some other parts of the world.

   Cf. noxious (under *obnoxious*, I, 6), *pernicious* (II, 9)

FIRST PRACTICE SET

Copy the *italicized* words. Beside each, write an appropriate definition.

1. The planter showed how *altruistic* he was by *emancipating* all of his slaves.

2. Congress did not *impeach* the senator, but many members *repudiated* his policies.

3. Mrs. Parks was *despondent* because she almost managed to *incinerate* the chicken instead of roasting it.

4. The commissioner's unwillingness to *mediate* in an *amicable* way irritated the labor leaders.

5. Junior tried to *temporize* when Mother threatened to *relegate* his toy guns to the basement if he made any more noise.

6. A dictator is too *astute* to *usurp* absolute power all at once.

7. The chief ranger knew that nothing would *vindicate* him if he failed to *evacuate* the inhabitants of the mountain before the fire got too close.

8. The plan to *subsidize* small businesses looked quite *innocuous*.

9. His action is somewhat less *heinous* because it was *inadvertent*.

10. We read a *didactic* essay about the *imperial* behavior of the king.

SECOND PRACTICE SET

Which base word in this unit best replaces each *italicized* word or phrase?

1. *Fond* sighs and *aptly-chosen* phrases marked romantic behavior in Shakespeare's day.

2. It was *crafty* of the speaker to stress his eagerness to *liberate* laborers from long hours and low pay.

3. The idea that the governor should be *tried for misconduct* is based on reports which are not *genuine*.

4. The coach had to *banish* to the bench the two players who could not *bring to agreement* their differences.

5. The doctor, who was always *unselfishly-concerned-for-others*, was glad to *serve as go-between* in the dispute.

6. By an *unintentional* remark, he revealed his plan to *seize wrongfully* his father's authority in the business.

7. The state's refusal to *grant financial aid to* the scientist's experiment made him *dejected*.

8. A fire cannot *burn to ashes* one's valuable papers if they are kept in a safe.

9. The politician was *friendly* and agreed to *disavow* his earlier critical remarks.

10. He told a parable, a *morally instructive* tale, which taught that one should not *pay back* evil for evil.

THIRD PRACTICE SET*

Which lettered pair of items has the same relation as the pair printed in capital letters?

1. MEDIATE : ARBITRATE :: (a) elect : usurp (b) incinerate : scorch (c) pacify : reconcile (d) repudiate : reciprocate

2. ELECT : IMPEACH :: (a) evacuate : emancipate (b) comprehend : reciprocate (c) assess : subsidize (d) decide quickly : temporize

3. ODIOUS : HEINOUS :: (a) intentional : inadvertent (b) unselfish : altruistic (c) amorous : felicitous (d) amicable : inimical

4. EGOTIST : ALTRUIST :: (a) amity : amicability (b) illumination : incineration (c) impeachment : vindication (d) usurpation : inheritance

---

* This is the first of several exercises which give you practice in finding a relationship or **analogy** between words paired together. Sometimes, the pair are related because they are synonyms (*cold : chilly*) or antonyms (*cold : hot*). Sometimes, one word in the pair may describe the other (*giant : large*), may indicate a product (*carpenter : porch*), or may influence the other (*comfort : fear, food : hunger*). You will be asked to find another pair of words in which there is the same relationship and the same relative position.

5. INNOCUOUS : INFANCY :: (a) amorous : courtship (b) impudent : impeachment (c) didactic : poetry (d) felicitous : arbitration

6. RELEGATE : FURNITURE :: (a) subsidize : government (b) incinerate : ashes (c) temporize : politicians (d) repudiate : agreement

7. SIGNATURE : AUTHENTICATE :: (a) party : reciprocate (b) corpse : cremate (c) reputation : vindicate (d) lawyer : mediate

8. AMICABLE : HOSTILITY :: (a) indebted : subsidy (b) didactic : foolishness (c) conciliatory : arbitration (d) humanitarian : usurpation

9. IMPERIAL : EMPIRE :: (a) despondent : mediation (b) authentic : letters (c) amicable : didacticism (d) humanitarian : altruism

10. UNHAPPINESS : FELICITY :: (a) slavery : emancipation (b) selfishness : egotism (c) usurpation : tyranny (d) public debt: subsidy

THE RIGHT WORD

Which word from this unit best replaces each *italicized* word or group of words?

1. The dictator strengthened his *wrongful seizure* of power by *favor-exchanging* defense agreements with neighboring countries.

2. Through *thoughtlessness*, the evidence for the *genuineness* of the document was lost.

3. The two men are *incapable of being brought into harmony*, even though both are *altruists who give large sums of money*.

4. The book is a *disavowal* of war in all its forms and a plea for *friendship* among nations.

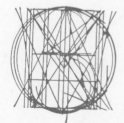

UNIT THREE

Choose the word from the list at the right which is the approximate opposite of each numbered item:

1. Stupidity, obtuseness: __?__

2. Long-windedness: __?__

3. Finality: __?__

4. Recuperation: __?__

5. Invariable state or condition: __?__

6. Unsound judgment: __?__

7. Scarcity: __?__

8. Prejudice: __?__

9. Upright position: __?__

10. Lack of fondness or of inclination toward: __?__

quintessence
surfeit
perspicacity
prostration
recumbency
tentativeness
predilection
sagacity
propensity
prerogative
succinctness
vicissitude

■ **Word List—NOUNS**

1. OVERTURE (ō′vĕr·tûr) . . . . . **proposition; offer, opening**

After the battle, the enemy made overtures of peace.

A national concern is making overtures to buy our local box factory.

The orchestra played the overture to *Tannhäuser* (Wagnerian opera).

The overture to an opera is the opening or introductory music.
Overture comes from a French verb meaning "open."

2. PAROXYSM (păr′ŏk·sĭz′m) . . . . **spasm, outburst**

The man's predicament in the water sent the girls into paroxysms of laughter.

The illness produces paroxysms or convulsions.

3. PERSPICACITY (pûr′spĭ·kăs′ĭ·tĭ) . **mental penetration, discernment**

Washington had the perspicacity to realize that the United States would someday be a great nation.

The two books about space travel are written with unusual perspicuity (clearness, lucidity).

▶ The big book is the more perspicuous of the two.

Perspicacity and **perspicuous** come from *per-*, "through" plus *-spic-*, "see" (I, 10). The first implies acuteness of discernment; the second, clarity and lucidity of expression.

4. PREDILECTION (prē′dĭ·lĕk′shŭn) . . . **preconceived preference or partiality**

Beth has a predilection for tall boys with dark hair and brown eyes.

A predilection is a favorable attitude, a **prejudice** is an unfavorable attitude.

A **bias** is a preconceived inclination or slant, either favorable or unfavorable. It keeps one from being impartial when impartiality is expected. See dictionary for literal meaning of *bias*.

5. PREROGATIVE (prė·rŏg′á·tĭv) . . . . . . privilege, right

Riding for half fare on the railroads is one of a clergyman's prerogatives.

Taking the initiative in dating is still a man's prerogative.

6. PROPENSITY (prò·pĕn′sĭ·tĭ) . . . . . natural tendency, bent

From the time he was able to walk, Jack had a propensity for getting into trouble.

A propensity for mathematics is an incentive to go into engineering or business.

Propensity and *penchant* both come from the Latin *pendere,* "hang or weigh." See *-pend-* (I, 9).

A **penchant** is a strong liking or inclination: Lucy has a penchant for walking in the rain.

Predispose means "incline beforehand or favorably": Jerome imagined that the teachers would be predisposed in his favor because of his curly hair.

A **proclivity** is a propensity for something objectionable, like swearing.

7. PROPRIETY (prò·prī′ĕ·tĭ) . . . conformity to accepted standards of behavior; rightness, suitability

An etiquette book gives rules of propriety.

All the proprieties, such as rising when a lady enters the room, are carefully observed in the best social circles.

Cf. decorum (I, 5)

8. PROSTRATION (prŏs·trā′shŭn) . . . a falling down in worship; exhaustion

In ancient Japan, the act of prostration before the emperor was one of the proprieties to be observed.

● Each visitor had to prostrate himself.

▶ The weary runner was lying prostrate on the ground.

Nervous prostration and heat prostration are forms of exhaustion.

9. QUINTESSENCE (kwĭnt·ĕs′ĕns) . . . . . the pure essence or perfect embodiment

The quintessence of Christian teaching may be found in the Sermon on the Mount and the Two Great Commandments.

The Homecoming Queen is the quintessence of modesty and charm.

► Love is undoubtedly the quintessential (most essential) requirement for a happy home.

Quintessence is a high powered word with celestial connotations. Its original meaning was "fifth essence." The ancient Greeks recognized four elements: fire, earth, air, and water. To these, Aristotle added a fifth, ether, of which, he believed, the stars were composed. Today, *quintessence* means "most t'ypical example" or "most concentrated essence."

An **epitome** (ĕ·pĭt'ŏ·mē) is a brief abstract or summary of a longer work, a part of which is typical of a whole, or an essence: Julie was the epitome of charm.

Cf. paragon (III, 4)

10. **RESTITUTION** (rĕs'tĭ·tū'shŭn) . . . . restoration; reparation

Police demanded immediate restitution of the stolen car to its owner.

The boys promised to make restitution for the damage they had done.

Cf. compensate and related words (II, 2)

11. **SAGACITY** (sȧ·găs'ĭ·tĭ) . . . . shrewdness, sound judgment

The old Indian chief's sagacity was well known.

► He could sum up years of patient observation in a single sagacious remark, such as, "White man do what woman say."

Emerson was called "the sage [profoundly wise man] of Concord."

► Franklin's *Autobiography* is full of sage advice.

Sagacity often implies farsightedness. It involves judgment as well as insight.

Perspicacity stresses insight, the understanding of dark and difficult matters.

Types of brain skill: **penetration, judiciousness, acumen** (III, 10), **perspicacity, astuteness** (III, 2), **acuteness**

12. **SURFEIT** (sûr'fĭt) . . . . . . excess; disgust from excess

Surfeit of praise had made him complacent and vain.

The result of years of constant travel was surfeit and a longing for a permanent home.

● A Thanksgiving dinner will surfeit (fill to excess) the stoutest eater.

Degrees of satiety: 1. *suffice* 2. *satisfy* 3. *satiate* (I, 4) or *sate* 4. *surfeit* 5. *cloy* (sicken with sweetness) 6. *glut* (fill disgustingly full)

13. VICISSITUDE (vĭ·sĭs′ĭ·tūd) . . . . change (often unpleasant), alternation

The vicissitudes of public life and the uncertainty of being being reelected were hard to endure.
Adolescence is a time of stress and disturbing vicissitudes.

The plural of this word, more often used than the singular, means "ups and downs" or "irregular and difficult changes."

▶ Word List—ADJECTIVES

1. LAMBENT (lăm′bĕnt) . . . . playing lightly over a surface or subject; softly radiant

The lambent firelight filled the room with dancing shadows.
His lambent wit delighted everyone.

2. LATENT (lā′tĕnt) . . . . . hidden, unrevealed; potential

Her latent executive ability came out when her husband died and she had to take over the business.
Coal contains latent heat. Bulbs contain latent flowers.

Cf. potential (I, 3, under *potent*), *dormant* (II, 12)

3. MOBILE (mō′bĭl) . . . . movable; changing readily, variable

A house trailer is more mobile than an Arab's tent.
Her face is mobile and her mind is equally so.

■ The mobility of the forest fire made it necessary to be ready for sudden changes of plans and positions.
The Indian's face was immobile, betraying no feeling.

To **mobilize** troops is to call them into service.
Review *Mov* Words (I, 9).
Cf. immobilize

4. **MORTAL (môr'tǎl)** . . subject to death; causing death, deadly

He realized that our mortal existence can easily be short-
ened by a mortal injury.

■ The mortality or death rate from tuberculosis was once very
high. Like the infant mortality rate, it is now very low.
Shakespeare wrote plays of immortal renown.

■ Socrates believed in the immortality of the soul.

Moribund means "near death, in a dying condition": Some thinkers
believe that European civilization is moribund.
Review *Mort* Words (I, 11).
Explain *mortuary, mortify, mortmain* and *amortize* (III, 9).

5. **PARTISAN (pär'tĭ·zǎn)** . . . . adhering to a party or cause

As elections approach, partisan politics requires one to
think and act with a political party.
He is a partisan of the public housing program.

Kinds of followers: *supporter, adherent, disciple, partisan*

6. **RECUMBENT (rē·kŭm'běnt)** . . . . reclining, leaning; inactive

The recumbent figure on the bed is my uncle taking his
Sunday afternoon nap.

■ He is often seen in a position of recumbency on a park
bench.
The lineman arranged himself in a recumbent position
against a telegraph post while he ate his lunch.

An **incumbent** duty is one which is obligatory; i.e., it lies upon a
person: It is incumbent upon the man to find a job so he can support
his family.
An incumbent is the holder of an office: Mr. Brown, who is a candidate for the office of mayor, denounces the present incumbent in
every speech.

7. **SALACIOUS (sá·lā'shŭs)** . . . . . . scandalous, obscene

Salacious books are banned from the mails.

■ The law is designed to curb salaciousness in printed matter.

8. **SALIENT (sā'lĭ·ěnt)** . . . . prominent, conspicuous

Major Richards outlined briefly the salient features of the
new recruiting plan.

One salient argument for a world government escaped all of the debaters—its convenience.

A **salient angle** is a projecting angle on a geometric figure.
The salient of a fortification or battle line is a projecting angle. (See dictionary.)

9. SEDITIOUS (sĕ·dĭsh′ŭs) . . . inciting discontent or rebellion

A wave of seditious whisperings swept through the crew.
■ Sedition was rife as authorities searched for its leaders.

Sedition is effort or activity intended to stir up discontent or rebellion.
Treason is overt action involving a betrayal to the enemy or an attempt to overthrow the government.
Cf. mutiny, anarchy, insurrection, and others (III, 4)

10. SUCCINCT (sŭk·sĭngkt′) . . . . terse, concise

The Indian's advice was admirably succinct: "Go home."
■ Succinctness is a quality the Spartans liked to cultivate. It is the opposite of prolixity, verbosity, and garrulousness.

Other Terse Words: *laconic* (II, 9), *brevity* (I, 2), *sententious* (compact or pompous)

11. TANGIBLE (tăn′jĭ·b′l) . . . . . real, substantial, palpable

The police could find no tangible evidence that the hobo shot the man—no fingerprints, no witnesses, no weapon.
■ The suspicions against him lack tangibility.
Faith and hope are intangible qualities which cannot be touched or measured.

Literally, *tangible* and *palpable* both mean "capable of being touched or recognized by the senses," but *palpable* is applied to something which may be grasped physically, and *tangible* to something which may be grasped physically or mentally.
Cf. perceptible, visible

12. TENTATIVE (tĕn′tȧ·tĭv) . . . . . provisional, experimental

This is a tentative draft of the new plan, which can be changed if you have any suggestions.
Our tentative method is to combine the two ingredients.
■ The tentativeness of the doctor's diagnosis makes him reluctant to tell the patient.

FIRST PRACTICE SET

Copy the *italicized* words. Beside each, write an appropriate definition.

1. It is a buyer's *prerogative* to demand *restitution* if a product is not satisfactory in every way.
2. Her *predilection* for light opera has some connection with her *propensity* for mimicry.
3. My favorite teacher had the *perspicacity* to realize that the Golden Rule is actually the *quintessence* of courtesy as well as *propriety*.
4. The rebels were using a *mobile* public address system for *seditious* purposes.
5. The *salient* feature of any strongly *partisan* viewpoint is its tendency toward bias.
6. The *lambent* glow of one neon sign is pleasing, but most towns suffer from a *surfeit* of such light.
7. It takes *sagacity* to see beyond the *vicissitudes* and know that always there's something better ahead—and something worse.
8. Her formerly *latent* skill in handling children had become her most *tangible* asset.
9. The city council has drawn up a *tentative* ordinance banning *salacious* magazines.
10. A *mortal* fear of seeming tedious makes him try too hard to to be *succinct*.

SECOND PRACTICE SET

Which base word from this unit best replaces each *italicized* word or group of words?

1. Being a teacher's son, he had a *preconceived preference* for friends with some *mental penetration*.
2. *Spasms* of weeping shook her and she was near *exhaustion*.
3. He said he would make *reparation* to anyone he had wronged, even if that person were his *deadly* enemy.

4. The *provisional* topic for the discussion was *conformity to accepted standards* in dress for business and sport.

5. It is an employer's *privilege* to seek *unrevealed* selling ability wherever he can find it.

6. The coach's *sound judgment* in planning a *readily changing* defense gave us an advantage in every game.

7. The *softly radiant* twilight fell and breezes fanned the *reclining* figure of the child.

8. Telegrams often achieve the *pure essence* of *conciseness*.

9. The *most conspicuous* argument of those interested in *inciting to rebellion* was that the king had usurped the throne.

10. A *scandalous* pamphlet was written to promote *adhering-to-a-cause* views.

THIRD PRACTICE SET

Which lettered pair of items has the same relationship as the pair printed in capital letters?

1. VERBOSITY : SUCCINCTNESS :: (a) aria : overture (b) nobility : prostration (c) problem : vicissitude (d) obtuseness : perspicacity

2. PROPENSITY : TINKERING WITH GADGETS :: (a) Indian chief : sagacity (b) prerogative : riding for half-fare (c) adolescence : vicissitude (d) propriety : argument

3. SAGACITY : FOOLISHNESS :: (a) salience : inconspicuousness (b) restitution : payment (c) etiquette : proprieties (d) Thanksgiving : surfeit

4. TANGIBLE : IMMATERIAL :: (a) sagacious : recumbent (b) treasonable : seditious (c) quintessential : most typical (d) revealed : latent

5. LACONIC : SUCCINCT :: (a) unwise : sagacious (b) grievous : immobile (c) latent : not hidden (d) quintessential : epitomized

6. PREDILECTION : PREJUDICE :: (a) partisanship : disinterest   (b) vicissitude : prerogative   (c) sagacity : perspicuity   (d) mortality : sedition

7. MOBILE : TRAILER :: (a) ancient : opera   (b) unconcealed : talent   (c) mortal : human being   (d) hateful : predilection

8. TENTATIVE DRAFT : FINAL DRAFT :: (a) candidate : incumbent   (b) succinct speech : concise speech   (c) lambent gazes : angry looks   (d) salaciousness : scandal

9. SHORTAGE : SURFEIT :: (a) epileptic fit : paroxysm   (b) partisanship : discipleship   (c) fixedness : vicissitude   (d) overture : prelude

10. LOYALTY : SEDITION :: (a) lack of propriety : breach of etiquette   (b) perspicacity : stupidity   (c) palpability : firmness   (d) irreverence : prostration

THE RIGHT WORD

Which word from this unit best replaces each *italicized* word or group of words?

1. *Terseness* is *obligatory* upon a person who composes telegrams.

2. A vulture *fills itself disgustingly full* on the *subject-to-death* remains of unburied human beings.

3. Morale is a rather *not-palpable* quality but a vital one to the troops we are about to *call into service*.

4. The book is written in a *lucid* style, and the *prominent* ideas are readily evident even to a very hasty reader.

5. The war left some countries *in a dying condition* and others in a state of *exhaustion*.

ᚢᚦᚨᚱᚲᚷ ᛟ
ᚹᚾᛁᛁᚺ ᛋᛟᛚ
ᛦᛋᛏᛒᛗᛗᛁ ᛝ

UNIT FOUR

Which word completes each statement best?

1. The proper treatment for a sorcerer is: (a) anathema (b) fetish (c) incubus (d) occultism.

2. Three countries, united to face a common enemy, form: (a) a covenant (b) a coalition (c) an insurrection (d) an incentive.

3. A crime that may be described as a kind of theft is: (a) aestheticism (b) exoticism (c) plagiarism (d) anathema.

4. A calm and musing state of mind may be found in: (a) a reverie (b) a solstice (c) a paradox (d) a covenant.

5. The weird masks worn on Hallowe'en are often: (a) ineffable (b) grotesque (c) recondite (d) impervious.

6. A word to describe foolishly sentimental behavior is: (a) sadistic (b) exotic (c) aesthetic (d) maudlin.

7. In a discussion, a question that has a bearing on the main subject is: (a) relevant (b) forensic (c) paradoxical (d) portentous.

8. An object worshipped for its magical power is: (a) a paradox (b) a solstice (c) a fetish (d) a paragon.

323

▪ Word List—NOUNS

1. **ANATHEMA** (á·năth'ê·má) . . . . solemn curse; person or
    object detested

    Anathemas did not discourage the leaders of the movement.
    The cut-rate store is anathema to its competitors.

    ● Newspapers anathematized the President for his foreign
    policy.

    Historically, anathema was a formal curse or ban issued by church
    authorities and accompanied by excommunication.
    Compare *execration,* a curse uttered with anger and loathing.

2. **COALITION** (kō'á·lĭsh'ŭn) . . combination or alliance (especially
    of opposing parties and usually temporary)

    A coalition of conservative Republicans and Southern
    Democrats defeated the measure in the Senate.

    ▶ After consultation with party leaders, the Premier of France
    set up a coalition cabinet.

    ● If you heat the crystals, they will coalesce (fuse, unite).
    Labor leaders proposed gradual coalescence of the two
    organizations.

    Merge Words: To **consolidate** three companies is to combine them,
    thus creating a unified and solid whole.
    To **amalgamate** two metals or two peoples is to combine them in a
    uniform whole.
    Cf. league, confederation, federation, union; miscegenation

3. **COVENANT** (kŭv'ĕ·nănt) . . . solemn agreement or compact

    Marriage is a covenant between two people who are in love.
    The Covenant of the League of Nations was its constitution.
    A church covenant is an agreement regarding church prac-
    tices and discipline.

    A covenant generally includes a solemn oath to uphold a principle
    or belief. What was a Covenanter? (See dictionary.)
    A **contract** is a legal agreement, usually written and often of a busi-
    ness nature.

4.   FETISH (fē'tĭsh) . . something worshipped for its magical power

The witch doctor held up his fetish, a carved boar tusk.
Among primitive tribes, fetishism may include the worship
of animals.
Lucy made a fetish of stylish clothes.

The word *fetish* is applied to anything which is the object of idolatrous devotion, whether a sport car or sunshine.
A **talisman** is a ring, stone, or other object, carved with symbols which are supposed to have magic powers. It may also be any good-luck token.
An **amulet** is a charm worn to ward off evil.

5.   INCENTIVE (ĭn·sĕn'tĭv) . stimulus, that which stirs one to do or be

The poetry prize provides an incentive for all the English
classes.
▶ Incentive pay increased production and made cost accounting easier.

Incentives ordinarily come from an exterior source (outside a person).
Motives arise from within a person, although they may result from outside influences.

6.   INCUBUS (ĭn'kû·bŭs) . . . . nightmare, depressing burden

An incubus of fear haunted the killer day and night.
France was staggering under an incubus of debt.

An incubus was originally a demon supposed to cause nightmare by lying upon a sleeping person.

7.   INSURRECTION (ĭn'sŭ·rĕk'shŭn) . . armed uprising or rebellion

Troops quickly quelled an insurrection in Honduras.
Three leading insurrectionists were captured and convicted.

Insurrection and **insurgent** come from the same Latin verb, *surgere*, "to rise." An **insurgent** may be a rebel, an insurrectionist, or one who rises up against his own political party in Congress.
Degrees of revolt: An **uprising** is an outbreak against the government, usually more deliberate and less spontaneous than a riot.
An **insurrection** is a more serious, armed revolt—one immediately successful or soon suppressed.
A **rebellion** is a revolt against an authority. The term is also applied to a revolt which has failed.
A **revolution** is bigger and more lasting than a rebellion. The term is often applied to a successful revolt.
Cf. resurrection (II, 8)

8. **PARADOX** (păr′à·dŏks) . . contradictory statement, contradiction

    The twofold action of mortar, which keeps bricks apart and at the same time holds them together, is a paradox.

    ▶ Marcus Aurelius, the Roman ruler, was a paradoxical man; he forgave his enemies, believed in the brotherhood of man, and yet hated the Christians.

    "The Language of Paradox," by Cleanth Brooks, is an important essay on modern poetry.

9. **PARAGON** (păr′à·gŏn) . . . . . perfect model or pattern

    The captain of the swimming team is a paragon of modesty.
    Shakespeare is the paragon of British dramatic poets.

10. **PLAGIARISM** (plā′jĭ·à·rĭz′m) . . . . . the stealing of ideas; the ideas stolen

    A similar story was published several years ago, and Jim must have read it. He is guilty of unconscious plagiarism.

    ● Composers sometimes plagiarize the old masters and modernize the music as their own.

    Plagiarism comes from the Latin word for "kidnapper."
    It has been said that there are no new plots, but a plagiarist not only steals another author's idea but also its treatment and often actual lines or passages.

11. **REVERIE** (rĕv′ẽr·ĭ) . . . . . . deep musing; a daydream

    The professor was in the midst of a reverie when the telephone rang.

    Ruminations are reflections or musings which are turned over and over in the mind: The doctor, in the course of his ruminations, remembered many remarkable cases.
    Review *meditate* (I, 2) and *contemplate* (III, 1).

12. **SOLSTICE** (sŏl′stĭs) . . . . . . point at which the sun is farthest from the equator

    In the northern hemisphere, the winter solstice comes just before Christmas. What are the dates? What is this solstice called in South America?

    Solstice may mean "the furthest limit, culmination, or turning point."

▶ Word List— ADJECTIVES

1. AESTHETIC (ĕs·thĕt'ĭk) . . of or responsive to beauty; artistsic

In order to help develop their children's aesthetic tastes, the Browns planned many family trips to art galleries and museums.

■ Contrast is an important principle of aesthetics (the study of the principles and theory of fine arts).

The term *aesthete* is applied to a person who cultivates his fondness for the arts. It may also be applied in an unfavorable sense to someone who has an exaggerated opinion of his own artistic sensitivity.

2. CHIMERICAL (kĭ·mĕr'ĭ·kăl) . . . . . . fantastic, imaginary

Her fears are as chimerical as the hallucinations of insanity.

■ Invasion of the earth by beings from Mars is one of the chimeras that haunt people today.

In Greek mythology, a **chimera** was a fire-breathing monster with a lion's head, goat's body, and serpent's tail. The name was later applied to any frightful or foolish creature of the imagination.
Other Imagination Words: A **visionary** person is a dreamer, often one whose schemes are not practical.
A **quixotic** person is either extravagantly chivalrous or very active in promoting impractical schemes. The word comes from the name of the absurd but charming figure, Don Quixote, invented by the Spanish author, Miguel de Cervantes.

3. EXOTIC (ĕks·ŏt'ĭk) . . . . strange, foreign

The odor of exotic flowers drifted in from the Oriental garden.
To an American, Chinese food looks and tastes exotic.

Exotic goes back to a Greek word meaning "outside."

4. FORENSIC (fô·rĕn'sĭk) . . pertaining to public debate, oratorical

Daniel Webster is remembered for his forensic skills.

– Cicero is also famous forensically.

Forensic derives from the Latin *forum* or market place.

5. **GROTESQUE** (grὂ·tĕsk') . . absurdly distorted, fantastic, bizarre

    Many medieval cathedrals are decorated with gargoyles:
    waterspouts carved to represent grotesque monsters.
    ▪ A similar grotesqueness sometimes appears in modern
    sculpture.

    Bizarre means "odd, strange, strikingly incongruous."

6. **INEFFABLE** (ĭn·ĕf'à·b'l) . . . . . unutterable, inexpressible

    The ineffable stillness of evening slowly enveloped the lake.
    ▪ The music of the waterfall was ineffably charming.

    Sometimes *ineffable* means "too sacred for utterance": The tribesmen
    never spoke aloud the ineffable name of their main deity.
    Cf. ethereal, heavenly, spiritual, airy, celestial (II, 8)

7. **MARITAL** (măr'ĭ·tăl) . . . . . . of a husband or marriage

    His new marital responsibilities had a steadying effect on
    him.
    A court of marital relations deals with problems of marriage.

8. **MAUDLIN** (môd'lĭn) . . weakly emotional, foolishly sentimental

    The party was almost over when Bill insisted on making a
    rather maudlin speech about "auld acquaintance" and
    "precious memories."
    The governor decided that much of the agitation in behalf
    of the killer was maudlin sympathy, and he refused to com-
    mute the sentence.

    Maudlin comes from the Old French name Maudelene or Madeleine,
    that is, Mary Magdalene, who was often represented in medieval art
    as having eyes red and swollen from weeping. The word acquired the
    meaning of "tearful," and later, "tearfully silly." The name of Magdalen
    College at Oxford University has the same pronunciation as *maudlin*.

9. **OCCULT** (ὂ·kŭlt') . . . . . of a magical nature, mysterious

    The palmist appeared to possess occult powers of some sort.
    ▪ Occultism, especially astrology, attracted Jane, because she
    wanted to get beyond the range of ordinary knowledge.

    Occult originally meant "covered up, hidden."
    Cf. recondite, esoteric, abstruse, mystical

10. **PORTENTOUS** (pŏr·těn'tŭs) . . foreshadowing evil; awe-inspiring

> The portentous black funnel of an approaching tornado sent most of the townspeople to their cellars.
> The first atomic explosion was a portentous event.
> ● Some people think that a black cat portends disaster.
> ■ The comet was regarded as a portent (omen) of evil.

11. **RECONDITE** (rĕk'ŭn·dīt) . . . . abstruse, obscure, difficult to understand

> The theory of relativity is a recondite topic.
> The professor delves into many recondite matters, such as the validity of stories about the so-called lost continent, Atlantis.

12. **RELEVANT** (rĕl'ē·vănt) . . pertinent; bearing on the case in hand

> Almost any topic is relevant in a writing class. In Latin class, however, a remark about baseball is most irrelevant.
> ■ Judge Horner questioned the relevance (relevancy) of the witness' testimony.

> *Cf. germane, apposite, apropos*

13. **SADISTIC** (să·dĭs'tĭk) . . . . cruel, fond of cruelty

> The man displayed a sadistic delight in mistreating animals.
> The sadistic horrors of Dachau were almost incredible.

> **Sadism** means "love of cruelty."

FIRST PRACTICE SET

Copy the *italicized* words. Beside each, write an appropriate definition.
1. A *coalition* of competing manufacturers seems like a *paradox*.
2. The medicine man waved a tribal *fetish* as he pronounced the *anathema* against strangers.
3. The tribal chiefs made a *covenant* not to take part in any future *insurrection*.

4. Herbert needs an *incentive* to cultivate his *forensic* talents.
5. The fear that his *plagiarism* would be discovered haunted the writer like an *incubus*.
6. A Joshua tree is a *grotesque* object with its awkward angles and its lack of *aesthetic* appeal.
7. The thunderstorm, with its *chimerical* cloud shapes, proved *portentous*, for it brought a flood that destroyed a village.
8. Aunt Sophie loves *exotic* clothes and dabbles in such *occult* arts as reading tea leaves.
9. A longing to study the *recondite* problems of space travel overpowered the youth's moments of *reverie*.
10. Nothing personal seemed *relevant* when he looked into the *ineffable* depths of the sky on a clear September night.

SECOND PRACTICE SET

Which word best replaces each *italicized* word or phrase?

1. Jacob and Laban made a *solemn agreement* that was quite *pertinent* to the peace and happiness of both.
2. A *temporary alliance* of Latin American countries was formed to implement their *solemn curse* against Communism.
3. The speaker used his *in-public-debate* skill to prevent an *armed uprising*.
4. Sometimes people under an anaesthetic have *fantastic-imaginary* dreams which seem *inexpressible* while they are taking place.
5. *Foreign* gestures and *abstruse* incantations marked the *magical* ritual of the witches.
6. Amid the *bizarre* ruins of shattered buildings, West Germany made *awe-inspiring* strides toward recovery.
7. The husband, who was rather *fond-of-cruelty*, finally caused a rift in his *marriage* happiness by beating his wife.
8. In her *deep musings*, Diane was a *perfect model* of pensiveness.
9. The memory of his *foolishly sentimental* remarks at the party gave him the *stimulus* to send his hostess a note of apology.
10. The carving has great *artistic* appeal and has become a sort of *object worshipped for its magical powers*.

THIRD PRACTICE SET

Which lettered pair of items has the same relationship as the pair printed in capital letters?

1. NOISE : SILENCE :: (a) curse : anathema (b) incubus : reverie (c) fetish : amulet (d) solstice : winter

2. INCENTIVE : MOTIVE :: (a) resentment : anathema (b) exotic food : native food (c) reverie : forensics (d) covenant : resolution

3. OMINOUS : PORTENTOUS :: (a) clear : chimerical (b) occult : rational (c) relevant : recondite (d) visionary : quixotic

4. LOVE : DUTY :: (a) aesthetics : morality (b) matter-of-factness : ineffability (c) union : coalition (d) paragon : motive

5. FUSION : COMBINATION :: (a) grotesqueness : incongruity (b) aesthetics : exoticism (c) coalescence : amalgamation (d) paragon : quintessence

6. RIOT : UPRISING :: (a) coalition : covenant (b) aesthetics : anathema (c) forensics : study (d) daydream : incubus

7. AMULET : FETISH :: (a) sadism : paradox (b) incentive : result (c) plagiarism : occultism (d) insurrection : revolution

8. SENTIMENTAL : MAUDLIN :: (a) fanciful : chimerical (b) native : exotic (c) relevant : evident (d) marital : moral

9. REVOLUTION : REBELLION :: (a) paradox : eternity (b) incubus : reverie (c) covenant : marriage (d) reconditeness : occultness

10. ABSURD : GROTESQUE :: (a) earthly : ineffable (b) relevant : unrelated (c) paradoxical : contradictory (d) quixotic : exotic

THE RIGHT WORD

Which word from this unit best replaces each *italicized* word or
group of words?

1. Does a red sky *foreshadow* evil?

2. Hearing the gangster's *profane curses*, the detective followed
   him to the hide-out.

3. A Democratic *rebel* in the Senate broke the tie by voting
   against his party.

4. The author was accused of *stealing another's ideas and using
   them as his own.*

5. Robert was full of *romantic, visionary, but impractical* schemes
   for making a living.

6. The fact that acute water shortages may affect the entire country seems more like a *frightful, foolish creature of the imagination* than a real possibility.

7. The new teacher is an *individual who cultivates his fondness
   for art, music, and poetry.*

8. The next step is to *strengthen by combining* the strong points
   of the three disarmament plans.

9. Someone interrupted the speaker to ask a question which was
   completely *without bearing on the case in hand.*

10. The idea of living in a cave instead of a tent during our camp-
    ing trip struck me as *wild and startling.*

UNIT FIVE

Which word best completes the sentence?

1. A taciturn nephew is (a) agile (b) quiet (c) tricky (d) suave.

2. An arrogant uncle is (a) fond of teasing (b) fond of asking questions (c) haughty (d) roguish.

3. A fastidious aunt is (a) unmarried (b) very fussy (c) rather giddy (d) too niggardly.

4. An ingenuous cousin is (a) clever (b) unimaginative (c) well born (d) artlessly frank.

5. A volatile niece is (a) even-tempered (b) changeable (c) condescending (d) too talkative.

6. A silly, self-satisfied brother-in-law is (a) astute (b) presumptuous (c) dogmatic (d) fatuous.

7. A sister-in-law fond of showing off is (a) ostentatious (b) sinuous (c) truculent (d) captious.

8. A mother-in-law who likes to go to social affairs is (a) garrulous (b) dogmatic (c) unctuous (d) gregarious.

9. A fault-finding father-in-law is (a) captious (b) jocular (c) fastidious (d) cynical.

10. An unduly positive grandfather is (a) tentative (b) aggressive (c) dogmatic (d) amicable.

▶ Word List— BEHAVIORISTICS

1. AGGRESSIVE (ă·grĕs'ĭv) . . . . . assertive, enterprising;
   quick to attack

   The new salesman was aggressive and self-confident.
   ▪ Aggressiveness is often necessary in business.
   ▪ The United Nations acted to prevent aggression (unprovoked attack or encroachment) in the Middle East.

   An aggressive person is disposed to attack and quick to take the initiative.
   A **forward** person is prompt, bold, advanced mentally, or impudent.
   An **officious** person is forward in a particularly meddlesome or objectionable manner (I, 6).
   An **assertive** person is forward, positive, or even dogmatic, but not quite officious.

2. ARROGANT (ăr'ô·gănt) . . . . . haughty, overbearingly proud

   The Nazis, with their delusions of being a master race, were arrogant as well as aggressive.
   ▪ The captain showed his arrogance by continually trying to usurp the coach's prerogatives.
   • Did the President arrogate (seize) to himself more power than the Constitution intended?

   A **presumptuous** person assumes too much about, or for, himself; i.e., is too bold or forward.
   A **supercilious** person has a scornful, aloof manner.
   A **disdainful** person is haughty or contemptuous, but not overbearing or aggressive.

3. CAPTIOUS (kăp'shŭs) . . . . . fault-finding, hard to please

   Ernest is often captious and too critical in his comments.
   ▪ The drama critic's captiousness makes his reviews interesting though often rather unfair.

   A **peevish** or **petulant** person is childishly sulky and fretful about small matters.
   Cf. hypercritical, cavilling (III, 1), *carping*

4. CYNICAL (sĭn'ĭ·kăl) . . scornfully distrustful of human motives

To a cynical person, all human actions are selfish.

■ Dorothy did not like the novel because of the author's cynicism.

Cf. pessimism (III, 8), *pessimistic, misanthropic, sarcastic, satirical* (II, 10)

5. DOGMATIC (dŏg·măt'ĭk) . . . . unduly positive

Uncle Bill is inclined to be quite dogmatic about what the British ought to do.

■ In discussing politics, Mrs. Werner avoids dogmatism.

● She does not often dogmatize because she knows there are good points on both sides.

The **dogma** of a church is its set of official doctrines or beliefs.
Cf. arbitrary, dictatorial, doctrinaire

6. EFFEMINATE (ĕ·fĕm'ĭ·nĭt) . . . . . . womanish, unmanly

Soft living made many of the wealthy Romans increasingly effeminate.

■ This effeminacy was reflected in the art of the period.

7. FASTIDIOUS (făs·tĭd'ĭ·ŭs) . . . hard to please; daintily refined; very discriminating

The actress is very fastidious about her make-up and dress.

■ Fastidiousness in preparing food makes it more appetizing.

A **particular** person is fussy about details.
A **squeamish** person is unduly sensitive to what is unsavory: Jane was so squeamish that the sight of a dead frog could make her feel ill.

8. FATUOUS (făt'ů·ŭs) . . . . . complacently stupid or silly

Nero was fatuous about his musical ability.

● The comedian's wit deteriorated into fatuousness.

Synonyms: *silly, stupid, foolish, oafish, asinine*
The Latin *fatuus* means "foolish." *Ignis fatuus,* "foolish fire," is the name given to the will-o'-the-wisp or glow which sometimes hovers over a swamp and which misleads foolish people.
Infatuation, often mistaken for love, is a foolish, unintelligent, or unreasoning fondness which tends to make up in intensity for what it lacks in durability.

9. **GARRULOUS** (găr′ʊ·lŭs) . . . . talkative

    Mrs. Jenks was a garrulous old gossip who haunted our neighborhood.

    ▪ Her garrulity was often annoying.

    > *Gobbledygook* is a popular word for "talking or writing which is long, pompous, vague, involved, usually with Latin-derived words." The word was coined by Representative Maury Maverick of Texas and compares wordiness with the gobbling of turkeys.
    > Talk Words: *loquacious, voluble, diffuse, glib, fluent, verbose, prolix*

10. **GREGARIOUS** (grĕ·gâr′ĭ·ŭs) . . . . inclined to go in groups

    Sheep, which are very gregarious, are more inclined than pigs or hens to stay together in flocks.

    Hermits are among the least gregarious of human beings.

    ▪ For high school students, gregariousness expresses itself in clubs, cliques, field trips, and parties.

11. **IMPETUOUS** (ĭm·pĕt′ʊ·ŭs) . . . . rushing with great force; headlong; rash, hasty

    Impetuous winds howled across the prairies.

    Shelley was an impetuous youth who acted impulsively.

    ▪ Maturity diminished his impetuosity somewhat.

    ▪ Robert Browning displayed a lover's impetuousness when he eloped with Elizabeth Barrett.

    > An **impulsive** person is quick to act on emotional incitement.
    > A **precipitate** person is rash and hasty, as well as sudden.
    > See *Pet* Words (II, 10).

12. **INGENUOUS** (ĭn·jĕn′ʊ·ŭs) . . . . . . free from reserve, straightforward; artless

    "I'd do the same thing myself," was Jim's ingenuous response to Bill's apology.

    ▪ The ingenuousness of the small boy's face and manner was very appealing.

    > In a play, the *ingénue* (ăN′zhā′nü′) is either an actress who plays the part of an ingenuous girl, or the part itself.
    > Do not confuse *ingenuous* with *ingenious* (II, 9).
    > Antonym: *disingenuous*
    > *Cf. naïve, unsophisticated, candid*

13.   IRASCIBLE (ĭ·răs'ĭ·b'l) . . . . easily angered, quick-tempered

Bad weather always made Tim irascible.

■ His family learned just when to expect such irascibility from him.

A **choleric** person is hot-tempered by nature.
An **irate** person is angry to the point of being enraged: The officer was irate because I stalled the car in traffic and could not get started.
Cf. petulant, peevish, and *Pet* Words (II, 10)

14.   NAIVE (nä·ēv') . . . . artless, unsophisticated

He had a naïve belief that joining the club would, in itself, make him popular.

She smiled with the naïveté (nä·ēv'tā') and simplicity of a child.

Synonyms: *natural, ingenuous, unaffected*

15.   OSTENTATIOUS (ŏs'tĕn·tā'shŭs) . . fond of display, pretentious

The newly rich are often more ostentatious in dress and behavior than the old, established families.

- A peacock strutted back and forth ostentatiously.
■ A fine, restrained ostentation marked the ceremony at Buckingham Palace.

16.   PHLEGMATIC (flĕg·măt'ĭk) . . . . . sluggish, unexcitable

The old dog, grown phlegmatic and lazy, ignored the squirrel completely.

- Fat people do not always behave phlegmatically.

Medieval doctors believed that a person's health and temperament were governed by four fluids, or **humors**, in his body. One of these was **phlegm**, too much of which supposedly caused a sluggish temperament.
Cf. apathy (I, 5), *imperturbable, impassive, stoical*

17.   SARDONIC (sär·dŏn'ĭk) . . . biting, sarcastic, bitterly scornful

A sardonic laugh echoed throughout the prison.

- Dyke smiled sardonically when the warden offered to put him on his honor.

Sardonic is a stronger word than *sarcastic* or *derisive*.

18. SATURNINE (săt′ẽr·nīn) . . . . . . gloomy, grave, morose

The prisoner watched with saturnine patience while the guards locked the cell door.

Mr. Whitford is a thin, dark, saturnine man, who rarely smiles.

Originally, a saturnine person was one supposedly born under the influence of the planet Saturn, named after a Roman god. This god, according to fable, ruled during a golden age; hence, a **Saturnian** era is any period of peace and prosperity.

In medieval alchemy, the name *saturn* was given to lead. *Saturnine* may thus mean "suffering from lead poisoning."

Antonym: *mercurial*

19. SINUOUS (sĭn′ů·ŭs) . . . . . . curving, winding; devious

Sinuous paths cross the mountain.

The language of diplomacy is indirect and sinuous (not straightforward).

Cf. insinuate, serpentine

20. SUPERCILIOUS (sū′pẽr·sĭl′ĭ·ŭs) . . . disdainful, scornfully aloof

With a supercilious frown, the great duke turned away from the beggar.

■ The superciliousness of the inspector irritated everybody.

Originally, *supercilious* meant "with raised eyebrows."

21. TACITURN (tăs′ĭ·tûrn) . . . habitually silent, uncommunicative

John Alden was a taciturn youth who found it difficult to tell Priscilla how much he liked her.

■ President Coolidge had a reputation for unusual taciturnity and terseness.

Tacit means "implied but not stated": With a nod, Mother gave her tacit consent to the plans for our skating party.

Synonyms: *reticent, reserved*

22. TRUCULENT (trŭk′ů·lĕnt) . . . . . . fierce, savage, cruel

A gang of truculent bullies robbed the candy store.

■ The big woman's truculence at being arrested did not frighten the policeman or the judge.

23. **UNCTUOUS** (ŭngk′tụ̇·ŭs) . . . . . excessively suave, bland; oily

The man's unctuous manner elicits favors he does not deserve.

■ A hypocritical neighbor informed Gordon with great unctuousness that he should always tell the truth.

■ The orator spoke with great unction (smooth manner) of our debt to the pioneers.

(See dictionary for other meanings of *unction.*)

24. **VERSATILE** (vûr′sȧ·tĭl) . . . . many-sided in abilities

A four-letter man is sure to be versatile in sports.

● A good general manager must be a man of great versatility: he must be skillful in finance, planning, personal relations, and many other matters.

25. **VOLATILE** (vŏl′ȧ·tĭl) . . . . changeable, flighty

She was volatile and carefree. Nothing troubled her very deeply or very long.

■ The Frenchman's volatility made him quite a dramatic figure, and he waved his arms like wings.

When used of a liquid, *volatile* means "quick to evaporate."

FIRST PRACTICE SET

Copy the *italicized* words. Beside each, write an appropriate definition.

1. Robert is a *gregarious* individual but not inclined to be *garrulous.*

2. The duke is *fastidious* about his clothes and *captious* toward his staff.

3. Mr. Jordan is *dogmatic* about the books one should read and *cynical* in his discussion of authors and writing.

4. The fighter's *irascible* disposition made him seem *truculent*.

5. "Bulldozer," our fullback, is *phlegmatic* and *taciturn*.

6. *Sardonic* wit befits a *saturnine* temperament.

7. The *ostentatious* Eagles played *aggressive* basketball.

8. The ostrich has a *fatuous* look but carries its head with an *arrogant* air.

9. The *unctuous* beggar appears *ingenuous,* but his police record shows how *sinuous* his dealings can be.

10. Rarely has anyone seen a man so *volatile* and so *supercilious*.

SECOND PRACTICE SET

Which base word from this unit best replaces each *italicized* word or group of words?

1. A *habitually silent* shopper might dislike a *talkative* clerk.

2. *Overbearingly proud* airs and a *bitterly scornful* sense of humor kept Joyce from making many friends.

3. The salesman does well because he is *assertive* in a brisk and *unsophisticated* way.

4. The *many-sided* artist is *fault-finding* and *disdainful* with his models.

5. The butler has an *excessively suave* voice and *fierce* manner.

6. Are small people more likely to be both *talkative* and *hasty?*

7. Though of a *sluggish* temperament, he is quite *inclined to join groups* in the evening.

8. The scout leader is *straightforward* in his ways but sometimes *hard to please*.

9. The foreman is *quick-tempered* about tardiness and sometimes *unduly positive* in political matters.

10. He justifies his *pretentious* behavior by being *scornfully distrustful* about modest people.

THIRD PRACTICE SET

Which lettered pair of items has the same relationship as the two words printed in capital letters?

1. CYNICAL : PESSIMISTIC :: (a) aggressive : unctuous (b) phlegmatic : apathetic (c) ostentatious : truculent (d) taciturn : naïve (e) presumptuous : precipitate

2. SARDONIC : SARCASM :: (a) fastidious : captiousness (b) impetuous : ingenuousness (c) sinuous : unction (d) dogmatic : dogma (e) ostentatious : naïveté

3. FATUOUS : INFATUATION :: (a) captious : captivation (b) taciturn : tacitness (c) dogmatic : dogmatism (d) ingenuous : ingenuity (e) volatile : volubility

4. VOLATILE : PHLEGMATIC :: (a) ostentatious : naïve (b) dogmatic : effeminate (c) gregarious : sociable (d) irascible : fatuous (e) garrulous : taciturn

5. IMPETUOUS : IMPULSIVE :: (a) ingenuous : ingenious (b) irresponsible : irascible (c) sardonic : sarcastic (d) timid : presumptuous (e) supercilious : meek

6. INGENUOUSNESS : DISINGENUOUS :: (a) arrogance : arrogant (b) femininity : effeminate (c) ostentation : unostentatious (d) gregariousness : aggregated (e) aggression : aggressive

7. NAÏVETÉ : ARTLESS :: (a) truculence : saturnine (b) irascibility : cynical (c) fatuousness : tranquil (d) gentleness : effeminate (e) taciturnity : reticent

8. SUPERCILIOUS : DISDAINFUL :: (a) volatile : changeless (b) versatile : gregarious (c) presumptuous : unctuous (d) ferocious : truculent (e) captious : fatuous

9. GREGARIOUS : UNSOCIABLE :: (a) garrulous : voluble
   (b) ingenuous : sinuous (c) irascible : impetuous (d) naïve :
   sincere (e) fastidious : undiscriminating

10. DOGMATIC : DOGMATIZE :: (a) presumptuous : presume
    (b) captious : capture (c) phlegmatic : emphasize (d) gar-
    rulous : notice (e) volatile : escape

THE RIGHT WORD

Which word from this unit best replaces each *italicized* word or
group of words?

1. She thinks she is *daintily refined* in matters of etiquette, but
   we think she is merely *irritable about small matters*.

2. Alcohol is very *quick to evaporate* and a very *adaptable-to-
   many-uses* solvent.

3. The ice cream man is *hot-tempered* and *fierce* toward anyone
   who treats him rudely.

4. We like Herb's *straightforwardness*, but he is sometimes inclined to be *forward in a meddlesome way*.

5. Is it his *quickness to act on emotional incitement* that makes
   him susceptible to *brief, unreasoning fondness?*

FAMILY REUNION

Write two paragraphs about an imaginary family reunion,
classifying each relative according to temperament.

1471-1528

UNIT SIX

Which word from the list at the right fits best in each blank?

The plot centers in an unusually __(1)__ German spy who tried to __(2)__ a British regiment. His plan was to infiltrate it and __(3)__ a mutiny. He made a very __(4)__ beginning when he was mistaken for a British lieutenant whom he had killed and whose uniform he had put on. He antagonized the commander, however, and tried to __(5)__ him with an apology. An __(6)__ slip of the tongue betrayed him, and his imperfect accent helped to __(7)__ his predicament. He realized that it would be __(8)__ to escape if he wanted to save his life, and he tried. Rifle fire began to __(9)__ upon him from several directions as he fled. He was injured and brought back. As there was nothing to __(10)__ his treachery, he was shot by a firing squad the next morning.

annihilate
extenuate
propitiate
converge
auspicious
meretricious
egregious
expedient
incongruous
aggravate
degenerate
instigate

343

• Word List— VERBS

1. AGGRAVATE (ăg′rà·vāt) . . . . make worse or more severe

Robert's irritability was aggravated by a persistent headache.

■ A cold winter brought aggravation of the suffering in the flood-devastated towns of New England.

2. ANNIHILATE (ă·nī′ĭ·lāt) . . . . destroy utterly

A few atomic bombs could annihilate the whole city.

■ Such annihilation would be more complete and more lasting than any other form of destruction could achieve.

Terrible Trio: To annihilate is to deprive something of its existence. To **obliterate** is to destroy by rendering unrecognizable: Rain obliterated every clue that would have helped police find the murderer.
One may obliterate an inscription, but one is more likely to burn, **raze, wreck** or **destroy** a building.
To **exterminate** is to wipe out, in the sense of killing: Madame Defarge wanted to exterminate an entire family, even though extermination would include a wife and child who were innocent of any crime.

3. ASSUAGE (ă·swāj′) . . . . soften, appease, pacify

Father's sympathy served to assuage Junior's disappointment over his stolen bicycle.

■ The assuagement of a nation's grief over the loss of its freedom is not achieved in a day or two.

Feelings are assuaged; people are comforted.
Cf. alleviate, allay, pacify, mitigate

4. CAPITULATE (kà·pĭt′ụ·lāt) . . . . surrender on certain terms

Although the principal refused, at first, to allow us to use the school gym for the party, he capitulated when we agreed to clean everything up before we left.

■ The capitulation of the enemy commander, on the condition that his men be unharmed, brought an end to the fighting.

5. **CONVERGE** (kŏn·vûrj′) . . come together, tend toward one point

They agreed to meet where the three paths converge.
Some thirty lives and thirty minds converge briefly in this English class.
- Will the convergence be a memorable one?
▸ In two convergent lines, students waited for food in the cafeteria.

6. **DEGENERATE** (dĕ·jĕn′ẽr·āt) . . . . deteriorate, grow worse

The morals of the city degenerated during the war.
- The degeneration among young people took various forms, such as narcotic addiction and alcoholism.
- The police arrested a degenerate (person of evil, unwholesome character).

7. **EXTENUATE** (ĕks·tĕn′ů·āt) . . . . make less serious, diminish

"Ignorance of the law does not extenuate a crime," the judge declared firmly.
▸ "Please consider the extenuating circumstances," the lawyer replied. "My client is young and new in this country."
- In extenuation of the crime, the lawyer also pleaded his client's lack of English.

Extenuate, like **tenuous**, comes from a Latin word meaning "thin."

8. **INSTIGATE** (ĭn′stĭ·gāt) . . . . provoke, incite

How did a false message instigate the attack?
- Max entered the contest at the instigation of a teacher.
- The instigator of a crime is as guilty as the actual miscreant.

Inciters: **impel, goad, spur, tempt**

9. **MITIGATE** (mĭt′ĭ·gāt) . . . . lessen, make milder

A large lake tends to mitigate extremes of climate along its shores.
- The governor would not discuss mitigation of the sentence.

Mitigate, like **assuage**, may be applied to emotions, but is more often used of the weather and outward events or conditions.

10. MOLLIFY (mŏl'ĭ·fī) . . . . **appease, pacify**

A piece of candy will often mollify a crying child.

■ Mollification of an angry adult requires tact, patience, and, perhaps, restitution or penance of some kind.

Mollify is used chiefly with reference to persons or animals and their feelings.

11. NEGOTIATE (nē·gō'shĭ·āt) . . . . . . **arrange, deal with**

The Secretary of State tried to negotiate a treaty with Pakistan.

The mine operators refused to negotiate with the strikers.

■ Later they relented, but negotiations broke off when the strikers presented their demands.

A negotiable bond, check, promissory note, or other paper is one which can be passed from one person to another as if it were money. (See dictionary for financial meanings of *negotiate*.)

12. PROCRASTINATE (prō·krăs'tĭ·nāt) . . . . **delay action, put off (from day to day)**

It is easy to procrastinate about seeing a dentist.

■ Uncle George worked out several European tours on paper, but procrastination kept him from ever going on them.

■ Queen Elizabeth I was a skillful procrastinator who often temporized or postponed decisions on difficult problems.

The Latin word *cras*, "tomorrow," is clearly visible in *procrastinate* and helps explain its meaning.

13. PROPITIATE (prō·pĭsh'ĭ·āt) . . . . . . **appease, conciliate**

The life of Charles Darnay was not enough to propitiate Madame Defarge's passion for vengeance.

► To the headman of the tribe, the dove was a propitious (favorable) sign, indicating that peace would continue.

Propitiate means "appease or conciliate" by somehow making amends for a shortcoming or misdeed. Unlike *mollify* and *assuage*, the word involves compensation or reparation.
Expiate means "attempt to undo a wrong" by suffering punishment or making reparation.
Cf. atone, placate

▸ Word List— ADJECTIVES

1. AUSPICIOUS (ôs·pǐsh′ǔs) . . . . . promising, favorable

Government spending made the year an auspicious one in which to launch a new business.

▪ The hobby show will be held under the auspices (sponsorship) of the Kiwanis Club.

Cf. propitious

2. EGREGIOUS (ė·grē′jǔs) . . . . . remarkably bad, flagrant

Dan made an egregious fool of himself when he jumped into the pool to save a floating dummy.

▪ Slowly, he realized the egregiousness of his blunder.

Egregious originally meant "out from the herd."
See also *Ex* Words (I, 9) and *Greg* Words (II, 12).

3. EQUIVOCAL (ė·kwǐv′ō·kăl) . . vague, ambiguous, questionable

The senator's equivocal reply to the reporter's question made it difficult to guess his true opinions.

He is a man of equivocal character, with a police record that may belie his trustworthiness.

● Do you ever equivocate to avoid embarrassment?

An **obscure** poem is one that can only be understood with great difficulty.
A **vague** poem is one that is hazy, indefinite, and unclear by its very nature.
An **enigmatic** poem is one that puzzles or perplexes. (See III, 1.)
A **cryptic** poem is one that is intentionally puzzling.

4. EXPEDIENT (ĕks·pē′dǐ·ĕnt) . . suitable, advisable; advantageous but not necessarily right

Is preparedness the most expedient way to avoid war?

▪ The expediency of the plan was evident, but it nevertheless seemed unjust.

▪ Bombing cities is an expedient (device for advantage) designed to cut off supplies before they reach the front.

5. **FORTUITOUS** (fôr·tū'ĭ·tŭs)   .   .   occurring by chance or accident

A fortuitous encounter with a beggar provided a valuable clue to the location of the lost mine.

■ Everyone commented upon the fortuitousness of his arrival.

Fortuitous implies good fortune as well as chance.
Cf. casual, adventitious

6. **INCONGRUOUS** (ĭn·kŏn'grŏŏ·ŭs)   .   .   .   discordant, ill-matched

It was incongruous to see the mayor wielding a shovel.

■ The incongruousness of the sight was unforgettable.

■ Incongruity (disproportion) is said to be the basis of humor.

Incongruous also means "inappropriate, inharmonious, unbecoming, inconsistent." It is not often used of persons.
Incompatible means incapable of being harmonized: Anger and serenity are incompatible.
Incompatibility is a cause of unhappiness in marriage.
Cf. compatible (III, 8)

7. **INTRINSIC** (ĭn·trĭn'sĭk)   .   .   .   .   .   actual; essential, inherent

Silver coins have an intrinsic value somewhat less than their face value.

A man's intrinsic qualities come to the surface sooner or later.

The intrinsic or **inherent** value of something is the value belonging to it by its very nature: The intrinsic value of a check is only that of a piece of paper.

8. **MERETRICIOUS** (měr'ē·trĭsh'ŭs)   .   .   .   .   deceptively alluring; gaudily ornamented

Mrs. Higgs lavishes upon her friends a meretricious sympathy which is unctuous and at times almost maudlin.

■ The meretriciousness of chain-letter schemes saves them from oblivion.

Cf. plausible (I, 3), *credible* (II, 8), *specious* (III, 8)

9. **PASTORAL** (pàs'tô·răl)   .   .   pertaining to shepherds or rural life

Mr. Stevens likes pastoral poetry and pastoral music.

Pastor originally meant "shepherd." Like **minister,** the more common designation, it now refers to the head of a Protestant church.

10. **SACRILEGIOUS** (săk'rĭ·lē'jŭs) . . . . irreverent, blasphemous

In Scotland, it was once considered sacrilegious to whistle on Sunday.

- The use of an organ in a church was once deemed a sacrilege.
- Sacrilegiousness was punished severely in Geneva during the sixteenth century.

11. **SALUBRIOUS** (så·lū'brĭ·ŭs) . . . . healthful, promoting health

The salubrious mountain air brings color to one's cheeks.

- The salubriousness of the climate draws many new residents to California each year.

Salutary means "conducive to health or well being": The sharp decrease of polio cases showed the salutary effects of Salk vaccine.

12. **SYNTHETIC** (sĭn·thĕt'ĭk) . . . . . . artificial, manufactured

The sympathy Mrs. Higgs offered was synthetic, not genuine.
Synthetic rubber is one of many products produced by chemicals rather than by nature.

- Such products are known as synthetics.
- A synthesis is a combining of parts into a new whole.

FIRST PRACTICE SET

Copy the *italicized* words. Beside each, write an appropriate definition.

1. The *expedient* thing to do is to clear up the *equivocal* parts of the agreement before you sign it.
2. A rebel general *instigated* the plan to *converge* on the city from four directions simultaneously.
3. Keeping active *mitigates* somewhat the tendency to *degenerate* physically.
4. Germany tried to *negotiate* a new treaty which would *mollify* her neighbor.

5. His first encounter was *auspicious* because it showed his *intrinsic* ability.

6. Her weeping was a *meretricious* device which served to elicit only *synthetic* sympathy.

7. The composer never finished his p*astoral* symphony because he had a tendency to *procrastinate*.

8. When his dog tore up the magazines, he tried to *propitiate* his sister and *assuage* her anger with a box of candy.

9. One may *extenuate* a man's faults but not *annihilate* them.

10. Mr. Forbes did not *capitulate* to his wife's demand because he thought it *incongruous*.

SECOND PRACTICE SET

Which base word from this unit best replaces each *italicized* word or group of words?

1. Nothing would *pacify* the manager or *lessen* his bitterness about losing his job.

2. Something *deceptively alluring* about the Pied Piper caused the rats to *tend toward one point* behind him.

3. The British Government finds it *advantageous* to *deal or treat* with the Chinese about a new trade agreement.

4. Mountain climbing is a *health-promoting* pastime capable of *lessening* even a fierce man's restlessness.

5. *Artificial* gasoline has *inherent* qualities equal to those of the natural product.

6. The knight tried to *conciliate* the angry king by *ambiguous* praise that sounded sincere.

7. The *occurring-by-chance* mistake proved *favorable* for the scientist because it led to the discovery of a new element.

8. Hitler was a *flagrant* example of a tyrant who almost managed to *destroy utterly* an entire people.

9. The behavior of radium *provoked* the study of atoms and the *discordant* nature of their behavior.

10. The governor's desire to *delay action* indefinitely will *make worse* the public dissatisfaction.

THIRD PRACTICE SET

Which pair of words *(a, b, c,* or *d)* best completes the meaning of each sentence?

1. The advent of the automobile served to __?__ the traffic problem at Haymarket Square where seven streets __?__.

   (a) mitigate—extenuate (b) negotiate—synthesize
   (c) aggravate—converge (d) capitulate—procrastinate

2. The assignment of traits from the reservoirs of heredity is a very __?__ process rather than one of __?__, such as one might desire.

   (a) fortuitous—expediency (b) egregious—incongruity
   (c) equivocal—degeneration (d) auspicious—negotiation

3. His grief was __?__ as he turned over in his mind the memories which nothing could ever __?__.

   (a) synthesized—exterminate (b) extenuated—mitigate
   (c) capitulated—annihilate (d) assuaged—obliterate

4. The __?__ message was too intentionally puzzling to __?__ the king's wrath; quite the contrary, his wrath grew.

   (a) obscure—propitiate (b) cryptic—mitigate
   (c) enigmatic—mollify (d) vague—aggravate

5. The inmates, who had taken over the prison, wanted to __?__ with the warden before talking of __?__.

   (a) extenuate—mitigation (b) procrastinate—propitiation
   (c) equivocate—assuagement (d) negotiate—capitulation

6. A Communist set out to __?__ various dramatic acts of violent __?__.

   (a) instigate—sacrilege (b) extenuate—mereticiousness
   (c) aggravate—egregiousness (d) assuage—degeneration

7. It would be __?__ folly to __?__ any longer about having the brakes fixed.

    (a) inexpedient—extenuate   (b) fortuitous—negotiate
    (c) egregious—procrastinate   (d) ambiguous—propitiate

8. The __?__ law to increase old-age pensions was passed to __?__ the elderly voters in the state.

    (a) expedient—instigate   (b) egregious—assuage
    (c) equivocal—aggravate   (d) meretricious—mollify

9. The girl had to __?__ in order to __?__ her rejected suitor's disappointment.

    (a) negotiate—instigate   (b) equivocate—assuage
    (c) extenuate—degenerate   (d) procrastinate—synthesize

10. Nothing could __?__ the crime he had committed, but he worked years to __?__ to some degree.

    (a) mollify—converge   (b) extenuate—expiate
    (c) annihilate—assuage   (d) aggravate—procrastinate

A WORD FOR IT

Which word from this unit best replaces each *italicized* word or group of words?

1. The powder will *wipe out* ants if you sprinkle it at the *coming together* of several lines of their traffic.

2. The new law is a *combining of ideas* of several different bills to *appease by making amends to* the farmers.

3. It was *advisable* for the skiers to find shelter before the blizzard grew worse. The *chance* discovery of a cave solved their problem.

4. The proposal has *inherent* merit; besides, this is a very *favorable* time for new legislation.

5. Nothing could *lessen* the seriousness of his *flagrant* error.

UNIT SEVEN

Which word at the right is indicated by each phrase?

1. He's a guardian of valuable treasures: __?__

2. He's a middle-class citizen: __?__

3. He goes on concert tours: __?__

4. He's a competent judge of painting: __?__

5. He's a wise counselor: __?__

6. This one specializes in retribution: __?__

7. He's a swift messenger or guide: __?__

8. He's uncultured: __?__

9. She's a society girl: __?__

10. She's a trifler at love: __?__

ballerina
curator
bourgeois
philistine
coquette
mercury
debutante
connoisseur
liaison
virtuoso
mentor
nemesis

▪ Word List—TEN WORDS OF FRENCH FAME

1.   BOURGEOIS (bo͞or·zhwä′) . . . (member of) the middle class

In France, a bourgeois is a member of the middle class.
▸ Bourgeois virtues include thrift, industriousness, and honesty.
Members of the bourgeoisie (middle class) are often conservative in their habits.

> Traditionally, society was divided into three clases: the **aristocratic** (patrician, landowning) class, the **bourgeois** class, and the **proletarian** (laboring) class. Does such a division exist in the United States today?

2.   CONNOISSEUR (kŏn′ĭ·sûr′) . . . . . competent judge

Dr. Weems, a connoisseur of classical music, has directed a symphony orchestra for many years.

> A connoisseur has abundant knowledge and sharp discrimination in some field, especially in one of the fine arts.
> A **gourmet** is a connoisseur of fine food and drink.
> A **gourmand** is a hearty or greedy eater.
> *Cf. epicure*

3.   COQUETTE (kȯ·kĕt′) . . . . . . flirt, female trifler at love

Julie is pretty enough to be quite a coquette.
▸ Myrna may grow less coquettish as she gets older.
▪ Her coquettishness may disappear when she really falls in love.

4.   COTERIE (kō′tĕ·rĭ) . . . . social set, clique

Carol's little coterie of artists is quite unfriendly to strangers.

> A coterie is a group of people who meet regularly for social purposes.
> A **clique** (klēk) is a small, exclusive coterie, often rather snobbish toward outsiders: In the senior class, there are several cliques, each with ten or twelve members.
> A **set** is a rather large group, often of society people linked together by common interests: The novel described the life of the smart set in New York.

5. CRITIQUE (krĭ·tēk') . . . . written analysis of a work of art

Each pupil did a critique of Browning's "Prospice."
The newspaper is famous for its literary critiques.

Critique means also "the art of criticism."

6. DEBUTANTE (dĕb'ů·tänt') . . . . society girl

Six debutantes were chatting gaily as they planned a charity ball.
One of them had made her debut (first appearance in society) only a few weeks before.
The pianist made his debut in Paris.

A **debut** (dā'bū) is any first appearance before the public.

7. INTRIGUE (ĭn·trēg') . . . . plotting, scheming

A state senator was the center of a political intrigue to get himself nominated for governor.
• As he grew older, realistic novels began to intrigue him (arouse his interest).

Intrigue may also mean "illicit love affair."

8. LIAISON (lē'ā·zŏn') . . . . unofficial linkage

The Department of the Army has a liaison with the State Department in order to coordinate its activities. In theory, the Secretary of the Army should always deal directly with the Secretary of the Navy, but in practice there must be numerous linkages that bypass the Secretaries.
▶ Col. Bridges is a liaison officer in the Pentagon.

Originally, *liaison* meant "illicit love affair."
How does this fact illuminate its present meaning?

9. PROTÉGÉ (prō'tĕ·zhā) . person under another's care or patronage

Joe gradually became the coach's protégé.
The singer is a protégé of a famous teacher, who found her in a little Hungarian village and adopted her when she was ten.

Protégée, like *fiancée,* is the feminine form of the word. It is seldom used in English.

10.   REPERTOIRE (rĕp′ĕr·twär) . . . list of operas, plays, etc., which
                                     a company or individual is prepared to perform

Most professional singers have an extensive repertoire,
ranging from operatic arias to folk songs.

▶ Because he belonged to a repertory company for some
years, the actor has played a wide variety of roles.

A **repertory** company is a theatrical group, organized on a more or less
permanent basis, which not only presents new plays but also maintains
a repertoire of classic plays. The Old Vic Theater in London and the
Comédie Française in Paris are famous repertory companies.

Word List—FROM NAMES

"I am become a name."—Tennyson's "Ulysses"

1.   ■ MALAPROPISM (măl′á·prŏp·ĭz′m) . . blunder in choice of words

In his talk, Phil accidentally used a malapropism: "The
police demanded immediate destitution of the stolen
goods." He meant to say "restitution."

Mrs. Malaprop, a pompous "she-dragon" in Sheridan's play, *The Rivals,*
had a great fondness for long words but a strong tendency to confuse
them, substituting for the word she intended another word of similar
sound but different meaning. For example, she declared that a girl
should have "a supercilious knowledge" of accounting, should know
something of "contagious countries," and should "reprehend the true
meaning of what she is saying." Mrs. Malaprop's name comes from
malapropos (originally French), which means "unseasonable, ill-
timed, inappropriate."
A *spoonerism* is another kind of verbal confusion: "A man rode down
the street on a well-boiled icicle." (See *facetiousness*, II, 10.)

2.   ■ MENTOR (mĕn′tẽr) .   .   .   . a wise, trusted adviser

The coach of a team or adviser of a school club is often
called its mentor.

Uncle Joe was my favorite uncle and most trusted mentor.

Mentor was the friend to whom the Greek hero Odysseus entrusted his
household and his son Telemachus before leaving for the Trojan War.

3. ■ MERCURY (mûr′kŭ·rĭ) . . . . . . heavy, metallic liquid;
messenger, carrier of news

The magazine publishers called their new periodical "The
Mercury," because they hoped that it would be a guide to
literature and world events.

► A mercurial person is volatile, quick-witted, changeable.

In Roman mythology, Mercury was the eloquent, clever, swift-footed
messenger of the gods. The planet was named in his honor. Medieval
alchemists gave the same name to the metal commonly known as
quicksilver.

4. ■ NEMESIS (něm′ė·sĭs) . . agent of retribution; a just punishment

As he was running away with Silas Marner's gold, Dunstan
met his nemesis when he fell into the quarry and drowned.
Brutus became Caesar's nemesis.

Nemesis was the Greek goddess of retribution or vengeance. The modern word may be applied to the retribution itself, or to the agent. (See
II, 8 for *retribution.*)

5. ► PROTEAN (prō′tė·ăn) . . . . exceedingly variable, readily
taking numerous forms

A science fiction writer needs a protean imagination.
Clark is a man of protean abilities: as actor, author, director, and producer, he has become a major figure in the
theatrical world.

In Greek mythology, Proteus was a sea-god who could assume many
different forms, among them that of a lion, a snake, a tree, and a fire.

6. ► STENTORIAN (stěn·tōr′rĭ·ăn) . . . . very loud or powerful

The foghorn gave forth a stentorian blast.
Mr. Eppling used to speak in stentorian tones.

In the *Iliad,* Stentor was a herald with a very powerful voice.

7. ● VULCANIZE (vŭl′kăn·īz) . . treat (rubber) with heat and sulfur

The machine vulcanizes rubber to make it more elastic and
durable. The process is also used to harden rubber.

■ Vulcanization of patches fuses them to the inner tube.

Vulcan was the Roman god of fire and metal working. The word *volcano* also comes from his name.

▪ Word List—EIGHT FROM FINE ARTS

1. **ALLEGORY** (ăl′ē·gō′rĭ) . . story in which characters are symbolic

   The Animal Farm, by George Orwell, is an allegory in which various animals symbolize social forces.
   Idylls of the King has an allegorical meaning.
   In "Gareth and Lynette," Death, the most terrible and formidable of the knights, turns out to be a young boy, easily overthrown. What does this allegory signify?

   The characters of an allegory are usually personified virtues or vices. Church pageants frequently include allegorical figures.

2. **BALLET** (băl′â) . . style of dancing; (a kind of) dance performance

   Ballet is an art which combines the beauty of music with the beauty of the dance.
   A ballet is an elaborate dance, using a special technique, which is presented upon a stage by a group of dancers. Many ballets tell a story, using movement and music instead of words.

   A **ballerina** (female dancer) needs years of training before she is able to execute the various ballet steps with ease and grace.
   The art of composing ballets is called *choreography* (kō′rē·ŏg′rá·fĭ).
   The composer of dances is the **choreographer.**

3. **CURATOR** (kû·rā′tēr) . . custodian of a museum or art collection

   The curator of the art gallery went to Paris to inspect a group of Renoir paintings.
   ▪ He has held the curatorship for ten years.

   In law, *curator* means "guardian of a minor or incompetent person," in which case, the word is accented on the first syllable.

4. **DENOUEMENT** (dà·nōō′mäN) . . outcome, solution (of a story or play)

   The denouement of a story plot must be believable as well as appropriate.

Discovery of the missing document brought the denouement of the prolonged litigation to settle the old man's
estate.

This word comes from a French verb meaning "unravel or untie."

5. OVATION (ō·vā′shŭn) . . . **enthusiastic reception or applause**

New York gives returning heroes a big ovation as they ride
down Fifth Avenue.
The Boston Symphony got a big ovation.

In ancient Rome, an ovation was a celebration for a general whose victory was not important enough to merit the celebration called a
"triumph."

6. PHILISTINE (fĭ·lĭs′tĭn; fĭl′ĭs·tĭn) . . . . **a person lacking in, or
indifferent to, culture**

Mrs. Gulch is a complete philistine when it comes to art,
literature, and music.
Have radio, television, and education reduced the philistine
tendencies in American life?

The Biblical Philistines were a warlike tribe who often attacked the
Israelites.

7. SYMMETRY (sĭm′ē·trĭ) . . . **balance, correspondence of parts**

The intricate symmetry of a snowflake shows up under
magnification.
▸ A maple leaf is relatively symmetrical.

Symmetry denotes a rather exact balance in the size, shape, and position of the parts on either side of a dividing line, which produces an
aesthetically satisfying whole that has regularity and proportion.

8. VIRTUOSO (vûr′tụ·ō′sō) . . . **person especially skilled in one
of the fine arts**

The violinist is a world-famed virtuoso.
He maintains his high level of virtuosity by practicing several hours every day.

Note: Each art has its own vocabulary, which requires some study of the art itself
and cannot be included in a book of general vocabulary such as this one.

FIRST PRACTICE SET

Copy the *italicized* words. Beside each, write an appropriate definition.

1. He looks like a *bourgeois* tradesman, but he is actually an art dealer and a *connoisseur* of Renaissance painting.

2. The young *debutante* is a *coquette* whose *coterie* of male admirers like to discuss her charms among themselves.

3. Queen Elizabeth I was fond of *intrigue,* and the question of her *liaison* with Essex has been carefully investigated.

4. The *critique* of the new play was written by a *protégé* of the author.

5. When the young soprano referred to the great *virtuoso* as her Stentor, she was using a *malapropism.*

6. Mr. Blake, the *mentor* of our debating team, advises against *stentorian* tones.

7. The company has a large *repertoire* of *ballets,* including several by its own choreographer.

8. An O. Henry story has a *symmetry* that is fairly regular and a *denouement* that is sudden and unexpected.

9. Even the *philistines* in the audience joined enthusiastically in the standing *ovation* at the close of the concert.

10. The *curator* of the city museum is writing an *allegory* in which Uncle Sam represents American common sense and generosity.

SECOND PRACTICE SET

Which base word from this unit best replaces each *italicized* word or group of words?

1. The *society girl* was not interested in *middle-class* life.

2. A *social set* of young people, who consider themselves *competent judges* of popular music, gathers weekly to play records.

3. The governor's political *trusted adviser* maintained *an unofficial linkage* with the judges of the state supreme court.

4. The refugee boy came to America as *a person under the care* of the *custodian* of the museum.

5. The play's *outcome* brought a great *burst of enthusiastic applause*.

6. The coach has a *very powerful* voice and uses it.

7. The *agent of retribution* of the Arthurian *story in which characters are symbolic* is a traitor knight.

8. The *Daily (Messenger)* contained a fine *analysis* of the play.

9. The *very variable* range of the *person-skilled-in-one-of-the-arts* impressed everyone.

10. To be aesthetically pleasing, a tower should have *correspondence of parts on either side.*

THIRD PRACTICE SET

Which lettered pair of items has the same relationship as the pair printed in capital letters?

1. CRITIC : PERFORMER :: (a) connoisseur : virtuoso (b) mercury : gods (c) philistine : debutante (d) concert : ovation

2. NEMESIS : RETRIBUTION :: (a) Vulcan : volcano (b) Mercury : newspaper (c) Stentor : herald (d) Proteus : variability

3. TEACHER : PROTÉGÉ :: (a) ballerina : ballet (b) debutante : coquette (c) mentor : virtuoso (d) bourgeois : denouement

4. AUTHOR : ALLEGORY :: (a) curator : museum (b) choreographer : ballet (c) coquette : admirers (d) actor : repertoire

5. MALAPROPISM : SPOONERISM :: (a) ovation : audience (b) liaison : army (c) scheme : intrigue (d) drama : ballet

6. ACTOR : REPERTOIRE :: (a) music : connoisseur (b) character : allegory (c) ballerina : ballets (d) curator : museum

7. PROTEUS : PROTEAN :: (a) Vulcan : vulgar (b) Stentor : senatorial (c) Odysseus : Trojan (d) Mercury : mercurial

8. COTERIE : CLIQUE :: (a) Proteus : Mercury (b) performer : virtuoso (c) debutante : society (d) ovation : Roman general

9. CURATOR : MUSEUM :: (a) Mentor : Telemachus (b) dividing line : symmetry (c) denouement : short story (d) choreographer : ovation

10. BOURGEOIS : ARISTOCRAT :: (a) Mercury : Olympus (b) debutante : virtuoso (c) philistine : connoisseur (d) ballet : opera

BONUS

(1) Make a list of Mrs. Malaprop's blunders and add a few that you have discovered or devised. Or take a dictionary of mythology and make a list of words that have come from mythological names.

(2) The word *impeccable* originally meant "free from sin." Dictionaries still include the positive form of this word, *peccable,* meaning "liable or prone to sin," but it has almost disappeared from current usage. David McCord, a well-known writer of verse, is waging a lighthearted campaign to restore such positive forms. By separating prefixes from the accompanying roots, Mr. McCord has discovered such words as *ept* and *ert* (from *inept* and *inert*). If you would like to join in the search for the Lost Positive, draw up a list of ten such forms. Then check your list with a dictionary to see whether these positive forms actually exist. Here are three to help you begin: *couth, sheveled, kempt.*

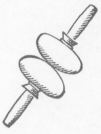

UNIT EIGHT

How many can you answer correctly?

1. A compatible person is (a) easy-going (b) easy to get along with (c) easy to dislike (d) easy to get rid of.
2. A person careful to observe the amenities is (a) very superstitious (b) very scrupulous (c) very polite (d) very sure to serve refreshments.
3. An option is (a) an exclamation (b) a curtain (c) a bill of sale (d) the right of choice.
4. A specious excuse is (a) prompt (b) evasive (c) deceptive (d) merely vague.
5. A criterion is (a) an animal (b) a critic (c) a model of perfection (d) a standard of judgment.
6. Comity pertains to (a) the theater (b) diplomacy (c) astronomy (d) beauty culture.
7. A crucial struggle is primarily (a) decisive (b) regrettable (c) injurious (d) prolonged.
8. Hyperbole is (a) a missile (b) cold weather (c) exaggeration (d) extravagance.
9. A nonchalant person is (a) indifferent (b) easy-going (c) negative (d) abstinent.
10. A deleterious substance is (a) hateful (b) laugh-producing (c) light and flaky (d) harmful to health.

▪ Word List—NOUNS

1. **AMENITY** (á·mĕn′ĭ·tĭ) . . . . . . **a pleasing way or custom**

   Saying "thank you" is an everyday amenity that makes life pleasanter.

   Visitors from Europe find the amenities here somewhat different from their own.

   ▸ Father is not always amenable (submissive) to suggestions.

   Amenable also means "liable": Speeders are amenable to arrest.
   Synonym: **civility**

2. **CRITERION** (krī·tḗr′ĭ·ŭn) . . . . . **basis or standard for judging**

   Vocabulary is one criterion of intelligence.

   Other criteria include mathematical skill and reading ability.

   The plural of *criterion* is **criteria.** The plural of *phenomenon* is *phenomena.* From what language do these words come?

3. **DIPLOMACY** (dĭ·plō′má·sĭ) . **skillful handling of touchy negotiations**

   Each international crisis demands patient diplomacy.

   Family arguments often require the patience and tact of a diplomat.

   Comity means "courtesy and civility," especially courtesy between nations in observing each others' laws and institutions.
   Protocol is the term given to the ceremonial forms and etiquette of diplomatic relations. For example, the rules of protocol determine who sits where at state dinners. (See dictionary for other meanings.)

4. **HYPERBOLE** (hī·pûr′bô·lē) . . . . . . **exaggeration for effect**

   "The waves were mountain-high" and "I almost died laughing" are common examples of hyperbole.

   ▸ Poets often use hyperbolical language.

   Litotes (lī′tô·tēz) is a kind of understatement in which one says the opposite of what one means, often using a negative. Thus, "Not a few came to the reception" means that many came.
   Hyper Words meaning "above, beyond normal": *hypertension, hypertrophy, hypersensitive, hyperacidity* (I, 12)

5. INTEGRITY (ĭn·tĕg′rĭ·tĭ) . . . . moral soundness, uprightness

The banker was a man of the utmost integrity, honest in all his dealings and unimpeachable in character.
The gate keeper showed his integrity when he refused to accept a bribe.

Integrity literally means "oneness or wholeness of character."
Cf. *integer*

6. INTUITION (ĭn′tŭ·ĭsh′ŭn) . . . . instinctive knowledge

She knew by intuition that she could not believe him.
► Religious faith is often largely intuitive.

Intuition literally means "untaught knowledge."
Cf. *tuition,* the charge for instruction in a college or private school.

7. NONCHALANCE (nŏn′shá·lăns) . . . indifference, unconcern

Bill's nonchalance under fire amazed his comrades.
- Nonchalantly, the man faced his accusers. Did his attitude result from knowledge of his innocence or from mere bravado (pretense of boldness)?
► The fighter remained as nonchalant in defeat as he had been in victory.

8. OPTIMISM (ŏp′tĭ·mĭz′m) . . . . tendency to expect the best

The doctor's optimism gave the sick man courage.
► Past victories made us optimistic about winning the pennant. He is an optimist because he can't see too many reasons why things should go wrong.

See also *optimum* "most favorable": The optimum temperature for a home is 68°-70°.
Review *sanguine* (II, 9).

9. OPTION (ŏp′shŭn) . . . . right of choice

Each buyer has the option of paying cash or making time payments.
► The searchlight is optional equipment (left to one's choice).

An option may also be the thing chosen: He prefers the second option, time payments.

10. **PERTINACITY** (pûr'tĭ·năs'ĭ·tĭ) . . . . stubborn perseverance

A salesman must have pertinacity because he meets so much resistance.

▶ Boswell was a pertinacious young man who never left Dr. Johnson's side.

Pertinacity is generally used in an unfavorable sense, **tenacity** in a favorable sense (II, 2).
Cf. *doggedness, persistence, resoluteness, stubbornness, obstinacy* (I, 8)

11. **PESSIMISM** (pĕs'ĭ·mĭz'm) . . . . tendency to expect the worst

He pictured all the catastrophes that might occur and his resulting pessimism made him very careful.

▶ Cloudy skies made everyone pessimistic about the picnic.
According to a popular definition, an optimist is a person who says, "Pass the sugar, please." A pessimist is a person who says, "There isn't any sugar left, I suppose?"

A **cynic** distrusts human motives and therefore takes a pessimistic view of mankind (III, 5).
A **misanthrope** is a hater of mankind.

12. **PRESTIGE** (prĕs·tēzh') . . . recognized influence or standing

This country has achieved great prestige in world affairs.
Advertising helped to give the product new prestige.

▶ Word List—ADJECTIVES

1. **CLANDESTINE** (klăn·dĕs'tĭn) . . . . secret, stealthy

The rebel leaders held a clandestine meeting in a cave.

▬ The drugs were brought into the country clandestinely.

Varieties of Secrecy: A **covert** glance is disguised, secret: The child threw covert glances at the forbidden box of candy.
A **furtive** glance is sly and wary: The pickpocket needed only one furtive glance to discover the location of the man's wallet.
A **surreptitious** visit is stealthy and concealed, although without the same sense of guilt that a clandestine visit might imply.

2. **COHERENT** (kō·hēr′ĕnt) . . . . sticking together, connected

The nurse tried to give a coherent account of what had happened.

■ Frank's explanation was confused and lacking in coherence (logical order).

The patient, though conscious, was incoherent with fever.

● A magnet makes iron filings cohere readily.

Coherence is usually applied to figurative or abstract things, *cohesion* to material things: The wet clay formed a cohesive mass.
Similar substances **cohere** when they stick together; dissimilar substances **adhere**.
Cf. adhesion, adhesiveness

3. **COMPATIBLE** (kŏm·păt′ĭ·b′l) . . capable of being harmonized

The hobo's garb is hardly compatible with his cultured way of speaking.

■ The speaker discussed different kinds of temperaments and their compatibility.

The optimistic and the pessimistic view are likely to be incompatible.

The term *congruous* has a similar meaning but is less frequently used than *compatible*.
Antonyms: *incongruous, incongruity* (III, 6), *incompatible, incompatibility*

4. **CRUCIAL** (krōo′shǎl) . . supremely important, decisive; severe

The third quarter proved to be crucial because we were one point behind.

Misfortune is a crucial test of character.

Crucial comes from the Latin word *crux,* "cross." Why does it suggest severe, climactic suffering?
Other Cross Words: *crucify, crucifix, cruciform, crucifer*

5. **DELETERIOUS** (dĕl′ē·tēr′ĭ·ŭs) . . . harmful to health, injurious

The new medicine sometimes has deleterious side effects.

■ The doctor stressed the deleteriousness of irregular habits of eating and sleeping.

Disease germs are **pernicious** (II, 9), and sewer gas is **noxious**.
An **obnoxious** (I, 6) person is merely **offensive** or **objectionable**.

6. **IMMUTABLE** (ĭ·mū′tȧ·b′l) . . . . unchangeable, changeless

The laws of the Medes were said to be immutable because not even the king could set aside one that he had made.

■ The immutability of the law of gravitation throughout the universe makes it possible to calculate one's weight on the moon.

A **mutation** is a variation, especially a departure from hereditary pattern in a plant or animal.
A **mutable** affection is a variable one.

7. **IMPERVIOUS** (ĭm·pûr′vĭ·ŭs) . . . impenetrable; unaffected by

Paraffin is impervious to water.

■ This imperviousness makes it useful in sealing jars of jelly. Her brother could have improved his manners if he had not been impervious to criticism.

Cf. Vi(a) Words (II, 10)

8. **IRIDESCENT** (ĭr′ĭ·dĕs′ĕnt) . . . . . . glistening with colors

Diamonds and dewdrops are remarkably iridescent.

■ Rainbows are caused by the iridescence of fine mist in sunlight.

In both Greek and Latin, the word *iris* means "rainbow"; thus *iridescent* means "shining like a rainbow."

9. **PEREMPTORY** (pēr·ĕmp′tȯ·rĭ) . . imperative, positive, dictatorial

The doctor's orders were peremptory: "No visitors under any circumstances."

■ The angry father ordered his son out of the house peremptorily.

A peremptory command or demand is absolute. It permits no refusal, denial, or delay.
For the legal meaning of this word, see dictionary.
Cf. imperious under *imperial* (III, 2)

10. **PERFUNCTORY** (pēr·fŭngk′tȯ·rĭ) . . . halfhearted, indifferent

The mayor's acceptance speech sounded perfunctory, as if he didn't want the job he had worked so hard to get.

■ On hot days, the men worked very perfunctorily.

11. **PREPOSTEROUS** (prė·pŏs'tēr·ŭs)   .   .   absurd, contrary to reason

At first, the demand for a thirty-two-hour week seemed preposterous.

■ Father saw clearly the preposterousness of the scheme to make a skating rink by flooding the main street.

A **ludicrous** plan is laughable chiefly because it is incongruous.
A preposterous plan is laughable because it is unsound. (Consult a dictionary for the meaning of the original Latin word.)

12. **RECALCITRANT** (rė·kăl'sĭ·trănt)   .   .   refusing to comply, defiant

It took a fire to start the recalcitrant mule.

■ The recalcitrance of Congress became a campaign issue.

Originally, *recalcitrant* meant "kicking back."
Antonyms: *tractable* (I, 9), *manageable, docile* (II, 12)
Cf. unruly, intractable, refractory

13. **SPECIOUS** (spē'shŭs)   .   .   .   .   .   .   fair-seeming; deceptive

Pat invented a specious excuse for not going to the party. The article was full of misleading statements and specious reasoning.

■ Not everyone recognized the speciousness of the prohibitively costly plan to get drinking water from the ocean.

Both a specious and a **meretricious** reason imply conscious fraud.
A **plausible** (I, 3) answer is one which seems reasonable at first hearing but may or may not be true.
An **ostensible** (II, 9) reason is a pretended one, not the real reason.

FIRST PRACTICE SET

Copy the *italicized* words. Beside each, write an appropriate definition.

1. *Compatibility* in tastes and habits is an important *criterion* for a happy marriage.
2. *Integrity* gives a person *prestige* throughout his life.
3. The universal *amenities* of gracious behavior play an important part in the processes of *diplomacy.*
4. She mistakes her father's *nonchalance* about his debts for *optimism* about getting them paid.

5. It is *preposterous* to think that such *specious* reasoning will fool anyone.
6. A will is almost *immutable* once the person who made it is dead.
7. The gem is *iridescent,* but it is not *impervious* to scratches.
8. The man is so *perfunctory* in his work that he is of little value, and he is *recalcitrant* toward criticism besides.
9. The *option* of getting married now or going on to college is a *crucial* one, but parents have no right to be *peremptory.*
10. Sports writers like *hyperbole.* One said that the home team handled the ball as if it were a wet cake of soap.

SECOND PRACTICE SET

Which base word from this unit best replaces each *italicized* word or group of words?

1. To call the loss of a *supremely important* football game "Mudville's Waterloo" was something of an *exaggeration for effect.*
2. Rising when ladies enter the room is the kind of *pleasing custom* which helps give a boy social *standing.*
3. Some employers regard punctuality as a *basis for judging* of a boy's *moral soundness.*
4. *Instinctive knowledge* told him that pills to keep one awake are *harmful to health* if taken too often.
5. Public opinion holds that *skillful handling of touchy negotiations* must not be *stealthy* or *dictatorial.*
6. *Stubborn perseverance* will no longer help a thrice-defeated candidate. He has no *right of choice* but to retire.
7. His arguments for *expecting the worst* about human nature are often very *logically connected.*
8. His apparent *unconcern* toward school work is not quite *capable of being harmonized* with the good grades he gets.
9. The decisions of the Supreme Court are *unchangeable* and its judges are virtually *unaffected by* political pressures.
10. It is *contrary to reason* to think that the *defiant* employee will get the promotion.

THIRD PRACTICE SET

Select the pair of words *(a, b, c,* or *d)* which best completes the meaning of each sentence.

1. One __?__ by which we may estimate the character of a man in public office is his __?__.

   (a) option–intuition   (b) amenity–prestige
   (c) criterion–integrity   (d) intuition–nonchalance

2. While __?__ often helps a person know what he ought to do, he must avoid __?__, knowing that the most inspired plans sometimes fail.

   (a) intuition–optimism   (b) nonchalance–pertinacity
   (c) prestige–pessimism   (d) diplomacy–intuition

3. The little __?__ of negotiation play an important part in the larger and more inclusive strategies of __?__.

   (a) criteria–optimism   (b) amenities–diplomacy
   (c) options–prestige   (d) pertinacities–integrity

4. The driver's account of the accident was __?__, but it was not __?__ with the victim's account.

   (a) preposterous–immutable   (b) iridescent–deleterious
   (c) specious–recalcitrant   (d) coherent–compatible

5. __?__ love affairs do not foster wisdom in one of life's most __?__ decisions.

   (a) recalcitrant–iridescent   (b) clandestine–crucial
   (c) deleterious–preposterous   (d) recalcitrant–perfunctory

6. Most voters thought the losing candidate's promises __?__ and his influence highly __?__.

   (a) crucial–impervious   (b) specious–deleterious
   (c) immutable–amenable   (d) preposterous–perfunctory

7. Because of his __?__ honesty, he was given the __?__ of paying either in cash or by check.

(a) perfunctory—amenity (b) preposterous—nonchalance
(c) immutable—option (d) specious—prestige

8. Is it __?__ to say that writers enjoy greater __?__ in America than they do in Europe?

(a) hyperbole—prestige (b) amenity—intuition
(c) pertinacity—pessimism (d) nonchalance—option

9. He thought he was __?__ to fear, but his __?__ disappeared when he saw that a crash was inevitable.

(a) immutable—diplomacy (b) amenable—criterion
(c) impervious—nonchalance (d) recalcitrant—option

10. Our worried __?__ about his future is based on the fact that he is so terribly __?__ in his work.

(a) criterion—recalcitrant (b) optimism—preposterous
(c) nonchalance—immutable (d) pessimism—perfunctory

A WORD FOR IT

Which word from this unit best replaces each *italicized* word or group of words?

1. The book club is not a very *sticking-together* group. The reading which was *left-to-one's choice* has been neglected.

2. A more *stubbornly persevering* reporter would have studied the principles of *civility between nations* in order to find out what was going to happen.

3. She knew *by instinctive knowledge* that her brother would not prove *submissive* to the inconveniences of wilderness life.

4. The foreman acted very *unconcerned* about the *harmfulness to health* of the fumes from the paints we are making.

5. The councilman's *refusal to comply* as far as the voters' wishes are concerned and his *impenetrability* to criticism may keep him from being reëlected this fall.

UNIT NINE

Which word from the list at the right gives the best answer to each question?

1. Which one applies to the Model T Ford?

2. Which one describes a plant that is native to the region where it is found?

3. Which one lessens pain?

4. Which one is on relief?

5. Which one is coarse?

6. Which one is jovial?

7. Which is very burdensome?

8. Which is indiscriminate?

9. Which is worldly?

10. Which secretly aids wrongdoing?

onerous
alleviate
connive
convivial
indigenous
amortize
promiscuous
indigent
mundane
obsolete
clement
ribald

• Word List—VERBS

1. ABROGATE (ăb′rô·gāt) . . . . abolish, annul, do away with

The new tax law abrogates several older ones.

▪ Abrogation of the treaty was inevitable because it no longer served our interests.

Cf. revoke (I, 10), *repeal, nullify, rescind, cancel, invalidate*

2. ADULTERATE (à·dŭl′tẽr·āt) . . . . cheapen or debase (with inferior or harmful ingredients)

Corn starch is sometimes used to adulterate ice cream.

▪ Pure food and drug laws control the adulteration of foods.

▪ Penalties are prescribed for the use of adulterants.

Adulterate goes back to the Latin *ad-*, "to," and *alter*, "other, different."

3. ALLEVIATE (ă·lē′vĭ·āt) . . . . lessen, make more endurable

A nurse tries to alleviate the patient's pain, mental as well as physical.

▪ Wide distribution of national income brings alleviation of poverty.

Relief Words: ***allay, mitigate, assuage*** (III, 6)
Cf. ameliorate (make better)

4. AMALGAMATE (à·măl′gà·māt) . . . . combine, unite, fuse

The two veterans' organizations voted to amalgamate.

▪ Details of the amalgamation were to be worked out by the two groups of officers.

An **amalgam** is an **alloy** or **fusion,** especially of mercury with some other metal. The amalgam fillings which a dentist uses are made of an alloy of mercury and silver.

The word **alloy** was originally applied to a base metal used to cheapen or adulterate other metals. Thus the word **unalloyed** has come to mean "genuine, sincere": Christmas brings unalloyed delight to children.

Combine Words: ***mix, blend, fuse, consolidate, alloy, coalesce*** (III, 4)

5. **AMORTIZE** (ăm′ẽr·tīz) . . write off a debt by regular payments

Mr. Burke can amortize the cost of his new house by paying one per cent a month.
- Amortization at this rate takes about twelve years.
- In a large corporation, the amortization of a new plant is a matter of bookkeeping. The company borrows from itself.

How do you account for the *-mort-* root in *amortize* and in *mortgage?* (See dictionary.)

6. **AMPLIFY** (ăm′plĭ·fī) . . . . make larger or fuller

Please amplify the account which you have already given.
- The apparatus for the amplification of sound is known as a sound amplifier or public address system.
- The amplitude of the layout for the new subdivision will make the cost of the lots rather high.
- During the summer, Mr. Williams will have ample (abundant, large) leisure for fishing.

7. **CONNIVE** (kŏ·nīv′) . . . . . approve or secretly aid the wrongdoing of another

The policeman was accused of conniving with the gamblers. George thought that his father would connive with him in planning the prank.
- Because of this connivance, he hoped to escape punishment.

Connive is followed by *at* or *with*. Originally, it meant "wink or shut the eyes."
For the legal meaning of *connivance*, see dictionary.
Cf. collusion (a secret agreement for fraudulent purposes)

8. **HIBERNATE** (hī′bẽr·nāt) . . . . spend the winter

Bears commonly hibernate in caves and logs. Human beings like to hibernate in Florida or Southern California.
- For people as for bears, hibernation means a more or less dormant condition.
- Hibernal (wintry) winds are usually chilling.

The opposite of *hibernate* is **aestivate.**
Cf. Hibernian (a native of Ireland)

9. **INAUGURATE** (ĭn·ô′gŭ·rāt) . . . make a formal beginning of; install in office

The company will inaugurate a new investment plan next year.

■ Inauguration of the officers took place at the last meeting.

► We plan to watch the President give his inaugural address.

Cf. initiation, inception, incipience (II, 8)

10. **NULLIFY** (nŭl′ĭ·fī) . . . . . . make ineffective; invalidate

A widespread refusal to obey the law practically nullified it.

■ Senator Whisk demanded the nullification of the treaty.

To nullify a law is to disregard it on a large scale, refuse to enforce it, or perhaps to pass another which largely cancels it.
To **annul** a marriage contract is to have it declared invalid by a legal authority.
See also the adjective *null,* "of no effect": The contract became null and void.

11. **PARAPHRASE** (păr′á·frāz) . . . . restate in different words

The newspaper paraphrases long legal decisions to make them more intelligible.

"For tomorrow, paraphrase this passage in your own words," the teacher said.

A paraphrase may be a "free" translation from a foreign language.

12. **REPRIEVE** (rĕ·prēv′) . . . . . . grant a delay or respite

The governor agreed to reprieve the condemned man so he could have one more Christmas with his family.

■ Vacation was a two-week reprieve (temporary escape) from the monotony of operating a machine.

Reprieve applies especially to a delay in inflicting punishment or to a temporary relief from something unpleasant.

13. **STULTIFY** (stŭl′tĭ·fī) . . . . . . render absurd or useless

The inattention and confusion on the floor of the House often seems to stultify speech-making.

■ His recent behavior has resulted in the stultification of his previous efforts.

▶ Word List— ADJECTIVES

1. **CLEMENT** (klĕm'ĕnt) . . . . **mild, merciful**

   That year, the weather was unusually clement in December, with fairly high temperatures and no storms.
   - The jury recommended clemency because the man had intended only to scare his victim.

   Review: *lenient, leniency, lenity* (I, 6)

2. **CONVIVIAL** (kŏn·vĭv'ĭ·ăl) . . . . . . **festive, jovial, gay**

   The Thanksgiving dinner was a convivial affair.
   - Even Grandfather joined in the conviviality.

   Congenial means "agreeable, compatible": My father and my grandfather are congenial spirits who like to hunt, fish, and golf together. What is the root? (See II, 11.)

3. **INDIGENOUS** (ĭn·dĭj'ĕ·nŭs) . . . . **native, characteristic of a specific region**

   The botanist has a catalogue of plants indigenous to North America.
   - Their indigenousness does not prevent their growing in other parts of the world.

   Indigenous, like *congenial*, traces its ancestry to the -*gen*- or birth words. (See II, 11.) For other native-locality words, see *aboriginal* and *endemic*.

4. **INDIGENT** (ĭn'dĭ·jĕnt) . . . . **needy, poor**

   Money was collected to provide Thanksgiving dinners for the indigent of the parish.
   - His parents' indigence (poverty) kept him from getting even a high school education.

   Poor Words: An **impoverished** person is one who formerly had wealth. An **impecunious** person never has much money, partly because of bad management.
   A **destitute** person is extremely poor, lacking even food.
   Cf. pecuniary, under *mercenary* (II, 5)

5. **INHERENT** (ĭn·hĕr′ĕnt) . . . . inborn; existing inseparably in

   Her inherent dislike for snakes created an irresistible temptation for her brother.
   - He is inherently mischievous.
   - Freedom and equality inhere in a democratic government.

   Synonyms: *innate, inbred, ingrained, intrinsic* (III, 6)

6. **MUNDANE** (mŭn′dān) . . . . earthly, worldly

   Einstein was not greatly concerned with the mundane details of daily living.
   John is painstaking about even the most mundane matters, such as keeping track of his expenses.

   Secular means "worldly," in the sense of "non-religious or spiritual":
   The church is concerned with religious, the state with secular affairs.
   Secularism is a preoccupation with worldly concerns.
   Sectarianism is excessive devotion to one sect or its beliefs.
   Pairs of Opposites: *earthly—heavenly; secular—sacred; terrestrial —celestial; temporal—eternal; sectarian—nonsectarian*

7. **OBSOLETE** (ŏb′sȯ·lēt) . . . . outmoded, out of use

   Armor began to be obsolete when gunpowder came into wide use.
   - Its obsoleteness dates from the sixteenth century.
   Machinery in a modern factory often becomes obsolescent (passing out of use) before it wears out.
   - Although this rapid obsolescence is costly, it is less costly than the operation of obsolescent equipment.

   Decadent (dē·kā′dĕnt, dĕk′á·dĕnt), meaning "on the decline," and *decadence* apply more to ideas, systems, and standards than to objects.

8. **ONEROUS** (ŏn′ēr·ŭs) . . . . burdensome, oppressive

   The onerous task of translating a four-volume novel kept his busy for several years.
   - The help of a collaborator would have reduced the onerousness of the project.

   The Latin word *onus,* "a load," has become an English word meaning "burden": The onus of arranging the reception fell upon the teacher.
   Exonerate comes from the same root.
   Cf. opus (a work or masterpiece)

9. **PACIFIC** (pá·sĭf′ĭk) . . . peaceable, peace-promoting, tranquil

• The United Nations exists to find pacific solutions to world problems.

• It tries to pacify warlike nations.

• It seeks to achieve pacification through justice.

> A **pacifist** rejects war and violence, believing that brotherly love and nonviolent resistance alone offer a final solution to man's conflicts.
> **Pacifism** is an important doctrine of the Society of Friends and certain other religious groups.

10. **PROMISCUOUS** (prô·mĭs′kû·ŭs) . . . mingling indiscriminately, indiscriminate

The children toss their clothes into a promiscuous heap when their mother is not watching.

• The cellar was cluttered—old bottles, rags, and broken tools were piled promiscuously in every corner.

> **Promiscuity** often means "loose and undiscriminating moral behavior."
> The root is *-misc-*, "mix," which appears also in **miscegenation.**
> Synonyms: *motley, miscellaneous, heterogeneous, haphazard*

11. **RIBALD** (rĭb′ăld) . . . . . . coarsely mocking, scurrilous

Ribald laughter greeted the remark of the drunken truck driver.

• Ribaldry ran riot in the tavern for several hours.

> Coarse Words: *indelicate, unrefined, vulgar, gross, obscene, scurrilous:* A ribald remark is one which provokes the laughter of people who enjoy coarse humor.
> A **scurrilous** remark is mockingly abusive.
> An **obscene** remark is loathsome and ugly.

12. **SEDATIVE** (sĕd′á·tĭv) . . . soothing, calming, pain-lessening

The sleeping pills in the red box have a sedative effect and are harmless.

• The doctor administered a sedative (pain killer) before the ambulance took the injured woman to the hospital.

> **Sedentary** employment is work at which one sits down all or most of the time.
> **Sedate** means "composed, serious": The new girl in my class at school is very sedate. *Cf. demure* (II, 4)

FIRST PRACTICE SET

Copy the *italicized* words. Beside each, write an appropriate definition.

1. She let suffering *adulterate* her happiness, a kind of suffering that nothing could *alleviate*.

2. Please *amplify* your confession by telling why you *connive* at your brother's wrongdoing.

3. The directors voted to *inaugurate* negotiations to *amalgamate* the two companies.

4. One of the directors is a *convivial* person who likes to *hibernate* on the French Riviera.

5. Your attempt to *paraphrase* the agreement appears to *nullify* the part about giving a month's notice.

6. The *clement* breezes of April make students reluctant to end the ten-day *reprieve* which the spring holiday offers.

7. Monkeys with an *inherent* immunity to the disease are not *indigenous* to the region.

8. The *mundane* routines of earning a living conspired to *stultify* his hopes of becoming a writer.

9. In time, the taking of morphine for its *sedative* effect may become *obsolete*.

10. If he can maintain *pacific* relations with his *ribald* acquaintances, he may escape their jibes.

SECOND PRACTICE SET

Which base word from this unit best replaces each *italicized* word or group of words?

1. The two organizations, both of which provide housing for the *poor,* will be *combined* next year.

2. Mr. Clayton will *make larger* his report on the plan to *write-off-by-regular-payments* the project.

3. He is afraid the City Council will *secretly help* the banks to *render useless* his committee's borrowing power.

4. He also fears the banks may *make a formal beginning of* a higher interest rate and thus make the financing too *burdensome.*

5. However, Mr. Clayton's ideas have an *inborn* logic. It is not likely that anything will *invalidate* his plan.

6. Most of the councilmen are rather *jovial* but not the *coarsely mocking* characters they are imagined to be.

7. Nothing can *debase* their honesty, and they do all they can to *lessen* the problems of the city.

8. The newspapers *restated in different words* Mr. Clayton's proposal to abolish *outmoded* housing.

9. The councilmen must decide whether or not to *annul* the old housing law. They may *grant a delay to* it for another year.

10. As the weather is *mild* here, people might prefer to *spend the winter* in a cave rather than live in inadequate dwellings.

THIRD PRACTICE SET

Which lettered pair of items has the same relationship as the pair printed in capital letters?

1. REFINED : RIBALD :: (a) reprieved : pardoned   (b) terrestrial : earthly   (c) affluent : indigent   (d) amplified : extended

2. CLEMENT : ALLEVIATE :: (a) dead : amortize   (b) ample : nullify   (c) separated : coalesce   (d) lenient : mitigate

3. SECULAR : RELIGIOUS :: (a) sacred : divine   (b) inborn : inherent   (c) convivial : austere   (d) promiscuous : heterogeneous

4. COALESCE : STULTIFY :: (a) gather : consolidate   (b) connive : pacify   (c) amalgamate : nullify   (d) adulterate : repeal

5. REPRIEVE : PARDON :: (a) crime : law (b) alleviation : assuagement (c) paraphrase : connivance (d) onerousness : respite

6. PACIFIC : MILITANT :: (a) convivial : congenial (b) demure : sedate (c) amalgamated : blended (d) pure : adulterated

7. TERMINATE : INAUGURATE :: (a) pacify : irritate (b) consolidate : amalgamate (c) enlarge : amplify (d) paraphrase : translate

8. SLEEPING PILL : SEDATIVE :: (a) gunpowder : obsoleteness (b) United Nations : federal government (c) summer : hibernation (d) payment : amortization

9. RIBALD : OBSCENE :: (a) obsolete : decadent (b) mundane : naïve (c) indigenous : foreign (d) indigent : destitute

10. HIBERNATE : AESTIVATE :: (a) mix : adulterate (b) inherit : inhere (c) amplify : condense (d) abrogate : annul

A WORD FOR IT

Which of the words in this unit best replaces each *italicized* word or group of words?

1. Writing is *sit-down-at-it* work, but many writers are not so *never-having-much money* as you may imagine.

2. Originality is a quality that *exists inseparably* in a good author, whether he is the *jovial* type or very much the opposite.

3. There was evidence of *secret agreement for fraudulent purposes* between the night watchman and the burglar, both of whom were fond of *coarse mockery*.

4. Birthday parties bring *genuine* pleasure to the children who attend them, from the most *composed* to the most excitable.

5. That college is *not devoted to one religious sect*, but it is by no means a *nonreligious* school.

UNIT TEN

What word from the list at the right fits best in each blank?

The author of this book thinks that vocabuarly is of __(1)__ importance because it enables one to think and express himself with greater __(2)__. The units require real __(3)__, especially the third practice sets, but those who complete them successfully deserve the __(4)__ of an *A*. In taking leave of this book, we beg __(5)__ for our failures and grumblings. We do not cast __(6)__s on the author. We know that in the modern world, vocabulary is almost __(7)__ to intelligence. We want to avoid the __(8)__ of failing to make the best use of our talents. We are __(9)__ in our refusal to give up. With a finer command of the English language, we shall be better able to meet each __(10)__ which may arise in the years to come.

catholicity
amnesty
exigency
clarity
aspersion
ignominy
accolade
paramount
adamant
analogy
tantamount
acumen

▪ Word List—NOUNS

1. ACCOLADE (ăk'ŏ·lād) . . . . award, recognition

The movie which received the top accolade of the motion picture industry that year was made abroad.

The Nobel prize in literature is the most cherished accolade a writer can achieve.

Accolade was originally the name of the ceremony conferring knighthood. The candidate received a ritual embrace (the word *accolade* comes from a verb meaning "embrace") and was given a light blow on the shoulder with the flat side of a sword. In modern usage, the word still carries an implication of high honor and recognition.

2. ACUMEN (ă·kū'měn) . . . . mental sharpness or acuteness

Mr. Wild's business acumen consisted of knowing how to make people want what he had to sell.

His wife's acuity helped him in selecting fabrics.

Acuity is sharpness of eye or mind.
Acumen and **acuteness** come from the Latin verb *acuere*, meaning "sharpen." *Acuity* comes from *acus*, "a needle."

3. AFFRONT (ă·frŭnt') . . . . . . open or intentional insult

His failure to greet you on the bus was not an affront. He just did not see you.

▪ Mr. Wild will not even affront a person he dislikes.

Affront is stronger than **offend** but hardly as strong as **insult**.

4. AMNESTY (ăm'nĕs·tĭ) . . . . general pardon (especially for political offenses)

After a civil war or revolt, the winning faction usually extends amnesty to former enemies on the condition that all resistance cease.

Such an act of amnesty heals wounds, unifies the country, and insures peace.

Amnesty comes from Greek *a-*, "not," and *mnasthai* "remember." It is not to be confused with **amnesia**, "loss of memory," from the same Greek root.

5. **ANALOGY** (á·năl′ô·jĭ) . . . . **partial similarity**

The hydrostatic analogy helps explain electricity.
► Voltage is analogous to water pressure.
The flow of water through the pipe is an analogue of the amperage or amount of electricity flowing.
► Arguing that a nation, like a person, grows old and dies is analogical reasoning.

6. **ASPERSION** (ăs·pûr′shŭn) . . . . . . **damaging criticism**

Joe did not hesitate to cast aspersions on his former teammate, declaring that the latter was lazy and cowardly.
"Line up and shut up," the sergeant shouted with his usual asperity (harshness).

Aspersion comes from Latin *ad-*, plus *spargere*, "sprinkle or strew." Other Unkind Remarks: An **innuendo** (from a Latin word for "nod") is an indirect aspersion. It may also be a meaningful smile, glance, or inflection.
An **insinuation** is a remark or suggestion which secretly hints at an idea unfavorable to someone. *Cf. sinuous* (III, 5)
A **reflection** is an expression of unfavorable opinion or reproach. It often defames its victim by implication rather than by direct criticism.
A **stricture** is a critical remark. It is definite and direct.
Cf. censure (I, 2), *animadversion, calumny* (III, 1), *defamation* under *libel* (II, 5)

7. **CLARITY** (klăr′ĭ·tĭ) . . . . **clearness**

The clarity of Burke's reasoning was not fully appreciated at the time he made his speeches.
● Writing helps to clarify (make clear) one's idea.
It fosters clarification.

A **clarion** was a kind of curved trumpet: The clarion (trumpet-clear) call to arms brought many volunteers.

8. **EXIGENCY** (ĕk′sĭ·jĕn·sĭ) . . . . . **urgent need, requirement**

The exigencies of the post-war situation in Holland called for the cooperation of both military and civil authorities.
► Widespread destruction, together with a shortage of supplies, helped create a crisis of truly exigent character.

Exigency implies a compelling necessity, usually the result of special circumstances, such as an accident, a crisis, an emergency.

9. **FRANCHISE** (frăn'chīz) . . . . . the right to vote; a business privilege granted by a government

In the United States, the franchise was extended to women after the First World War.

This enfranchisement was achieved by means of the Nineteenth Amendment.

*   If Congress decides that boys old enough to be soldiers are old enough to vote, eighteen-year-olds will be enfranchised some day.

The city refused to renew the bus company's franchise.

Cf. disenfranchisement

10. **ICONOCLASM** (ī·kŏn'ô·klăsm) . . . attacking of cherished beliefs

The writer's iconoclasm was revealed in all his books. No idea or social institution was too sacred for him to mock.

He was a perennial iconoclast.

▶   One of his most iconoclastic ideas was that schools should be closed, and young people should educate themselves through reading and individual research.

Iconoclasm is literally "image breaking." The original iconoclasts were those who denounced as idolatrous the use of images or icons in the churches.

Iconolatry is the worship of images.

Iconology is the study of images, pictures, and symbolic representation generally.

The **iconoscope,** or image-viewing part of a television set, is the picture tube.

11. **THERAPY** (thĕr'á·pĭ) . . . . treatment, healing, cure

Therapy by drugs is not the only method of combating illness.

Psychotherapy, or mental treatment, is an important branch of therapeutics.

▶   At times, rest and sleep alone have therapeutic value.

A person specially trained to give treatments is a therapist.

Therapeutics is the branch of medicine concerned with the treatment of disease.

Hydrotherapy, treatment with warm baths and mineral waters, was in use as far back as ancient Greek times.

Radiotherapy is important in treating cancer.

▸ Word List—ADJECTIVES

1. **ADAMANT** (ăd′á·mănt) . . . . unyielding

   Lincoln was adamant on matters of moral principle.

   The boys tried to convince their mother to allow them to go on the trip, but she was adamant in her refusal.

   It took adamantine courage for the Marines to storm Mt. Suribachi on Iwo Jima.

   The name *adamant,* originally that of an imaginary stone of extreme hardness, was later applied to the diamond. In time, the word was used to describe any object, feeling, or opinion of unyielding hardness.

2. **ALLERGIC** (ă·lûr′jĭk) . . . . abnormally sensitive

   Our neighbor says that she is allergic to cat's fur and that it causes her skin to become inflamed.

   ▪ Hay fever is the result of a common allergy or hypersensitiveness to certain kinds of pollen in the air.

   Allergy is a medical term, but in popular usage, it is applied to an aversion to such annoyances as egotists, billboards, and spoiled children.

3. **BAROQUE** (bá·rōk′) . . . . overdecorated; irregular in shape

   Nineteenth century mansions often had a baroque appearance.

   Modern architecture, with its emphasis on simplicity, is the antithesis of the baroque (special art style developed in the sixteenth century).

   Cf. rococo (rô·kō′kō), *grotesque* (III, 4)

4. **CATHOLIC** (kăth′ô·lĭk) . . . . . universal, widely inclusive

   The president of a large university must be a man of catholic interests—scientific, cultural, artistic, financial, and political.

   ▪ The catholicity of his tastes makes him feel at ease in any surroundings.

   Curio: ***catholicon*** means "a panacea or cure-all."

5. HALCYON (hăl'sĭ·ŭn) . . . . calmly happy, tranquil

The halcyon days of autumn and Indian summer passed much too swiftly.

The halcyon years are the later years, when life is less hectic than it is in youth.

This word comes from a legend. (See dictionary.)

6. HISTRIONIC (hĭs'trĭ·ŏn'ĭk) . . of play acting, theatrical; affected

He won quite a bit of undeserved admiration by his histrionic accounts of the dangers a reporter must face.

■ When her request was refused, Mary's histrionics did not impress her family.

This word goes back to the Latin *histrio*, meaning "an actor." Today, *histrionic* is often used in a derogatory sense.
Thespian means "dramatic," and has no unfavorable connotations. Thespis was a sixth century Greek poet who is supposed to have been the inventor of tragedy.

7. IGNOMINIOUS (ĭg'nô·mĭn'ĭ·ŭs) . . . humiliating, contemptible

The British withdrawal from Dunkirk might have been an ignominious failure had not the weather been favorable.

■ Judith's attempts to play the violin ended in ignominy because she did not practice faithfully.

8. IMPECCABLE (ĭm·pĕk'á·b'l) . . . . . . blameless, flawless

The judge's behavior throughout his long term of office was impeccable. He never showed the slightest partiality or accepted a favor that could possibly appear to influence him.

■ The employer was impressed by the impeccability of the applicant's dress and general appearance.

9. PARAMOUNT (păr'á·mount) . . . . chief, supreme

The mayor declared that the city's paramount need was better housing.

Her husband's health was her paramount concern in planning the meals, and he did not always like the food he was served.

Cf. pre-eminent

10. SUCCULENT (sŭk'ů·lĕnt) . . . . juicy

Al brought home a pail of succulent blackberries.

■ The succulence of ripe melons tempted the two boys.

11. TANTAMOUNT (tăn'tà·mount') . . . . equivalent

The suspect's explanation was tantamount to a confession of guilt.

In the case of Smith's application for the job, recommendation by his Congressman was tantamount to appointment.

The word is applied to equivalence in value, effect, or meaning, not to a similarity between objects.

12. ULTERIOR (ŭl·tẽr'ĭ·ẽr) . . . . beyond what appears, hidden

His mother wanted Billy to enjoy the summer, but she also had an ulterior reason for sending him to camp. She felt that he needed exercise.

Ulterior planning comes at a later, more remote, and therefore, subsequent time.

13. UTOPIAN (ů·tō'pĭ·ăn) . . . charactertistic of an ideal society

The Oneida Community in New York State was founded as a utopian project.

■ The utopianism of Robert Owen led him to found a colony at New Harmony, Indiana.

■ The Amana Society near Buffalo was another nineteenth century utopia.

In 1516, Sir Thomas More's book *Utopia* was first published. In it, he described an ideal commonwealth, located on an imaginary island. The name of this perfect society, Utopia, was formed of the Greek *ou-*, meaning "not," and *topas*, "a place."

14. VICARIOUS (vī·kâr'ĭ·ŭs) . . . . taking the place of, or
experiencing through, another

Books and plays give one vast quantities of vicarious experience in travel, suffering, success, and failure.

⁻ One can live vicariously in any country and any period.

What is meant by vicarious atonement in a theological sense?
Why is a vicar so called?

FIRST PRACTICE SET

Copy the *italicized* words. Beside each, write an appropriate definition.

1. The scientist was *adamant* in refusing a decoration or any other kind of *accolade* from an unfriendly foreign country.
2. The unfriendly countries considered his refusal an *affront,* but his friends lauded his *acumen.*
3. The decree of *amnesty* which followed the revolt included restoration of the *franchise* to the rebels.
4. A mild stroke creates an *exigency* for which no *therapy* exists.
5. In a crises, one's mental *clarity* may help but *histrionic* behavior will not.
6. An *analogy* between life and a sea voyage attaches *paramount* importance to the possession of a purpose or direction.
7. It is a misfortune to be *allergic* to such *succulent* delicacies as fresh pineapple.
8. His refusal to tell whether he had a part in the *ignominious* plot to kill his uncle is *tantamount* to an admission of guilt.
9. His guilt gave him *ulterior* motives for wanting to set up a *utopian* colony in Antarctica.
10. One can cast no *aspersions* on the *impeccable* workmanship of the *halcyon* era between the wars.

SECOND PRACTICE SET

Which base word from this unit best replaces each *italicized* word or group of words?

1. The *recognitions* of the scientific world are often bestowed on those who are daring in their *attacking of cherished beliefs.*
2. *General pardon for political offenses* after a revolt, armed or parliamentary, is a form of political *healing.*
3. The privilege of the universal *right to vote* was once only a *characteristic-of-an-ideal-society* dream.
4. She met each *urgent need* or crisis with *theatrical* sobs.
5. The *damaging criticism* regarding his honesty was an *intentional insult* he would not soon forget.

6. A person with the *mental acuteness* to play chess well can see the *partial similarity* between chess and the structure of British society.
7. The *chief* value of these *tranquil* weeks of vacation is the relaxation they offer.
8. Failure to do your best is *equivalent* to *humiliating* surrender.
9. The teacher is *unyielding* about not letting Marilyn appear on the program until her performance is *flawless*.
10. A *juicy* steak distracted his thoughts for a few moments from the *hidden* meaning of the doctor's words.

THIRD PRACTICE SET

Which lettered pair of items has the same relationship as the pair printed in capital letters?

1. AFFRONT : INSULT :: (a) theatricality : histrionics (b) amnesty : amnesia (c) asperity : aspersion (d) disease : therapy

2. IGNOMINY : DEFEAT :: (a) disgrace : accolade (b) ulterior motive : franchise (c) catholicity : idea (d) shrewdness : acumen

3. HAY FEVER : ALLERGY :: (a) adamant : Lincoln (b) acuity : needle (c) clarity : iconoclasm (d) Oneida Community : utopia

4. ASPERSION : CENSURE :: (a) impeccability : artist (b) catholicity : universality (c) steak : succulency (d) analogy : electricity

5. EXIGENCY : EMERGENCY :: (a) iconoscope : iconoclasm (b) amnesty : ignominy (c) sword on shoulder : accolade (d) amendment : franchise

6. PRACTICAL : UTOPIAN :: (a) acute : sharp (b) stormy : halcyon (c) impeccable : paramount (d) ignominious : brave

7. THERAPIST : THERAPY :: (a) clarity : clarion (b) anes-thetist : amnesty (c) emigrant : exigency (d) iconoclast : iconoclasm

8. ICON : ICONOSCOPE :: (a) franchise : disenfranchisement (b) front : confrontation (c) therapy : psychotherapy (d) book : clarification

9. BAROQUE : ARCHITECTURE :: (a) Thespian : Greek poetry (b) catholic : books (c) iconoclastic : sculpture (d) succulent : steaks

10. UTOPIA : SIR THOMAS MORE :: (a) Amana : Buffalo (b) New Harmony : Robert Owen (c) Oneida : New York (d) Greece : Thespis

A WORD FOR IT

Which word from this unit best replaces each *italicized* word or group of words?

1. A liberal arts college fosters *wide inclusiveness* in one's knowledge and capacities, but it may actually discourage *attacking-of-cherished-beliefs* thinking and other forms of originality.

2. The study of English should help one *make clear* his thinking and make easier the *comparing-by-partial-similarities* presentation of ideas.

3. Reading good novels often has *healing* value and increases one's *sharpness of eye or mind* in understanding human problems.

4. The soldier who took his friend's place when an *urgent need* arose knew that his friend would face *in-place-of-another* suffering.

5. He always preferred direct, straightforward criticism to sly *disparagement full of secret hints* or *indirect aspersion by word or look.*

FINAL TESTS—

UNIT 1

Which base word in the unit best replaces each *italicized* word or group of words?

1. Bad weather did not *restrain through fear* the Canadian explorers, and they did not *find fault frivolously* about the inconveniences of primitive living conditions.

2. The two scientists can *work together* readily because their theories about the new metal *match remarkably*.

3. The dishonest fighter's *situation from which there is no escape* led him to *meditate* emigration to another country.

4. The doctor would sometimes *object to* the unwise advice of a rival physician, but he would never *belittle* another doctor.

5. He learned with *amazement* that a tank containing a cupful of gasoline will *explode* with greater violence than one that is full.

6. Mr. Wilson will *excuse* the faults of his own children with great *willingness*.

7. With *shame*, he heard the prosecuting attorney *dig up* old accusations which he thought had been entirely forgotten.

8. Telepathy remains a great *source of perplexity* as investigators seek *fulfillment* of their experiments.

9. The attacker's *boldness* in assailing the strongest part of the fort created a new *predicament* for the decimated defenders.

10. Many kinds of *false and malicious statement* about the United States *issue forth* from foreign enemies.

UNIT 2

1. Gov. Barton tried to *bring to agreement* the enemies who wanted to *bring accusation against* him for misconduct in office.

2. Senator Patton decided to *act evasively to gain time* but not to vote for any bill that would *grant financial aid to* importers of foreign cars.

3. These *loving* letters, supposedly from Lincoln to Anne Rutledge, are not *genuine*.

4. Mr. Simmons is *unselfishly concerned for others* in his actions and is seldom *morally instructive* in his talk.

5. She was *shrewd* enough to wait for the most *appropriate* moment to ask her father for a larger allowance.

6. The magnate could not *disavow* his *unintentional* outburst because too many people had heard it.

7. Mr. Simmons' generosity made the ex-convict *dejected* because he could not *pay back*.

8. Someone must *act as harmonizing agent in* the railroad dispute if we are to have a prompt and *peaceable* settlement.

9. The antique dealer's praise of the old clock served to *justify* Mrs. Brown's insistence that it should not be *banished* to the attic.

10. The order to *withdraw from* the town came just as Major King was about to *seize wrongfully* the authority to rule it.

UNIT 3

1. Being president of a large corporation requires *sound judgment* as well as *mental penetration*.

2. Deserts suffer from *death-causing* and continual *excess* of sunshine.

3. Since *restoration* of the embezzled money was impossible, it was the victim's *right* to sue.

4. The man's *hidden* hatred of his employer was finally expressed in a *spasm* of anger.

5. Mr. Norton has a *preconceived preference* for such *palpable* rewards as money and stocks.

6. The *opening* of the opera suggests the *falling down in worship* of the worshipers as they enter the temple.

7. The *adhering-to-a-party* argument for government spending disregards the most *prominent* objections.

8. An ambulance is a very *movable* resting place for *reclining* victims of illness and accidents.

9. People expect the author of an etiquette book to be the *perfect embodiment* of *conformity to expected standards of behavior.*

10. The *provisional* wording of the new law is remarkably *concise.*

UNIT 4

1. The contract is a *solemn agreement* which gives each party a great *stimulus* to meet the prescribed requirements.

2. The dictator's enemies formed a *temporary alliance,* the thought of which began to haunt him like some strange *nightmare.*

3. It is not *stealing-of-ideas* to take a story from history, but *artistic* factors often require changes in the story.

4. It would seem like a *contradiction* to have the December *point at which the sun is farthest from the equator* bringing summer weather.

5. Is a question about *marriage* problems *pertinent* to a discussion of education?

6. The debate champion is a *perfect model* of *oratorical* effectiveness.

7. The *fantastic* costumes and *strange* rhythms of the Indian ceremonial draw many spectators.

8. Her *foolishly sentimental* pleas had no effect on the *cruel* tribesmen.

9. To the chieftain, who was versed in *mysterious* knowledge, the horse's lameness seemed to be *foreshadowing-evil.*

10. Chess is a *difficult-to-understand* pastime which offers *inexpressible* enjoyment to those who play it well.

UNIT 5

1. He watched the *pretentious* display of new clothes with a smile that was *sneeringly distrustful of human motives.*

2. Many dislike the foreman because he is *fault-finding* and *haughty.*

3. The faded actress thought she was being *straightforward* rather than *complacently stupid.*

4. The doctor's temperament was more than *unexcitable;* it was truly *gloomy and grave.*

5. The book expresses a *scornfully aloof* point of view and is written in a rather *womanish* style.

6. Chaucer's nun was *daintily refined* and somewhat *unsophisticated* about the world's evils.

7. The politician with the *excessively suave* manner was quite *unduly positive* about his opinions.

8. She has a *lively, changeable* nature and is given to making *rushing-with-great-force* decisions.

9. He was a man of *devious* schemings and *sarcastic* scorn for his victims.

10. The *habitually silent* football player seems mild, but he can be quite *savage* in a game.

UNIT 6

1. It is *advisable* that persons with a rheumatic heart condition seek a more *healthful* climate.

2. One hydrogen bomb is enough to *utterly destroy* the city and all of its *remarkably bad* architectural monstrosities.

3. The warden refused to *deal* with the rioting prisoners or to *surrender* to any of their demands.

4. The suspect's actions *made more severe* the policeman's suspicion, in spite of all the *making-it-less-serious* circumstances.

5. The *occurring-by-chance* remark about a drop in prices led Mr. Clark to *delay action* about buying a new car.

6. Should the fact that the peddler *provoked* but did not commit the crime *make milder* the penalty?

7. The *irreverent* play has many *deceptively alluring* lines in it.

8. Nylon is one of the *artificial* fabrics which appeared on the market at a very *promising* time.

9. It is hard to estimate the *actual* worth of such *ambiguous* statements about the new method of making soap.

10. During the post-war period, as streams of refugees *came together* in the city, social conditions began to *deteriorate*.

UNIT 7

1. The president's *trusted adviser* is a *competent judge* of good cooking.

2. Milton's father belonged to the *middle class*, but he was not a *person lacking cultivation in the arts*.

3. The poet has a *clique* of admirers who touch off quite an *enthusiastic applause* whenever he speaks.

4. The professor's *written analysis of a work of art* exposed the *plottings* of the artist's friends.

5. The young *person especially skilled in one of the fine arts* is a *person under the patronage* of a wealthy manufacturer.

6. The *dance* has a *correspondence of parts* which is well worth studying.

7. The *custodian* of the rare book collection makes a hobby of collecting *blunders in the choice of words.*

8. The *society girl* liked poetry and she had a large *list she could recite.*

9. The government maintains *an unofficial linkage* with the Vatican and the man chosen serves as a kind of *carrier of news.*

10. The *outcome* of the *story in which characters are symbolic* is that the land freezes permanently.

UNIT 8

1. Tact is an important *standard for judging* of one's *skillful handling of touchy negotiations.*

2. *Instinctive knowledge* somehow told him that the applicant was not a man of sufficient *moral soundness* for the important position.

3. In certain Asiatic countries, a woman's *right of choice* in the *supremely important* matter of marriage is somewhat circumscribed.

4. Laziness is hardly ever *capable of being harmonized* with the *connected* analysis of a problem.

5. The stars seem *changeless* and *unaffected by* time or accident.

6. Gratitude is more than a mere *pleasing custom*, and *indifference* is often pretended.

7. His egotism is *absurd* and his influence *injurious* because others imitate him.

8. Carol's statement that she would "make hay while the sun shone" proved to be as *deceptive* as it was *halfhearted*.

9. The captain's *dictatorial* order was of the nature of *exaggeration for effect*.

10. In spite of the *stealthy* nature of their activities, the resistance fighters were full of *expectation of the best* and hoped for a speedy end to the war.

UNIT 9

1. In order to *lessen* unemployment, the union voted to *do away with* its demand for higher wages.

2. The new plan to *write off by regular payments* the national debt would require *oppressive* taxation.

3. A *worldly* view of life was *inseparably existing* in Roman society.

4. Before kerosene lamps became *outmoded* and automobiles became common, gasoline was sometimes used to *cheapen* kerosene.

5. Franklin, who was naturally *festive,* found that his social life helped *enlarge* his knowledge of people.

6. Carelessness tends to *invalidate* brilliant plans, and stupidity may *render absurd* many proposals.

7. The next expedition will *make formal beginning of* a study of fur-bearing animals *native* to the coldest climates.

8. Bears *spend the winter* in caves until the *mild* weather returns.

9. The Community Chest *combines* the charitable appeals of several agencies, some of which help *needy* families.

10. He *secretly plans wrongdoing* with his brother in the illegal sale of a *pain-lessening* drug.

UNIT 10

1. The artist expected an *award* from the judges, but he received an *open insult* instead.

2. Newspapers added their *damaging criticisms* to the *humiliating* rejection of the artist's best work.

3. He was accused of *beyond-what-appears* motives that were *equivalent* to Communistic plotting.

4. He blamed the treatment he had received on the *clearness* of his *attacking of cherished beliefs.*

5. His *theatrical* behavior under this kind of treatment did not foster *general pardon* for him.

6. He claimed that his pictures were *characteristic of an ideal society,* as well as *flawless* in craftsmanship.

7. With what must be called desperate *mental sharpness,* he found for his humiliation a kind of *partial similarity* in the persecution of Socrates by his fellow citizens.

8. He wanted his declining years to be a *calmly happy* epoch, but his need for approval was *supreme.*

9. He was *abnormally sensitive* to ridicule, yet most connoisseurs laughed at the *overdecorated* style of his paintings.

10. The most *widely inclusive* of art critics felt that his art was important chiefly as a form of *healing treatment* that kept the artist from being dangerous.

DIVISION TESTS

On a separate sheet, write the numbers of the *italicized* words. Beside each, write the number of the matching word or words.

SECTION 1

1. *Disparage* one's usefulness
2. *Usurp* the host's prerogatives
3. Unwilling to *reciprocate*
4. Orders that *emanate* daily
5. *Subsidize* research
6. *Cavil* about taxes
7. *Reconcile* enemies
8. *Demur* firmly
9. *Mediate* an agreement
10. *Construe* instructions

1. quibble or find fault
2. interpret
3. recover or restore
4. object or take exception
5. dismiss or banish
6. belittle, speak slightingly of
7. flow or issue forth
8. pay back
9. bring to agreement
10. grant financial aid to
11. seize wrongfully
12. bring about as go-between

SECTION 2

1. Alarming *consternation*
2. *Perspicacity* of the unlearned
3. A *propensity* for deceit
4. *Impasse* in his affairs
5. *Surfeit* of food
6. A baseless *calumny*
7. Expected *vicissitude*
8. The loser's *chagrin*
9. *Quintessence* of depair
10. *Enigma* of destiny

1. suspicion, distrust
2. slander, malicious statement
3. situation from which there is no escape
4. the pure essence, embodiment
5. shame, vexation, humiliation
6. puzzle, source of perplexity
7. mental penetration, discernment
8. lack of skill or training
9. excess, disgust from excess
10. change or alternation
11. amazement, terror, dread
12. bent, natural tendency

Section 3

1. *Heinous* exploit
2. *Lambent* candlelight
3. An *innocuous* pastime
4. *Recumbent* giant
5. *Seditious* thoughts
6. An *astute* buyer
7. *Succinct* comments
8. *Altruistic* motives
9. A *didactic* approach
10. *Salacious* whisperings

1. unselfishly concerned for others
2. shrewd, crafty
3. morally instructive
4. hateful, odious
5. harmless
6. playing lightly over a surface or subject
7. quick, hurried, sudden
8. scandalous, obscene
9. ugly, disgusting
10. reclining, leaning, inactive
11. inciting discontent or rebellion
12. terse, concise

UNITS 4, 5, 6, 7

Section 4

1. *Ineffable* loveliness
2. *Recondite* sayings
3. *Maudlin* laughter
4. *Arrogant* disgust
5. *Cynical* politics
6. *Gregarious* ants
7. *Chimerical* delusions
8. *Irascible* captors
9. A *taciturn* editor
10. *Relevant* decisions

1. fantastic, imaginary
2. instructive, intelligible
3. unutterable, inexpressible
4. abstruse, obscure
5. pertinent, bearing on the case in hand
6. weakly emotional, foolishly sentimental
7. habitually silent
8. haughty, overbearingly proud
9. inclined to go in groups or herds
10. sneering, distrustful of human motives
11. easily angered
12. awkward, clumsy

Section 5

1. *Expedient* action
2. *Salubrious* weather
3. A *captious* sister
4. *Dogmatic* in opinions
5. *Intrinsic* merit
6. *Garrulous* sailors
7. *Equivocal* answers
8. A *truculent* bulldog
9. *Egregious* misdeeds
10. *Fatuous* followers

1. real, true, actual
2. talkative
3. marvelous, remarkable
4. vague, ambiguous
5. complacently stupid or silly
6. unduly positive
7. suitable, advisable
8. fault-finding, hard to please
9. healthful, promoting health
10. fast-acting, treacherous
11. fierce, savage, cruel
12. remarkably bad, flagrant

Section 6

1. The *incubus* of guilt
2. A gaudy *fetish*
3. A *coterie* of painters
4. Poetic *paradox*
5. An absurd *malaproprism*
6. Once a *paragon*
7. A complicated *allegory*
8. Sooth sayer's *anathema*
9. Accidental *symmetry*
10. The hour of his *nemesis*

1. contradictory statement
2. perfect model or pattern
3. punishment, agent of retribution
4. story in which characters are symbolic
5. balance, correspondence of parts
6. social set, clique
7. nightmare, or depressing burden
8. something worshipped for its magical powers
9. solemn curse; person or object detested
10. collection, assortment
11. damaging statement or accusation
12. blunder in choice of words

Section 7

1. *Mollify* an irate customer
2. *Proscrastinate* unduly
3. *Extenuate* one's failure
4. *Instigate* a proposal
5. *Propitiate* the manager
6. *Aggravate* one's suffering
7. *Annihiliate* a city
8. *Capitulate* graciously
9. *Negotiate* endlessly
10. *Mitigate* the penalty

1. destroy utterly
2. weaken or reduce
3. settle a claim for damage
4. surrender
5. make worse or more severe
6. arrange or deal with
7. lessen or make milder
8. appease or pacify
9. conciliate (as result of misdeed)
10. make less serious, diminish
11. delay action
12. provoke or incite

UNITS 8, 9, 10

Section 8

1. *Impervious* to insult
2. *Indigenous* talent
3. A *mundane* motive
4. *Compatible* ideas
5. *Indigent* relatives
6. The *onerous* illness
7. A *deleterious* chemical
8. *Ribald* grimaces
9. *Specious* apologies
10. *Iridescent* vapor

1. capable of being harmonized
2. fair seeming, deceptive
3. native, characteristic of (a specific region)
4. burdensome, oppressive
5. rustic, rural, coarse
6. harmful to health, injurious
7. shiny, gaudy, garish
8. impenetrable, changeless
9. earthly, worldly
10. glistening with colors
11. coarsely mocking, scurrilous
12. needy, poor

SECTION 9

1. *Alleviate* discomfort
2. *Abrogate* a covenant
3. *Enfranchise* aliens
4. *Stultify* an opposing argument
5. *Affront* a guest
6. *Amortize* a bond issue
7. *Adulterate* dog food
8. *Paraphrase* a message
9. *Connive* shamelessly
10. *Hibernate* abroad

1. abolish, annul, do away with
2. insult (openly)
3. restate in different words
4. save from disgrace or death
5. cheapen or debase
6. give the right to vote to
7. render absurd or useless
8. approve or secretly aid another in wrongdoing
9. write off by regular payments
10. lessen, make more endurable
11. cheat or lie to
12. spend the winter

SECTION 10

1. A lover's *pertinacity*
2. A heart of *adamant*
3. Undeserved *amnesty*
4. Inventor's *prestige*
5. Youthful *iconoclasm*
6. A new kind of *therapy*
7. A necessary *amenity*
8. Stupid *nonchalance*
9. Imaginary *exigency*
10. A voter's *option*

1. pardon for political offense
2. stubborn perseverance
3. impenetrably hard stone
4. easy-going forgetfulness
5. right of choice
6. harsh or stubborn pride
7. attacking of cherished beliefs
8. indifference, unconcern
9. pleasing way or custom
10. urgent need
11. recognized influence or standing
12. treatment, healing, cure

PRONUNCIATION KEY

Symbol	Example	Symbol	Example	Symbol	Example
ā	āle	h	hat	o͞o	fo͞od
ȧ	chȧotic	ī	īce	o͝o	fo͝ot
â	câre	ĭ	ĭll	ou	out
ă	ădd	ĭ	charĭty (ital.)	p	pen
ă	ăccount (ital.)	j	joke	r	rat
ä	ärm	k	keep	s	sit
ȧ	ȧsk			sh	she
ȧ	sofȧ (ital.)	K	= ch in German *ich*	t	to
b	but	l	late	th	thin
ch	chair	m	man	~~th~~	~~then~~
d	day	n	nod	tu̬	natu̬re
du̬	verdu̬re	N	French *bon*	ū	cūbe
ē	ēve	ng	sing	u̇	u̇nite
ę	hęre	ō	ōld	û	ûrn
ė	ėvent	ȯ	ȯbey	ŭ	ŭp
ĕ	ĕnd	ô	ôrb	ŭ	circŭs (ital.)
ĕ	silĕnt (ital.)	ŏ	ŏdd	ü	German *grün*
ē	makēr	ǫ	sǫft	v	van
f	fill	ȯ	cȯnnect (ital.)	w	win
g	go	oi	oil	y	yet
				z	zone

The system of indicating pronunciation is used by permission of the publishers of Webster's New International Dictionary, Second Edition, Copyright 1934, 1939, 1945, 1950, 1953, 1954, 1957 by G. & C. Merriam Co.

zh = z in azure

APPENDIX 1

SUFFIXES

Here are five groups of common suffixes, with examples of each. They are accompanied by questions and comments and followed by practice exercises.

Group I ■ MAKERS OF NOUNS

-al : arrival, betrayal, portrayal, refusal

This suffix is often used to form nouns from verbs.

-ance : connivance, maintenance, nonchalance, obeisance
-ence : acquiescence, incipience, iridescence, transcience

The two forms of this suffix originally represented two different conjugations in Latin. There is no dependable rule for spelling them in English.

-dom : Christendom, kingdom, officialdom, wisdom
-hood : brotherhood, fatherhood, manhood, neighborhood, womanhood
-ship : discipleship, friendship, partisanship

From what language did these three suffixes and most of the roots in the example words originally come? Notice that most of the roots are nouns.

-ee : appointee, devotee, draftee, nominee, repartee, trainee

Which of these words does not denote a person? From what language did the suffix *-ee* originally come?

407

| *-er* | : | abstainer, embezzler, loiterer, transformer, transmitter |
| *-ess* | : | mistress, poetess, princess, sorceress, stewardess |

These suffixes denote persons. The suffix *-ess* is used to make feminine nouns. What word in the list undergoes a slight spelling change when the suffix is added?

| *-ice* | : | apprentice, avarice, novice, service |

| *-ism* | : | fetishism, galvanism, Hitlerism, pessimism, truism, witticism |

Each of these words denotes a set of beliefs, a saying, or a process. Can you add ten more *-isms* to the list?

| *-ist* | : | antagonist, dogmatist, plagiarist, psychiatrist, therapist |

Each of these words denotes a person. How many others can you add?

| *-ity* | : | agility, possibility, versatility, virility |
| *-ty* | : | fealty, liberty, loyalty, novelty |

| *-ment* | : | abridgment, chastisement, curtailment, enticement, resentment |

Which of the example words varies slightly from the expected spelling? Can you give a very familiar legal noun which is often misspelled because it varies in the same way?

| *-ness* | : | furtiveness, gruesomeness, hopefulness, pensiveness |

From what language did *-ness* originally come? Notice that each example word is formed by adding this suffix to an adjective.

| *-or* | : | incisor, innovator, mediator, proprietor, speculator |

| *-sion* | : | depression, diversion, obsession, suspension |
| *-tion* | : | abolition, coalition, sedition; liberation, mediation |

| *-y, -ry* | : | empathy, irony, sympathy; husbandry, rivalry |
| *-cy* | : | adjacency, bankruptcy, complacency, consistency, constancy |

Group II ► MAKERS OF ADJECTIVES

-able	:	consolable, disposable, readable, reconcilable
-ible	:	contemptible, discernible, irresistible, reducible

-al	:	abysmal, epochal, fiscal, hexagonal, nocturnal
-ial	:	connubial, custodial, menial, mercurial, parochial
-ual	:	casual, gradual, manual, perpetual, visual

Which words are used both as adjectives and as nouns? What *-al, -ial,* and *-ual* words can you name that serve as nouns? What did *individual* originally mean? Note: The suffix *-al* (p. 407) sometimes serves as a noun suffix: *dispersal, recital, reversal.*

-ic	:	nomadic, prosaic, soporific, sporadic, symphonic
-tic	:	aromatic, dogmatic, pathetic, synthetic, traumatic

The suffix *-ic* is often used with *-ist* nouns, such as *imperialistic* and *futuristic.* Can you think of other examples?

-ine	:	bovine, equine, labyrinthine, porcine, serpentine
-ile	:	ductile, infantile, puerile, senile, servile, sterile

Each of these suffixes has two possible pronunciations. If you are not sure of the pronunciation of the example words, consult your dictionary.

-ive	:	cursive, festive, pensive, pervasive, regressive, sedative

Which word has usurped "noundom"? Note: For the use of this suffix in making verbs and nouns, see Group V.

-ish	:	bookish, fiendish, greenish, peevish, womanish
-ful	:	delightful, graceful, neglectful, resentful, rueful, sinful
-less	:	defenceless, graceless, guileless, hapless, relentless
-like	:	homelike, sylphlike, zephyrlike

From what language do *-ish, -ful, -less,* and *-like* derive? Do most of the roots derive from the same source? Notice that you can add *-ness* to most of these words and make nouns.

-ous	:	analogous, rapturous, rigorous, solicitous, tempestuous
-ious	:	devious, tedious; sacrilegious, specious, meretricious

Group III   ● MAKERS OF VERBS

-ate : alleviate, amalgamate, annihilate, compensate, prevaricate

Many words ending in -*ate* are not verbs. See Group V.

-ify : amplify, deify, gratify, humidify, nullify, pacify
-ize : amortize, burglarize, ostracize, subsidize, temporize

Group IV   ▫ MAKERS OF ADVERBS

-ly : adroitly, astutely, complacently, defiantly, warily

This suffix, added to adjectives, produces virtually all of the adverbs in the English language. Occasionally, the suffix makes an adjective: *comely, heavenly, homely, leisurely*.

Group V   VERSATILE SUFFIXES

Certain suffixes may be used to make more than one part of speech. The following suffixes make verbs, nouns, and adjectives, but NOT adverbs.

-ant : ■ assailant, claimant, occupant; savant
▶ exultant, radiant, self-reliant, valiant

In verbs such as *warrant, decant, recant,* and *supplant,* the -*ant* is part of the root and not a suffix.

-ary : ■ aviary, functionary, notary
▶ arbitrary, mercenary, military, subsidiary

What does each word mean? Which of the adjectives are also used as nouns?

-ate : ● abrogate, deviate, emanate, mediate, perpetrate, terminate

See also -*ate* under Group III.

■ advocate, candidate, mandate, palatinate, potentate

Which of the nouns can also function as a verb?

▶ collegiate, desolate, intermediate, intimate; sedate

Which may be used as a different part of speech without change of form or spelling? What variations in the pronunciation of the suffix do you notice in this list?

-ent : ■ portent, solvent, superintendent
▶ evident, insistent, subsequent

Can you define each one? Can you add ten more to the list, with or without the aid of a dictionary of rhymes?

-ite : ● expedite, incite, ignite, unite
■ Benthamite, Israelite, parasite, satellite
▶ exquisite, favorite; finite, tripartite

In chemistry, this suffix has a special meaning in such words as *nitrite, ferrite,* and *fluorite.* Compare *nitrate, ferrate,* and *carbonate.*

-ive : ■ derivative, expletive, substantive
▶ affirmative, conclusive, decisive, excessive, restive

The ending -*ive* in verbs such as *arrive, survive, contrive,* and *derive* belongs to the root and is not a suffix.

-ory : ■ directory, factory; oratory, purgatory
▶ advisory, auditory, commendatory, dilatory, inflammatory

-(r)ior : ■ interior, exterior, posterior
▶ anterior, inferior, ulterior

The ending -*(r)ior* is the comparative form of Latin adjectives. It provides a pattern for comparative adjectives in English, such as *prettier, happier, merrier.*

SUFFIX EXERCISES

Most of the words in these exercises are base words. The addition of suffixes will often produce variant forms which you have studied in the units.

1. Give a ■ noun form which corresponds to each of the following ● verbs:

   1. abate
   2. abolish
   3. acquiesce
   4. acquit
   5. bereave

   6. connive
   7. defer
   8. disburse
   9. indict
   10. infer

2. What is the ■ noun form which corresponds to each of the following ► adjectives?

   1. avaricious
   2. arrogant
   3. authentic
   4. complacent
   5. despotic

   6. grotesque
   7. partisan
   8. ribald
   9. sovereign
   10. versatile

3. Cite a ■ noun—person or agent form—which corresponds to each of the following words:

   1. ● abet
   2. ● appoint
   3. ● assail
   4. ■ counsel (also ● verb)
   5. ■ custody

   6. ► imperial
   7. ● loiter
   8. ► optimistic
   9. ► skeptical
   10. ► tyrannical

4. What ► adjective form, other than an *-ing* form, corresponds to each of the following ● verbs?

1. congratulate
2. console
3. discern
4. err
5. indulge

6. pervade
7. relent
8. reproach
9. reverse
10. surmount

5. Cite a familiar ► adjective form which corresponds to each of the following ■ nouns. Which of these adjectives may be changed into - adverbs?

1. amenity
2. chaos
3. coquette
4. guile
5. hypocrisy

6. libel
7. mercury
8. puerility
9. rigor
10. sacrilege

6. What is the ● verb form of each of the following ■ nouns?

1. alien
2. antagonist
3. brevity (with prefix)
4. hybrid
5. indemnity

6. proximity (with prefix)
7. reciprocity
8. satire
9. subsidy
10. vigor (with prefix)

7. What is the ● verb form which corresponds to each of the following ► adjectives?

1. domestic
2. fatuous (with prefix)
3. galvanic
4. immune
5. iterative

6. luminous (with prefix)
7. mobile
8. recuperative
9. synthetic
10. tolerant

APPENDIX 2

KEYS to Tests in Part I

UNIT TESTS

UNIT 1

Pretest	Third Practice Set	Antonyms
(1) divulge	(1) c	(1) b
(2) implore	(2) e	(2) a
(3) adapt	(3) d	(3) d
(4) affirm	(4) b	(4) d
(5) curtail	(5) c	(5) a
(6) acquire	(6) d	(6) c
(7) coerce	(7) b	(7) e
(8) defer	(8) c	(8) e
(9) designate	(9) d	(9) d
(10) admonish	(10) c	(10) b
(11) abolish		

UNIT 2

Pretest	Third Practice Set		A Word For It
(1) esteem	(1) 12	(1) 3	(1) discern
(2) salvage	(2) 8	(2) 7	(2) appreciate
(3) redeem	(3) 5	(3) 11	(3) censorious
(4) counsel	(4) 2	(4) 2	(4) dawdles
(5) custody	(5) 10	(5) 4	(5) pondered
(6) appall	(6) 6	(6) 6	(6) feint
(7) deluge	(7) 9	(7) 1	(7) cherish
(8) obsess	(8) 4	(8) 12	(8) muse
(9) havoc	(9) 7	(9) 5	(9) guerdon
(10) cherish	(10) 1	(10) 8	(10) dally
(11) chaos			
(12) wrest			

UNIT 3

Pretest		*Third Practice Set*			
(1) b	(6) a	(1)	5	(6)	1
(2) d	(7) b	(2)	9	(7)	12
(3) c	(8) b	(3)	7	(8)	2
(4) a	(9) a	(4)	10	(9)	4
(5) d		(5)	8	(10)	6

UNIT 4

Pretest		*Third Practice Set*			
(1) a	(6) a	(1)	7	(6)	11
(2) d	(7) d	(2)	6	(7)	3
(3) c	(8) b	(3)	8	(8)	5
(4) b	(9) d	(4)	9	(9)	12
(5) c		(5)	10	(10)	2

UNIT 5

Pretest	*Third Practice Set*						
(1) a	(1)	8	(11)	17	(1)	11	
(2) b	(2)	14	(12)	5	(2)	9	
(3) c	(3)	12	(13)	6	(3)	4	
(4) d	(4)	15	(14)	7	(4)	1	
(5) c	(5)	10	(15)	9	(5)	12	
(6) d	(6)	16			(6)	2	
(7) b	(7)	13			(7)	3	
(8) b	(8)	4			(8)	5	
	(9)	1			(9)	6	
	(10)	2			(10)	8	

UNIT 6

Pretest	*Third Practice Set*				*Antonyms*	
(1) b	(1)	6	(1)	11	(1)	7
(2) a	(2)	10	(2)	6	(2)	4
(3) d	(3)	4	(3)	1	(3)	8
(4) b	(4)	2	(4)	9	(4)	10
(5) c	(5)	1	(5)	12	(5)	3
(6) b	(6)	11	(6)	8	(6)	2
(7) d	(7)	12	(7)	4	(7)	12
(8) a	(8)	8	(8)	5	(8)	1
	(9)	3	(9)	2	(9)	5
	(10)	5	(10)	3	(10)	6

UNIT 7

Pretest	*Third Practice Set*	
(1) c	(1) 7	(1) 3
(2) a	(2) 10	(2) 8
(3) d	(3) 6	(3) 6
(4) c	(4) 1	(4) 7
(5) d	(5) 11	(5) 10
(6) c	(6) 2	(6) 1
(7) b	(7) 12	(7) 9
(8) b	(8) 3	(8) 12
(9) a	(9) 4	(9) 4
	(10) 8	(10) 2

UNIT 8

Pretest	*Third Practice Set*	
(1) b	(1) 5	(11) 14
(2) a	(2) 9	(12) 16
(3) d	(3) 2	(13) 13
(4) a	(4) 1	(14) 17
(5) c	(5) 10	(15) 15
(6) b	(6) 12	
(7) d	(7) 4	
(8) a	(8) 6	
(9) c	(9) 3	
	(10) 8	

UNIT 9

Pretest	*Second Practice Set*	*Third Practice Set*	*Antonyms*
(1) not	(1) counterspy	(1) not	(1) disconnect
(2) wrongly	(2) nonviolent	(2) under	(2) illogical
(3) against	(3) antipathy	(3) out	(3) antiseptic
(4) against	(4) impending	(4) not	(4) disapproval
(5) shut away	(5) motive	(5) against	(5) misbehavior
(apart)	(6) pensive	(6) make	(6) exclude
(6) against	(7) dissolve	(7) throw...out	(7) counterproposal
(7) away from	(8) antiwar	(8) putting	(8) nonmetal
	(9) illegible	(9) sent	(9) eject
	(10) exclusion	(10) moving...down	(10) irreligious
	(11) miscalculate		
	(12) extortion		
	(13) distractions		
	(14) selection	―――	
	(15) suspension	(18) dejection	
	(16) emissary	(19) fiction	
	(17) supposition	(20) delusion	

UNIT 10

Pretest	*Second Practice Set*		*Third Practice Set*	
(1) to	(1) circumscribe	(11) subservient	(1) 6	(6) 9
(2) between	(2) contain	(12) visualize	(2) 4	(7) 11
(3) through	(3) aspire	(13) convocation	(3) 1	(8) 3
(4) before	(4) infuse	(14) translate	(4) 10	(9) 8
(5) behind	(5) precede	(15) introspection	(5) 12	(10) 5
(6) carry	(6) prospect	(16) dispel		
(7) write	(7) pertain	(17) recede	*The Right Word*	
(8) bearing	(8) interscholastic	(18) egress	(1) symposium	
(9) turn	(9) duct	(19) aversion	(2) commotion	
(10) breath	(10) portage	(20) aggressive	(3) procrastinate	
			(4) preclude	
			(5) proconsul	

UNIT 11

Pretest	*Second Practice Set*	*Third Practice Set*		*The Right Word*
(1) anaesthetic	(1) cursory denouncing innovations	(1) 7	(1) 8	(1) 6
(2) astringent		(2) 11	(2) 9	(2) 11
(3) post-mortem		(3) 9	(3) 10	(3) 9
(4) rectitude	(2) infractions mortality	(4) 8	(4) 11	(4) 2
(5) countermand		(5) 12	(5) 2	(5) 10
(6) penitentiary	(3) perfidy antipathy	(6) 10	(6) 4	(6) 12
(7) thanatopsis		(7) 2	(7) 3	(7) 4
(8) placebo	(4) dissecting incisions	(8) 4	(8) 6	(8) 5
(9) necrolatry		(9) 1	(9) 1	(9) 3
(10) cardiogram	(5) cardiac rupture	(10) 5	(10) 5	(10) 8
	(6) fidelity inherent			
	(7) homicide penitentiary	(9) immerse conflagration	(11) sanctimonious rectitude	
	(8) luminous sympathy	(10) placate victor	(12) placid depressed	

UNIT 12

Pretest		*Third Practice Set*	
(1) two	(7) one hundred	(1) centenarian	(9) polygamy patriarchs
(2) hundredth	(8) sixth	(2) equilateral	
(3) ninety	(9) one	(3) enneagon	(10) pliable
(4) eighty	(10) seventh	(4) demigod	(11) sesquicentennial
(5) one	(11) seven	(5) pentameter	(12) semicircle hemisphere
(6) four		(5) Decalog(ue)	
		(7) hectograph	(13) polygon polyhedron
		(8) milleniums (millenia)	(14) November
			(15) hyperacidity

FINAL TESTS

Unit 1	*Unit 2*	*Unit 3*	*Unit 4*
(1) zephyrs verge	(1) discern epoch	(1) plaintive furtive	(1) pestilence abate
(2) adapt abolish	(2) demeanor meditate	(2) placid weird	(2) pulverized potion
(3) affirms curtail	(3) deluge chaos	(3) pensive rigorous	(3) fiend abyss
(4) designate remnants	(4) citadel obsesses	(4) motley wanton	(4) epithet reproach
(5) defer acquired	(5) counsel err	(5) wily rueful	(5) anecdote derelict
(6) labyrinth hazards	(6) salvage censure	(6) pungent dour	(6) resent abet
(7) jargon interim	(7) feign custody	(7) lucid ghastly	(7) cited omens
(8) divulge guile	(8) redeem havoc	(8) droll canine	(8) lament purge
(9) admonish robot	(9) appall esteem	(9) mature candid	(9) manifest pervades
(10) implore rapture	(10) regale wrest	(10) plausible potent	(10) entice frustrated

Unit 5	*Unit 6*	*Unit 7*	*Unit 8*
(1) defiance assailed	(1) luminous hostile	(1) indignation acute	(1) liberated relinquish
(2) dexterity elude	(2) lurid vindictive	(2) adjacent inferior	(2) martial segregate
(3) discretion dispersed	(3) languid nomadic	(3) exultantly fugitives	(3) remonstrate predatory
(4) antagonists extricate	(4) copious obnoxious	(4) errant retinue	(4) vaunts precarious
(5) adhered adorned	(5) perpetual homely	(5) insolence incognito	(5) requiting retards
(6) emulate exertions	(6) eminent regal	(6) visage incessant	(6) inquisitive surmount
(7) augmented elation	(7) roguish officious	(7) agile exorbitant	(7) massive terminated
(8) intimated alter	(8) vehement lenient	(8) implicit succor	(8) vanquish servile
(9) enhance conjectures	(9) domestic laudable	(9) repose infernal	(9) valiant obstinate
(10) accomplices conflagration	(10) zealous vociferous	(10) inert rendezvous	(10) negligent intricate

Unit 9	**Unit 10**	**Unit 11**	**Unit 12**
(1) absolution	(1) interfused	(1) sentimentally apathy	(1) millipede
(2) extraction	(2) propels	(2) penitence announces	(2) monarchy
(3) distortion	(3) import	(3) suppress sympathize	(3) octagon
(4) emotion	(4) transference	(4) disrupt concord	(4) quadrennial
(5) evolution	(5) report	(5) fidelity inherent	(5) hectometer
(6) deposition	(6) inscription	(6) excursions subaqueous	(6) nonagenarian
(7) seclusion	(7) regression	(7) sanctity rectitude	(7) biology
(8) opponent	(8) periscope	(8) mortality cardiac	(8) equilateral
(9) dismissal	(9) circumspection	(9) dictated invincible	(9) pliable
(10) mobile	(10) aspires toward	(10) stringent loquacious	(10) bigamy

DIVISION TESTS

	Section 1	*Section 2*	*Section 3*	*Section 4*	*Section 5*	*Section 6*
(1)	5	3	2	5	4	4
(2)	8	5	4	3	6	5
(3)	1	4	11	6	9	8
(4)	11	10	6	1	2	3
(5)	12	9	3	8	3	9
(6)	7	8	1	10	10	1
(7)	2	6	10	4	5	11
(8)	6	11	5	7	12	10
(9)	10	2	9	11	8	7
(10)	3	12	7	9	1	6

	Section 7	*Section 8*	*Section 9*	*Section 10*	*Section 11*	*Section 12*
(1)	3	4	3	1	5	3
(2)	6	8	5	4	6	4
(3)	5	10	8	8	1	5
(4)	10	1	4	5	2	10
(5)	1	12	10	3	7	2
(6)	9	7	9	9	3	11
(7)	2	11	1	12	8	6
(8)	11	9	7	6	11	9
(9)	7	6	12	11	10	7
(10)	4	3	2	2	9	12

KEYS to Tests in Part II

UNIT TESTS

UNIT 1

Pretest	*Third Practice Set*	*The Right Word*	
(1) corroborate	(1) b	(1) 8	(1) 5
(2) dubious	(2) c	(2) 7	(2) 8
(3) depreciate	(3) a	(3) 9	(3) 12
(4) discriminate	(4) c	(4) 1	(4) 6
(5) acquiesce	(5) b	(5) 12	(5) 7
(6) banish	(6) d	(6) 11	(6) 10
(7) indulgent	(7) b	(7) 2	(7) 11
(8) livid	(8) b	(8) 3	(8) 2
(9) hysterical	(9) d	(9) 5	(9) 3
(10) console	(10) c	(10) 4	(10) 1

UNIT 2

Pretest	*Third Practice Set*	*Antonyms*
(1) accelerate	(1) 6	(1) d
(2) improvise	(2) 12	(2) a
(3) simulate	(3) 10	(3) b
(4) similes	(4) 9	(4) c
(5) exaggerate	(5) 1	(5) a
(6) recuperate	(6) 2	(6) e
(7) resuscitate	(7) 11	(7) b
(8) humiliate	(8) 5	(8) d
(9) retaliate	(9) 8	(9) c
	(10) 3	(10) c

UNIT 3

Pretest	*Third Practice Set*	*The Right Word*	
(1) d	(1) b	(1) 4	(1) 7
(2) b	(2) d	(2) 10	(2) 10
(3) c	(3) a	(3) 9	(3) 9
(4) a	(4) c	(4) 12	(4) 8
(5) b	(5) c	(5) 7	(5) 11
(6) d	(6) e	(6) 6	(6) 2
(7) b	(7) a	(7) 8	(7) 6
(8) b	(8) e	(8) 2	(8) 4
	(9) c	(9) 11	(9) 5
	(10) d	(10) 1	(10) 1

UNIT 4

Pretest	*Second Practice Set*		*Third Practice Set*
(1) c	(1) 10	(1) 11	(1) c
(2) b	(2) 12	(2) 7	(2) b
(3) a	(3) 8	(3) 8	(3) b
(4) d	(4) 7	(4) 9	(4) d
(5) c	(5) 3	(5) 1	(5) b
(6) b	(6) 9	(6) 3	(6) a
(7) a	(7) 4	(7) 12	(7) a
(8) c	(8) 5	(8) 4	(8) d
	(9) 1	(9) 2	(9) c
	(10) 2	(10) 6	(10) b

UNIT 5

Pretest	*Second Practice Set*		*Third Practice Set*
(1) c	(1) 10	(1) 10	(1) b
(2) b	(2) 7	(2) 9	(2) c
(3) a	(3) 6	(3) 8	(3) a
(4) d	(4) 8	(4) 11	(4) e
(5) c	(5) 11	(5) 1	(5) c
(6) a	(6) 12	(6) 4	(6) b
(7) c	(7) 9	(7) 2	(7) b
	(8) 2	(8) 6	(8) c
	(9) 5	(9) 3	(9) e
	(10) 4	(10) 5	(10) a

UNIT 6

Pretest	*Third Practice Set*	*The Right Word*	
(1) c	(1) c	(1) 6	(1) 6
(2) a	(2) c	(2) 8	(2) 10
(3) c	(3) e	(3) 10	(3) 9
(4) d	(4) b	(4) 1	(4) 1
(5) d	(5) b	(5) 2	(5) 2
(6) b	(6) d	(6) 11	(6) 5
(7) d	(7) a	(7) 12	(7) 12
(8) a	(8) c	(8) 5	(8) 3
	(9) a	(9) 7	(9) 8
	(10) b	(10) 4	(10) 4

UNIT 7

Pretest	Third Practice Set	The Right Word	Replacements
(1) c	(1) b	(1) 11	(1) an expatriate
(2) a	(2) d	(2) 12	(2) devout
(3) d	(3) a	(3) 10	(3) turbid
(4) d	(4) e	(4) 2	(4) galvanic
(5) b	(5) e	(5) 1	(5) deport him
(6) d	(6) b	(6) 3	(6) metamorphosed
(7) b	(7) c	(7) 6	(7) exempt
(8) a	(8) a	(8) 7	(8) vicious
	(9) d	(9) 4	(9) intolerance
	(10) a	(10) 8	(10) banish

UNIT 8

Pretest	Second Practice Set	Third Practice Set	The Right Word
(1) veracity	(1) 9	(1) insurrection civil	(1) c
(2) metamorphosis	(2) 11		(2) b
(3) ardent	(3) 6	(2) zealous fervent	(3) a
(4) retribution	(4) 8		(4) e
(5) indolence	(5) 10	(3) traditions fluctuate	(5) c
(6) fluctuation	(6) 12		(6) e
(7) morale	(7) 3	(4) passionate imply	(7) b
(8) futile	(8) 1		(8) a
(9) civil	(9) 4	(5) ruse temerity	(9) b
(10) celestial	(10) 2		(10) d

UNIT 9

Pretest	Third Practice Set
(1) rancor	(1) b
(2) morose	(2) d
(3) vigilant	(3) c
(4) sanguine	(4) c
(5) perversity	(5) d
(6) militant	(6) b
(7) insidious	(7) a
(8) oblivion	(8) b
	(9) c
	(10) b

UNIT 10

Pretest	Third Practice Set	Matching Words	The Right Word
(1) burlesque	(1) c	(1) 5	(1) sun
(2) derision	(2) a	(2) 8	(2) heat or temperature
(3) hilarity	(3) b	(3) 11	(3) saying
(4) cajolery	(4) d	(4) 1	(4) full
(5) levity	(5) c	(5) 9	(5) attacks
(6) ludicrousness	(6) e	(6) 2	(6) knowledge
(7) satire	(7) d	(7) 12	(7) sun(light)
(8) jocularity	(8) e	(8) 4	(8) talking or conference
(9) repartee	(9) d	(9) 7	(9) time
(10) bathos	(10) c	(10) 6	(10) caricature

UNIT 11

Pretest	Third Practice Set	Replacements
(1) terminus	(1) b	(1) superfluous
(2) maternity	(2) e	(2) somnambulist
(3) congenital	(3) a	(3) fortified
(4) anthropoid	(4) b	(4) fraternity
(5) patrimony	(5) d	(5) persona non grata
(6) terrestrial	(6) a	(6) transmute
(7) perambulate	(7) c	(7) aquamarine
(8) maritime	(8) a	(8) congenital
(9) amphibious	(9) e	(9) retrogress
	(10) c	(10) manual

UNIT 12

Pretest	Third Practice Set	Matching Words
(1) panchromatic	(1) c	(1) 8
(2) homogeneous	(2) a	(2) 6
(3) neolithic	(3) b	(3) 9
(4) omniscient	(4) e	(4) 12
(5) seismographic	(5) b	(5) 1
(6) gregarious	(6) d	(6) 7
(7) ephemeral	(7) a	(7) 11
(8) somnolent	(8) c	(8) 2
(9) amorphous	(9) c	(9) 4
	(10) e	(10) 5

FINAL TESTS

Unit 1	*Unit 2*	*Unit 3*	*Unit 4*
(1) contrive depreciate	(1) nonentity moron	(1) denizens kinship	(1) austere deficient
(2) senile constitute	(2) simulate sovereign	(2) opulence illusion	(2) avid inexorable
(3) arid chronic	(3) exaggerate retaliate	(3) prodigious posterity	(3) competent explicit
(4) discriminate ferocious	(4) accelerate humiliation	(4) precision proximity	(4) demure capricious
(5) dilate virtually	(5) rostrum improvise	(5) adroit feline	(5) querulous stringent
(6) overt internal	(6) tenacity compensate	(6) facile impromptu	(6) punctilious meticulous
(7) hysterical acquiesce	(7) promulgate a simile	(7) prosaic mediocre	(7) pugnacious plebeian
(8) dubious lethal	(8) satellite a parity	(8) vengeance spontaneous	(8) inscrutable lugubrious
(9) allude corroborate	(9) resuscitate recuperated	(9) virile subtle	(9) inveterate melancholy
(10) banished nuptial	(10) quorum jeopardize	(10) reminiscences transient	(10) opportune formidable

Unit 5	*Unit 6*	*Unit 7*	*Unit 8*
(1) litigation fiscal	(1) abstain elicit	(1) vacillates skeptical	(1) incipient morale
(2) actuarial legitimate	(2) condescend to duplicity	(2) gratify vindicate	(2) indolence fallacy
(3) libel lucrative	(3) dissipate emaciated	(3) prevaricate vitiates	(3) fluctuation alternate
(4) prosecute perjures	(4) exhorted cupidity	(4) tolerate provident	(4) ardent futile
(5) embezzled deficit	(5) exasperates dominate	(5) turbulent vicious	(5) liberal subterfuge
(6) indicted acquitted	(6) deprecate façade	(6) protuberant pallid	(6) culpable eccentric
(7) alleges bequeathed	(7) clairvoyant altercation	(7) monotonous inarticulate	(7) benign complacent
(8) incriminated disbursed	(8) apprehended apparitions	(8) ostracize (re)iterating	(8) civil credible
(9) epitaph bereavement	(9) concede barrage	(9) intermittent transfigured	(9) tradition retribution
(10) interment condolences	(10) confederate alien	(10) scrutinize juvenile	(10) temerity veracity

Unit 9	**Unit 10**	**Unit 11**	**Unit 12**
(1) morose belligerent	(1) animation hilarity	(1) marine nautical	(1) journal or diary autobiography
(2) venial rancor	(2) derision levity	(2) manual persist	(2) benefactors potent
(3) hypocrisy gluttony	(3) cajolery jocularity	(3) territory magnitude	(3) anonymous autocrat
(4) ingenious laconic	(4) burlesque petulant	(4) retrogress ascend	(4) amorphous homogeneous
(5) intrepid venomous	(5) repartee animus or animosity	(5) ambulatory fraternity	(5) migrate telepathy
(6) heresy depravity	(6) incarnate irony	(6) heterogeneous commuted	(6) omniscient consecutively
(7) insidious pernicious	(7) chronological cognomen	(7) malady anthropology	(7) panacea pseudo
(8) vigilant ostensible	(8) corporal derogatory	(8) terminate suburban	(8) neologism acronym
(9) sanguine ubiquitious	(9) trivial facetiousness	(9) renascence gratify	(9) jurisprudence neophyte
(10) militant oblivious to	(10) heliotropes thermal	(10) fortitude dominant	(10) dehydrated dormant

DIVISION TESTS

Section 1	*Section 2*	*Section 3*	*Section 4*	*Section 5*	*Section 6*
(1) 10	(1) 4	(1) 12	(1) 9	(1) 5	(1) 7
(2) 4	(2) 10	(2) 1	(2) 6	(2) 11	(2) 3
(3) 6	(3) 5	(3) 10	(3) 1	(3) 10	(3) 9
(4) 11	(4) 6	(4) 5	(4) 10	(4) 2	(4) 8
(5) 2	(5) 9	(5) 4	(5) 8	(5) 12	(5) 11
(6) 1	(6) 12	(6) 7	(6) 11	(6) 3	(6) 1
(7) 9	(7) 1	(7) 2	(7) 4	(7) 8	(7) 4
(8) 12	(8) 2	(8) 11	(8) 3	(8) 9	(8) 5
(9) 7	(9) 8	(9) 6	(9) 2	(9) 4	(9) 10
(10) 8	(10) 7	(10) 3	(10) 5	(10) 1	(10) 12

Section 7	*Section 8*	*Section 9*	*Section 10*	*Section 11*	*Section 12*
(1) 2	(1) 4	(1) 11	(1) 5	(1) 9	(1) 3
(2) 4	(2) 8	(2) 9	(2) 12	(2) 6	(2) 10
(3) 6	(3) 12	(3) 2	(3) 3	(3) 1	(3) 7
(4) 3	(4) 7	(4) 10	(4) 8	(4) 12	(4) 5
(5) 7	(5) 1	(5) 6	(5) 11	(5) 3	(5) 9
(6) 5	(6) 11	(6) 8	(6) 9	(6) 7	(6) 2
(7) 12	(7) 10	(7) 1	(7) 2	(7) 4	(7) 11
(8) 8	(8) 2	(8) 5	(8) 6	(8) 10	(8) 4
(9) 11	(9) 6	(9) 12	(9) 1	(9) 2	(9) 8
(10) 9	(10) 5	(10) 7	(10) 4	(10) 8	(10) 6

KEYS to Tests in Part III

UNIT TESTS

UNIT 1

Pretest	*Third Practice Set*	*The Right Word*
(1) collaborate	(1) b	(1) collaborator
(2) disparage	(2) d	audacious
(3) exhume	(3) b	(2) exhumation
(4) fruition	(4) c	quandary
(5) detonate	(5) a	(3) disparagement
(6) deter	(6) b	chagrined
(7) homage	(7) d	(4) exemplary
(8) an impasse	(8) a	calumniate
(9) calumny	(9) d	(5) emanations
(10) consternation	(10) c	detonation

UNIT 2

Pretest	*Third Practice Set*	*The Right Word*
(1) emancipate	(1) c	(1) usurpation
(2) reconcile	(2) d	reciprocal
(3) evacuate	(3) b	(2) inadvertence
(4) reciprocate	(4) c	authenticity
(5) incinerate	(5) a	(3) irreconcilable
(6) impeach	(6) d	philanthropists
(7) relegate	(7) c	(4) repudiation
(8) subsidize	(8) b	amity
(9) repudiate	(9) d	
(10) usurp	(10) a	

UNIT 3

Pretest	*Third Practice Set*	*The Right Word*
(1) perspicacity	(1) d	(1) succinctness
(2) succinctness	(2) b	incumbent
(3) tentativeness	(3) a	(2) gluts
(4) prostration	(4) d	mortal
(5) vicissitude	(5) d	(3) intangible
(6) sagacity	(6) a	mobilize
(7) surfeit	(7) c	(4) perspicuous
(8) predilection	(8) a	salient
(9) recumbency	(9) c	(5) moribund
(10) propensity	(10) b	prostration

426

UNIT 4

Pretest	*Third Practice Set*	*The Right Word*
(1) a	(1) b	(1) portend
(2) b	(2) b	(2) execrations
(3) c	(3) d	(3) insurgent
(4) a	(4) a	(4) plagiarism
(5) b	(5) c	(5) quixotic
(6) d	(6) a	(6) chimera
(7) a	(7) d	(7) aesthete
(8) c	(8) a	(8) consolidate
	(9) d	(9) irrelevant
	(10) c	(10) fantastic

UNIT 5

Pretest	*Third Practice Set*	*The Right Word*
(1) b	(1) b	(1) fastidious
(2) c	(2) a	petulant or peevish
(3) b	(3) c	(2) volatile
(4) d	(4) e	versatile
(5) b	(5) c	(3) choleric
(6) d	(6) c	truculent
(7) a	(7) e	(4) ingenuousness
(8) d	(8) d	officious
	(9) e	(5) impulsiveness
	(10) a	infatuation

UNIT 6

Pretest	*Third Practice Set*	*A Word For It*
(1) egregious	(1) c	(1) exterminate
(2) annihilate	(2) a	convergence
(3) instigate	(3) d	(2) synthesis
(4) auspicious	(4) b	propitiate
(5) propitiate	(5) d	(3) expedient
(6) incongruous	(6) a	fortuitous
(7) aggravate	(7) c	(4) intrinsic
(8) expedient	(8) d	auspicious
(9) converge	(9) b	(5) mitigate
(10) extenuate	(10) b	egregious

UNIT 7

Pretest		*Third Practice Set*	
(1) connoisseur	(6) nemesis	(1) a	(6) c
(2) bourgeois	(7) mercury	(2) d	(7) d
(3) virtuoso	(8) philistine	(3) c	(8) b
(4) curator	(9) debutante	(4) b	(9) a
(5) mentor	(10) coquette	(5) c	(10) c

UNIT 8

Pretest	_Third Practice Set_	_A Word For It_
(1) b	(1) c	(1) cohesive
(2) c	(2) a	optional
(3) d	(3) b	(2) pertinacious
(4) c	(4) d	comity
(5) d	(5) b	(3) intuitively
(6) b	(6) b	amenable
(7) a	(7) c	(4) nonchalant
(8) c	(8) a	deleteriousness
(9) a	(9) c	(5) recalcitrance
(10) d	(10) d	imperviousness

UNIT 9

Pretest	_Third Practice Set_	_A Word For It_
(1) obsolete	(1) c	(1) sedentary
(2) indigenous	(2) d	impecunious
(3) alleviate	(3) c	(2) inheres
(4) indigent	(4) c	convivial
(5) ribald	(5) b	(3) collusion
(6) convivial	(6) d	ribaldry
(7) onerous	(7) a	(4) unalloyed
(8) promiscuous	(8) d	sedate
(9) mundane	(9) d	(5) nonsectarian
(10) connive	(10) c	secular

UNIT 10

Pretest	_Third Practice Set_	_A Word For It_
(1) paramount	(1) a	(1) catholicity
(2) clarity	(2) d	iconoclastic
(3) acumen	(3) d	(2) clarify
(4) accolade	(4) b	analogical
(5) amnesty	(5) c	(3) therapeutic
(6) aspersions	(6) b	acuity
(7) tantamount	(7) d	(4) exigency
(8) ignominy	(8) c	vicarious
(9) adamant	(9) d	(5) insinuation
(10) exigency	(10) b	innuendo

FINAL TESTS

Unit 1
(1) deter
    cavil
(2) collaborate
    coincide
(3) impasse
    contemplate
(4) demur at
    disparage
(5) consternation
    detonate
(6) condone
    alacrity
(7) chagrin
    exhume
(8) enigma
    fruition
(9) audacity
    dilemma
(10) calumny
    emanate

Unit 2
(1) reconcile
    impeach
(2) temporize
    subsidize
(3) amorous
    authentic
(4) altruistic
    didactic
(5) astute
    felicitous
(6) repudiate
    inadvertent
(7) despondent
    reciprocate
(8) mediate
    amicable
(9) vindicate
    relegated
(10) evacuate
    usurp

Unit 3
(1) sagacity
    perspicacity
(2) mortal
    surfeit
(3) restitution
    prerogative
(4) latent
    paroxysm
(5) predilection
    tangible
(6) overture
    prostration
(7) partisan
    salient
(8) mobile
    recumbent
(9) quintessence
    propriety
(10) tentative
    succinct

Unit 4
(1) covenant
    incentive
(2) coalition
    incubus
(3) plagiarism
    aesthetic
(4) paradox
    solstice
(5) marital
    relevant
(6) paragon
    forensic
(7) chimerical
    exotic
(8) maudlin
    sadistic
(9) occult
    portentous
(10) recondite
    ineffable

Unit 5
(1) ostentatious
    cynical
(2) captious
    arrogant
(3) ingenuous
    fatuous
(4) phlegmatic
    saturnine
(5) supercilious
    effeminate
(6) fastidious
    naive
(7) unctuous
    dogmatic
(8) volatile
    impetuous
(9) sinuous
    sardonic
(10) taciturn
    truculent

Unit 6
(1) expedient
    salubrious
(2) annihilate
    egregious
(3) negotiate
    capitulate
(4) aggravated
    extenuating
(5) fortuitous
    proscrastinate
(6) instigated
    mitigate
(7) sacrilegious
    meretricious
(8) synthetic
    auspicious
(9) intrinsic
    equivocal
(10) converged
    degenerate

Unit 7
(1) mentor
    connoisseur
(2) bourgeoisie
    philistine
(3) coterie
    ovation
(4) critique
    intrigues
(5) virtuoso
    protégé
(6) ballet
    symmetry
(7) curator
    malapropisms
(8) debutante
    repertoire
(9) liaison
    mercury
(10) denouement
    allegory

Unit 8	**Unit 9**	**Unit 10**
(1) criterion diplomacy	(1) alleviate abrogate	(1) accolade affront
(2) intuition integrity	(2) amortize onerous	(2) aspersions ignominious
(3) option crucial	(3) mundane inherent	(3) ulterior tantamount
(4) compatible coherent	(4) obsolete adulterate	(4) clarity iconoclasm
(5) immutable impervious to	(5) convivial amplify	(5) histrionic amnesty
(6) amenity nonchalance	(6) nullify stultify	(6) utopian impeccable
(7) preposterous deleterious	(7) inaugurate indigenous	(7) acumen analogy
(8) specious perfunctory	(8) hibernate clement	(8) halcyon paramount
(9) peremptory hyperbole	(9) amalgamates indigent	(9) allergic baroque
(10) clandestine optimism	(10) connives sedative	(10) catholic therapy

DIVISION TESTS

Section 1	*Section 2*	*Section 3*	*Section 4*	*Section 5*
(1) 6	(1) 11	(1) 4	(1) 3	(1) 7
(2) 11	(2) 7	(2) 6	(2) 4	(2) 9
(3) 8	(3) 12	(3) 5	(3) 6	(3) 8
(4) 7	(4) 3	(4) 10	(4) 8	(4) 6
(5) 10	(5) 9	(5) 11	(5) 10	(5) 1
(6) 1	(6) 2	(6) 2	(6) 9	(6) 2
(7) 9	(7) 10	(7) 12	(7) 1	(7) 4
(8) 4	(8) 5	(8) 1	(8) 11	(8) 11
(9) 12	(9) 4	(9) 3	(9) 7	(9) 12
(10) 2	(10) 6	(10) 8	(10) 5	(10) 5

Section 6	*Section 7*	*Section 8*	*Section 9*	*Section 10*
(1) 7	(1) 8	(1) 8	(1) 10	(1) 2
(2) 8	(2) 11	(2) 3	(2) 1	(2) 3
(3) 6	(3) 10	(3) 9	(3) 6	(3) 1
(4) 1	(4) 12	(4) 1	(4) 7	(4) 11
(5) 12	(5) 9	(5) 12	(5) 2	(5) 7
(6) 2	(6) 5	(6) 4	(6) 9	(6) 12
(7) 4	(7) 1	(7) 6	(7) 5	(7) 9
(8) 9	(8) 4	(8) 11	(8) 3	(8) 8
(9) 5	(9) 6	(9) 2	(9) 8	(9) 10
(10) 3	(10) 7	(10) 10	(10) 12	(10) 5

INDEX